THE GULF OF ALASKA
BIOLOGY AND OCEANOGRAPHY

PHILLIP R. MUNDY, EDITOR

Exxon Valdez Oil Spill Trustee Council

Published by Alaska Sea Grant College Program, University of Alaska Fairbanks

Elmer E. Rasmuson Library Cataloging in Publication Data

The Gulf of Alaska : biology and oceanography / Phillip R. Mundy, ed. – Fairbanks : Alaska Sea Grant College Program, University of Alaska Fairbanks 2005.

p. : ill., maps ; cm. – (Alaska Sea Grant College Program ; AK-SG-05-01)

Includes bibliographical references and index.

ISBN 1-56612-090-x

1. Marine biology—Alaska, Gulf of. 2. Oceanography—Alaska. 3. Ecosystem health—Alaska, Gulf of. I. Title. II. Mundy, Phillip R. (Phillip Roy). Series: Alaska Sea Grant College Program report ; AK-SG-05-01.

QH95.35.G845 2005

Citation: Mundy, Phillip R. (ed.). 2005. The Gulf of Alaska: Biology and Oceanography. Alaska Sea Grant College Program, University of Alaska Fairbanks.

CREDITS

Work for this book was supported by a grant from the *Exxon Valdez* Oil Spill Trustee Council, Anchorage, Alaska. The *Exxon Valdez* Oil Spill Trustee Council oversees restoration of the injured ecosystem through a civil settlement that includes the State of Alaska, the U.S. Federal Government, and the Exxon Company. Please see http://www.evostc.state.ak.us.

Publisher of the book is the Alaska Sea Grant College Program, supported by the U.S. Department of Commerce, NOAA National Sea Grant Office, grant NA16RG2321, project A/161-01; and by the University of Alaska Fairbanks with state funds. The University of Alaska is an affirmative action/equal opportunity employer and educational institution.

Sea Grant is a unique partnership with public and private sectors combining research, education, and technology transfer for public service. This national network of universities meets changing environmental and economic needs of people in our coastal, ocean, and Great Lakes regions.

Alaska Sea Grant College Program
University of Alaska Fairbanks
P.O. Box 755040
Fairbanks, Alaska 99775-5040
Toll free (888) 789-0090
(907) 474-6707 • fax (907) 474-6285
www.alaskaseagrant.org

Contents

PREFACE

The knowledge and experience gained during years of science studies in the aftermath of the *Exxon Valdez* oil spill (EVOS) confirmed that understanding the sources of changes in marine resources and ecosystems requires putting those changes into a historical context. Toward this end, in 1999 the EVOS Trustee Council dedicated funds for long-term monitoring and ecosystem-based research in the area affected by the 1989 oil spill, which is the northern Gulf of Alaska (GOA), including Prince William Sound, Cook Inlet, Kodiak Island, and the Alaska Peninsula. This program is called the GEM (Gulf of Alaska Ecosystem Monitoring and Research) Program. GEM's mission is to sustain a healthy and biologically diverse marine ecosystem in the northern GOA and to sustain human use of the marine resources in the ecosystem through greater understanding of how productivity is influenced by natural changes and human activities.

As part of the GEM Program, scientists cooperated to compile the scientific knowledge of the GOA. That scientific compilation, updated, makes up the content of this book, *The Gulf of Alaska: Biology and Oceanography*.

ACKNOWLEDGMENTS

The scientific leadership for the Gulf of Alaska Ecosystem Monitoring and Research Program (GEM) was provided by Phillip R. Mundy and Robert Spies. Molly McCammon provided policy leadership. Editors for the version of the manuscript reviewed by the National Research Council were Molly McCammon, Phil Mundy, Katharine Miller, and Bob Walker. Sue Keller edited this Alaska Sea Grant publication. Book cover design is by Dixon Jones; cover image is from Mountain High Maps ® Copyright © 1993 Digital Wisdom, Inc. Text formatting is by Kathy Kurtenbach.

Past and present members of the *Exxon Valdez* Trustee Council and their alternates during development of GEM are gratefully acknowledged: Jim Balsiger, Bruce Botelho, Michele Brown, Dave Gibbons, Marilyn Heiman, Drue Pearce, Steve Pennoyer, Frank Rue, and Craig Tillery.

Special thanks to the volunteer scientists of the National Research Coucil's Committee to Review the Gulf of Alaska Ecosystem Monitoring Program: Michael Roman (chair), Don Bowen, Andria A. Elskus, John J. Goering, George Hunt, Seth Macinko, Donal Manahan, Brenda Norcross, J. Steven Picou, Thomas C. Royer, Jennifer Ruesink, and Karl Turekian. The committee was ably staffed by Chris Elfring, David Policansky, and Ann Carlisle.

Because GEM was developed in an open and collaborative process that spanned nearly three years, many people had occasion to make material and intellectual contributions. The efforts of the following are gratefully acknowledged: Alisa Abookire, Ken Adams, Vera Alexander, Jennifer Allen, Fred Allendorf, Paul Anderson, Peter Armato, Shannon Atkinson, Kerim Aydin, Jim Ayres, Michael Baffrey; Torie Baker, Kris Balliet, Hal Batchelder, Bill Bechtol, Catherine Berg, Brock Bernstein, Chris Blackburn, Jim Blackburn, John Blaha, Jim Bodkin, Dede Bohn, James Brady, Stephen Braund, Evelyn Brown, Patty Brown-Schwalenberg, Al Burch, Vern Byrd, Robin Carlson, Rob Cermak, Veronica Christman, Robert Clark, Dave Cobb, Ken Coyle, Ted Cooney, Seth Danielson, Tom Dean, Robert DeVelice, Jane DiCosimo, Gary Drew, Janet Duffy-Anderson, Doug Eggers, Greg Erickson, Dave Eslinger, Charles Falkenberg, Gary Fandrei, Bob Foy, Steve Frenzel, Carol Fries, Fritz Funk, Dan Gillikin, David Goldstein, Andy Gunther, Gary Gury, Ed Harrison, Bill Hauser, Robert Henrichs, Carrie Holba, Ken Holbrook, Anne Hollowed, Brett Huber, Gary Hufford, Charlie Hughey, Dan Hull, Joe Hunt, Henry Huntington, Steve Ignell, David Irons, Lisa Ka'aihue, Tom Kline, Gary Kompkoff, Jan Konigsberg, Gordon Kruse, Kathy Kuletz, Pat Lavin, Pat Livingston, Lloyd Lowry, Allen Macklin, Tom Malone, Suzanne Marcy, Richard Marasco, Michael H. Martin, Paul McCollum, Walter Meganack Jr., Jennifer Nielsen,

Gordon Nelson, Pat Norman, Phil North, Worth Nowlin, Peter Q. Olsson, Gretchen Oosterhout, Ted Otis, Paul Panamarioff, Kent Patrick-Riley, Charles Peterson, John Piatt, Josie Quintrell, Terry Reed, Bud Rice, Stanley Rice, Jim Richardson, Evan Richert, Monica Riedel, George Rose, Dave Roseneau, Susan Saupe, Andy Schmidt, Carl Schoch, Sandra Schubert, Marianne See, Stan Senner, Bob Shavelson, Jeff Shester, Hugh Short, Jeff Short, Claudia Slater, Bob Small, Alan Springer, Robert Spies, Stacy Studebaker, Arliss Sturgulewski, Joe Sullivan, Kevin Summers, Gary Thomas, Glenn VanBlaricom, Shari Vaughan, Gale Vick, Jia Wang, Sarah Ward, Tom Weingartner, Steve Weisberg, David Welch, Kent Wohl, Cherri Womac, Bruce Wright, and Kate Wynne.◆

This book is dedicated to the memory of our friend, colleague, and coauthor, Dr. Charles Falkenberg, who died with his wife and two daughters in the crash of American Airlines flight 77 at the Pentagon, September 11, 2001. Dr. Falkenberg, his family, and the others who perished on that date will dwell in our collective memory forever.

Introduction

Phillip R. Mundy and Robert Spies

1.1 THE GOA AT A GLANCE

The conceptual foundation for the Gulf of Alaska (GOA) ecosystem explains how its plant and animal populations are controlled through time. The conceptual foundation is the product of syntheses of the latest scientific information and an assessment of leading ecological hypotheses. It encapsulates our understanding of how the GOA operates as an ecological system and how its biological resources, including highly valued populations of animals, are regulated. Citations to scientific literature are omitted in the following paragraphs for the sake of brevity.

If watersheds and marine areas of the GOA are looked at together, the importance of key geological features in shaping the natural physical and biological forces that control productivity is apparent (Figure 1.1). **Features illustrated in Figure 1.1 are in bold in the following text.** Natural forces are shaped by the surface topography of the GOA. Storm tracks moving across the North Pacific from west to east can drive **Aleutian low pressure systems** (Aleutian Low) deep into the GOA until the encounter with **boundary mountains** causes the release of **precipitation** and **airborne contaminants**. Freshwater runoff strengthens the **Alaska Coastal Current** (ACC) even as it brings airborne and terrestrial pollutants into the **watersheds** and **food webs**.

Natural forces that control biological productivity are also shaped by the submarine topography (bathymetry) of the **continental shelf**. Deep waters **upwell** across the **continental shelf break**, subsequently being carried across the **photic boundary** into areas of photosynthetic activity by the motion of surface currents (**ACC, Alaska Current [AC]**), **lunar forcing**, the motion of the earth, and **tidal mixing**. These deep waters carry **old carbon and nutrients** up into the food webs of the shelf and onshore areas. Where the deep waters encounter islands, seamounts, and **sills**, the resulting currents may deform the boundaries of the frontal zones of the ACC (**mid-shelf front**) and AC (**shelf-break front**), creating **eddies** that entrain plankton and other plants and animals for long periods of time.

Natural physical forces control productivity by limiting the amount of food and availability of habitats. During the winter especially, the **Aleutian Low** produces **wind**-driven transport of surface marine waters (**Ekman transport**), bringing water onshore. Movement of water onshore creates **downwelling** that takes plankton and associated nutrients out of the photic zone. On the other hand, the wind may act to hold the nutrients dissolved in water and held in **detritus** in the photic zone in some areas, because wind also produces **turbulence** that mixes the surface water. Turbulent mixing causes nutrients to be retained in surface waters, and retention increases production of **phytoplankton**, the base of the food web in surface waters. Production of **zooplankton**, secondary productivity, is the trophic connection (linkage) of phytoplankton to production of **forage fish**, which in turn links primary productivity to **seabirds**, **large fish**, **marine mammals**, and **benthic and intertidal communities**.

The biogeochemical cycle is an important collection of natural biological and physical processes controlling the productivities of both marine and terrestrial environments. The mechanisms that move carbon from the surface to the deep waters are known collectively as the **carbon pump**. Atmospheric carbon moves into seawater as carbon dioxide to be incorporated by phytoplankton during photosynthesis. Carbon also enters the sea as carbonates leached from the land by freshwater runoff as plant debris, and as other biological input such as immigrations of salmon (**salmon fry**) and other anadromous species. Carbon moves to benthic communities and to deep water as detritus and emigrant animals (**overwintering copepods** and migrating fish such as myctophids). Emigrant animals (**adult salmon** and other anadromous species) also move marine carbon (and phosphorus and nitrogen) into the watersheds.

As illustrated by the interactions of biological and physical components of the biogeochemical cycle, natural biological forces modify the effects of natural physical forces on birds, fish, and mammals. Because of biological-physical interactions, natural physical forces that cause changes in **primary productivity** do not necessarily cause proportional changes in populations of birds, fish, mammals, and benthic animals. For example, the effects of physical forces on the amount of food available from primary productivity are modified through other natural forces, such as **predation and competition** among individuals, collectively known as the **trophic linkages**. Populations that respond strongly to physical forcing of primary productivity on approximately the same time scales are termed "strongly coupled," and those that exhibit variable responses are termed "weakly coupled" with respect to those physical variables. Note that physical forcing changes not only the food available from primary productivity, but also the extent of habitats available for reproduction and feeding.

Human actions also serve to change the ways in which populations of plants and animals respond to the natural physical forces that affect the responses of reproduction, growth, and survival through limiting food and habitat. Human actions such as water withdrawals, sewage discharge, and development of **coastal communities** change productivity by altering habitat availability and trophic linkages. The economy of Alaska depends heavily on extraction of natural resources (primarily oil, fish, and shellfish followed by timber and minerals). Fishing and other extractive uses (**subsistence, sport, commercial**) affect death rates through removals. Other forms of human action are more subtle, but no less effective, controls on productivity. In the northern GOA, recreation and tourism, oil and gas development, logging, road building and urbanization, marine transportation, and subsistence harvests are all activities that have the potential to affect fish and wildlife populations and habitat. **Recreation and tourism** may alter growth and reproduction by disturbing rookeries and introducing pollutants. **Commercial marine transport** may alter productivity by introducing pollutants (oil spills) and noxious exotic species as competitors and predators. Currently, the human impact on Alaska's marine ecosystems is relatively small compared to impacts in most of the developed world. Even here, however, natural resource managers have concerns about localized pollution, the potential impacts of some fisheries, extreme changes in some fish and wildlife populations, and the little known impacts of contaminants and global warming.

In summary, Figure 1.1 shows that the GOA and its watersheds are part of a larger oceanic ecosystem in which natural physical forces such as currents, upwelling, downwelling, precipitation, and runoff, acting over large and small distances, play impor-

tant roles in determining basic biological productivity. Natural physical forces respond primarily to seasonal shifts in the weather, and in particular to long-term changes in the intensity and location of the Aleutian Low in winter. Increased upwelling offshore appears to increase inputs of nutrients to surface waters, which increases productivity of plankton. Increased winds appear to increase the transport of zooplankton shoreward toward and past the shelf break. How often and how much offshore zooplankton sources contribute to coastal food webs depends on natural physical and biological forces such as predation, migration, currents and structure of the fronts, formation and stability of eddies, degree and extent of turbulence, and responses of plankton to short and long-term changes in temperature and salinity.

A wide range of human impacts interacts with natural biological and physical forces to change productivity and community structure in the GOA. Approximately 71,000 full-time residents live within the area directly affected by the 1989 oil spill and two to three times that number use the area seasonally for work and recreation. The spill area population, combined with that of the nearby population centers of Anchorage and Wasilla, totals more than 60 percent of Alaska's 627,000 permanent residents. When the resident population is combined with the more than one million tourists who visit the state each year, it becomes clear that the natural resources of the GOA cannot be immune to the pressures associated with human uses and activities.

Because of the tremendous uncertainty about sources of long-term changes, the conceptual foundation does not provide a specific model (testable hypothesis) for ecosystem change. Rather, the conceptual foundation is designed to be broad enough to serve as a tool to encompass ecosystem interconnections, and to link information from traditional knowledge and scientific disciplines. It takes into account both oceanic and terrestrial ecosystems and addresses the influence of climate and human activity in influencing biological productivity within these interconnected systems.

As a start on a central hypothesis, consider the one provided by the National Research Council (NRC 2002, p. 27), as follows:

The Gulf of Alaska, its surrounding watersheds, and human populations are an interconnected set of ecosystems that must be studied and monitored as an integrated whole. Within this interconnected set, at time scales of years to decades, climate and human impacts are the two

Figure 1.1. The physical and biological elements of the ecosystems of the northern Gulf of Alaska from the mountains surrounding the watersheds to the ocean waters offshore.

most important driving forces in determining primary production and its transfer to upper-trophic-level organisms of concern to humans.

The NRC summary identifies climate and human impacts as the two most important determinants of biological production, among the many forcing factors recognized as significant in the conceptual foundation. Nonetheless, the biological communities that support the birds, fish, and mammals are subject to a variety of biological and physical agents and factors of change, any one of which can at times play an important, and even dominant, role in controlling populations of birds, fish, shellfish, and mammals. A central hypothesis that starts with and considers the full suite of forcing factors is needed to identify the most important forcing factors for species and habitats of the region.

1.2 LEADING HYPOTHESES

This section reviews leading hypotheses that explain changes in biological production as a result of natural and human activities.

1.2.1 Match-Mismatch Hypothesis

The essence of the match-mismatch hypothesis follows.

- Populations of organisms are adapted to certain environmental conditions.

- When those conditions change rapidly, predator and prey populations may not track in the same way.

- As a result, transfer of energy into the higher levels of the food web is compromised.

This hypothesis has been proposed by Mackas to explain changes in production with the slow shift to earlier emergence of *Neocalanus* copepods at Ocean Station P in the last several decades (Mackas et al. 1998). The match-mismatch hypothesis was also invoked by Anderson and Piatt to explain ecological changes observed in a long time series of small-mesh trawl sampling around Kodiak Island and the Alaska Peninsula (Anderson and Piatt 1999).

1.2.2 Pelagic-Benthic Split

Eslinger et al. (2001) suggested that strong inshore blooms of spring phytoplankton that occur in conditions of strong stratification put more biological production into the benthic ecosystem, in contrast to weaker, but more prolonged, blooms that occur in cool and windy growing seasons. Under the latter conditions, it has been proposed that biological production is more efficiently used by the pelagic ecosystem and that relatively less of the production reaches the benthos. It is conceivable that during a series of years in which one condition is much more prevalent than the other, food might be reallocated between pelagic-feeding and benthic-feeding species and be reflected in changes in these populations. Strong year classes of particular long-lived species also might result from conditions of strong stratification causing more biological production or weaker blooms, leading to dominance of the system by certain suites of species.

1.2.3 Optimum Stability Window Hypothesis

Gargett (1997) proposed that there is a point in the range of water stability below which water is too easily mixed downward, resulting in less than maximum productivity, and above which the water is stratified to the extent that it resists wind mixing. Gargett proposed that the fluctuating differences in salmon production between the California Current and subarctic gyre domains are ultimately the result of these two systems being on different parts of this response curve at different times.

1.2.4 Physiological Performance and Limits Hypothesis

A number of explanations for long-term change more simply propose that the abundance of certain species, mainly fish, is a direct response to their physiological performance at different temperatures. Under this hypothesis, the changes in dominance of cod-like fishes and crustaceans that were seen in the northern GOA around 1978 and in eastern Canada around 1990 were initially a response to warm (ascendancy of gadids) or cold (ascendancy of crustaceans) water temperatures. In other words, the main agents of change are the direct effects of water temperatures acting on physiological functions of individuals, in addition to the combined effects of freshwater input, winds, and temperature on ecological processes.

1.2.5 Food Quality Hypothesis

The food quality hypothesis is also referred to as the junk food hypothesis. It attributes declines of many higher-trophic-level organisms observed in the last several decades (harbor seals, sea lions, and many seabirds) to the predominance of suites of forage species that have low energy content (less lipid) than previous food sources (for example, gadids and flatfishes). Consistent with this hypothesis is evidence from the *Exxon Valdez* Trustee Council's Alaska Predator Ecosystem Experiment program, which showed that it takes about twice as much pollock as herring to raise a kittiwake chick to fledging during the nesting season (Piatt and Van Pelt 1998, Piatt 2000, Romano et al. 2000). With the relative rarity of capelin and sand lance in the diets of seabirds in Prince William Sound (PWS) during the last several decades, it seems that many of the population declines might be at least partially attributable to the role of these fatty fish in seabird diets. The change in food sources has been advanced for marine mammal populations that have been in decline.

1.2.6 Fluctuating Inshore and Offshore Production Regimes Hypothesis

Although the fluctuating inshore and offshore production regimes model is closely related to the Gargett hypothesis of an optimum stability window, it proposes that under the same set of atmospheric forcing conditions opposite production effects are seen inshore and offshore. Figures 1.2a-d illustrate some features of this model.

The model was developed from observations during the last several decades that populations of many seabirds, harbor seals, and sea lions, which forage mainly in inshore waters, have been declining while marine survival of salmon and high levels of offshore plankton and nekton suggested that offshore productivity was very high. It is proposed that the various manifestations of climate forcing have combined since about 1978 (positive Pacific decadal oscillation [PDO]) to make the ocean more productive offshore.

Characteristics of the offshore ocean include more upwelling of deep nutrients and a mixed surface layer that is shallower and more productive. These same climatic conditions are proposed to have made the inshore areas of the GOA less productive. During the positive PDO (Figure 1.2 A,B), greater freshwater supply (precipitation on the ocean and terrestrial runoff) results in greater-than-optimal nearshore stratification. Also, during the positive PDO , greater winds cannot overcome the stratification during the growing season, but do inhibit the relaxation of downwelling. Therefore, fewer nutrients are supplied to the inshore regime from the annual run-up of deep water onto the shelf. During a negative PDO (Figure 1.2 C,D), the opposite pattern in biological response results from a colder, less windy, and drier maritime climate.

1.2.7 Human Impacts Hypotheses

Hypotheses on human impacts explain alterations of ecosystems as the result of human activities. Changes in species composition, alteration of the relative abundances of species and their food species, and changes in production and productivities of populations of plants and animals are widely accepted as being consequences, to some degree, of human activities (Jackson et al. 2001). An important, constant dilemma in the history of natural resource management is distinguishing between human and non-human causes of fluctuations in production of biological resources through time (Mangel et al. 1996, NRC 1999). Indeed, this classic dilemma is the origin of the central hypothesis. A large body of existing hypotheses, summarized below, view specific human activities, such as harvesting and pollution, as causes of changes in biological production that are direct or indirect sources of mortality for plant and animal populations, including those of humans.

1.2.7.1 Theory of Sustainable Fishing

According to the theory of sustainable fishing, it is possible to strike a balance between the losses caused by human and natural forces, and the gains due to reproduction and growth, such that the abundance of a species in an area remains constant through time. Also known as the deterministic theory of fishing (Quinn and Deriso 1999), this theory has intellectual origins in the equation of logistic population growth first introduced in this context in 1837 (Quinn and Deriso 1999), and in even older concepts of population regulation that can be traced

to the late eighteenth century (1798). It is well known that the ideal of a constant population size regularly producing predictable amounts of biomass for human consumption in perpetuity is rare in the case of wild populations (1973) (Ricker 1975, Quinn and Deriso 1999). Nonetheless, this ideal is the basis for the legal, scientific, and popular concepts of sustainable uses of all types of renewable natural resources, and it motivates the need to distinguish between, and to help quantify, natural and human caused sources of mortality.

The original basic theory of sustainable fishing has been expanded to include the concept that the process of fishing sustainably for one species may not constitute fishing sustainably for other species (Quinn and Deriso 1999). For example, one of the operating hypotheses for investigations of causes for decline of the Steller sea lion in the GOA by the National Marine Fisheries Service (NMFS 2002) is that the declines are due to commercial fisheries out-competing the sea lion for food. Starvation and associated nutritional stress are hypothesized to be direct agents of mortality and causes of lowered reproductive rates.

Fisheries are also hypothesized to compete with terrestrial species by lowering the overall productivity of watersheds in the region and adjacent areas, thereby also reducing the production of salmon that originate in those watersheds (Finney 1998; Gresh et al. 2000; Finney et al. 2000, 2002). Transport of nutrients from the marine environment to the watersheds by anadromous species, principally Pacific salmon, is thought to be important for sustaining the overall productivity of some types of watersheds, including the salmon species themselves (Mathisen 1972; Kline et al. 1990, 1993; Bilby et al. 1996; Mathisen et al. 2000). Note that application of the deterministic theory of fishing without inclusion of nutrient effects could lead to a downward spiral in the annual production of the salmon species being managed, instead of the constant population predicted by the theory (Finney et al. 2000). As the salmon fishery removes nutrients from the watershed, the carrying capacity of the watershed for salmon is lowered, thereby causing the deterministic theory of fishing to prescribe to managers a lower "sustainable" level of spawners. The lower level of spawners means even less nutrients and a lower level of productivity for the watershed. Lower productivity means an even lower estimate of "sustainable" spawners from the theory, leading to less nutrients for the watershed, and a downward spiral in salmon production.

A.

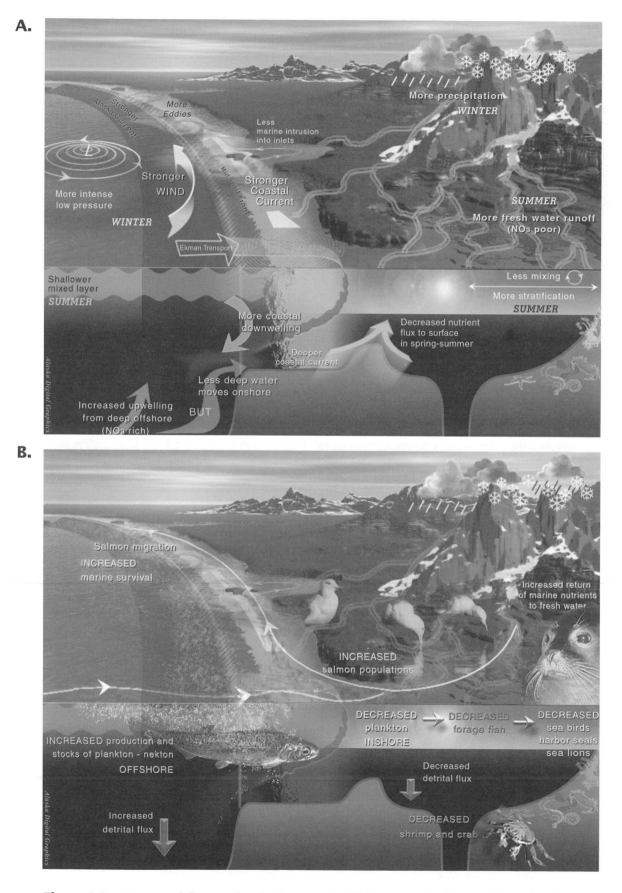

Figure 1.2.   **Proposed fluctuating inshore and offshore production regimes in the Gulf of Alaska showing relative changes in the physical processes during a**

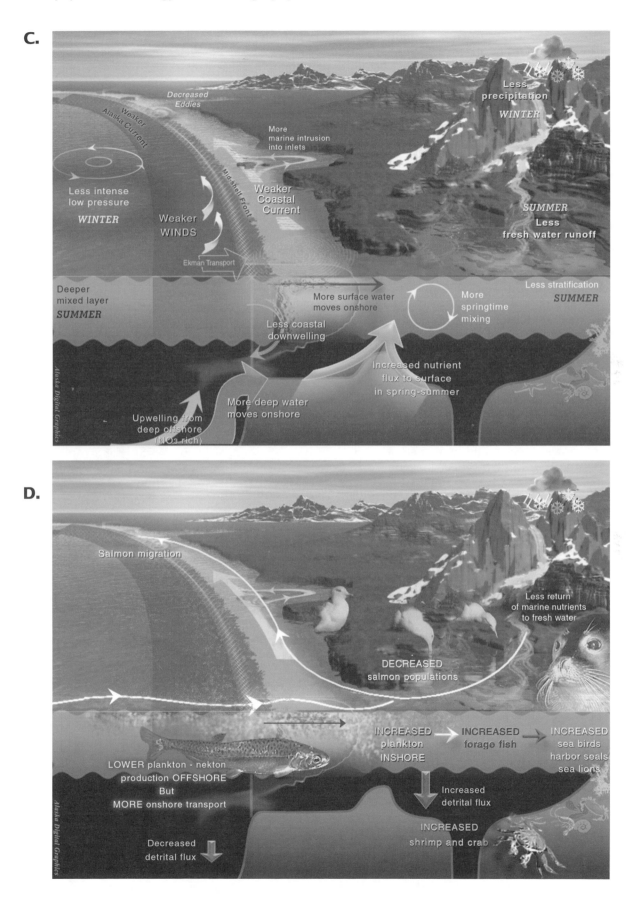

positive Pacific decadal oscillation (PDO; strong winter low pressure) (A,B) and a negative PDO (weak winter low pressure) (C,D).

1.2.7.2 Ubiquitous Distribution and Northern Concentration of Anthropogenic Contaminants Hypothesis

Transport of contaminants from sites of release in lower latitudes by atmospheric and oceanic processes and through biologic pathways concentrates anthropogenic contaminants in northern ecosystems in even the most remote, uninhabited regions of the Northern Hemisphere, including the GOA (Crane and Galasso 1999). Contaminants produced by human activities in human-populated areas, principally radionuclides, organochlorines, and heavy metals, alter ecosystems in all parts of the world by changing rates of biological production (productivities), as agents of direct and indirect mortality. For example, one of the operating hypotheses for investigations of causes for decline of the Steller sea lion in the GOA by the National Marine Fisheries Service (NMFS 2002) is that the declines are due to reproductive impairment and mortality resulting from contaminants from distant and local sources. Also in the GOA region, two organochlorines, polychlorinated biphenyls (PCBs) and the pesticide dichlorodiphenyltrichloroethane (DDT), were found to be transported to remote localities in the Copper River drainage (near 63°N 145°W) by migratory fish species and by wind (Ewald et al. 1998). Both DDT and PCB concentrations per individual increase as they move through the food chain, with both at times being found in very high concentrations near the top of the food chain in birds and mammals, including humans. DDT is well known to cause reproductive impairment, especially in birds. Metabolites of DDT (p,p'-DDE) were found in blubber taken by biopsy of killer whales in PWS in concentrations high enough (21-210 ppm) to suggest reproductive impairment and infant mortality, and relatively high concentrations of other organochlorines were also found (Ylitalo et al. 2001). PCB is known to cause pathological changes in reproductive and immune systems. For example, relatively high concentrations of PCB in the milk fat of Inuit women are consistent with the high incidence of infectious disease among Inuit infants in arctic Quebec, Canada (Dewailly et al. 1993).

1.2.7.3 Anthropogenic Distribution of Exotic Species Hypothesis

According to this hypothesis, human transport of vertebrate and invertebrate species causes changes in ecosystems by radically changing species composition and relative abundances of species through alterations of food web (trophic) pathways and interactions. The food webs of the GOA appear to be susceptible to alteration by certain freshwater and anadromous fish species that are known to be able to complete their life cycles at these latitudes: Atlantic salmon, northern pike, and yellow perch (ADF&G 2002). Anthropogenic introductions of both northern pike and yellow perch have been documented, and Atlantic salmon have become established to the south in British Columbia as a result of failed pen rearing operations. In addition, a number of other vertebrate and invertebrate animal species and a number of freshwater and salt marsh plants may be able to establish themselves in the region if introduced (ADF&G 2002).

1.2.7.4 Cumulative Human Effects Hypothesis

Individual instances of fishing, introduction of contaminants, transport of exotic species, and other human impacts that are not alone sufficient to cause discernible changes in the ecosystem are inexorably accumulated through time to levels that can and do profoundly alter the habitats and trophic pathways of the ecosystem, thereby reducing production of many animal and plant species. As a corollary, cumulative effects are directly proportional to human population density and they can reach levels that prohibit any sustainable human use of certain species (Mangel et al. 1996). For example, many salmon populations near and adjacent to human centers in the Pacific Northwest (California, Oregon, Washington, Idaho) are now categorized by the federal government as threatened or endangered, and can no longer provide a harvestable surplus with respect to humans (Stouder et al. 1997), whereas salmon populations in areas of low human densities are producing historical record-high levels of harvest (Mundy 1996). Further, it is evident that environments around urbanized areas (such as Los Angeles, Puget Sound, Boston Harbor, San Francisco Bay, and New York Bight) and watershed systems (Columbia River Basin and San Joaquin River) have highly altered ecosystems that contain invasive exotic species, individuals impaired by contamination, and fish populations that have been altered by the combined effects of various human impacts. It appears that this degradation occurred over a long period of time and as a result of the combined impacts of many different human activities.

1.3 PRINCIPAL ECOLOGICAL CONCEPTS

Production at the base of the food web, primary productivity, is strongly influenced by physical forces, and ultimately determines ecosystem productivity. However, the abundance of any particular population within the food web depends on three things: immediate food supply (prey), removals (mortality), and habitat.

All animals and plants in the oceans ultimately rely on energy from the sun or, in some special cases, on chemical energy from within the earth. The amount of solar energy converted to living material determines the level of ecosystem production (total amount of living material and at what rate it is produced). As a rule of thumb, populations of individual species (such as salmon, herring, and harbor seals) cannot exceed about 10 percent of the biomass of their prey populations (about the average conversion of prey to predator biomass). Therefore, the amount of energy that gets incorporated into living material and the processes that deliver this material as food and energy to each species are key factors influencing reproduction, growth, and death in species of concern. Increases in prey, with other factors such as habitat being equal, generally allow populations to increase through growth and reproduction of individual members. At the same time, there are factors that lead to decreases in populations, loss of suitable habitat, decreases in growth, reproduction, and immigration, and increases in the rate of removal (death and emigration) of individuals from the population. As a result, the combined effects of natural forces and human activities that determine food supply (bottom-up forces), habitat (bottom-up and top-down forces), and removals (top-down forces) determine the size of animal populations by controlling reproduction, growth, and death.

1.3.1 Physical Forcing and Primary Production

The vast majority of the energy that supports ecosystems in the GOA comes from capture, or fixation, of solar energy in the surface waters. How much of this energy is captured by plants in the ocean's surface layer and watersheds and passed on ultimately determines how much biomass and production occur at all levels in the ecosystem. Capture of solar energy by plants in the oceans and watersheds and the conversion of solar energy to living tissue (primary production) depends on several interacting forces and conditions that vary widely from place to place, season to season, and year to year as well as between decades. The process of capturing solar energy is explained below.

First, in the ocean, primary production occurs only in the shallowly lit photic zone (a few hundred feet). In watersheds, cloud cover and shading play a larger role in variability of productivity. Second, plants that fix this energy, by using it to make simple sugars out of carbon dioxide and water, depend on nutrients that are absorbed by the plants as they grow and reproduce. Solar energy that is not captured by plants in the ocean warms the surface waters, making it less dense than the water beneath the photic zone, which causes layering of the water masses. A continuous supply of nutrients to the surface waters is necessary to maintain plant production. Likewise, terrestrial plants depend on nutrients carried from the ocean by anadromous fish. Because the deep water of the GOA is the main reservoir of nutrients for shallow waters, and apparently also an important source for watersheds, the processes that bring nutrients to the surface and into the watersheds are key to understanding primary ecosystem productivity. Changes in nutrient supply on time scales of days to decades and spatial scales from kilometers to hundreds of kilometers have important impacts on primary production, generating as much as a thousand-fold difference in the amount of solar energy that is captured by the living ecosystem. Nutrient supply from the deep water is influenced by the properties of the shallower water above (mainly because of the decreasing density of the water toward the surface). Nutrient supply is also influenced by physical forces that can overcome the density differences between deep and shallow water—namely, wind acting on the water surface and tidal mixing. For watersheds, nutrient supply apparently depends strongly on biological transport of marine nitrogen by salmon, which die and release their nutrients in freshwater, as well as other sources (such as nitrogen fixers).

As demonstrated in the following scientific chapters of this book, the knowledge of nutrient supply in the GOA, both how it occurs and how it may be changed on multi-year and multi-decadal scales, is very rudimentary. As the energy of the wind and tides mixes surface and deeper water, it not only brings nutrients to the surface layers, but also mixes algae that fix the solar energy down and out of the photic zone, which tends to decrease primary production. Therefore, other factors being equal, continuous high primary production in the spring-summer growing season is a balance between enough wind and tidal mixing to bring new nutrients to the surface, but not so much wind or tidal mixing that would send algal populations to deep water. The seasonal changes in downwelling, solar energy, and water stratification that set up the annual plankton bloom are described in chapter 6 of this book. As noted, it is not well understood how differences in physical forces from year to year and decade to decade change primary production manifold in any particular place.

1.3.2 Food, Habitat, and Removals

Increases in immediate food supply (prey) will translate to population increase, all other factors being equal. The allocation of energy in each individual is key to growth of the population it belongs to. Food supply is converted into population biomass through growth and reproduction of individuals in specific favorable habitats. Therefore, factors in the habitat such as water temperature, distribution of prey, and contaminants that can influence the allocation of food energy to the following activities will influence the population size: chasing and capturing prey, maintaining body temperature (for homeotherms and other physiological processes), growth, and reproduction.

Removals are all the processes that result in loss of individuals from the population, or mortality. These processes include death from contamination, human harvest, predation, disease, and competition. For example, harvest of a large proportion of the largest and most fecund fish in a population will soon decrease the population, as will a virulent virus or the appearance of a voracious predator in large numbers.

Also included under the category of removals is any factor that negatively affects growth or reproductive rate of individuals, because such factors can decrease population size. Contaminants are considered potential removals because of the following possible effects:

- Causing damage that makes energy utilization less efficient and requires energy for repairs;

- Interfering with molecular receptors that are part of the regulatory machinery for energy allocation;

- Damaging immune systems that make disease more likely; and

- Outright killing of organisms at high concentrations.

Habitats in marine and freshwater environments are ultimately controlled by temperature and salinity, as modified by many other biological, physical, and chemical factors. Basic physiological functions such as respiration and assimilation of nutrients from food occur only within certain boundaries of temperature and salinity. A number of hypotheses on the origins of long-term change relate the abundance of certain aquatic species to their physiological performance in different temperatures. For example, changes in dominance of cod-like fishes and crustaceans in the northern GOA around 1978, and in eastern Canada around 1990, were explained as positive responses of gadids to increasingly warm temperatures. Using the same reasoning, the ascendancy of crustaceans such as shrimp in the GOA in the 1950s and 1960s, and in eastern Canada during the 1990s, have been attributed to cooling water temperatures.

On the basis of the first principles of physics, chemistry, and biology, temperature and salinity must be agents of change in biological resources through effects relating to physiological functions in individual plants and animals. Effects on individuals add to the combined effects of freshwater input, winds, and temperature on ecological processes. The preceding ecological concepts have been applied directly to the GOA ecosystems to show how the system and its plant and animal populations are controlled in the conceptual foundation.

1.3.3 Trophic Structure

The principal trophic groups of the northern GOA are represented by the analysis of Okey and Pauly for PWS (Okey and Pauly 1999). The upper trophic levels (3.5+) are dominated by large vertebrates, including toothed whales, harbor seals and sea lions, seabirds, sharks, and fish species that are large as adults (Table 1.1). Primary consumers on trophic levels between 1 (primary producers) and 3 (tertiary) include jellyfish, zooplankters (including larvae of crustaceans and fish), infauna, and meiofauna. The primary sources of food in the northern GOA are phytoplankton, macroalgae and eelgrass, and detritus. The species of the dominant biomass are macroalgae and eelgrass, followed closely by shallow and deep infauna, deep epibenthos, and herbivorous zooplankton. In terms of production per biomass (P/B), the dominant species groups are clearly the phytoplankton, followed by the herbivorous zooplankton. In terms of food consumption per biomass (Q/B), invertebrate-eating birds top the list, followed by small cetaceans and pinnipeds, and herbivorous zooplankton. Using this concept of the trophic structure of the northern GOA, data on the lower trophic levels (< 3.5) are extremely important to detecting and understanding change in valued marine-related resources.

The GOA and its watersheds are part of a larger oceanic ecosystem in which natural physical forces such as currents, upwelling, downwelling, precipitation, and runoff, acting over large and small distances, play important roles in determining basic biological productivity. Natural physical forces respond

Table 1.1. Representative Trophic Groups of the Northern Gulf of Alaska Arranged in Descending Order by Trophic Level.

Group name	Trophic level	Biomass (t km^{-2} year^{-1})	P/B (yr^{-1})	Q/B (yr^{-1})
Orcas	4.98	0.003	0.050	8.285
Sharks	4.81	0.700	0.100	2.100
Pacific halibut	4.59	0.677	0.320	1.730
Small cetaceans (porpoises)	4.52	0.015	0.150	29.200
Pinnipeds (harbor seal & sea lion)	4.45	0.066	0.060	25.550
Lingcod	4.33	0.077	0.580	3.300
Sablefish	4.29	0.293	0.566	6.420
Arrowtooth flounder adult	4.25	4.000	0.220	3.030
Salmon adult	4.17	1.034	6.476	13.000
Pacific cod	4.14	0.300	1.200	4.000
Arrowtooth flounder juvenile	4.01	0.855	0.220	3.030
Avian predators	3.89	0.002	5.000	36.500
Seabirds	3.78	0.011	7.800	150.60
Deep demersal fish (skates and flatfishes)	3.78	0.960	0.930	3.210
Pollock age 1+	3.76	7.480	0.707	2.559
Rockfish	3.74	1.016	0.170	3.440
Baleen whales	3.65	0.149	0.050	10.900
Salmon fry 0-12 cm	3.51	0.072	7.154	62.800
Nearshore demersal fish (greenling and sculpin)	3.35	4.200	1.000	4.240
Squid	3.26	3.000	3.000	15.000
Eulachon	3.25	0.371	2.000	18.000
Sea otters	3.23	0.045	0.130	117.000
Deep epibenthos	3.16	30.000	3.000	10.000
Capelin	3.11	0.367	3.500	18.000
Adult herring	3.10	2.810	0.540	18.000
Pollock age 0	3.07	0.110	2.340	16.180
Shallow large epibenthos	3.07	3.100	2.100	10.000
Invertebrate eating bird	3.07	0.005	0.200	450.500
Sand lance	3.06	0.595	2.000	18.000
Juvenile herring	3.03	13.406	0.729	18.000
Jellies	2.96	6.390	8.820	29.410
Deep small infauna	2.25	49.400	3.000	23.000
Near omni-zooplankton	2.25	0.103	7.900	26.333
Omni-zooplankton	2.25	24.635	11.060	22.130
Shallow small infauna	2.18	51.500	3.800	23.000
Meiofauna	2.11	**4.478**	4.500	22.000
Deep large infauna	2.10	28.350	0.600	23.000
Shallow small epibenthos	2.05	26.100	2.300	10.000
Shallow large infauna (clams, etc.)	2.00	12.500	0.600	23.000
Near herbi-zooplankton	2.00	0.136	27.000	90.000
Herbi-zooplankton	2.00	30.000	24.000	50.000
Near phytoplankton	1.00	**5.326**	190.000	0.000
Offshore phytoplankton	1.00	**10.672**	190.000	0.000
Macroalgae/eelgrass	1.00	125.250	5.000	0.000
Inshore detritus	1.00	3.000	–	–
Offshore detritus	1.00	4.500	–	–

Notes: Bold values were calculated by the Ecopath software.

P/B is production per biomass. Q/B is food consumption per biomass.

Source: Table 74 (Okey and Pauly 1999)

primarily to seasonal shifts in the weather, and in particular to long-term changes in the intensity and location of the Aleutian Low system in winter. Increased upwelling offshore appears to increase inputs of nutrients to surface waters, which increases productivity of plankton. Increased winds appear to increase the transport of zooplankton shoreward toward and past the shelf break. How often and how much offshore zooplankton sources contribute to coastal food webs depends on natural physical and biological forces such as predation, migration, currents and structure of the fronts, formation and stability of eddies, degree and extent of turbulence, and responses of plankton to short and long-term changes in temperature and salinity.

A wide range of human impacts interacts with natural biological and physical forces to change productivity and community structure in the GOA. Human activities have the most direct and obvious impacts at those sites in watersheds and intertidal areas where human populations are high. Nonetheless, some human activities affect populations of birds, fish, shellfish, and mammals far offshore, and also have impacts far from the sites of the actions. In short, human activities and natural forces together act over global to local scales to drive and shape marine and terrestrial life in the GOA and its tributary watersheds. Natural forces and human impacts, as exemplified by heat and salt distribution, insolation, biological energy flow, biogeochemical cycling and food web structure, fishery removals, pollutant inputs, and the relationships among them over time define the state of the marine ecosystem. Natural forces and human impacts bring about changes in populations of birds, fish, shellfish, and mammals by altering the relationships among variables that define the marine ecosystem. This understanding of the mechanisms affecting change in the GOA provides the basis for developing key hypotheses about the GOA ecosystem.

1.4 THE CENTRAL HYPOTHESIS AND HABITAT TYPES

Identifying the forcing factors, human and natural, that drive biological production requires framing hypotheses and questions. The central hypothesis states widely held beliefs about what drives changes in living marine-related resources in time and space:

Natural forces and human activities working over global to local scales bring about short-term and long-lasting changes in the biological communities that support birds,

fish, shellfish, and mammals. Natural forces and human activities bring about change by altering relationships among defining characteristics of habitats and ecosystems such as heat and salt distribution, insolation, biological energy flow, freshwater flow, biogeochemical cycles, food web structure, fishery impacts, and pollutant levels.

Although widely accepted as fact, the specific mechanisms that cause change are largely untested in the GOA region, and the relative importance of the forcing factors is unknown. Current speculations, supported by limited observations, are that forcing by winds, precipitation, predation, currents, natural competitors for food and habitat, fisheries, and pollutants change living marine-related resources over different scales of time and space through alteration of critical properties of habitats and ecosystems (Figures 1.3 and 1.4).

Although the central hypothesis may appear to be a bland statement of the obvious, it is an essential first step in applying the scientific method to address the many open, and sometimes highly contentious, scientific questions about whether, and to what extent, human activities are responsible for degradation of habitats and declines in populations of animals. The central hypothesis states what is thought to be known in general, preparing the way for questions that test the validity of this knowledge. For example it is reasonable to ask of the central hypothesis, "What are the natural forces and are they equally important in all types of habitat?" Critically examining the starting point, through posing and answering questions, is intended to point out the need for more specific hypotheses, which in turn lead to more specific questions, and so forth.

The central hypothesis is given more specificity through adaptation to habitat types in the following section. Before adding specificity to the central hypothesis, the habitat types need definition, and the context of conducting studies at time-space scales appropriate to the phenomenon needs to be provided.

Four habitat types, representative of the GOA region, have been identified: watersheds, intertidal and subtidal areas, ACC, and offshore areas (the continental shelf break and the Alaska Gyre). These habitats were selected after evaluating information about how natural forces and human activities control biological productivity in the northern GOA. The habitats are composed of identifiable, although not rigid, collections of characteristic microhabitats, resident and migratory species, and physical features.

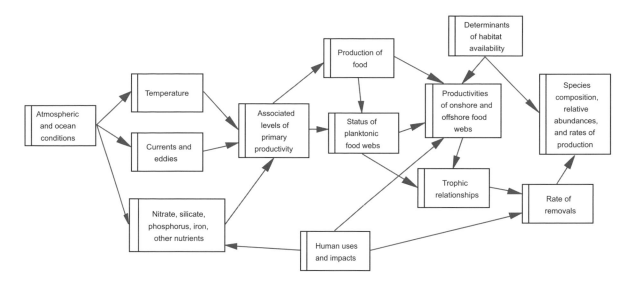

Figure 1.3.   Possible connections among specific mechanisms and agents of change in living marine-related resources.

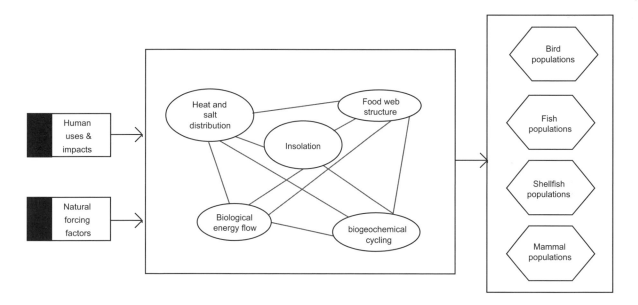

Figure 1.4.   Relations among major parts of the Gulf Ecosystem Monitoring (GEM) Program conceptual foundation.

- *Watersheds*—freshwater and terrestrial habitats from the mountains to the extent of a river's plume.

- *Intertidal and subtidal areas*—brackish and saltwater coastal habitats that extend offshore to the 20 m depth contour.

- *Alaska Coastal Current (ACC)*—a swift coastal current of lower salinities (25 to 31 psu) typically found within 35 km of the shore.

- *Offshore*—the continental shelf break (between the 200 m and 1,000 m depth contours) and the Alaska Gyre in waters outside the 1,000 m depth contour.

To understand the composition and extent of ecosystems, it is necessary to ask and answer questions about the distances and time associated with the variation in the biological and physical phenomena. As stated eloquently by Ricklefs (1990, p. 169), "Every phenomenon, regardless of its scale in space and time, includes finer scale processes and patterns and is embedded in a matrix of processes and patterns having larger dimensions." Indeed, spatial and temporal scales are part of the definitions of physical and biological processes such as advection and growth. Taking account of spatial and temporal scales is critical to studying linkages between natural forces and biological responses (Francis et al. 1998).

Cross-habitat linkages and processes are described in more detail in later chapters. It is assumed that modeling efforts are regional in focus rather than habitat specific.

The central hypothesis is adapted to each habitat type:

Watersheds—Natural forces (such as climate) and human activities (such as habitat degradation and fishing) serve as distant and local factors in causing short-term and long-lasting changes in marine-related biological production in watersheds.

Intertidal and Subtidal—Natural forces (such as currents and predation) and human activities (such as increased urbanization and localized pollution) serve as distant and local factors, in causing short-term and long-lasting changes in community structure and dynamics of the intertidal and subtidal habitats.

Alaska Coastal Current (ACC)—Natural forces (such as variability in the strength, structure, and dynamics of the ACC) and human activities (such as fishing and pollution) cause local and distant changes in production of phytoplankton, zooplankton, birds, fish, and mammals.

Offshore—Natural forces (such as changes in the strength of the Alaska Current and Alaskan Stream, mixed layer depth of the gyre, wind stress, and downwelling) and human activities (such as pollution) play significant roles in determining production of carbon and its shoreward transport.

CHAPTER 2

Physical and Biological Background

Phillip R. Mundy and Robert T. Cooney

2.1 INTRODUCTION

The cold and turbulent Gulf of Alaska (GOA) is one of the world's most productive ocean regions. It sustains immense populations of seabirds, marine mammals, and fishes, and provides a way of life for tens of thousands of Alaskans. Indeed, the GOA is still wild, full of life, and deserves protection and wise management as one of the bio-gems of the planet.

Just why the GOA is so unusually productive remains unclear. The fish, birds, and mammals at the top of the food chain are supported by a diverse marine food web (Table 1.1 in chapter 1), dependent on the physical characteristics of an ever-changing ocean—one that experiences seasonal, annual, and longer-period extremes in weather and climate. The plant nutrients come from deep water, fueling production at the base of the marine food web. This production is eventually expressed in the stock size and production of higher-level consumers. Somehow, physical conditions in this region promote sufficient exchange between deep and shallow waters to bring these fertilizing elements to the surface, where they stimulate plant growth each year. To understand the GOA's complex ecosystem, and the productivity of its species big and small, requires more precise knowledge about the interactions between many biological and physical factors.

Recent studies on how selected species interact with prey, predators, and competitors—and most important, how these associations are influenced by shifts in ocean climate and human activities—provide exciting new possibilities for understanding this great ecosystem. This knowledge will help resource managers sustain populations of these species despite growing human influence in the region (possible climate change and elevated pollution levels) and the pressure of increased human use (harvests, recreational impacts, and population).

The following summary describes the northern GOA ecosystem as it is now understood, and reveals gaps in current knowledge about the dynamics of higher-level productivity.

2.2 PRINCIPAL HABITATS AND LIVING RESOURCES

The extent of damage resulting from the massive oiling of Prince William Sound and the coastal waters to the west in spring 1989 will never be fully known. In the short term, scientific studies focus on the spill-affected resources that remain at risk. But the *Exxon Valdez* Oil Spill Trustee Council has committed its long-term support to a program of broader ecological research and environmental monitoring. The effort centers on the major physical and biological phenomena that influence marine productivity in the principal habitats of the northern GOA. These habitats can be identified as:

- Coastal watersheds;

- Intertidal and shallow subtidal zones to a depth of 20 meters;

- Alaska Coastal Current (ACC); and

- Offshore areas embracing the continental shelf break and beyond to the continental slope and deep ocean basin.

In these interacting environments, scientists understand only to a limited extent how the dominant fishes, seabirds, and marine mammals use critical habitats to sustain populations in face of cyclic ocean climate, extensive commercial and subsistence harvests, and threats from pollution and diseases.

2.2.1 Watersheds

The extensive coastal watersheds that drain into the northern GOA represent spawning and rearing habitat for anadromous species like Pacific salmon and eulachon, and nesting habitat for some seabirds like marbled murrelets. The carcasses of spawned-out salmon supply substantial amounts of marine-derived nutrients to the poorly nourished streams, lakes, and rivers used for their reproduction. In addition, dying salmon provide a food supply for many birds and mammals throughout the coastal range. Bears, eagles, and many gulls benefit locally from this extensive forage resource. Analyses have also shown that marine-derived nitrogen from anadromous fishes leaves a detectable signal in many coastal plant communities.

The human harvest of anadromous species may affect not only those species, but also all of the plants and animals touched by marine nutrients. Therefore, understanding the distribution of marine nutrients by anadromous fish species puts a new dimension on fisheries management. So, it is reasonable to ask to what extent human consumption of salmon affects the production of other plants and animals in the coastal watersheds. Moving beyond single-species management toward ecosystem-based management in coastal watersheds would require long-term monitoring of the flux of marine nutrients.

These same watersheds experience extensive human activity in addition to fishing. Large-scale logging and commercialization, including coastal settlements and towns, can alter or destroy some habitats. Expanding recreational activities in the coastal zone between Prince William Sound and Kodiak Island also will include additional land uses. Compared with other regions in North America, however, most watersheds in the periphery of the GOA are remote and relatively undisturbed.

2.2.2 Intertidal and Subtidal

The intertidal and shallow subtidal habitats are represented by a variety of nearshore estuarine, fjord, and exposed coastal settings. These habitats range from precipitous and rocky, to gently sloping with muddy or sandy bottoms. The intertidal and shallow subtidal zones are among the most productive of marine habitats in the GOA. Here the annual growth of microalgae, seaweeds, and seagrasses supports many invertebrates that, in turn, are food for fishes, marine birds, and mammals. Guillemots and sea otters, for example, depend on the crabs, clams, and mussels, along with small benthic fishes found in the intertidal and subtidal habitats. This specialized edge-zone habitat is also a nursery for juvenile pink and chum salmon and juvenile Pacific herring for several months each year. Huge schools of spawning herring and capelin deposit their eggs in the shallows each spring. These mass spawnings induce a feeding frenzy that may last for a week or more. Gulls, kittiwakes, seals, sea lions, fishes, and a variety of large invertebrates gather to feed on the egg masses. The fish eggs are often eaten in huge numbers by shorebirds and other species that stop over in the region during the spring migration.

The intertidal and shallow subtidal zones may be at greatest risk to human activities. Increasing use of vehicles, boats, and aircraft by recreationists and sport fishermen exploits these areas. In addition, floating pollutants and refuse, particularly plastic materials from the fishing industry, make landfall in the intertidal zone. Unlike the coastal watersheds that remain relatively unaltered at many locations, it is rare to walk the intertidal zone anywhere in the GOA without seeing evidence of human activity. The degree to which these "footprints" result in environmental degradation is clear in the case of oil and toxic spills, but largely unknown for other pollution.

2.2.3 Alaska Coastal Current

Hugging the inner third of the continental shelf, the ACC provides a sizeable and ecologically important transition zone between the shallow, nearshore communities and the huge outer-shelf and oceanic pelagic ecosystems. Fed by runoff from glaciers, snowmelt, and rainfall, the well-defined coastal current is a nearshore "river in the sea" with a freshwater output about one-and-a-half times that of the Mississippi River. It flows consistently to the north and west around the northern GOA from British Columbia to Unimak Pass on the Aleutian Islands chain. The ACC, urged along by coastal winds, distributes subarctic plankton communities around the region and into protected inside waters such as Prince William Sound and lower Cook Inlet. During the summer months, the ACC has local reversals and small eddies, which can concentrate plankton and small fishes in convergence zones, for foraging fish, birds, and marine mammals.

The ACC is an important feeding habitat for many fish, birds, and mammals. Most seabirds nest in coastal colonies or on islands where protection from predators is afforded by the isolation of rocky cliffs. Because of this nesting behavior, the distribution and abundance of seabirds during their reproductive season is governed primarily by the availability of suitable, safe nesting sites and access to adequate prey. Seabirds in the GOA are often grouped on the basis of their foraging behavior. Surface feeders like kittiwakes obtain prey mostly in the upper 1 meter (m), coastal divers such as guillemots and murrelets exploit the shallow water column and nearshore seabed, while murres are deep divers capable of feeding in the water or on the bottom to depths of 200 m. Seabirds feed close to colonies when opportunities arise, but most are also capable of flying a long distance to feed. It is not unusual for coastal seabirds to fly to the outer shelf and shelf-break regions to feed themselves and their offspring.

Marine mammals residing in the ACC are primarily fish eaters, although a few feed on bottom-dwelling invertebrates and some hunt other marine mammals or even seabirds. Killer whales are either resident (fish eaters primarily) or transient (feeding mostly on other marine mammals). Seals, sea lions, and sea otters bear and protect their offspring in coastal rookeries sprinkled around the edge of the GOA and influenced by the ACC. Fur seals and sea lions exploit a broad array of nearshore and oceanic habitats, although the juveniles appear to be more confined to the waters near rookeries. By comparison, sea otters and harbor seals are almost sedentary in habit, usually ranging only short distances for food. Juvenile and adult harbor seals hunt and consume a variety of fishes, squids, and octopus in mostly coastal habitats. While sea otters can retrieve food from depths to 100 m, they rarely leave the shallow coastal areas where they live as generalist predators on a broad array of sessile or slow-moving macro-invertebrates, including clams, mussels, crabs, sea urchins, and sea stars.

Many fishes and shellfishes also live, feed, and reproduce in the ACC. Coastal rockfishes, Pacific herring, juvenile and adult walleye pollock, juvenile and adult salmon, adult cod, and many species of shrimps and crabs occur in protected fjords, inlets, bays, and sounds where they forage and/or reproduce, and where their early life stages feed and grow. Halibut and lingcod occur abundantly in some seasons, and king crabs that feed and grow in deeper shelf and slope environments visit the shallower inner shelf to reproduce each year. Because the eggs and larvae of many marine invertebrates and fishes drift with the plankton for weeks or even months, the flow of the ACC serves to distribute these forms to the variety of coastal habitats found around the edge of the GOA.

The same coastal flow that benefits so many species may also serve to distribute marine pollutants. Oil spilled in the northeastern corner of Prince William Sound by the *Exxon Valdez* in 1989 entered the coastal flow and was carried hundreds of miles to the west, fouling beaches along the outer Kenai Peninsula, in lower Cook Inlet, on Kodiak Island, and along the southern Alaska Peninsula. A future toxic spill in shelf or coastal waters southeast of Prince William Sound could conceivably be spread across the entire northern GOA by the coastal flow.

2.2.4 Offshore: Mid-shelf and Deeper Waters

Offshore waters, which begin at the outer edge of the adjacent Alaska Coastal Current region—about 20 to 30 miles offshore—delineate a huge marine ecosystem. East of Prince William Sound, the shelf is narrow, so the mid-shelf and deeper waters are close to the coast, about 30 to 50 miles. South and west of the sound, the shelf broadens to 100 to 120 miles in width before narrowing again south of the Alaska Peninsula and Aleutian Islands. These differences in shelf width provide seabirds, seals, and sea lions at some coastal locations with easy access to the deepwater environments for feeding purposes when needed; at other sites, access to the shelf edge and open ocean is much farther away. Spatial differences of this kind may be important to recognize when comparing the reproductive successes of birds and mammals in rookeries from different locations in the GOA. Arrowtooth flounder, Pacific ocean perch, walleye pollock, Pacific halibut, and Pacific cod (in descending order of importance) composed the bulk of the trawl-caught stock of groundfishes in shelf and continental slope environments of the GOA in 1996.

The dominant flow in the offshore is counterclockwise, and it is designated the Alaska Current. Because the Alaska Current has its southern origins in the oceanic Subarctic Current, marine pollution and floating refuse from as far away as Asia, or originating from deliberate deep-ocean dumping or accidents at sea, can be swept north and westward around the shelf edge in the GOA. Trash from the international fishing industry operating 200 miles offshore is commonly found on beaches. Some of these pollutants also can be carried westward to the GOA in the atmosphere.

2.3 INTERMEDIATE LEVELS OF THE FOOD WEB

Food webs are really pyramids with seabirds, marine mammals, and fishes at the top that depend initially on energy captured by marine plants at their base. Although there are hundreds—perhaps thousands—of different plant and animal plankters involved in the synthesis and initial transfer of organic matter through the food web, the pyramid of herbivores and predators narrows quickly.

The diets of seabirds, marine mammals, and fishes are composed of a relatively modest variety of small schooling fishes and macroplankters, but they are consumed in very large numbers. Seabirds are the clearest illustration. Out of the hundreds of fish species in the GOA, a substantial portion of the diets of seabirds consists mainly of smelts (capelin, eulachon, and rainbow smelt), juvenile herring, pollock and salmon, Pacific sand lance, Pacific sandfish, lanternfishes, and adult euphausiids. In shallow waters, small benthic fishes like pricklebacks and gunnels are also important. Many of these forage species are rich in fats, and almost all exhibit schooling behaviors that concentrate them for their bird, mammal, and larger fish predators. Herring, capelin, sand lance, and lanternfish are probably preferred for their high caloric content. Juvenile pollock, cod, and salmon are less preferred, despite their abundance, because of their lower energy content.

Despite the ecological importance of macroplankton and small schooling fishes, the distributions, abundances, and forage requirements of these species are poorly understood. The influence of climate change on their populations is also poorly known. This is partly because routine censusing techniques are used primarily to count and map adult stocks of commercial importance, and ignore the smaller forage fishes. Modern techniques that use high-speed mid-water and surface trawls, marine acoustics, LIDAR (light detection and ranging), aerial surveys, and monitoring the diets of top consumers like birds and large commercial fishes will make it possible to learn more about this vital link in the food web.

Forage fishes are often taken in the bycatch of federal- and state-regulated fisheries in the GOA, and while the proportion relative to the target species tends to be small, it may be ecologically significant in some cases. Fisheries targeting herring, salmon, and pollock all have incidental catches of juveniles that might be avoided as the industry develops new equipment and techniques to minimize the impact of bycatch mortality. Mortality of forage fishes associated with marine pollution and diseases is also poorly understood. There is some evidence that the failure of herring in Prince William Sound to recover from oil spill injuries may be due, in part, to an abnormally high incidence of viral hemorrhagic septicemia (VHS) and a marine fungus plaguing these stocks.

2.4 PLANKTON AND LINKAGES TO PHYSICAL OCEANOGRAPHY

Oceanic, shelf, and coastal plankton are the base of a vast food web supporting most seabirds, marine mammals, and fishes. These tiny drifters are supplemented by rich populations of plants and mostly small benthic invertebrates that feed higher-level consumers in intertidal and shallow subtidal areas. Although adult birds, fishes, and mammals rarely feed directly on plankton, there are notable exceptions, such as adult walleye pollock, Pacific herring, baleen whales, and some seabirds. On the other hand, the plankton community does play a direct and important role during the early life history of most fishes. Ichthyoplankters—larval and juvenile fishes and shellfishes—derive critical nutrition from the plankton, but are themselves also preyed upon by plankters, mostly small jellyfish.

Because fish are highly vulnerable in the egg, larval, and early juvenile stages, only a fraction survive to join the adult populations. Traditionally, this survival rate was estimated in field studies of the early life stages of fish, including the physical and chemical characteristics of the rearing waters. These studies have led to several important ideas about critical ecological bottlenecks in the early development of fish larvae and juveniles linking changes in ocean currents and climate with distribution, growth, and survival. This direct tie to ocean climate creates an important "handshake" that extends through the food web to adult fish stocks. Unfortunately, the small number and patchy distribution of ichthyoplankters relative to the non-fish plankton creates some extremely serious difficulties with sampling and data interpretation that limit the early life history approach.

The bloom of plankton each spring defines the cycle of marine production for that and succeeding years as the impact of the planktonic biomass moves through the food web. The plankton communities undergo huge seasonal changes in rates of photosynthesis and growth, and in their standing stocks each year. Initiated in the spring by a stabilizing upper layer and increasing ambient light levels, the phytoplankton community undergoes explosive growth during April, May, and June before being controlled by nutrient depletion, sinking, and zooplankton grazing. The organic matter produced in this burst of productivity mostly comprises a relatively small number of dominant species. In a similar way, shallow-water plants—microalgae, seaweeds, and seagrasses—provide much of the plant-derived organic matter in intertidal and shallow subtidal areas. In the late fall, plankton stocks plummet dramatically and remain low during winter and early spring.

The timing, duration, and intensity of marine plant blooms are controlled largely by the physical structure of the water column. Depending on the variable conditions of any given spring, the plant bloom may be early or late by as much as three weeks. Warming and freshening of the surface layers in response to longer and brighter days promote intense photosynthesis. However, the seasonal stability of the upper layers that initiates the growth of phytoplankton stocks also restricts the vertical movement of dissolved nitrogen, phosphate, and silicon, resulting in a dramatic slowing of growth in early and mid-summer. Previous work suggests that winter-conditioned temperature and salinity influences plankton production, working in concert with spring weather conditions to establish the overall success of the spring bloom. Recent observations from moorings that monitor chlorophyll in the water indicate that a fall phytoplankton bloom also occurs in Prince William Sound in some years, but not others. This burst of production peaks in September and can last through November. The ecological importance of this late-season production and the physical forces that unleash the bloom are not yet understood.

By definition, the plankton are drifters; they have little or no mobility. Therefore, their geographical locations are determined primarily by ocean currents. However, because many zooplankters are capable of daily and/or seasonal vertical migrations of 100 m or more, these migrations may interact with vertical or horizontal currents in ways that create localized swarms and layers (patches) of plankton in the ocean. These patches provide food for birds, fishes, and marine mammals. Whales feeding on surface or subsurface swarms of large copepods or euphausiids, and adult pollock and herring filtering or gulping large calanoid copepods in surface layers, are examples of patch feeding. Because the plankton can be concentrated or dispersed by ocean currents, fronts, and eddies, the physical oceanography plays a huge role in creating and maintaining "feeding stations" for marine birds, mammals, and fishes.

The marine production cycle beyond the shelf edge is exceptionally complex. Photic zone levels of nitrogen, phosphate, and silicon are apparently available in sufficient quantities to promote phytoplankton production during the spring, summer, and fall. However, levels of chlorophyll (a measure of the concentration of living phytoplankton in the water) in the upper layers remain very low throughout the year at many locations. In the coastal regions and inner shelf, there is a burst of chlorophyll—the "bloom"—each spring. This bloom results from an imbalance between rates of phytoplankton growth and rates of plant loss to grazers or sinking. Over the deep ocean and outer shelf, this burst/bloom does not usually occur, meaning that growth and loss rates of the plants are nearly equal, and that there is very little "excess" plant matter in the water to sink to the deep seabed. This balancing act in offshore waters has generally been attributed to the ability of the micrograzers to efficiently "crop down" the plant stocks and prevent blooms.

It has been suggested that inorganic iron from atmospheric sources is limiting plant productivity to very small cell sizes at the ocean surface. These microscopic plants are cropped efficiently by oceanic protozoans and other microconsumers. Unlike the shelf and coastal plankton, where large chain-forming diatoms feed the macrozooplankton directly, the oceanic food web instead supports an additional level of tiny consumers that are then grazed by larger zooplankters. On the basis of food-chain theory, this additional step at the base of the food web should reduce the open ocean's ability to feed consumer stocks higher in the food web. The fact that the open GOA is the preferred feeding ground for a majority of salmon stocks with origins in North America and Asia suggests that an additional step in the food web does not compromise the region's ability to feed hundreds of millions of these fish each year.

Very little is known about how the plankton community responds to human activity. Some recent and dramatic shifts in phytoplankton stocks in the Bering Sea, associated with a summer warming trend, were accompanied by very noticeable declines in seabird survivals in the shelf environment. These observations suggest that any increased climate warming due to human influence could alter high-latitude food webs with drastic effects for some consumers.

2.5 INFLUENCES OF WEATHER AND CLIMATE

GOA organisms are influenced by a variety of currents, frontal regions, eddies, water temperatures, and salinities. These conditions define the ocean state and reflect the influence of weather and climate. From September through April each year, weather in the GOA region responds to the position and intensity of the Aleutian low pressure system (Aleutian Low). The cyclonic storms that develop in and around the GOA in association with the Aleutian Low cause strong easterly winds to blow along the northern coastline. The friction of these winds on the sea surface promotes a net shoreward flow in the upper 60 to 90 meters, and a counter-clockwise drift of the Alaska Gyre, the Alaska Current, Alaskan Stream, and Alaska Coastal Current. The frequency and intensity of storms establishes a "conveyor belt," carrying ocean-derived plankton stocks shoreward, some reaching as far as the protected coastal waters. With use of carbon isotopes as indicators, a strong offshore signal can be found in inshore zooplankton and fishes at some locations. In contrast, during June, July, and August, the conveyor belt slows or weakly reverses in response to the appearance of the North Pacific high-pressure system in the GOA. The reversal of the conveyor belt over the outer shelf allows deep water below the surface to overrun the shelf break at some locations, providing a crucial source of deep nutrients and oxygen renewal for deep coastal areas.

The location and intensity of the Aleutian Low is not constant. When the low is intense, the weather is stormy with increased precipitation in the coastal mountains, and elevated sea levels and warmer water temperatures in the eastern GOA. Under these conditions, described as the positive phase of a weather phenomenon called the Pacific decadal oscillation (PDO), the wind-induced cross-shelf transport increases, as does flow in the Alaska Coastal Current. During the long term, these conditions seem to favor production of salmon, pollock, cod, and flounder, but other species are disadvantaged, such as seabirds at many locations, some forage fishes, and shellfish like shrimp and crab. When the PDO cycles back to its next negative phase—as it is predicted to do, with colder, less stormy, lower sea levels—conditions should favor the recovery of shellfish stocks, with salmon and gadid populations expected to slip into decline. Why these populations fluctuate the way they do in response to changes in ocean climate is unknown. However, the cycling of nature's laboratory from year to year, and through longer periods, provides a strong basis for a number of intriguing studies to search for and describe the underlying mechanisms that create change, and sometimes complete reversals, in fish, bird, and mammal abundance.

2.6 TOWARD A MORE FUNCTIONAL UNDERSTANDING OF GOA ECOSYSTEMS

Current knowledge about coastal, shelf, and oceanic ecosystems supporting the living marine resources of the GOA is limited and skewed heavily toward structural elements—species lists, historical patterns of production (catch and harvest statistics), crude maps of distribution and abundance, some diet information, migratory behaviors, and in a few cases, rates of production. At the level of plankton, the seasonal cycle is quite well understood in relationship to factors like light and nutrients, but higher in the food web at the zooplankton level and also the small schooling fishes, little information is available. Therefore, with a few exceptions, the "puzzle pieces" are beginning to form reasonably coherent pictures at the top and bottom of the food web, but are absent or mostly missing from the middle regions of the web.

The challenge for researchers is to understand how the major physical and biological components interact dynamically to produce the historical patterns in stock size and production of key species. Conventional population theory teaches that variability at the highest levels in food webs reflects the balance between reproduction and mortality (due to natural causes, predation, harvests, diseases, and pollution). A few statistical analyses point to significant correlations, however, between population levels and weather, climate, or physical oceanographic conditions, some apparently tied to recurring cycles like the PDO, the North Pacific index (NPI), the 18.6 year lunar nodal tidal cycle, and episodic events like El Niño/La Niña. Unfortunately these intriguing and often ephemeral correlations suggest, but do not identify, the mechanisms behind these relationships. This critical missing information should be obtained at some point in comprehensive field and modeling studies that focus on selected ecosystem processes.

To be successful, these studies must identify and collect the relevant data, and be supported over time periods that bridge the cycles in climate and ocean conditions. Few studies anywhere have been able to sustain their activities long enough, or were sufficiently comprehensive to meet these criteria. Bold steps, which are being taken in marine ecological research to more fully exploit emerging research directions for studies of large ecosystems, are described in the following paragraphs.

2.6.1 Nature Is Complex

Food web theory has played a major role in shaping quantitative approaches to studying marine systems. Since the early 1940s, when aquatic communities were perceived as a linear series of interconnected levels—producers (plants), first-order consumers (herbivores), higher-level consumers (predators), and recyclers (bacteria)—this powerful idea has pointed to ever more sophisticated inquiries about how matter and energy are cycled through these systems. However, in the last few years, there has been a growing awareness that the inability to more fully understand how nature works may be tied to a number of simplifying assumptions that have always been made about living systems. It is now understood that at some level of detail, natural processes cannot all be adequately explained by strict linear theory. This means that unless the complexity of nature is acknowledged and that constraint dealt with in a realistic manner, the research will fall short, as will the ability to resolve resource management and other issues.

2.6.2 Survival Strategies Define Habitat Dependencies

There is a growing need to more fully understand what has been passed over as mostly "old science"—how the life history of a target species exploits the marine ecosystem during its entire life span. For example, most marine fishes begin life as tiny pelagic or demersal eggs followed by a drifting larval stage that may last for weeks or months. The drifting period is followed by successive juvenile and maturing older stages that may use different parts of the ecosystem from those that host the adults. Understanding the entire ecological domain of a particular species will help establish the "connectiveness" needed to more fully understand how human influences and perturbations in climate and weather work their way though the marine ecosystem in the GOA.

2.6.3 Use of Common Biological Currency

Oceanographers have traditionally used measures of carbon or nitrogen as common denominators to describe processes of organic matter synthesis and transfer at lower trophic levels. At the other end of the food web, the fisheries literature tracks the abundance and biomass of exploited stocks, usually expressed in numbers or weight. Recently, the energy content of species has been suggested as a useful measure for assessing the status of stocks and their principal prey. Bioenergetic modeling is becoming more common and measures of whole body energy content easier to obtain. For instance, the overwintering starvation mortality of juvenile Pacific herring residing in Prince William Sound can now be estimated through numerical analysis of the fat stores of the herring as they go into winter and the winter water temperatures.

2.6.4 Problems of Time and Space

Attempts to understand how marine ecosystems react to climate and human influences pose huge sampling problems for systems on the scale of the GOA. Current understanding suggests that the impacts of large-scale climate shifts and pollution are not uniform, but seem to be temporally and spatially distributed in ways that are not fully understood. For example, seabird colonies at some locations do well, while others do not. Two aspects may be impor-

tant contributors to this uncertainty: (1) variability in the timing, location, and duration of primary productivity each year as influenced by weather—a kind of "timing is everything" issue; and (2) spatial patchiness on a variety of length scales in forage stocks responding locally to changing temperature, salinity, currents, and other ocean characteristics.

2.6.5 Immigration or Emigration

The mobile nature of most animal populations provides challenges and opportunities for any scientific monitoring activity seeking to build or use long time series of observations on abundance. Such problems are particularly noticeable for seabirds and marine mammals that are often counted at nesting sites and rookeries. Population trends in bird and mammal species that are measured at nursery sites in dynamic habitats, such as sedimentary sea front bluffs and ice floes, need to be carefully examined to see if trends in population size might be explained by loss or addition of habitats. Permanent relocations of rookeries could pose serious problems in the interpretation of historical trends in the GOA. It is probable that fish or shellfish stocks would also shift their distributions in response to compelling environmental change, such as permanent or chronic shifts in sea temperature, leading to increases in some areas and declines in others, although the overall stock production might remain unaltered. Shifts in the distribution of fish/shellfish prey species also have consequences in the form of apparent trends in populations of birds and mammals. Hence potential causes of misinterpretation of population trends due to shifts in the distributions of species within the GOA must be addressed by monitoring projects.

Animal migrations between marine and freshwater habitats provide important geochemical pathways for carbon, nitrogen, sulfur (C, N, S) and other elements that are important for production in near shore marine habitats and coastal watersheds. Feeding migrations, such as those of river otters and harlequin ducks, and breeding migrations, such as those of salmon and eulachon (smelt), are common marine-terrestrial life history strategies in the GOA. The role of marine inputs to the watershed phase of regional biogeochemical cycles has been recognized for some time (Mathisen 1972). Experiments in artificial and natural streams have shown that chlorophyll *a* and the biomasses of the biofilm (bacteria and molds) and aquatic macroinvertebrates, such as insects, increase as the amount of salmon carcass biomass increases (Wipfli et al. 1998). Chlorophyll *a* has been observed to increase over the full range of carcass biomass, whereas increases in macroinverte-brates stop at some limiting value of carcass loading (Wipfli et al. 1998, 1999). Salmon carcasses stimulate production of multiple trophic levels, including decomposers, in watersheds by providing carbon and nutrients. In earlier studies of an Alaskan stream containing chinook salmon, Piorkowski (1995) supported the hypothesis of Wipfli et al. (1998) that salmon carcasses can be important in structuring aquatic food webs. In particular, microbial composition and diversity may determine the ability of the stream ecosystem to use nutrients from salmon carcasses, a principal source of marine nitrogen.

Marine nutrients and carbon (C, N, S) move from the marine environment into terrestrial species in the watersheds of the GOA (Wipfli et al. 1999), as has been shown to be the case in anadromous fish-bearing watersheds elsewhere in the North Pacific region (Bilby et al. 1996). The following species have been found to transport marine nutrients within watersheds:

- Anadromous species, such as salmon (Kline et al. 1993, Ben-David et al. 1998b);

- Marine-feeding land animals, such as river otters (Ben-David et al. 1998a) and coastal mink (Ben-David et al. 1997b);

- Opportunistic scavengers such as riverine mink (Ben-David et al. 1997b), wolf (Szepanski et al. 1999), and martens (Ben-David et al. 1997a); and

- Riparian zone plants such as trees (Bilby et al. 1996).

In theory, any terrestrial plant or animal species that feeds in the marine environment or that receives nutrients from anadromous fish, such as harlequin duck or Sitka spruce, is a pathway to the watersheds for marine carbon and nutrients. Species that contain marine nutrients are widely distributed throughout watersheds, as determined from levels of marine nitrogen in juvenile fish, invertebrates, and aquatic and riparian plants (Piorkowski 1995; Bilby et al. 1996; Ben-David et al. 1998a,b). The role of marine nutrients in watersheds is key to understanding the relative importance of climate and human-induced changes in population levels of birds, fish, and mammals. Indeed, losses of basic habitat productivity because of low numbers of salmon entering a watershed (Mathisen 1972, Kline et al. 1993, Piorkowski 1995, Finney et al. 2000) may be confused with the effects of fisheries interceptions or marine climate trends. Comparison of anadromous fish-bearing streams to non-anadromous streams has demonstrated differences in productivities

related to marine nutrient cycling. Import of marine nutrients and food energy to the lotic (flowing water) ecosystem may be retarded in systems that have been denuded of salmon for any length of time (Piorkowski 1995).

Paleoecological studies (which focus on ancient events) in watersheds bearing anadromous species can shed light on long-term trends in marine productivity. Use of marine nitrogen in sediment cores from freshwater spawning and rearing areas to reconstruct prehistoric abundance of salmon offers some insights into long-term trends in climate, as well as how to separate the effects of climate from human impacts such as fishing and habitat degradation (Finney 1998, Finney et al. 2000).

Watershed studies linking the freshwater and marine portions of the regional ecosystem could pay important benefits to natural resource management agencies. As agencies grapple with implementation of ecosystem-based management, conservation actions are likely to focus more on ecosystem processes and less on single species (Mangel et al. 1996). In the long-term, protection of Alaska's natural resources will require extending the protection now afforded to single species, such as targeted commercially important salmon stocks, to ecosystem functions (Mangel et al. 1996). In process-oriented conservation (Mangel et al. 1996), production of ecologically central vertebrate species is combined with measures of the production of other species and measures of energy and nutrient flow among trophic levels to identify and protect ecological processes such as nutrient transport. Applications of ecological process measures in Alaska ecosystems have shown the feasibility and potential importance of such measures (Mathisen 1972; Kline et al. 1990; Kline et al. 1993; Piorkowski 1995; Ben-David et al. 1997a,b, 1998a,b; Szepanski et al. 1999), as have applications outside of Alaska (Bilby et al. 1996, Larkin and Slaney 1997).

2.6.6 Top-Down and Bottom-Up Controls

Historical approaches to studies of marine systems have led to a dichotomy of disciplines. Oceanographers have focused on the base of the food web and relationships with ocean physics and chemistry, whereas fisheries scientists have studied exploited stocks and, occasionally, the forage resources that support them. Top-down or bottom-up control has been debated endlessly for years without resolution. It is now beginning to be understood that this is not an either/or problem, but rather one of process interaction. Top-down and bottom-up control of populations occurs simultaneously in all living systems and must be studied as such to refine understandings of system function. For example, recent studies of juvenile pink salmon in Prince William Sound have demonstrated that top-down losses to fish predators, such as adult pollock and herring, are modulated by the kinds and amounts of zooplankton available, a bottom-up function. The opportunistic pollock and herring prefer to feed on macrozooplankton when it is plentiful, thereby improving the chance of juvenile salmon to fatten up and escape their role as prey. However, when macrozooplankton is not abundant, pollock and herring begin augmenting their diets by feeding more heavily on small fishes, including juvenile salmon. In this way, bottom-up processes affecting the production of copepods not only help feed and fatten young salmon, but top-down processes of pollock feeding on copepods help protect the salmon fry.

2.7 CONCLUSION

In the final analysis, the GOA is a complex ecosystem—a product of evolutionary adaptation through many thousands of years. This robust living assemblage exhibits different characteristics of species dominance, distribution, and abundance in response to short-term and longer-period changes in climate forcing and human influences. These different "states" have most recently been described as regimes. In the GOA, at least two dominant physical states—El Niño/La Niña and Pacific decadal oscillation—are known to affect the production cycles of several marine species.

CHAPTER 3

Climate and Weather

Phillip R. Mundy and Peter Olsson

3.1 DESCRIPTION OF THE GULF OF ALASKA

The Gulf of Alaska (GOA) encompasses watersheds and waters south and east of the Alaska Peninsula from Great Sitkin Island (176°W), north of 52°N to the Canadian mainland on Queen Charlotte Sound (127°30'W). Twelve-and-a-half percent of the continental shelf of the United States lies within GOA waters (Hood 1986).

The area of the Gulf of Alaska directly affected by the 1989 *Exxon Valdez* oil spill (Figure 3.1) encompasses broadly diverse terrestrial and aquatic environments. Within the four broad habitat types—watersheds, intertidal-subtidal, Alaska Coastal Current (ACC), and offshore (continental shelf break and Alaska Gyre)—the geological, climatic, oceanographic, and biological processes interact to produce the highly valued natural beauty and bounty of this region.

Human uses of the GOA are extensive. The GOA is a major source of food and recreation for the entire nation, a source of traditional foods and culture for indigenous peoples, and a source of food and enjoyment for all Alaskans. Serving as a "lung" of the planet, GOA components are part of the process that provides oxygen to the atmosphere. In addition, the GOA provides habitat for diverse populations of plants, fish, and wildlife and is a source of beauty and inspiration to those who love natural things.

The eastern boundary of the GOA is a geologically young, tectonically active area that contains the world's third largest permanent ice field, after Greenland and Antarctica. Consequently, the watersheds of the eastern boundary of the GOA lie in a series of steep, high mountain ranges. Glaciers head many watersheds in this area, and the eastern boundary mountains trap weather systems from the west, making orographic, or mountain-directed, forcing important in shaping the region's climate. From the southeastern GOA limit (52°N at landfall) moving north, the eastern GOA headwater mountain ranges and height of the highest peaks are the Pacific Coast (3,136 m), St. Elias (5,486 m), and

Wrangell (4,996 m). Northern boundary mountain ranges from east to west are the Chugach (4,016 m), Talkeetna (2,682 m), and Alaska (6,194 m). The western boundary of the GOA headwaters is formed in the north by the Alaska Range and to the south-southwest by the Aleutian Mountains (2,312 m).

Relatively few major river systems manage to pierce the eastern boundary mountains, although thousands of small independent drainages dot the eastern coastline and islands of the Inside Passage. Major eastern rivers from the south moving north to the perimeter of Prince William Sound (PWS) are the Skeena and Nass (Canada), the Stikine, Taku, Chilkat, Chilkoot, Alsek, Situk, and Copper. All major and nearly all smaller watersheds in the GOA region support anadromous fish species. For example, although PWS proper has no major river systems, it does have more than 800 independent drainages that are known to support anadromous fish species.

To the west of PWS lie the major rivers of Cook Inlet. Two major tributaries of Cook Inlet, the Kenai and the Kasilof, originate on the Kenai Peninsula. The Kenai Peninsula lies between PWS, the northern GOA and Cook Inlet. Cook Inlet's largest northern tributary, the Susitna River, has headwaters in the Alaska Range on the slopes of North America's highest peak, Mt. McKinley. Moving southwest down the Alaska Peninsula, only two major river systems are found on the western coastal boundary of the GOA, the Crescent and Chignik, although many small coastal watersheds connected to the GOA abound. Kodiak Island, off the coast of the Alaska Peninsula, has a number of relatively large river systems, including the Karluk, Red, and Frazer.

The nature of the terrestrial boundaries of the GOA is important in defining the processes that drive biological production in all environments. As described in more detail below, the ice cap and the eastern boundary mountains create substantial freshwater runoff that controls salinity in the nearshore GOA and helps drive the eastern boundary current. The eastern mountains slow the pace of and deflect weather systems that influence productivity in freshwater and marine environments.

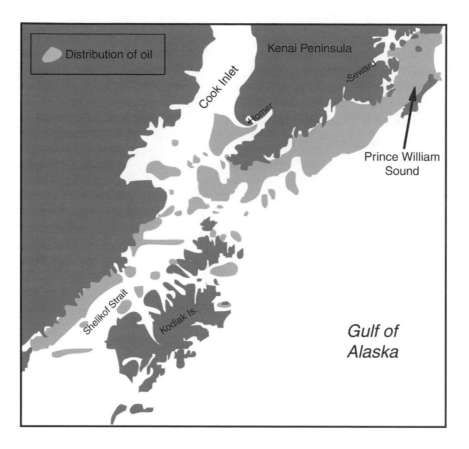

Figure 3.1.   Distribution of oil from the 1989 *Exxon Valdez* oil spill.

The GOA shoreline is bordered by a continental shelf ranging to 200 meters (m) in depth (Figure 3.2). Extensive and spectacular shoreline has been and is being shaped by plate tectonics and massive glacial activity (Hampton et al. 1986). In the eastern GOA, the shelf is variable in width from Cape Spencer to Middleton Island. It broadens considerably in the north between Middleton Island and the Shumagin Islands and narrows again through the Aleutian Islands. The continental slope, down to 2,000 m, is very broad in the eastern GOA, but it narrows steadily southwestward of Kodiak, becoming only a narrow shoulder above the wall of the deep Aleutian Trench just west of Unimak Pass. The continental shelf is incised by extensive valleys or canyons that may be important in cross-shelf water movement (Carlson et al. 1982), and by very large areas of drowned glacial moraines and slumped sediments (Molnia 1981).

3.2 WEATHER AND CLIMATE

The weather in the northern Gulf of Alaska, and by extension that of adjacent regions such as Prince William Sound, is dominated for much of the year by extratropical cyclones. These storms typically form well to the south and east of the region over the warm waters of the central North Pacific Ocean and propagate northwestward into the cooler waters of the GOA (Wilson and Overland 1986, Luick et al. 1987). Eventually these storms make landfall in Southcentral or Southeast Alaska where their further progress is impeded by the extreme terrain of the St. Elias Mountains and other coastal ranges. In fact, weather forecasters call the coastal region between Cordova and Yakutat "Coffin Corner," in reference to the frequency of decaying extratropical storms found there.

The high probability of cyclonic disturbances in the northern GOA is significant to the local weather and climate of PWS. Associated with these storms are large offshore-directed, low-level pressure gradients (tightly packed isobars roughly parallel to the coast). Depending on other factors (such as static stability, upper-level wind profile) these gradients can produce strong gradient-balance winds parallel to the coastline or downslope (offshore-directed) wind events (Macklin et al. 1988). Further, because of the complex glacially sculptured nature of the terrain in

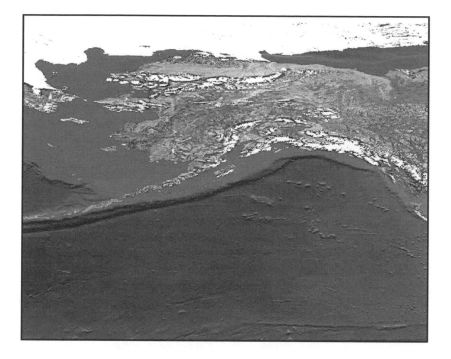

Figure 3.2. Satellite radar image of the Gulf of Alaska. Continental shelf, seamounts, and abyssal plain can be seen in relief. Composite image from Sea-viewing Wide Field-of-view Sensor (SeaWiFS), a National Aeronautics and Space Administration remote-sensing satellite.

PWS, several regions experience significant upslope winds in certain favorable storm situations. This wind configuration, in concert with steep terrain and nearly saturated, low-level air masses, produces the local extreme in precipitation responsible for tidewater glaciers of PWS.

The combination of general storminess, significant windiness (and concomitant wave generation), and orographically enhanced precipitation are essential features of the northern GOA and PWS, and have a strong impact on the variety and composition of the biota supported by this region. In addition, the annual melting of seasonal snowfall accumulations, in combination with glacial ablation, is responsible for the bulk of freshwater input into PWS. In this context, any changes in climate—naturally induced or anthropogenic—that substantively alter the frequency and duration of these common yet transient weather features should also affect related parts of the regional ecosystem. In the following discussion, the factors responsible for climate change are identified and explained on a general level in preparation for specific relationships among climate, physical, and chemical oceanography, species, and groups of species that follow. Climate is recognized to be a

major natural force influencing change in biological resources.

Climatic forcing is an important natural agent of change in the region's populations of birds, fish, mammals, and other plant and animal species (Mantua et al. 1997, Francis et al. 1998, Hare et al. 1999, Anderson and Piatt 1999). Human activities (anthropogenic forcing) may have profound effects on climate. There is growing evidence that human activities producing "greenhouse gases" such as carbon dioxide may contribute to global climate change by altering the global carbon cycle (Sigman and Boyle 2000, Allen et al. 2000). Understanding how natural and human forcing influences biological productivity requires knowledge of the major determinants of climate change described here.

Climate in the GOA results from the complex interactions of geophysical and astrophysical forces, and also in part by biogeochemical forcing. Physical processes acting on the global carbon cycle and its living component, the biological pump, drive oscillations in climate (Sigman and Boyle 2000). The most prominent geophysical feature associated with climate change in the GOA is the Aleutian Low (Wilson and

Overland 1986). The location and intensity of this system affects storm tracks, air temperatures, wind velocities, ocean currents, and other key physical factors in the GOA and adjacent land areas. Sharp variations, or oscillations, in the location and intensity of the Aleutian Low are the result of physical factors operating both proximally and at great distances from the GOA (Mantua et al. 1997). Periodic changes in the location and intensity of the Aleutian Low are related to movements of adjacent continental air masses and the jet stream to oceanography and weather in the eastern tropical Pacific.

Astrophysical forces contribute to long-term trends and periodic changes in the climate of the GOA by controlling the amount of solar radiation that reaches the earth, or insolation (Rutherford and D'Hondt 2000). Climate also depends on the amount of global insolation and the proportion of the insolation stored by the atmosphere, oceans, and biological systems (Sigman and Boyle 2000). Changes in climate and biological systems occur through physical forcing of controlling factors, such as solar radiation, strength of lunar mixing of water masses, and patterns of ocean circulation. Periodic variations in the earth's solar orbit, the speed of rotation and orientation of the earth, and the degree of inclination of the earth's axis in relation to the sun result in periodic changes in climate and associated biological activity.

Understanding climatic change requires sorting out the effects of physical forcing factors that operate simultaneously at different periods. Periodicities of physical forcing on factors potentially controlling climate and biological systems include 100,000 years, 41,000 years, 23,000 years, 10,000 years, 20 years, 18.6 years, and 10 years, among many others. For example, Minobe (1999) identified periods of 50 and 20 years in an analysis of the North Pacific index (NPI) (Minobe 1999). The NPI is a time series of geographically averaged sea-level pressures representing a univariate (depending on only one random variable) measure of location for the Aleutian Low (Trenberth and Hurrell 1994).

Advances and retreats of ice fields and glaciers mark major changes in weather and biology. Changes in the seasonal and geographic distribution of solar radiation are thought to be primarily responsible for the periodic advance and recession of glaciers during the past two million years (Hays et al. 1976). The amount of solar radiation reaching the earth changes periodically, or oscillates, in response to variations in the path of the earth's orbit about the sun. Geographic and seasonal changes in solar radiation caused by periodic variations in the earth's orbit around and

orientation toward the sun have been labeled "Milankovich cycles," which are known to have characteristic frequencies of 100,000, 41,000, and 23,000 years (Berger et al. 1984). Shifts in the periodicity of long-term weather patterns correspond to shifts from one Milankovich cycle to another. How and why shifts from one Milankovich cycle to another occur are among the most important questions in paleoclimate research (Hays et al. 1976, Rutherford and D'Hondt 2000).

3.2.1 Long Time Scales
3.2.1.1 Orbital Eccentricity and Obliquity

Shifts in the periodicity of glaciation from 41,000 to 100,000 years between 1.5 and 0.6 million years before present (Myr bp) emphasize the importance of the atmosphere and oceans in translating the effects of physical forcing into weather cycles. Glacial cycles may have initially shifted from the 41,000-year period of the "obliquity cycle" to the 100,000-year period of the "orbital eccentricity" perhaps caused initially by changes in the heat flux, from the equator to the higher latitudes (Rutherford and D'Hondt 2000). (Obliquity is the angle between the plane of the earth's orbit and the equatorial plane.) According to the theory advanced by Rutherford and D'Hondt (2000), interactions between long-period physical forcing (Milankovich cycles) and shorter-period forcing (precession) may have been a key factor in lengthening the time period between glaciations in the transition period of 1.5 and 0.6 Myr bp. Transitions from glacial to interglacial periods may be triggered by factors such as the micronutrient iron (Martin 1990) that control the activity of the biological pump in the Southern Ocean, described below.

Theories about regulation of heat flux from the equator to northern latitudes are central to understanding climate change. For example, the heat flux that occurs when the Gulf Stream moves equatorial warmth north to surround the United Kingdom, Iceland, and Northern Europe defines comfortable human life styles in these locations. Anything that disrupts this heat flux process would drastically alter climate in Northern Europe.

3.2.1.2 Day Length

Day length is increasing by one to two seconds each 100,000 years primarily because of lunar tidal action (U.S. Naval Observatory). Understanding the role of day length in climate variation is problematic because the rotational speed of the earth cannot be predicted exactly due to the effects of a large number of poorly understood sources of variation. Short-term effects are probably inconsequential biologically, because variations in daily rotational speed are very small, but cumulative effects could be more substantial in the long term.

3.2.1.3 The Biological Pump and Carbon Cycling

Changes in the amount of solar radiation available to drive physical and biological systems on earth are not the only causes of climate oscillations in the GOA, or elsewhere on earth. Of critical importance to life on earth, changes in insolation result in changes in the amount of a "greenhouse gas" carbon dioxide in the atmosphere resulting from changes in physical properties, such as ocean temperature, and due to biological processes collectively known as the biological pump (Chisholm 2000). The importance of the biological pump in determining levels of atmospheric carbon dioxide is thought to be substantial, since the direct physical and chemical effects of changes in insolation on the carbon cycle alone (Sigman and Boyle 2000) are not sufficient to account for the magnitude of the changes in atmospheric carbon dioxide between major climate changes, such as glaciations.

The Biological Pump. Photosynthesis and respiration by marine plants and animals play key roles in the global carbon cycle by "pumping" carbon dioxide from the atmosphere to the surface ocean and incorporating it into organic carbon during photosynthesis. Organic carbon not liberated as carbon dioxide during respiration is "pumped" (exported) to deep ocean water where bacteria convert it to carbon dioxide. Over a period of about 1,000 years, ocean currents return the deep water's carbon dioxide to the surface (through upwelling) where it again drives photosynthesis and ventilates to the atmosphere. The degree to which this deep water's carbon dioxide is "pumped" back into the atmosphere or "pumped" back into deep water depends on the intensity of the photosynthetic activity, which depends on availability of the macronutrients phosphate, nitrate, and silicate, and on micronutrients such as reduced iron (Chisholm 2000).

Areas where nitrates and phosphates do not limit phytoplankton production, such as the Southern Ocean (60°S), can have very large effects on the global carbon cycle through the action of the biological pump. When stimulated by the micronutrient iron, the biological pump of the Southern Ocean becomes very strong because of the presence of ample nitrate and phosphate to fuel photosynthesis, as demonstrated by the Southern Ocean Iron Release Experiment

(SOIREE) at 61°S 140°E in February 1999 (Boyd et al. 2000). SOIREE stimulated phytoplankton production in surface waters for about two weeks fixing up to 3,000 metric tons (t) of organic carbon. Although it has not been demonstrated that "iron fertilization" increases export of carbon to deep waters (Chisholm 2000), it clearly does enhance surface production. The Southern Ocean and much of the GOA share the equality of being "high nitrate, low chlorophyll" waters, so it is tempting to speculate that iron would play an important role in controlling production, if not export production, in the GOA.

The Carbon Cycle. An accounting of changes in the amount of carbon in each component of the earth's terrestrial and ocean carbon cycles, as influenced and represented by the physical and chemical factors of ocean temperature, dissolved inorganic carbon, ocean alkalinity, and the deep reservoir of the nutrients phosphate and nitrate, has to incorporate changes in the strength of the ocean's biological pump to be complete (Sigman and Boyle 2000). The amount of atmospheric carbon dioxide decreases during glacial periods. Because physical-chemical effects do not fully account for these changes, the ruling hypothesis is that the biological pump is stronger during glaciations. But why would the biological pump be stronger during glaciations?

Two leading theories explain decreases in atmospheric carbon dioxide by means of increased activity in the ocean's biological pump during glaciations (Sigman and Boyle 2000). Both theories explain how increased export production of carbon from surface waters to long-term storage in deep ocean waters can lower atmospheric carbon dioxide during glacial periods. The Broecker theory develops mechanisms based on increasing export from low- to mid-latitude surface waters (Broecker 1982, McElroy 1983), and the second theory relies on high-latitude export production of direct relevance to the GOA. Patterns and trends in nutrient use in high latitude oceans, such as the GOA, where nutrients usually do not limit phytoplankton production, could hold the key to understanding climate oscillations.

3.2.1.4 Ocean Circulation

Because of the heat energy stored in seawater, oceans are vast integrators of past climatic events, as well as agents and buffers of climate change. Wind, precipitation, and other features of climate shape surface ocean currents (Wilson and Overland 1986), and ocean currents in turn strongly feed back into climate. Deep ocean waters driven by thermohaline

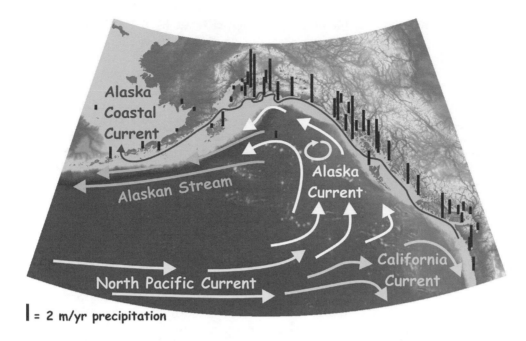

I = 2 m/yr precipitation

Figure 3.3. **Surface circulation fields in the Gulf of Alaska and mean annual precipitation totals from coastal stations (black vertical bars) and for the central gulf (Seth Danielson after Baumgartner and Reichel 1975).**

circulation in the Atlantic and southern oceans influence air temperatures over these portions of the globe by transporting and exchanging large quantities of heat energy with the atmosphere (Peixoto and Oort 1992). Patterns of thermohaline (affected by salt and temperature) ocean circulation probably change during periods of glaciation (Lynch-Stieglitz et al. 1999). The nature of changes in patterns of thermohaline circulation appear to determine the duration and intensity of climate change (Ganopolski and Rahmstorf 2001). Although the climate of the GOA is not directly affected by thermohaline circulation, climate in the GOA is influenced by thermohaline circulation through climatic linkages to other parts of the globe.

Teleconnection between the North Pacific and the Tropical Pacific can periodically strongly influence levels of coastal and interior precipitation. Because changing patterns in precipitation alter the expression of the Alaska Coastal Current (Figure 3.3), which is largely driven by runoff (Royer 1981a), periodically changing weather patterns such as the Pacific Decadal Oscillation (PDO) and the El Niño Southern Oscillation (ENSO) can profoundly alter the circulation and biology of the GOA (see section 3.2.2.3.)

The effects of the cool ACC and the warmer Alaskan Stream moderate air temperatures. GOA ocean temperatures are important in determining climate in the fall and early winter in the northern GOA and may be influential at other times of the year. Because the cool glacially influenced waters of the ACC moderate air temperatures along the coast, the strength and stability of the ACC are important in determining climate.

3.2.2 Multi-Decadal and Multi-Annual Time Scales

3.2.2.1 Precession and Nutation

Short period changes in the seasonal and geographic distribution of solar radiation are also due to changes in the earth's orientation and rotational speed (day length) (Lambeck 1980). Wobbling (precession) and nodding (nutation) of the earth as it spins on its axis are primarily due to the fluid nature of the atmosphere and oceans, the gravitational attraction of sun and moon, and the irregular shape of the planet.

Small periodic variations in the length of the day occur with periods of 18.6 years, 1 year, and 60 other periodic components. The periodic components are due to both lunar and solar tidal forcing. In addition to its effect on day length, lunar tidal forcing with a period of 18.6 years has been associated with high-latitude climate forcing, periodic changes in intensity of transport of nutrients by tidal mixing, and

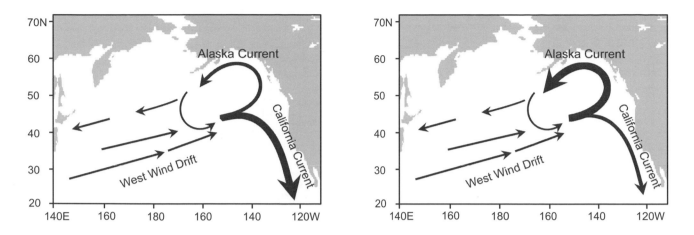

Figure 3.4.   Oceanic circulation patterns in the far eastern Pacific Ocean proposed for negative PDO (Pacific decadal oscillation; left) and positive PDO (right) (Hollowed and Wooster 1992).

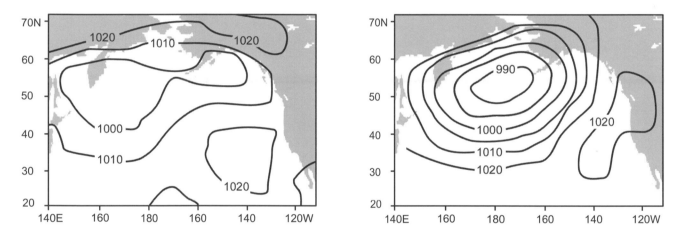

Figure 3.5.   Mean sea-level pressure patterns, in millibars, from the winters of 1972 (left) and 1977 (right) (Emery and Hamilton 1985).

periodic changes in fish recruitment (Royer 1993, Parker et al. 1995). Biological and physical effects of the lunar tidal cycle may extend beyond effects associated with tidal mixing. About one-third of the energy input to the sea by lunar forcing serves to mix deepwater masses with adjacent waters (Egbert and Ray 2000). Oscillations in the lunar energy input could contribute to oscillations in biological productivity through effects on the rate of transport of nutrients to surface waters. The lunar tidal cycle appears to be approximately synchronous with the PDO.

Contemporary climate in the GOA is defined by large-scale atmospheric and oceanic circulation on a global scale. Two periodic changes in ocean and

atmospheric conditions are particularly useful for understanding change in the climate of the GOA: the PDO and the ENSO. Although weather patterns in the Arctic and North Atlantic are also correlated with weather in the North Pacific, these relations are far from clear. The PDO, ENSO, and other patterns of climate variability combine to give the GOA a variable and sometimes severe climate that serves as the incubator for the winter storms that sweep across the North American continent through the Aleutian storm track (Wilson and Overland 1986).

Increased understanding of the PDO has been made possible by simple yet highly descriptive indices of weather, such as the North Pacific index (NPI).

Positive PDO Index
Physics

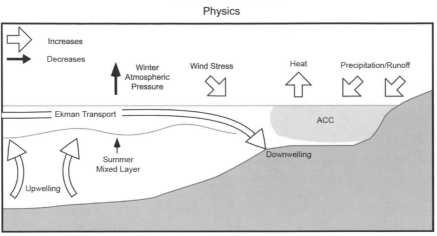

Positive PDO Index
Biological Production/Transport

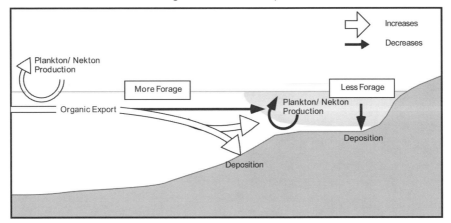

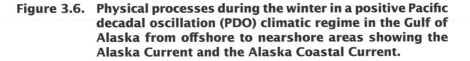

Figure 3.6. Physical processes during the winter in a positive Pacific decadal oscillation (PDO) climatic regime in the Gulf of Alaska from offshore to nearshore areas showing the Alaska Current and the Alaska Coastal Current.

These indices are discussed below. Changes in the annual values of these indices led to the realization that weather conditions in the GOA sometimes change sharply from one set of average conditions to a different set during a period of only a few years. These rapid climatic and oceanographic regime shifts are associated with similarly rapid changes in the animals and plants of the region that are of vital interest to government, industry, and the general public.

3.2.2.2 Pacific Decadal Oscillation

The Pacific decadal oscillation (PDO) and associated phenomena appear to be major sources of oceanographic and biological variability (Mantua et al.

1997). Associated with the PDO are three semi-permanent atmospheric pressure regions dominating climate in the northern GOA: the Siberian and East Pacific high-pressure systems and the Aleutian Low. These regions have variable, but characteristic, seasonal locations. A prominent feature of the PDO and the climate of the GOA is the Aleutian Low, for which average geographic location changes periodically during the winter. Wintertime location of the Aleutian Low affects ocean circulation patterns and sea-level pressure patterns. It is characteristic of two climatic regimes: a southwestern locus called a negative PDO regime (as in 1972) and a northeastern locus called a positive PDO (1977) (Figures 3.4 and 3.5). The location of the Aleutian Low in

Negative PDO Index

Physics

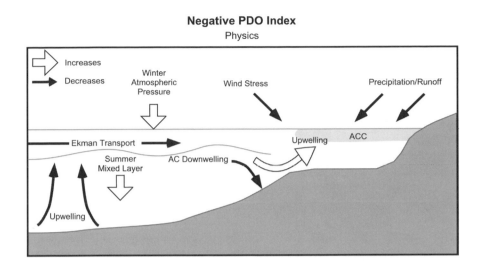

Negative PDO Index

Biological Production/Transport

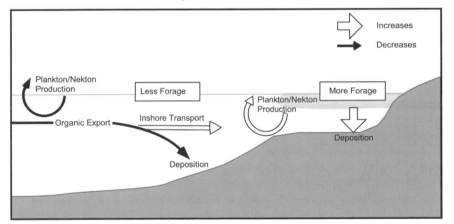

Figure 3.7. Physical processes during the winter in a negative Pacific decadal oscillation (PDO) climatic regime in the Gulf of Alaska from offshore to nearshore areas showing the Alaska Current and the Alaska Coastal Current.

the winter appears to be synchronized with annual abundances and strength of recruitment of some fish species (Hollowed and Wooster 1992, Francis and Hare 1994). The Aleutian Low averages about 1,002 millibars (Favorite et al. 1976), is most intense in winter, and appears to cycle in its average position and intensity with about a 20- to 25-year period (Rogers 1981, Trenberth and Hurrell 1994).

The PDO is studied with multiple indices, including the anomalies of sea level pressure (as in the NPI, which is discussed below), anomalies of sea surface temperature, and wind stress (Mantua et al. 1997, Hare et al. 1999). The PDO changes, or oscillates, between positive (warm) and negative (cool) states

(Figures 3.6 and 3.7). In decades of positive PDOs, below-normal sea surface temperatures occur in the central and western North Pacific and above normal temperatures occur in the GOA. An intense low pressure is centered over the Alaska Peninsula, resulting in the GOA being warm and windy with lots of precipitation. In decades of negative PDOs, the opposite sea surface temperature and pressure patterns occur.

The NPI, a univariate time series representing the strength of the Aleutian Low, shows the same twentieth-century regimes defined by the PDO. The NPI is the anomaly, or deviation from the long-term average, of geographically averaged sea-level pressure in the region from 160°E to 140°W, 30° to 65°N, for the years 1899 to 1997 (Trenberth and Paolino 1980, Trenberth and Hurrell 1994). The NPI was used to identify climatic regimes in the twentieth century, for the years 1899 to 1924, 1925 to 1947, 1948 to 1976, and 1977 to 1997, and to explore the interactions of short (20-year) and long (50-year) period effects on the timing of regime shifts. Negative (cool) PDOs occurred during 1890 to 1924 and 1947 to 1976, and positive (warm) PDOs dominated from 1925 to 1946 and from 1977 to about 1995 (Mantua et al. 1997, Minobe 1997). Minobe's analysis of the NPI identified a characteristic S-shaped waveform with a 50-year period (sinusoidal pentadecadal). His analysis pointed out that rapid transitions from one regime to another could not be fully explained by a single sinusoidal-wavelike effect. The speed with which regime shifts occurred in the twentieth century led Minobe to suggest that the pentadecadal cycle is synchronized or phase locked with another climate variation on a shorter bidecadal time scale (Anderson and Munson 1972).

In addition to periodic and seasonal changes, there is evidence that the Aleutian storm track has shifted to an overall more southerly position during the twentieth century (Richardson 1936, Klein 1957, Whittaker and Horn 1982, Wilson and Overland 1986).

3.2.2.3 El Niño Southern Oscillation

The El Niño southern oscillation (ENSO) is a weather pattern originating in the equatorial Pacific with strong influences as far north as the GOA (Emery and Hamilton 1985). ENSO is marked by three states: warm, normal, and cool (Enfield 1997). Under normal conditions, the water temperatures at the continental boundary of the eastern Pacific are around 20°C, as cold bottom waters (8°C) mix with warmer surface water to form a large pool of relatively cool water off the coast of Peru. When an El Niño (warm) event starts, the pool of cool coastal water at the continental boundary becomes smaller and smaller as warm water masses (20°C to 30°C) from the west move on top of them, and the sea level starts to rise. At full El Niño, increases in the surface water temperatures of as much as 5.4°C have been observed very close to the coast of Peru. El Niño also brings a sea level rise along the equator in the eastern Pacific Ocean of as much as 34 cm, as warm buoyant waters moving in from the west override cooler, denser water masses at the continental boundary. In a cool La Niña event, the sea levels are the opposite from an El Niño, and relatively cool (less than 20°C) waters extend well offshore along the equator. Note that the sea surface temperature changes associated with ENSO events extend well into the GOA.

The ENSO has effects in some of the same geographic areas as PDO, but there are two major differences between these patterns. First, an ENSO event does not last as long as a PDO event, and second an ENSO event starts, and is easiest to detect, in the eastern equatorial Pacific; whereas PDO dominates the eastern North Pacific, including the GOA. The simultaneous occurrence of two major weather patterns in one location illustrates Minobe's point that multiple forcing factors with different characteristic frequencies must be operating simultaneously to create regime shifts.

Physical and Geological Oceanography: Coastal Boundaries and Coastal and Ocean Circulation

Thomas Weingartner

4.1 Physical Setting, Geology, and Geography

The Gulf of Alaska (GOA) includes the continental shelf, slope, and abyssal plain of the northern part (north of 50°N) of the northeastern Pacific Ocean. It extends 3,600 kilometers (km) westward from 127°30′ W near the northern end of Vancouver Island, British Columbia, to 176°W along the southern edge of the central Aleutian Islands (Figure 4.1). It includes a continental shelf area of about 3.7×10^5 km^2 (110,000 square nautical miles [Lynde 1986]). The area of the shelf amounts to about 17 percent of the entire Alaskan continental shelf area (2.86×10^6 km^2 total) and approximately 12.5 percent of the total continental shelf of the United States (McRoy and Goering 1974). This vast oceanic domain sustains a rich and diverse marine life that supports the economic and subsistence livelihood for both Alaskans and people living in Asia and North America. The GOA is also an important transportation corridor for vessels carrying cargo to and from Alaska and vessels traveling the Great Circle Route between North America and Asia.

The high-latitude location and geological history of the GOA and adjacent landmass strongly influence the present-day regional meteorology, oceanography, and sedimentary environment. The northern extension of the Cascade Range, with mountains ranging in altitude from 3 to 6 km, rings the coast from British Columbia to Southcentral Alaska (Royer 1982). The Aleutian Range spans the Alaska Peninsula in the western GOA and contains peaks exceeding 1,000 m in elevation. All of the mountains are young and therefore provide plentiful sources of sediment to the ocean. The region is seismically active because it lies within the converging boundaries of the Pacific and North American plates. The motions of these plates control the seismicity, tectonics, volcanism, and much of the morphology of the GOA and make this region one of the most tectonically

active regions on earth (Jacob 1986). Indeed, tectonic motion continuously reshapes the seafloor through faulting, subsidence, landslides, tsunamis, and soil liquefaction. For example, as much as 15 m of uplift occurred over portions of the shelf during the Great Alaska Earthquake of 1964 (Malloy and Merrill 1972, Plafker 1972, von Huene et al. 1972). These geological processes influence ocean circulation patterns, delivery of terrestrial sediments to the ocean, and reworking of seabed sediments.

Approximately 20 percent of the GOA watershed is covered by glaciers today (Royer 1982) making the region the third greatest glacial field on earth (Meier 1984). The glaciers reflect both the subpolar maritime climate, and the regional distribution of mountains, or orography, of the GOA (see chapter 3). The climate setting includes high rates of precipitation and cool temperatures, especially at high altitudes, that enhance the formation of the ice fields and glaciers. The ice fields are both a source and sink for the freshwater delivered to the ocean. In some years the glaciers gain and store the precipitation as ice and snow; in other years, the stored precipitation is released into the numerous streams and rivers draining into the GOA. Glacial scouring of the underlying bedrock provides an abundance of fine-grained sediments to the GOA shelf and basin (Hampton et al. 1986). The major inputs of glacial sediment are the Bering and Malaspina glaciers and the Alsek and Copper rivers in the northern GOA and the Knik, Matanuska, and Susitna rivers that feed Cook Inlet in the northwestern GOA (Hampton et al. 1986).

The bathymetry, or bottom depth variations, of the GOA reflects the diverse and complex geomorphological processes that have worked the region during millions of years. The GOA abyssal plain gradually shoals from a 5,000 m depth in the southwestern GOA to less than 3,000 m in the northeastern GOA. Maximal depths exceed 7,000 m near the central Aleutian Trench along the continental slope south

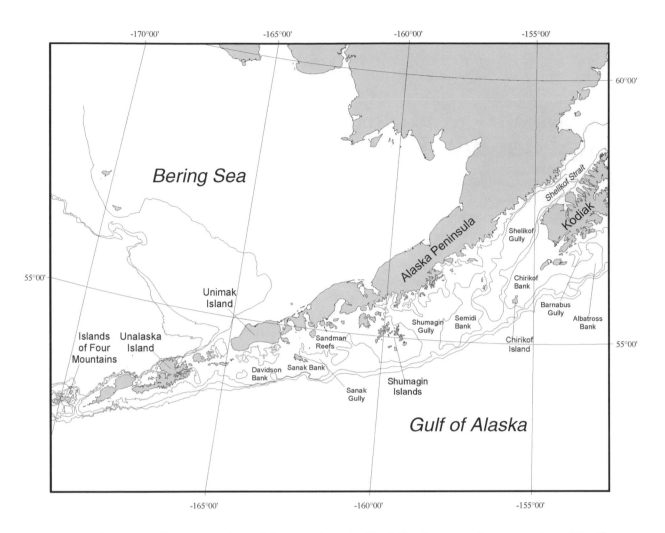

Figure 4.1a.   Shelf topography of the northern Gulf of Alaska and adjacent waters (Martin 1997).

of the Aleutian Islands. Numerous seamounts, remnants of subsea volcanoes associated with spreading centers in the Pacific lithospheric plate (at the earth's crust), are scattered across the central basin. Several of the seamounts or guyots (flat-topped seamounts) rise to within a few hundred meters of the sea surface and provide important mesopelagic (middle depth of the open sea) habitat for pelagic (open sea) and benthic (bottom) marine organisms.

The continental shelf varies in width from about 5 km off the Queen Charlotte Islands in the eastern GOA to about 200 km north and south of Kodiak Island. Along the Aleutian Islands, the shelf break is extremely narrow or even absent, as depths plunge rapidly north and south of the island chain. The numerous passes between these islands control the flow between the GOA and the Bering Sea, with depths (and inflow) generally increasing in the westerly direction (Favorite 1974). In the eastern

Aleutians, most of the passes are shallow and narrow, the largest being Amukta Pass with a maximal depth of 430 m and an area of about 20 km^2 (Favorite 1974). Unimak Pass is the easternmost pass (of oceanographic significance) and connects the southeast Bering Sea shelf directly to the GOA shelf near the Shumagin Islands. This pass is about 75 m deep and has a cross-sectional area of about 1 km^2 (Schumacher et al. 1982).

The shelf topography in the northern GOA is enormously complex because of both tectonic and glacial processes (Figures 4.1a and b). Numerous troughs and canyons, many oriented across the shelf, punctuate the seafloor. Subsea embankments and ridges abound as a result of subsidence, uplift, and glacial moraines. These geological processes have also shaped the immensely complicated coastline that includes lots of silled and unsilled fjords, embayments, capes, and island groups.

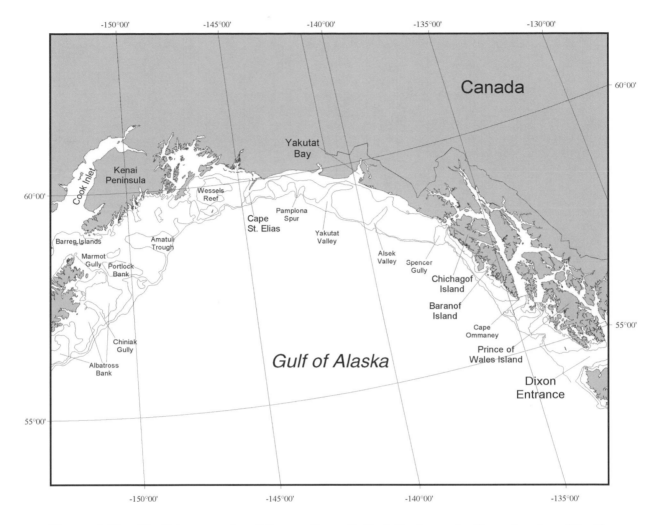

Figure 4.1b.   Shelf topography of the northern Gulf of Alaska and adjacent waters (Martin 1997).

The northwestern GOA includes several prominent geological features that influence the regional oceanography. Kayak Island, which extends about 50 km across the shelf east of the mouth of the Copper River, can deflect inner shelf waters offshore. Interaction of shelf currents with this island can also spawn eddies that transport nearshore waters, which have a high suspended sediment load, onto the outer shelf (Ahlnäes et al. 1987).

Prince William Sound (PWS), which lies west of Kayak Island, is a large, complex, fjord-type estuarine system with characteristics of an inland sea (Muench and Heggie 1978). PWS communicates with the GOA shelf through Hinchinbrook Entrance in eastern PWS and Montague Strait and several smaller passes in western PWS. The shelf is relatively shallow (about 125 m deep) south of Hinchinbrook Entrance and along the eastern shore

of Montague Strait. Hinchinbrook Canyon, however, has depths of about 200 m and extends southward from Hinchinbrook Entrance and opens onto the continental slope. This canyon is a potentially important conduit by which slope waters can communicate directly with PWS. Central PWS is about 60 km by 90 km with depths typically in excess of 200 m and a maximal depth of about 750 m in northern PWS. The entrances to PWS are guarded by the shelf, sills, or both, of about 180 m depth. Many islands are scattered throughout PWS, and bays, fjords, and numerous glaciers are interspersed along its rugged coastline.

Several silled fjords indent the northern GOA coast, between PWS and Cook Inlet. Inner fjord depths can exceed 250 m, which are greater than the depths over the adjacent shelf. To the west of the Kenai Peninsula is Cook Inlet, which extends about 275 km from its mouth to Anchorage at its head. The inlet is about 90 km wide at its mouth, narrows to about 20 km at the Forelands some 200 km from the mouth, and then widens to about 30 km near Anchorage. Upper Cook Inlet branches into two narrow arms (Turnagain and Knik) that extend inland another 70 km. Depths range from 100 m to 150 m at the mouth of Cook Inlet to less than 40 m in the upper end, with the upper arms being so shallow that extensive mudflats are exposed during low tides. The bottom topography throughout the inlet reflects extensive faulting and glacial erosion (Hampton et al. 1986).

At its mouth, Cook Inlet communicates with the northern shelf through Kennedy Entrance to the east, and with Shelikof Strait to the west. The latter is a 200 km by 50 km rectangular channel between Kodiak Island and the Alaska Peninsula with many fjords indenting the coast along both sides of the strait. The main channel, with depths between 150 and 300 m, veers southeastward at the lower end of Kodiak Island and intersects the continental slope west of Chirikof Island. Southwest of Shelikof Strait bottom depths shoal to 100 to 150 m, and the shelf is complicated by the passes and channels associated with the Shumagin and Semidi islands.

4.2 ATMOSPHERIC FORCING OF GOA WATERS

The climate over the GOA is largely shaped by three semipermanent atmospheric pressure patterns: the Aleutian Low, the Siberian High, and the East Pacific High (Wilson and Overland 1986). These systems represent statistical composites of many individual pressure cells moving across the northern North Pacific. The climatological position of these pressure systems varies seasonally, as shown in Figure 4.2. From October through April, the cold air masses of the Siberian High deepen over northeastern Siberia, and the East Pacific High is centered off the southwest coast of California. From May through September, the Siberian High weakens and the East Pacific High migrates northward to about 40°N and attains its greatest intensity (highest pressure) in June. The seasonal changes in intensity and position of these high-pressure systems influence the strength and propagation paths of low-pressure systems (cyclones) over the North Pacific. In winter, the Siberian High forces storms into the GOA, and lows are strong; in summer, these systems are weaker and propagate along a more northerly track across the Bering Sea and into the Arctic Ocean.

The low-pressure storm systems that make up the Aleutian Low form in three ways. Many are generated in the western Pacific when cold, dry air flows off Asia and encounters northward-flowing, warm ocean waters along the Asian continent. Additional formation regions occur in the central Pacific along the Subarctic Front (near 35°N) where strong latitudinal temperature gradients in the ocean interact with unstable, winter air masses (Roden 1970). Finally, the GOA can also be a region of active cyclogenesis (low-pressure formation), particularly in winter when frigid air spills southward over the frozen Bering Sea, the Alaska mainland, or both (Winston 1955). Such conditions can be hazardous to mariners because the accompanying high wind speeds and subfreezing air temperatures can lead to rapid vessel icing (Overland 1990).

Regardless of origin, these lows generally strengthen as they track eastward across the North Pacific. This intensification results from the flux of heat and moisture from the ocean to the atmosphere. The lows attain maximal strength (lowest pressure) in the western and central GOA. Once in the GOA, the coastal mountains inhibit inland propagation, so that the storms often stall and dissipate here. Indeed, Russian mariners refer to the northeastern GOA as the "graveyard of lows" (Plakhotnik 1964).

The mountains also force air masses upward, resulting in cooling, condensation, and enhanced precipitation. The precipitation feeds a large number of mountain drainages that feed the GOA or, in winter, is stored in snowfields and glaciers where it can remain for periods ranging from months to years.

Seasonal variations in the intensity and paths of these low-pressure systems markedly influence meteorological conditions in the GOA. Of particular importance to the marine ecosystem are the seasonal changes in radiation, wind velocity, precipitation, and coastal runoff.

The incoming short-wave radiation that warms the sea surface and provides the energy for marine photosynthesis is strongly affected by cloud cover. Throughout the year, cloud cover of more than 75 percent occurs over the northern GOA more than 60 percent of the time (Brower et al. 1988), and cloud cover of less than 25 percent occurs less than 15 percent of the time. Interannual variability in cloud cover, especially in summer, can affect sea-surface temperatures and possibly the mixed-layer structure (which also depends heavily on salinity distribution). The anomalously warm surface waters observed in

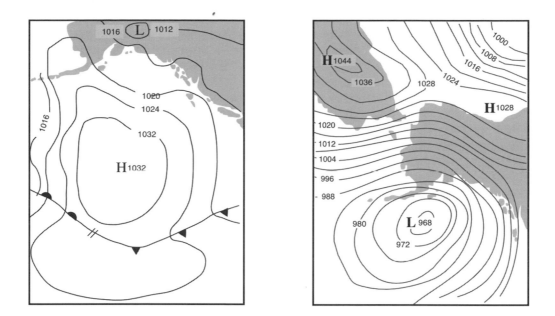

Figure 4.2. Typical summer (left) and winter (right) examples of the Aleutian Low and Siberian High pressure systems (Hollowed and Wooster 1987). Contours are sea-level pressure in millibars.

the summer and fall of 1997 were probably due to unusually low cloud cover and mild winds (Hunt et al. 1999). The characteristic cloud cover is so heavy that it hinders the effective use of passive microwave sensors, such as Advanced Very High Resolution Radar and Sea-viewing Wide Field of view Sensor (SeaWiFS), in ecosystem monitoring.

The cyclonic (counterclockwise) winds associated with the low-pressure systems force an onshore surface transport (Ekman transport) over the shelf and downwelling along the coast. Figure 4.3 shows the mean monthly upwelling index on the northern GOA shelf. This index is negative (implying downwelling) in most months, indicating the prevalence of onshore Ekman transport and coastal convergence. Downwelling favorable winds are strongest from November through March, and feeble or even weakly anticyclonic (upwelling favorable) in summer when the Aleutian Low is displaced by the East Pacific High (Royer 1975, Wilson and Overland 1986). Over the central basin, these winds exert a cyclonic torque (or wind-stress curl) that forces the large-scale ocean circulation.

The high rates of precipitation are evident in long-term average measurements. Figure 4.3 is a composite of long-term average annual precipitation measurements from stations around the GOA. Precipitation rates of 2 to 4 meters per year (m yr^{-1}) are typical throughout the region, but rates in Southeast

Alaska and Prince William Sound exceed 4 m yr^{-1}. Except over the Alaska Peninsula in the western GOA, the coastal precipitation rates are much greater than the estimated net precipitation rate of 1 m yr^{-1} over the central basin (Baumgartner and Reichel 1975). The coastal estimates are undoubtedly biased because most of the measurements are made at sea level and therefore do not fully capture the influence of altitude on the precipitative flux.

Figure 4.3 also includes the mean monthly coastal discharge from Southeast and Southcentral Alaska as estimated by Royer (1982). On an annual average this freshwater influx is enormous and amounts to about 23,000 m^{3}s^{-1}, or about 20 percent greater than the mean annual Mississippi River discharge, and accounts for nearly 40 percent of the freshwater flux into the GOA. This runoff enters the shelf mainly through many small (and ungauged) drainage systems, rather than from a few major rivers. Consequently, the discharge can be thought of as a diffuse, coastal "line" source around the GOA perimeter, rather than arising from a few, large "point" sources. The discharge is greatest in early fall and decreases rapidly through winter, when precipitation is stored as snow. There is a secondary runoff peak in spring and summer, because of snowmelt (Royer 1982). The phasing and magnitude of this freshwater flux is important, because salinity primarily affects water densities (and therefore ocean dynamics) in the northern GOA.

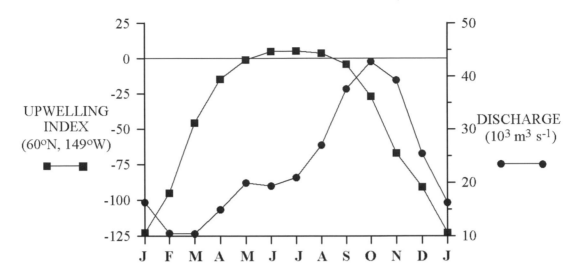

Figure 4.3. Mean monthly upwelling index, 1946-1999, and mean monthly coastal discharge, 1930-1999 (Royer 1982; T. Royer, Center for Coastal Physical Oceanography, Old Dominion University, Norfolk, Virginia, pers. comm., 2000) in the northern Gulf of Alaska. Negative values of the index imply onshore Ekman transport and coastal downwelling. Discharge is shown in cubic meters per second, a measure of flow.

Figure 4.3 shows that the seasonal variation in wind stress and freshwater discharge is large, but also that these variables are not in phase with one another; downwelling is maximal in winter and minimal in summer, whereas discharge is maximal in fall and minimal in late winter. Both winds and buoyant discharge affect the vertical density stratification and contribute to the formation of horizontal pressure (and density) gradients over the shelf and slope. The wind field over the shelf is spatially coherent (Livingstone and Royer 1980) because the scales of the storm systems that enter the GOA are comparable to the size of the basin. The alongshore coherence of the wind field and the distributed nature of the coastal discharge suggest that forcing by winds and buoyancy is approximately uniform along the length of the shelf. Both the winds and buoyant flux force the mean cyclonic alongshore flow over the GOA shelf and slope (Reed and Schumacher 1986, Royer 1998), as shown schematically in Figure 3.4 (chapter 3). On the inner shelf, the flow consists of the Alaska Coastal Current, and over the slope it consists of the Alaska Current (eastern and northeastern GOA) and the Alaskan Stream (northwestern GOA). These current systems are extensive, swift, and continuous over a vast alongshore extent. Thus, the shelf and slope are strongly affected by advection (transport of momentum, energy, and dissolved and suspended materials by ocean currents), implying that climate perturbations can be efficiently communicated into the northwestern GOA by the ocean circulation.

The strong advection also implies that processes occurring far upstream might substantially influence biological production in the GOA.

4.3 PHYSICAL OCEANOGRAPHY OF THE GULF OF ALASKA SHELF AND SHELF SLOPE

The GOA shelf can be divided on the basis of water-mass structure and circulation characteristics into three domains:

- The inner shelf (or Alaska Coastal Current domain) consisting of the ACC;

- The outer shelf, including the shelf-break front; and

- The mid-shelf region between the inner and outer shelves.

Because the boundaries separating these regions are dynamic, their locations vary in space and time. Although dynamic connections among these domains undoubtedly exist, the nature of these links is poorly understood.

The ACC is the most prominent aspect of the shelf circulation. It is a persistent circulation feature that flows cyclonically (westward in the northern

GOA) throughout the year. This current originates on the British Columbian shelf (although in some months or years, it might originate as far south as the Columbia River [Thompson et al. 1989, Royer 1998]), about 2,500 km from its entrance into the Bering Sea through Unimak Pass, in the western GOA (Schumacher et al. 1982).

The ACC is a swift (20 to 180 centimeters per second [cm s^{-1}] [0.4 to 3.6 knots]), coastally trapped flow typically found within 35 km of the shore (Royer 1981b, Johnson et al. 1988, Stabeno et al. 1995). Much or all of the ACC loops through southern PWS, entering through Hinchinbrook Entrance and exiting through Montague Strait (Niebauer et al. 1994). Therefore, the ACC potentially is important to the circulation dynamics of PWS; clearly, it is a critical advective and migratory path for material and organisms between the GOA and PWS. West of PWS, the ACC branches northeast of Kodiak Island. The bulk of the current curves around the mouth of Cook Inlet and continues southward through Shelikof Strait (Muench et al. 1978); the remainder flows southward along the shelf east of Kodiak Island (Stabeno et al. 1995). Although there are no long-term (multiyear) estimates of transport in the ACC, direct measurements (Schumacher et al. 1990, Stabeno et al. 1995) along the Kenai Peninsula and upstream of Kodiak suggest an average transport of about 0.8 Sverdrup (Sv, a unit of flow equal to 1 million cubic meters per second [1 Sv equals 10^6 m^{3}s^{-1}]), with a maximum in winter and a minimum in summer.

The large annual cycle in wind and freshwater discharge is reflected in the mean monthly temperatures and salinities at hydrographic station GAK 1, near Seward, on the inner shelf (Figure 4.4). Mean monthly sea-surface temperatures range from about 3.5°C in March to about 14°C in August. The amplitude of the annual temperature cycle, however, diminishes with depth, with the annual range being only about 1°C at depths greater than 150 m. Surface temperatures are colder than subsurface temperatures from November through May, and the water column has little thermal stratification from December through May.

Surface salinities range from a maximum of about 31 practical salinity units (psu) in late winter to a minimum of 25 psu in August. Vertical salinity (density) gradients are minimal in March and April and maximal in the summer months. Surface stratification commences in April or May (somewhat earlier in PWS), as cyclonic wind stress decreases and runoff increases, and is greatest in mid- to late summer.

The inner shelf and PWS stratify first, because runoff initially is confined to nearshore regions and only gradually spreads offshore through ocean processes. Solar heating provides additional surface buoyancy by warming the upper layers uniformly across the shelf. However, the thermal stratification remains weak until late May or June. As winds intensify in fall, the stratification erodes, resulting from stronger vertical mixing and increased downwelling, which causes surface waters to sink along the coast.

Within the ACC, the annual amplitude in salinity diminishes with depth and has a minimum of about 0.5 psu at about the 100 m depth. At greater depths, the annual amplitude increases but the annual salinity cycle is out of phase with near-surface salinity changes. For example, at and below the 150 m depth, the salinity is minimal in March and maximal in late summer–early fall. The phase difference between the near-surface and near-bottom layers reflects the combined influence of winds and coastal discharge. In summer, when downwelling relaxes, salty, nutrient-rich water from offshore invades the inner shelf (Royer 1975). The upper portion of the water column is freshest in summer, when the winds are weak (little mixing) and coastal discharge is increasing. Vertical mixing is strong through the winter and redistributes freshwater, salt, and possibly nutrients throughout the water column.

The effects of the seasonal cycle of wind and buoyancy forcing are also reflected in both the hydrographic properties and the along-shore velocity structure of the shelf. The seasonal transitions in temperature and salinity properties are shown in Figure 4.5, which is constructed from cross-shore sections along the Seward Line in the northern GOA for April (representative of late winter), August (summer), and October (fall).

The ACC domain, or inner shelf, is within 50 km of the coast. From February through April, the vertical and cross-shelf gradients of salinity and temperature are weak, and the ACC front lies within about 10 km of the coast and extends from the surface to the bottom. Vertical shears (gradients) of the along-shelf velocity are weak and the current dynamics are primarily wind-driven and barotropic (controlled by sea-surface slopes set up by the winds) at this time (Johnson et al. 1988, Stabeno et al. 1995). In summer (late May to early September), the vertical stratification is large, but cross-shelf salinity (and density) gradients are weak. The ACC front extends from 30 to 50 km offshore and usually no deeper than 40 m. The along-shelf flow is weak, although highly variable, in summer. Vertical stratification

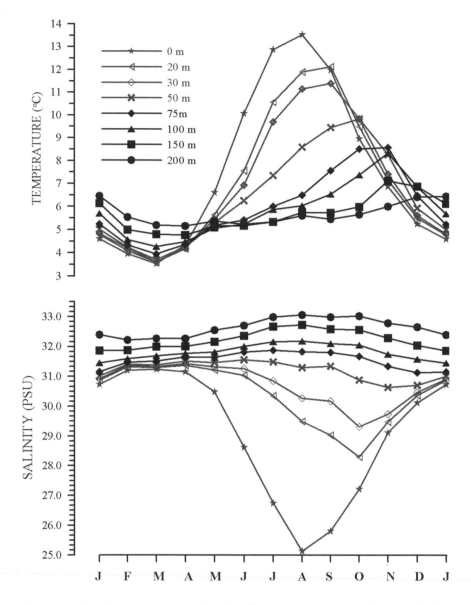

Figure 4.4. The mean annual cycle of temperature (upper) and salinity (lower) at various depths at station GAK1 on the inner shelf of the northern Gulf of Alaska. The monthly estimates are based on 1970-1999 data. The figure includes information from Xiong and Royer 1984.

weakens in fall, but the cross-shelf salinity gradients and the ACC front are stronger than at other times of the year. As coastal downwelling increases, the front moves shoreward to within 30 km of the coast and steepens so that the base of the front intersects the bottom between the 50 and 100 m isobaths.

Theory (Garrett and Loder 1981, Chapman and Lentz 1994, Yankovsky and Chapman 1997, Chapman 2000) suggests that seasonal variations in the ACC frontal structure should strongly influence the vertical and horizontal transport and mixing of

dissolved and suspended material, both across and along the inner shelf. Royer et al. (1979) showed that surface drifters released seaward of the ACC front first drifted onshore (in accordance with Ekman dynamics) and then drifted along-shore upon encountering the ACC front. Conversely, Johnson et al. (1988) showed that, inshore of the front, the surface layer spreads offshore, with this offshore flow increasing as discharge increases in fall. Taken together, these results suggest cross-frontal convergence arising from differing dynamics on either side of the ACC front. Buoyancy effects dominate

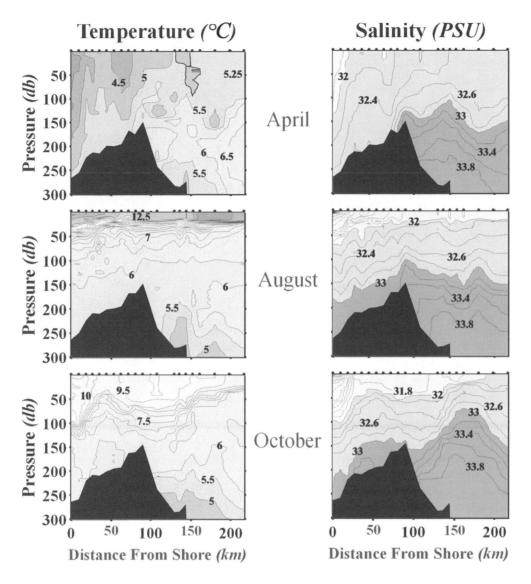

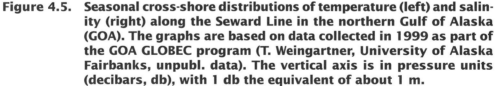

Figure 4.5. **Seasonal cross-shore distributions of temperature (left) and salinity (right) along the Seward Line in the northern Gulf of Alaska (GOA). The graphs are based on data collected in 1999 as part of the GOA GLOBEC program (T. Weingartner, University of Alaska Fairbanks, unpubl. data). The vertical axis is in pressure units (decibars, db), with 1 db the equivalent of about 1 m.**

at the surface inshore of the front (at least for part of the year); wind forcing dominates offshore of the front. Convergence across the front would tend to accumulate plankton along the frontal boundary, possibly attracting foraging fish, seabirds, and marine mammals (L. Haldorson, University of Alaska, Juneau, pers. comm.). The front might also be a region of significant vertical motions. Downwelling velocities of about 30 meters per day (m d^{-1}) in the upper 30 m of the water column are possible in fall. (This estimate is based on the assumption that the cross-frontal convergence occurs over a frontal width

of 15 km with an onshore Ekman flow of 3 cm s^{-1} seaward of the front and an offshore flow of ~15 cm s^{-1} [Johnson et al. 1988] inshore of the front.)

PWS is an important part of the GOA ecosystem providing both habitat to a multitude of organisms and being a potential sink and source for dissolved and suspended materials carried by shelf waters. PWS has a large central basin of about 60 by 90 km. Depths in the central basin are about 350 m. However, maximum depths exceed 750 m in northwestern PWS and are typically about 500 m along the western side of PWS. It is surrounded by many bays and fjords that provide a diversity of habitats for marine organisms (Schmidt 1977, Niebauer et al. 1994, Gay and Vaughan 2001). The mountains and glaciers that ring PWS make up its watershed and provide a plentiful supply of freshwater and sediment to PWS through many streams and rivers. Flow through this semi-enclosed sea is generally counterclockwise with shelf waters entering through Hinchinbrook Entrance in the east and exiting through Montague Strait in the west. The circulation varies seasonally in accordance with the seasonal cycle of winds and runoff, and it appears that the clockwise circulation might reverse seasonally, or at least occasionally, in summer with surface waters exiting through Hinchinbrook Entrance and entering through Montague Strait (Vaughan et al. 2001). Most of the exchange with the shelf occurs with the ACC as indeed at least a portion if not most of the ACC flows through lower PWS. However, Hinchinbrook Entrance can also communicate directly with the continental slope through Hinchinbrook Canyon, which extends from the entrance southward for more than 100 km to the shelf break. Deep water exchange appears to be most prominent in the summer; however, deep water inflow events occur throughout the year (Niebauer et al. 1994, Vaughan et al. 2001). The canyon therefore represents a potential conduit by which slope waters can enter PWS. Because these deep waters are relatively rich in nutrients they could be important to the nutrient budgets of PWS and may provide an advective pathway by which oceanic plankton can be carried into PWS. Reliable transport estimates of mass and property exchanges between PWS and the shelf are not available, although Niebauer et al. (1994) suggest that as much as 40 percent of the sound's volume is exchanged in summer (May-September) and 200 percent of the volume is exchanged in winter (October through April). While these estimates need to be verified, they nevertheless suggest efficient exchange between the shelf and sound and imply that the PWS ecosystem is intimately linked to shelf processes. Water property distributions and stratification in PWS are generally similar to those of the ACC on the shelf. However, because of the sheltering effects of land, the PWS water column stratifies earlier in spring and persists longer in fall than does the shelf.

Although the mid-shelf region is poorly studied and understood compared to other portions of the GOA shelf and slope, it is critically involved in the cross-shelf transport and vertical mixing of nutrients, sediments, organisms, heat, and salt. At the very least it serves as an important link between the inner shelf and the continental slope.

The mid-shelf domain covers the region between 50 and 125 km from the coast. Here cross-shelf temperature and salinity gradients are weak in all seasons. In general, the strongest horizontal density gradients occur within the bottom 50 m of the water column, probably associated with the inshore location of the shelf-break front (which does not always have a surface expression). The bottom of the shelf-break front is generally found farther inshore in summer than in fall or winter. Over the upper portion of the mid-shelf water column, the vertical stratification is largely controlled by salinity in most months, although vertical salinity gradients are weaker here in summer and fall than on the inner shelf. Consequently, in summer, thermal stratification plays an important role in stratifying the mid-shelf water column. Here, the along-shelf flow is weakly westward on average because of the feeble horizontal density gradients. Both the flow and horizontal density gradients are highly variable, however, because of energetic mesoscale (10 to 50 km) flow features. Potential sources for the mesoscale variability are as follows:

1. Separation of the ACC from capes (Ahlnäes et al. 1987);

2. Instabilities of the ACC (Mysak et al. 1981, Bogard et al. 1994);

3. Interactions of the shelf flow with topography (Lagerloef 1983); and

4. Meandering of the Alaska Current along the continental slope (Niebauer et al. 1981).

This mesoscale variability is very difficult to quantify, because it depends on spatial variations in the coastline and the bottom topography and on seasonal variations in the winds and shelf density structure. Nevertheless, these mesoscale features appear to be biologically significant. For example, Incze et al. (1989), Vastano et al. (1992), Schumacher and Kendall (1991), Schumacher et al. (1993), and Bogard et al. (1994) show the coincidence between larval pollock numbers and the presence of eddies in Shelikof Strait. Moreover, the nutritional condition of first-feeding larvae is significantly better inside than outside of eddies (Canino et al. 1991).

The inner and mid-shelf domains share two other noteworthy characteristics. First, during much of the year, the cross-shelf sea surface temperature contrasts are generally small (about 2°C). The small thermal gradients and heavy cloud cover reduce the utility of thermal infrared radiometry in assessing circulation features and frontal boundaries in the northern GOA.

Second, the bottom-water properties of the shelf change markedly throughout the year. The above figures show that the high-salinity bottom waters carried inshore are drawn from over the continental slope in summer. This inflow occurs annually and probably exerts an important dynamical influence on the shelf circulation by modifying the bottom boundary layer (Gawarkiewicz and Chapman 1992, Chapman 2000, Pickart 2000). It might also serve as an important seasonal onshore pathway for oceanic zooplankton. These animals migrate diurnally over the full depth of the water column; during the long summer day length, the zooplankton will spend more time at the bottom than at the surface. The bottom flow that transports the high-salinity water shoreward might then result in a net shoreward flux of zooplankton in summer. The summertime inflow of saline water onto the inner shelf is one means by which the slope and basin interior communicates directly with the nearshore, because (as discussed below) this water is drawn from within the permanent halocline (depth horizon over which salinity changes rapidly) of the GOA. The deep summer inflow is a potentially important conduit for nutrients from offshore to onshore. Inflow, however, is not the only means by which nutrient-rich offshore water can supply the shelf. Other mechanisms include flow up canyons intersecting the shelf break (Klinck 1996, Allen 1996, Hickey 1997, Allen 2000), topographically induced upwelling (Freeland and Denman 1982), and shelf-break eddies and flow meanders (Bower 1991).

The third domain, consisting of the shelf break and continental slope, is influenced by the Alaska Current, which flows along the northeastern and northern GOA, and its transformation west of 150°W, into the southwestward-flowing Alaskan Stream. These currents make up the poleward limb of the North Pacific Subarctic Gyre and provide the oceanic connection between the GOA shelf and the Pacific Ocean. The Alaska Current is a broad (300 km), sluggish (5 to 15 cm s^{-1}) flow with weak horizontal and vertical velocity shears. The Alaskan Stream is a narrow (100 km), swift (100 cm s^{-1}) flow with large velocity shear over the upper 500 m (Reed and Schumacher 1986). The stream continues westward along the southern flank of the Alaska Peninsula and Aleutian Islands and gradually weakens west of 180°W (Thomson 1972). The convergence of the Alaska Current into the Alaskan Stream probably entails concomitant changes in the velocity and thermohaline gradients along the shelf break. Insofar as these gradients influence fluxes between the shelf and slope (Gawarkiewicz 1991), the transformation of the Alaska Current into the Alaskan Stream implies that shelf-break exchange mechanisms are not

uniform around the GOA. Moreover, the effects of these exchanges on the shelf will also be influenced by the shelf width, which varies from 50 km or less in the eastern and northeastern GOA to about 200 km in the northern and northwestern GOA.

The Alaskan Stream has a mean annual volume transport (flow of water) of between 15 and 20 Sv (Reed and Schumacher 1986, Musgrave et al. 1992), and although seasonal transport variations appear small, interannual transport variations may be as great as 30 percent (Royer 1981a). Thomson et al. (1990) found that the Alaska Current is swifter and narrower in winter than in summer. Surface salinities within the Alaska Current vary by only about 0.5 psu throughout the year, whereas the seasonal change in sea surface temperature (SST) is comparable to that of the shelf (about 10°C). Nevertheless, horizontal and vertical density gradients are controlled by the salinity distribution. Maximal stratification occurs between depths of 100 and 300 m and is associated with the permanent halocline of the GOA. Halocline salinities range between 33 and 34 psu, and temperatures are between 5°C and 6°C (Tully and Barber 1960, Dodimead et al. 1963, Reid 1965, Favorite et al. 1976, Musgrave et al. 1992). These water-mass characteristics are identical to the properties of the deep water that floods the shelf bottom each summer (Figure 4.5.)

Although eddy energies of the Alaskan Stream appear small (Royer 1981a, Reed and Schumacher 1986), significant alteration of the slope and shelf-break circulation is likely during occasional passage of large (200 km diameter) eddies that populate the interior basin (Crawford et al. 1999). Musgrave et al. (1992) show considerable alteration in the structure of the shelf-break front off Kodiak Island during the passage of one such eddy. These eddies are long-lived (two to three years) and energetic, having typical swirl speeds of 20 to 50 cm s^{-1} (Tabata 1982, Musgrave et al. 1992, Okkonen 1992, Crawford et al. 1999). They form in the eastern GOA, primarily in years of anomalously strong cyclonic wind forcing along the eastern boundary (Willmott and Mysak 1980, Melsom et al. 1999, Meyers and Basu 1999) and then propagate westward at about 2 to 3 cm s^{-1}. Most of the eddies remain over the deep basin and far from the continental slope; however, some propagate along the slope, requiring several months to transit from Yakutat to Kodiak Island (Crawford et al. 1999; S. Okkonen, University of Alaska Fairbanks, pers. comm., 2001).

Eddies that impinge upon the continental slope could significantly influence the shelf circulation and exchanges between the shelf and slope of salt, heat, nutrients, and plankton. Their influence on shelf-slope exchange in the northern GOA has not been ascertained, but because they propagate slowly, are long-lived, and form episodically, they could be a source of interannual variability for this shelf. These eddies have many features in common with the Gulf Stream rings that significantly modify shelf properties along the East Coast of the United States (Houghton et al. 1986, Ramp 1986, Joyce et al. 1992, Wang 1992, Schlitz 1999). In the eastern GOA, Whitney et al. (1998) showed that these eddies cause a net off-shelf nutrient flux. In the northern GOA, they might have the opposite effect, because nutrient concentrations are generally higher over the slope than on the shelf (T. Whitledge and A. Childers, University of Alaska Fairbanks, pers. comm., 2000).

4.4 BIOPHYSICAL IMPLICATIONS

The magnitude of the spring phytoplankton bloom depends on surface nutrient concentrations and water-column stability. The annual resupply of nutrients to the euphotic zone is not understood for the inner shelf, however. Cross-shelf, surface Ekman transport in winter cannot account for the high nutrient concentrations observed on the inner shelf in spring (T. Whitledge and A. Childers, University of Alaska Fairbanks, pers. comm., 2000). Turbulent mixing during late fall and winter could mix the nutrient-rich deep water (brought onto the shelf in summer) up into the surface layer in time for the spring bloom. If so, vernal nutrient levels might result from a two-stage preconditioning process occurring during the several months preceding the spring bloom. The first stage occurs in summer and is related to the on-shelf movement of saline, nutrient-rich, bottom water as described above. The quantity of nutrients carried onshore then depends upon the summer wind field and the properties of the slope source water that contributes to this inflow. The second step occurs in fall and winter and depends on turbulence. Current instabilities, downwelling-induced convection, and diffusion accomplish the vertical mixing. The extent of this mixing depends upon the seasonally varying stratification and the vertical and horizontal velocity structure of the ACC. Each of these mechanisms probably varies from year to year, suggesting that spring nutrient concentrations will also vary.

Another potentially important nutrient source for the inner shelf in spring is PWS. Winter mixing in PWS could bring nutrient-rich water to the surface, where it is exported to the shelf by that portion of the ACC that loops through PWS.

The timing of the spring bloom depends on development of stratification within the euphotic zone. The euphotic zone extends from the surface to a depth where sufficient light still exists to support photosynthesis. Stratification within the euphotic zone is influenced by freshwater discharge and solar heating. Preliminary GLOBEC data (T. Whitledge and D. Stockwell, University of Alaska Fairbanks, pers. comm., 2000) suggest that the spring bloom begins in protected regions of PWS in late March as day length increases and stratification builds as a result of snowmelt, rainfall, and the sheltering effect of PWS from winds. The bloom on the shelf lags that of PWS by two to six weeks and may not proceed simultaneously across the shelf. This delay results from the time required to stratify the shelf. Because density is strongly affected by salinity and, therefore, by the spreading of freshwater on the shelf, stratification does not evolve by vertical (one-dimensional) processes phase-locked to the annual solar cycle. Rather, stratification depends primarily on the rate at which freshwater spreads offshore, which is a consequence of three-dimensional circulation and mixing processes intimately associated with ocean dynamics.

Several implications follow from this hypothesis. First, spring bloom dynamics on the shelf are not as tightly coupled to the solar cycle as on mid-latitude shelves where temperature controls density. Second, mixed-layer development depends on processes operating spanning a range of time scales and involves a plethora of variables that affect vertical mixing and the offshore flux of freshwater from the nearshore. These variables include the fractions of winter precipitation delivered to the coast as snow and rain, the timing and rate of spring snowmelt (a function of air temperature and cloudiness), and the wind velocity. The relevant time scales range from a few days (storm events) to seasonal or longer. The long time scales follow from the fact that the shelf circulation, particularly the ACC, can advect the freshwater that contributes to stratification from very distant regions. Third, interannual variability in the onset and strength of stratification on the GOA continental shelf is probably greater than for mid-latitude shelves. This expectation follows from the fact that several potentially interacting parameters affect stratification, and each or all can vary considerably from year to year. Therefore, application of Gargett's (1997) hypothesis of the optimal stability window to the GOA shelf involves more degrees of freedom than its use on either mid-latitude shelves or the central GOA (where temperature exerts primary control on stratification in the euphotic zone).

All of these considerations suggest that stratification probably does not develop uniformly in space or time on the GOA shelf. The implications are potentially enormous with respect to feeding opportunities for zooplankton in spring. These animals must encounter abundant prey shortly after migrating to the surface from their overwintering depths. Emergence from diapause (a period of reduced metabolism and inactivity) is tightly coupled to the solar cycle, rather than the onset of stratification. Conceivably, then, zooplankton recruitment success might depend on shelf physical processes occurring over a period of several months prior to the onset of the bloom. In particular, the magnitude and phasing of the spring bloom might be preconditioned by shelf processes that occurred throughout the preceding summer and winter. Perturbations in the magnitude and phasing of the spring bloom might propagate through the food chain and affect summer and fall feeding success of juvenile fishes (Denman et al. 1989).

4.5 TIDES

The tides in the GOA are of the mixed type with the principal lunar semi-diurnal (M_2) tide being dominant and the luni-solar diurnal (K_1) tide being, in general, of secondary importance. Tidal characteristics (amplitudes and velocities) are strongly influenced by the complex shelf and slope bathymetry and coastal geometry, however. Consequently, spatial variations in the tidal characteristics of these two species are large. For example, Anchorage has the largest tidal amplitudes in the northern GOA, with the M_2 tide being about 3.6 m and the K_1 tide being about 0.7 m. In contrast, the amplitudes of both of these constituents in Kodiak and Seward are less than half those of Anchorage. Foreman et al. (2000) found that the cross-shelf flux of tidal energy onto the northwest GOA shelf is enormous and is accompanied by high (bottom) frictional dissipation rates. Their model estimates indicate that the tidal dissipation rate in Kennedy Entrance accounts for nearly 50 percent of the total dissipation of the M_2 constituent in the GOA. Further, about one-third of the energy of the K_1 tide in the GOA is dissipated in Cook Inlet. Some of the energy lost from tides is available for mixing, which would reduce vertical stratification and enhance the transfer of nutrients into the euphotic zone.

The interaction of the tidal wave with varying bottom topography can also generate shelf waves at the diurnal frequency and generate residual flows. The waves are a prominent feature of the low-frequency circulation along the British Columbian shelf (Crawford 1984, Crawford and Thomson 1984, Flather 1988, Foreman and Thomson 1997, Cummins and Oey 2000) and could affect pycnocline displacements. (The pycnocline is a vertical layer across which water density changes are large and stable.) The model of Foreman et al. (2000) predicts diurnal-period shelf waves in the northwest GOA and especially along the Kodiak shelf break. Although no observations are available to confirm the presence of such waves along the Kodiak shelf, their presence could influence biological production here as well as the dispersal of planktonic organisms. Residual flows resulting from nonlinear tidal dynamics could (locally) influence the transport of suspended and dissolved materials on the shelf.

Seasonal changes in water-column stratification can also affect the vertical distribution of tidal energy over the shelf through the generation of internal (baroclinic) waves of tidal period. Such motions are likely to occur in summer and fall in the northwestern GOA where the flux of barotropic tidal energy (which is nearly uniformly distributed over the water column) across the shelf break (Foreman et al. 2000) interacts with the highly stratified water column on the shelf. The internal waves generated can have small spatial scales (tens of kilometers) in contrast to the large scale (thousands of kilometers) of the generating barotropic tidal waves. Moreover, the phases and amplitudes of the baroclinic tides will vary with seasonal changes in stratification. Although no systematic investigation of internal tides on the GOA shelf has been conducted, S. Danielson (University of Alaska Fairbanks, pers. comm., 2000) found that the tidal velocities in the ACC near Seward in winter are about 5 cm s^{-1} and are barotropic. However, in late summer, tidal velocities in the upper 50 m are about 20 cm s^{-1} whereas below 100 m depth they are about 5 cm s^{-1}. Internal tides will also displace the pycnocline sufficiently to have biological consequences, including the pumping of nutrients into the surface layer, the dispersal of plankton and small fishes, and the formation of transitory and small-scale zones of horizontal divergence and convergence that affect feeding behaviors (Mann and Lazier 1996). Stratified tidal flows might also be significant for some silled fjords. The interaction of the tide with the sill can enhance mixing and exchange (Farmer and Smith 1980, Freeland and Farmer 1980) and can resupply the inner fjord with nutrient-rich, high-salinity water and plankton through Bernoulli suction effects (Thompson and Golding 1981, Thomson and Wolanski 1984).

4.6 GULF OF ALASKA BASIN

The circulation in the central GOA consists of the cyclonically (counterclockwise) flowing Alaska Gyre, which is part of the more extensive subarctic gyre of the North Pacific Ocean. The center of the gyre is at about 53°N, and 145° to 150°W. The gyre includes the Alaska Current and Alaskan Stream and the eastward-flowing North Pacific Current along the southern boundary of the GOA. The latter is a trans-Pacific flow that originates at the confluence of the northward-flowing Kuroshio Current and the southward-flowing Oyashio Current in the western Pacific. Some water from the Alaskan Stream apparently recirculates into the North Pacific Current, but the strength and location of this recirculation is poorly understood and appears to be extremely variable (Favorite et al. 1976). The North Pacific Current bifurcates off of the western coast of North America, with the northward flow feeding the Alaska Gyre and the southward branch entering the California Current. The bifurcation zone is located roughly along the zero line in the climatological mean for the wind stress curl. The gyral flow reflects the large-scale cyclonic wind-stress distribution over the GOA. Mean speeds of drifters deployed in the upper 150 m of this gyre (far from the continental slope) are 2 to 10 cm s^{-1}, but the variability is large (Thomson et al. 1990). These cyclonic winds also force a long-term average upwelling rate of about 10 to 30 m yr^{-1} in the gyre center (Xie and Hsieh 1995).

The vertical thermohaline structure of the Alaska Gyre is described by Tully and Barber (1960) and Dodimead et al. (1963) and consists of the following components:

- A seasonally varying upper layer that extends from the surface to about the 100 m depth;

- A halocline that extends from 100 m to about the 200 m depth over which salinity increases from 33 to 34 psu and temperatures decrease from 6 to 4°C; and

- A deep layer, extending from the bottom of the halocline to about the 1,000 m depth, over which salinity increases more slowly to about 34.4 psu and temperatures decrease from 4° to 3°C.

Below the deep layer salinity increases more slowly to its maximal value of about 34.7 psu at the bottom.

The seasonal variations of the upper layer reflect the effects of wind-mixing and heat exchange with the atmosphere—essentially one-dimensional mixing processes. The ocean loses heat to the atmosphere from October through March and gains heat from April through September. The upper layer is isohaline and isothermal in winter down to the top of the halocline. At this time, upper-layer salinities range from 32.5 to 32.8 psu, and temperatures range from 4° to 6°C. The upper layer is fresher and colder in the northern GOA and saltier and warmer in the southern GOA. The upper layer gradually freshens and warms in spring, as wind speeds decrease and solar heating increases. A summer mixed layer forms that includes a weak secondary halocline and a strong seasonal thermocline, with both centered at about the 30 m depth. The seasonal pycnocline erodes and upper layer properties revert to winter conditions as cooling and wind-mixing increase in fall.

The halocline is a permanent feature of the subarctic North Pacific Ocean and represents the deepest limit over which winter mixing occurs within the upper layer. The halocline results from the high (compared with other ocean basins) rates of precipitation and runoff in conjunction with large-scale, three-dimensional circulation and interior mixing processes occurring over the North Pacific (Reid 1965, Warren 1983, Van Scoy et al. 1991, Musgrave et al. 1992). The strong density gradient of the halocline effectively limits vertical exchange between saline and nutrient-rich deep water and the upper layer. The deep waters of the GOA consist of the North Pacific Intermediate Water (formed in the northwestern Pacific Ocean) and, at greater depths, contributions from the North Atlantic. Mean flows in the deep interior are feeble (1 cm s^{-1}), and the flow dynamics are governed by both the climatological wind stress distribution (Koblinsky et al. 1989) and the global thermohaline circulation (Warren and Owens 1985) modified by the bottom topography. The thermohaline circulation carries nutrient-rich waters into the North Pacific and forces a weak and deep upwelling throughout the region (Stommel and Arons 1960a,b; Reid 1981).

CHAPTER 5

Biological and Chemical Oceanography
Robert T. Cooney

5.1 MARINE NUTRIENTS

The overall fertility of the Gulf of Alaska (GOA) depends primarily on nutrient resupply from deep-water sources to the surface layer where plants grow. Rates of carbon fixation by phytoplankton in the euphotic zone are limited seasonally and annually by changing light levels and the kinds and supply rates of several dissolved inorganic chemical species. Three elements—nitrogen, phosphorus, and silicon—are essential for photosynthesis (Parsons et al. 1984). Other dissolved inorganic constituents such as iron are also believed to control rates of photosynthesis at some locations and times (Martin and Gordon 1988, Freeland et al. 1997, Pahlow and Riebsell 2000).

Organic matter synthesized by plants in the lighted surface layer is consumed there or sinks down into the deeper water where some may eventually reach the seabed. The unconsumed portion is oxidized to inorganic dissolved forms by bacteria at all depths. In the euphotic zone, inorganic nutrients excreted by zooplankton and fish, or liberated by bacterial oxidation (a process referred to as remineralization), are used immediately by phytoplankton. In contrast, living cells, organic detritus (remains of dead organisms), and fecal pellets that escape the euphotic zone by sinking are remineralized below the lighted upper layer, and the resulting inorganic forms are temporarily lost to surface plant stocks. These combined processes lead to vertical distributions of dissolved inorganic nitrogen, phosphorus, and silicon in which the surface concentrations are much lower than those found deeper in the water column (Reeburgh and Kipphut 1986). Geostrophic (shaped by the earth's rotation) and wind-forced upwelling and deep seasonal overturn provide mechanisms that bring nutrient-enriched deep water back into the surface layer each year (Schumacher and Royer 1993). Also, at depths shallower than about 100 m, tidal mixing resulting from friction across the bottom can interact with the wind-mixed surface layer to provide an intermittent avenue for surface nutrient replenishment during all seasons.

Concentrations of the dissolved inorganic forms of nitrogen (nitrate, nitrite, and ammonia), phosphorus (phosphate), and silicon (silicate) occur at some of the highest levels measured anywhere in the deep waters of the GOA (Mantyla and Reid 1983). A permanent strong pycnocline, resulting from the low salinity of the upper 120 to 150 m, limits access to this valuable pool; deep winter mixing rarely reaches below about 110 m in waters over the deep ocean (Dodimead et al. 1963, Favorite et al. 1976). Although upwelling occurs in the center of the Alaska Gyre, it is believed to be only on the order of a meter (or considerably less) per day (Sugimoto 1993, Xie and Hsieh 1995), a relatively modest rate compared to some regions of high productivity like the Peru or Oregon coastal upwellings. Away from the Alaska Gyre along the northern continental margin of the GOA, the prevailing winds drive a predominately downwelling environment over the continental shelf for seven to eight months each year. Although this condition usually moderates during the summer, there is little evidence that wind-forced coastal upwelling is ever well developed. Instead, during the period of relaxed downwelling a rebound of isopycnal (density boundaries; waters having the same densities) surfaces along the shelf edge permits the run-up of dense slope water onto and across the shelf. This subsurface water, containing elevated concentrations of dissolved nutrients, flows into the deeper coastal basins and fjords (Muench and Heggie 1978, Heggie and Burrell 1981). Presumably the timing and duration of this coastal bottom water renewal is related to the reversal of the Pacific high pressure dominance in the GOA each summer.

The nearshore waters in the northern GOA are also influenced by runoff from a large number of streams, rivers, and glaciers in the rugged coastal margin. In these areas, which are largely untouched by agriculture, this input probably contributes little to the coastal nutrient cycle, except possibly as a source for silicon and iron (Burrell 1986). Therefore, the major pool of plant nutrients for water column production in ocean, shelf, and coastal regions is derived from marine sources and resides in the deep waters below the surface production zone.

Because light limits carbon fixation during the winter months, there is a strong seasonal signal in nutrient concentrations in the euphotic zone in upper-layer shelf, coastal, and inside waters. During the winter, dissolved inorganic plant nutrients build their concentrations in the deepening wind-mixed layer as deeper, nutrient-rich water becomes involved in the seasonal overturn when uptake by phytoplankton is minimal. Under seasonal light limitation, surface nutrient concentrations usually peak in March, just before the onset of the annual plankton production cycle. By mid- to late May and early June, euphotic zone nutrients are drawn down dramatically to seasonal lows as the stratification that initiates the spring "bloom" of plant plankton severely restricts the vertical flux of new nutrients (Goering et al. 1973). Nitrate can become undetectable or nearly so during the summer months in many shelf and coastal areas, and ammonia (excreted by grazers) becomes important in sustaining the much reduced primary productivity. Later in fall, with the onset of the Aleutian Low and the storms that it produces, a cooling and deepening wind-mixed layer can reinject sufficient new nutrients into a shrinking euphotic zone to initiate a fall plant bloom in some years (Eslinger et al. 2001).

The strong seasonal signal of nutrients and plant stocks evident on the continental shelf is somewhat diminished in surface waters seaward of the shelf break in the GOA. The region beyond the continental shelf break is described as "high nutrient, low chlorophyll." It was believed historically that large calanoid copepods (species of zooplankton endemic to the subarctic Pacific) consumed sufficient plant biomass each year to control the overall productivity below levels needed to completely exhaust the surface nitrogen (Heinrich 1962, Parsons and Lalli 1988).

More recently, iron limitation has been posed as a mechanism controlling primary production in the GOA and in several other offshore regions of the world's oceans (Martin and Gordon 1988). Contemporary research in the GOA has revealed that control of the amount of food produced by phytoplankton through grazing of zooplankters is probably important, although the species of zooplankton involved are not the large calanoid copepods (Dagg and Walser 1987, Frost 1991, Dagg 1993). Production of phytoplankton is now thought to be controlled by an assemblage of microconsumers, represented by abundant ciliate protozoans and small flagellates (Booth et al. 1993). Because the growth rates of these grazers are about the same as those of the plants, it is hypothesized that these microconsumers

are capable of efficiently tracking and limiting the overall oceanic production by eating the primary producers (Banse 1982). This control mechanism is possible because the plant communities are dominated by very small cells, 10 microns or less, that serve as food for the microconsumers.

A related hypothesis asserts that the small size of the plants is actually in response to low levels of iron. It is known that faced with nutrient limitation, phytoplankton communities generally shift to small-sized species whose surface-area-to-volume ratios are high.

Surprising recent observations demonstrate a trend in increasing temperatures in the upper layers that may be causing a shift in the seasonal nutrient balance offshore (Polovina et al. 1995, Freeland et al. 1997). For the first time, there are reports that nitrogen has been drawn down to undetectable levels along "Line P" in the southern GOA out to a distance of 600 km from the coast. Line P is an oceanographic transect occupied by the Canadian government which is the oldest source of data from the southern GOA. The evidence indicates that the winter mixed layer is shoaling under long-term warming conditions.

An essential continuing issue is to understand how, at a variety of spatial and temporal scales, the supply rates of inorganic nitrogen, phosphorus, silicon, and other essential nutrients for plant growth in the euphotic zone are mediated by climate-driven physical mechanisms in the GOA. Inorganic nutrient supplies might be influenced by climate changes in the following ways:

- Upwelling in the Alaska Gyre;

- Deep winter mixing;

- Shelf and coastal upwelling and downwelling;

- Vertical transport in frontal zones and eddies; and

- Deep and shallow cross-shelf transports.

In addition to these mechanisms, the Alaska Coastal Current may play a role that has yet to be determined in the supply rates of dissolved inorganic nutrients to nearshore habitats (Schumacher and Royer 1993). Finally, the import of marine-derived nitrogen associated with the spawning migrations of salmon and other anadromous fishes has been described as a novel means by which the oceanic GOA enriches the terrestrial margin each year. This allochthonous input (food from an outside source) to the drainages bordering the GOA is clearly important in many freshwater nursery areas hosting the early life stages of Pacific salmon (Finney 1998) and probably varies with interannual and longer-term changes in salmon abundance.

5.2 PLANKTON AND PRODUCTIVITY

Much of what is presently understood about the plankton communities and their productivity in the GOA has arisen from several programs examining the open ocean and shelf environments. These programs have included the following:

- U.S.-Canada NORPAC surveys (LeBrasseur 1965);

- Subarctic Pacific Ecosystem Research (SUPER) project of the National Science Foundation (NSF) (Miller 1993);

- The multi-decadal plankton observations from Canadian Ocean Station P (OSP) and Line P (McAllister 1969, Fulton 1983, Frost 1983, Parsons and Lalli 1988);

- Annual summer Japanese vessel surveys by Hokkaido University (Kawamura 1988);

- The Outer Continental Shelf Energy Assessment Program (OCSEAP) by Minerals Management Service (MMS) and National Oceanic and Atmospheric Administration (NOAA) (Hood and Zimmerman 1986); and

- The Shelikof Strait Fisheries Oceanography Cooperative Investigation (FOCI) study by NOAA and NMFS (Kendall et al. 1996).

Additional and more recent programs include the North Pacific GLOBEC and those supported by the EVOS Trustee Council. The above mentioned programs and a few other studies provide a reasonably coherent first-order view of the structure and function of lower trophic levels in the northeastern subarctic Pacific Ocean. A serious gap in the detailed understanding of relationships between the observed inshore and offshore production cycles remains, however—namely how these quite different marine ecosystems are phased through time and interact at their boundaries over the shelf. As a result, information is now lacking about how the effects of future climate change may manifest in food webs supporting higher level consumers, except in a very general way.

5.2.1 Seasonal and Annual Plankton Dynamics

The composition, distribution, abundance, and productivity of plant and animal plankton communities in the GOA have been reviewed by Sambrotto and Lorenzen (1986), Cooney (1986), Miller (1993), and Mackas and Frost (1993). In general, dramatic differences are observed between pelagic communities over the deep ocean, and those found in shelf, coastal, and protected inside waters (sounds, fjords, and estuaries). Specifically, the euphotic zone seaward of the shelf edge is dominated year-round by very small phytoplankters—tiny diatoms, naked flagellates, and cyanobacteria (Booth 1988). Most are smaller than 10 microns in size, and their combined standing stocks (measured as chlorophyll concentration) occur at very low and seasonally stable levels. It was originally hypothesized that a small group of large oceanic copepods (*Neocalanus* spp. and *Eucalanus bungii*) limited plant numbers and open ocean production by efficiently controlling the plant stocks through grazing (Heinrich 1962). More recent evidence, however, indicates the predominant grazers on the oceanic flora are not the large calanoids (Dagg 1993), but instead abundant populations of ciliate protozoans and heterotrophic microflagellates (Miller et al. 1991a,b; Frost 1993). It has been further suggested that in these high nutrient, low chlorophyll oceanic waters, very low levels of dissolved inorganic iron (coming mainly from atmospheric sources) are ultimately responsible for structuring the composition of the primary producers and consumers (Martin and Gordon 1988, Martin 1991). Close reproductive and trophic coupling between the nanophytoplankton and microconsumers appears to restrict levels of primary productivity below that needed to exhaust all of the seasonally available nitrogen each year (Banse 1982). Moreover, the excreta of the microconsumers is diffuse, with low sinking rates, and is easily oxidized by bacteria. Ammonia (derived from protein metabolism, urea) is a preferred plant nutrient and the first oxidation product recycled in this way. Wheeler and Kokkinakis (1990) demonstrated that as long as ammonia is available for the plants, nitrate uptake in the euphotic zone is much reduced. Together, these findings are demonstrating new relationships and nutrient balances at the base of the offshore pelagic ecosystem in the GOA.

In contrast, some shelf, and most coastal, and inside waters host a more traditional plankton community in which large and small diatoms and dinoflagellates support a copepod-dominated grazing assemblage

(Sambrotto and Lorenzen 1986, Cooney 1986). Here, the annual production cycle is characterized by well-defined spring (and sometimes fall) blooms of large diatom species (many larger than 50 microns) whose productivities are limited seasonally by the rapid utilization of dissolved inorganic nitrogen, phosphorus, and silicon in the euphotic zone (Ward 1997, Eslinger et al. 2001). These blooms typically begin in late March and early April in response to a seasonal stabilization of the winter-conditioned deep mixed layer. High rates of photosynthesis usually last only four to six weeks (Goering et al. 1973). Strong periods of wind, tidal mixing, or both during the bloom can prolong the production by interrupting the conditions of light and stability needed to support plant growth. When the phytoplankton bloom is prolonged in this way, its intensity is lessened, but considerably more organic matter is directed into pelagic food webs, rather than sinking to feed seabed consumers (Eslinger et al. 2001). Accelerated seasonal warming and freshening of the upper layers in May and June provide increasing stratification that eventually restricts the vertical flux of new nutrients and limits summer primary productivity to very low levels. In some years, a fall bloom of diatoms occurs in September and October in response to a deepening wind-mixed layer and enhanced nutrient levels. The ecological significance of the fall portion of the pelagic production cycle remains undescribed.

In both the ocean and shelf domains, strong seasonal signals occur in standing stocks and estimates of daily and annual rates of production for the phytoplankton and zooplankton. Some of the earliest measurements of photosynthesis at Canadian Ocean Station P (OSP) placed the annual primary production in the southern part of the Alaska Gyre at about 50 grams of carbon per square meter per year (g C $m^{-2}y^{-1}$) (McAllister 1969), or somewhat lower than the overall world ocean average of about 70 g C $m^{-2}y^{-1}$. More recent studies using other techniques, however, have suggested higher annual rates, somewhere between 100 and 170 g C $m^{-2}y^{-1}$ (Welschmeyer et al. 1993). Unlike the production cycle over the shelf, the oceanic primary productivity does not produce an identifiable spring/summer plant bloom. Instead, the oceanic phytoplankton stock remains at low levels (about 0.3 milligrams [mg] of chlorophyll *a* m^{-3}) year-round for reasons discussed above. In stark contrast, oceanic stocks of zooplankton (upper 150 m) do exhibit marked seasonality. Late winter values of 5 to 20 mg m^{-3} (wet weight) rise to 100 to 500 mg m^{-3} in mid-summer, when upper-layer populations of large calanoids dominate the standing stock. Assuming the zooplankton production is roughly 15 percent of the oceanic primary productivity

(Parsons 1986), annual estimates of zooplankton carbon production arising from primary productivity range between 8 and 26 g C m^{-2}. Given the carbon content of an average zooplankter is approximately 45 percent of the dry weight, and that dry weight is about 15 percent of the wet weight (Omori 1969), annual carbon production can be converted to crude estimates of biomass. Results from this calculation suggest that between 119 and 385 g of biomass m^{-2} may be produced each year in the upper layers of the oceanic regime from sources thought to be largely zooplankton.

The shelf, coastal, and inside waters present a mosaic of many different pelagic habitats. The open shelf (depths less than 200 m) is narrow in the east between Yakutat and Kayak Island (20 to 25 km in some places), but broadens in the north and west beyond the Copper River (about 100 to 200 km). The shelf is punctuated by submarine canyons and deep straits, but also rises to extensive shallow banks at some locations. The rugged northern coastal margin is characterized by numerous islands, coastal and protected fjords, and estuaries. Only Prince William Sound (PWS) is deeper than 400 m.

Although the measurements are sparse, the open shelf and coastal areas of the northern GOA are believed to be quite productive, particularly the region between PWS and Shelikof Strait (Sambrotto and Lorenzen 1986). Coastal transport and turbulence along the Kenai Peninsula, in lower Cook Inlet, and around Kodiak and Afognak islands appears to enhance nutrient supplies during the spring and summer. Annual rates of primary production approaching 200 to 300 g C $m^{-2}y^{-1}$ have been described. In other coastal fjords, sounds, and bays, the estimates of annual primary production range from 140 to more than 200 g C $m^{-2}y^{-1}$ (Goering et al. 1973, Sambrotto and Lorenzen 1986). Assuming again that the annual zooplankton production is roughly 15 percent of the primary productivity, yearly zooplankton growth in shelf and coastal areas probably ranges between 21 and 45 g C $m^{-2}y^{-1}$, or 311 to 667 g $m^{-2}y^{-1}$ wet weight. In PWS, the wet-weight biomass of zooplankton caught in nets in the upper 50 m varies from a low in February of about 10 mg m^{-3} to a high of more than 600 mg m^{-3} in June and July (Cooney et al. 2001a). For selected other coastal areas outside PWS, the seasonal range of zooplankton biomass includes winter lows of about 40 mg m^{-3} to spring/summer highs approaching 5,000 mg m^{-3}.

In addition to strong seasonality in standing stocks and rates of production, plankton communities also exhibit predictable seasonal species succession each year. Over the shelf, the large diatom-dominated spring bloom gives way to dinoflagellates and other smaller forms as nutrient supplies diminish in late May and early June. Ward (1997) described the phytoplankton species succession in PWS. She found that early season dominance in the phytoplankton bloom was shared by the large chain-forming diatoms *Skeletonema*, *Thalassiosira*, and *Chaetoceros*. Later in June, under post-bloom nutrient restriction, diatoms were dominated by smaller *Rhizosolenia* and tiny flagellates. This seasonal shift in dominance from larger to smaller plant species in response to declining nutrient concentrations and supply rates is commonly observed in other high-latitude systems and is believed to be at least partially responsible for driving the succession in the grazing community.

The zooplankton succession is somewhat more complex and involves interchanges between the ocean and shelf ecosystems. In the winter and spring, the early copepodite stages of *Neocalanus* spp. begin arriving in the upper layers from deepwater spawning populations (Miller 1988, Miller and Nielsen 1988, Miller and Clemons 1988). This arrival occurs in some coastal areas (at depths of more than 400 m) in late February and early March, but is delayed about thirty days in the open ocean. Both *Neocalanus* spp. and *Eucalanus bungii* are interzonal seasonal migrators, living a portion of their life cycle in the upper layers as developing copepodites, and later resting in diapause in the deep water preparing for reproduction. While maturing in the oceanic surface water, *Neocalanus plumchrus* and *N. flemingeri* inhabit the wind-mixed layer above the seasonal thermocline (upper 25 to 30 m), while *N. cristatus* (the largest of the subarctic copepods) and *Eucalanus bungii* are found below the seasonal stratification (Mackas et al. 1993). The unusual partitioning of the surface ocean environment by these species has not yet been verified for shelf and coastal waters, although it has been suggested that the partitioning may occur in the deepwater fjords and sounds (T. Cooney, University of Alaska Fairbanks, unpubl. data).

Along with the early copepodites of the interzonal migrators, the late winter and spring shelf zooplankton community also hosts small numbers of *Pseudocalanus* spp., *Metridia pacifica*, *M. okhotensis*, and adult *Calanus marshallae*. Because these copepods must first feed before reproducing, their seasonal numbers and biomass are set by the timing, intensity, and duration of the diatom bloom. By May and early June, the abundances of small copepods like *Pseudocalanus* and *Acartia* are increasing, but the community biomass is often dominated by

relatively small numbers of very large developmental stages (C4 and C5) of *Neocalanus* (Cooney et al. 2001a). After *Neocalanus* leaves the surface waters in late May and early June for diapause below the surface, *Pseudocalanus*, *Acartia*, and *Centropages* (small copepods); the pteropod *Limicina pacifica*; and larvaceans (*Oikopleura* and *Fritillaria*) occur in increasing abundance. Later, from summer to fall and extending into early winter, carnivorous jellyplankters represented by ctenophores and small hydromedusae, and chaetognaths (*Sagitta elegans*) become common. These shifting seasonal dominants are joined by several different euphausiids (*Euphausia* and *Thysanoessa*) and amphipods (*Cyphocaris* and *Parathemisto*) throughout the year. Despite the fact that the subarctic net-zooplankton community consists of a large number of different animal taxa, most of the biomass and much of the abundance in the upper 100 m is accounted for by fewer than two or three dozen species (Cooney 1986).

5.2.2 Interannual and Decadal-Scale Variation in Plankton Stocks

Few measurements and estimates are available for year-to-year and decadal-scale variability in primary and secondary productivity in all marine environments in the northern GOA (Sambrotto and Lorenzen 1986). Fortunately, some information is available about variable levels of zooplankton stocks. Frost (1993) described interannual changes in net-zooplankton sampled from 1956 to 1980 at OSP. Year-to-year variations in stocks of about a factor of five were characteristic of that data set, and a slight positive correlation with salinity was observed. Cooney et al. (2001b) examined an 18-year time series of settled zooplankton volumes from eastern PWS collected near salmon hatcheries by the personnel of the Prince William Sound Aquaculture Corporation, Cordova. Once again, annual springtime differences of about a factor of five were encountered in these data. In addition, from 1981 to 1991, settled zooplankton volumes in PWS were also strongly and positively correlated with the strength of the Bakun upwelling index calculated for a location near Hinchinbrook Entrance. This correlation completely disappeared after 1991 (Eslinger et al. 2001). Also, the years of highest settled volumes in eastern PWS (1985 and 1989) were only moderate years for zooplankton reported by Incze et al. (1997) for Shelikof Strait, suggesting the Kodiak shelf and PWS populations were phased differently for at least those years. Sugimoto and Tadokoro (1997) report a regime shift in the subarctic Pacific and Bering Sea in the early 1990s that generally resulted in lower zooplankton stocks in both regions. Perhaps in response to this phenomenon, springtime settled zooplankton volumes in PWS also declined by about 50 percent after 1991 (Cooney et al. 2001b).

The most provocative picture of decadal-scale change in zooplankton abundance in the GOA is provided by Brodeur and Ware (1992) (Figure 5.1). Using spatially distributed oceanic data sets reporting zooplankton biomass from 1956 to 1962, and again from 1980 to 1989, these authors were able to capture the large-scale properties of the pelagic production cycle during both positive and negative aspects of the Pacific decadal oscillation (PDO) (Mantua et al. 1997). A doubling of net-zooplankton biomass was observed under conditions of increased winter winds responding to an intensified Aleutian Low (the decade of the 1980s). This sustained doubling of biomass was also reflected at higher trophic levels in the offshore food web (Brodeur and Ware 1995). It was believed the observed production stimulation during the decade of the 1980s was created by increased nutrient levels associated with greater upwelling in the Alaska Gyre. The observed horizontal pattern of upper layer zooplankton stocks (Figure 5.1) was an impressive areal expansion (positive PDO) or contraction (negative PDO). Under periods of intensified winter winds, some of the highest oceanic zooplankton concentrations were developed in a band along the shelf edge in the northern regions in the GOA. Unfortunately, data from the shelf itself during this same time period are not sufficient to ascertain how this elevated biomass may have reached the coastal areas, perhaps intruding PWS.

5.2.3 Factors Affecting Trophic Exchanges between the Plankton and Larger Consumers

Most would concede that the general theory of trophodynamics articulated by Lindeman (1942) sixty years ago to represent ways in which matter and energy are transferred through aquatic communities (by different levels of producers and consumers) is an overly simplistic picture of the complex interactions and nonlinear relationships we see today. Useful in the lecture hall as a teaching tool, and successfully applied to certain problems where first-order estimates of production at hypothetical levels are sought based on estimates of plankton productivity, these formulations usually lack any dynamic connection with the physical environment or nutrient levels. They also generally fail to delineate seasonality or other important temporal variability. Nonetheless, because of the ease of their application and the acceptance of certain simplifying assumptions

(generalized ecological transfer efficiencies and lumping taxa within trophic levels), the linear food-web or carbon budget approach continues to be used for selected purposes.

Bottom-up trophic models of food web structure supporting the production of fishes, birds, and mammals in open ocean, slope, estuarine, and fjord environments in the GOA were formulated by Parsons (1986) in a synthesis of information compiled primarily as the result of the Minerals Management Service (MMS)–funded Outer Continental Shelf (OCS) studies. More recently Okey and Pauly (1998) developed a mass balance formulation with the Ecopath model of trophic mass balance for a PWS food web as the result of the EVOS Restoration Program. These models are certainly instructive at some level of generality, but their usefulness for describing specific climate-related mechanisms that might modify food-web transfers is limited by their detachment from the physical environment and their reliance on annually or seasonally averaged stock sizes and productivities.

Instead, it may be more instructive to examine how evolved behavioral traits and other aspects of the life histories of the dominant plankters (and other forage taxa) lend themselves to food-web transfers that could be affected by climate change. To do this, it will be important to study how the biology at lower trophic levels interacts (on a variety of time and space scales) with the physical environment to create enhanced (or diminished) trophic opportunities in the consumer matrix of different habitats and seasonal characterizations that pervade the marine ecosystem in the northern GOA. The compressed nature of the annual plankton production cycle in oceanic, shelf, and coastal waters seemingly places a premium on "timing" as a strategy to maximize the chances for successfully linking consumers to each year's burst of organic matter synthesis. Paul and Smith (1993) found that yellowfin sole replenished their seasonally depleted energy reserves each year in a short period of about one month following the peak in primary productivity. This rapid replenishment of energy reserves is presumably possible because of the structural properties of forage populations that occur abundantly during the short and intense production cycle. Patch-dependent feeding is a term used to describe how many consumers respond to the grainy time and space distributions of food in their feeding environments (Valiela 1995). In the case of plankters, which by definition move with the water, temporal and spatial patchiness can be created or dissipated through interactions with (1) physical processes such as vertical and horizontal transport

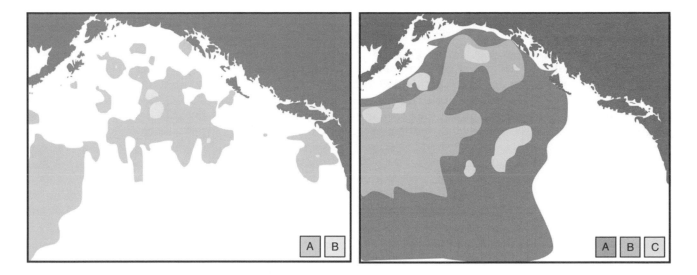

Fig. 5.1. Biomass of plankton for spring and summer period contrasted for a negative Pacific decadal oscillation (PDO) period (left) and a positive PDO period (right). The shaded boxes present zooplankton biomass as follows: A represents 100 to 200 g 1,000 m⁻³, B represents 201 to 300 g 1,000 m⁻³, and C represents more than 300 g 1,000 m⁻³ (Brodeur and Ware 1992).

and diffusion, and (2) biological attributes such as rapid growth and swarming or layering in association with feeding and reproductive behaviors.

For example, the more than two month maturation process for the large oceanic copepods (*Neocalanus* spp.) growing in the near-surface of the open ocean, shelf, and some coastal environments concludes with a short period (twenty to thirty days) in which the biomass peaks each year, is concentrated in the largest (C5) copepodites, and is compressed into relatively thin layers and swarms contiguous for tens, possibly hundreds of kilometers (Cooney 1989, Mackas et al. 1993, Coyle 1997, Kirsch et al. 2000). In its most concentrated form, this seasonally ephemeral biomass is an important source of food for diving seabirds (Coyle 1997), whales, and planktivorous fishes such as adult Alaska pollock and Pacific herring (Willette et al. 1999). Acoustic observations suggest the degree of plankton swarming or layering depends, in part, on the strength of water column mixing and stability. Numerical models of the production cycle in PWS demonstrated that interannual variations in the timing of the annual biomass peak in zooplankton probably reflects differences in the timing of the earlier phytoplankton bloom each year. Eslinger et al. (2001) reported that the spring diatom bloom varied by as much as three weeks from year to year in PWS, but that the annual peak in zooplankton always lagged the plants by about twenty-five to thirty days. Year-to-year shifts of a week or more in the peak of zooplankton biomass may profoundly

influence the effectiveness of food-web transfers to fishes, birds, and other consumers with severe consequences. For example, Pacific herring have apparently evolved a reproductive strategy to place age-0 juveniles in the water column precisely at the time of the mid-summer peak in plankton forage. Failure to successfully provision themselves by missing the most optimal summer feeding conditions may contribute to high rates of winter starvation for age-0 herring in PWS (Cooney et al. 2001b).

In another example, Cooney (1983) reported a possible interaction between the movements occurring over the life cycle of large oceanic calanoid, ontogenetic migrations, and an enrichment of feeding habitats for fishes, birds, and mammals over the shelf forced by localized convergences in the late winter and spring months. As previously mentioned, *Neocalanus* spp. arrive in the surface waters of the deep ocean in March and April each year. Early copepodite stages are presumably carried across the shelf in the wind-forced Ekman flow (upper 60 to 90 m) where they eventually encounter zones of surface convergence (Cooney 1986). *Neocalanus* spp. in the shelf environment depends on the spring diatom bloom for growth and maturation. Because the developing copepodites have an affinity for the upper layers where the phytoplankton production occurs (Mackas et al. 1993), they may be able to counteract regions of downwelling and convergence by continuing to migrate upward in these zones (a few tens of meters per day at most). Where they successfully detach themselves from the downwelling water, populations advected shoreward into convergences (possibly in the frontal region of the Alaska Coastal Current [ACC]) will accumulate. These zones of high copepod (and perhaps other taxa) biomass should represent regions of potentially high trophic efficiency for planktivores built and maintained for a few weeks by wind-forced horizontal and vertical transport.

Cooney (1988) calculated that nearly 10 million metric tons of zooplankton could be introduced to the shelf annually over 1,000 km of coastline in the northern GOA by the wind-forced shoreward Ekman transport each year. If only a portion of this biomass is retained in shelf and coastal food webs, the "lateral input" of ocean-derived zooplankton (much of it represented by the large interzonal calanoids) may partially explain how the seasonally persistent downwelling shelf sustains the observed high annual production at higher trophic levels. Kline (1999), in studies of carbon and nitrogen isotopes of zooplankton sampled in Prince William Sound, found that 50 percent or more of the diapausing *Neocalanus cristatus* overwintering in the deep water originated from populations outside PWS each year. Similar isotopic signals in herring and other coastal fishes seem to confirm a partial role for the bordering ocean in "feeding" some coastal habitats.

Coyle (1997) described the dynamics of *Neocalanus cristatus* in frontal areas along the northern and southern approaches to the Aleutian Islands. In regions near water column instabilities that fostered nutrient exchange for nearby stratified phytoplankton populations, these large oceanic copepods occurred along pycnoclines in subsurface swarms and layers that were attractive feeding sites for diving least auklets. These trophic associations (observed acoustically) formed and dissipated in response to weather and tidal modified forcing of the waters over the shelf north and south of the Aleutian Islands.

Kirsch et al. (2000) described dense layers (10 to 20 m in vertical extent) of C4 and C5 *Neocalanus plumchrus*, *N. flemingeri*, and *Calanus marshallae* in the upper 50 m of PWS that serve as seasonally important feeding zones for adult Alaska pollock and Pacific herring. Swarming behavior in the upper layers by these copepods, responding to the distribution of their food in the euphotic zone, compresses *Neocalanus* into layers stretching for tens of kilometers that are readily located and utilized by planktivores. Other observations at the time found these layers were absent or only weakly developed in areas with high mixing energy like outer Montague Strait.

Diel migrations of many taxa bring deep populations into the surface waters each night. The large bodied copepod *Metridia* spp. and many Pacific euphausiids (*Euphausia* and *Thysanoessa*) represent zooplankters that undergo substantial daily migrations from deep to shallow waters at night. A variety of reasons have been proposed for this behavior (Longhurst 1976). Regardless of the "why," vertically migrating populations that build local concentrations near the sea surface during darkness represent another way that behavioral traits are responsible for creating patchiness that probably enhance trophic exchange. Cooney (1989) and Stockmar (1994) studied diel and spatial changes in the biomass of net-zooplankton and micronekton in the upper 10 m of the open ocean and shelf habitats in the northern GOA. They found a consistent enrichment of biomass in the surface waters at night caused by *Metridia pacifica* and several different euphausiids that often exceeded daylight levels by a factor of five or six.

Springer et al. (1996) make a strong case for the enhancement of primary and secondary productivity along the shelf edge of the southeastern Bering Sea. Citing tidal mixing, transverse circulation, and eddies as mechanisms to increase nutrient supplies, this so-called "greenbelt" is described as 60 percent more productive than the outer-shelf environment and 270 percent more productive than the bordering deep ocean. Earlier, Cooney and Coyle (1982) documented the presence of a high-density band of upper-layer zooplankton along the shelf edge of the eastern Bering Sea. Composed primarily of *Metridia* spp., *Neocalanus* spp., and *Eucalanus bungii*, this narrow zone of elevated biomass is apparently also a part of the greenbelt. Although these features have yet to be described for the northern GOA, the present North Pacific GLOBEC study is monitoring primary productivity and zooplankton stocks along cross-shelf transects that should intercept a shelf-edge greenbelt if one is present in the northern GOA.

Finally, meso- and large-scale eddy formation over the shelf and slope regimes may also influence the patchiness of plankton in ways that could be susceptible to changing climate forcing. A permanent eddy in the coastal water west of Kayak Island is often visible because of entrained sediment from the Copper River. Formed by a branch of the ACC, this eddy may help concentrate plankton populations of the upper layer in ways that could later influence PWS (Reed and Schumacher 1986). Vaughan et al. (2001) and Wang (2001) describe surface eddies in the central region of PWS with implications for the transport and retention of ichthyoplankton. These eddies (cyclonic and anticyclonic) are believed to form in response to seasonal changes in freshwater outflow and wind forcing. Large-scale coastal and shelf eddies apparently form near Sitka and propagate north and west around the periphery of the GOA (Musgrave et al. 1992). Similar features on the East Coast of the United States have been shown to be long-lived (many months) and capable of sustaining unique biological assemblages as they move through time and space. These same characteristics are also expected for the northern GOA.

5.2.4 Climate Forcing of Plankton Production in the Gulf of Alaska

A major challenge for investigators is to eventually produce a detailed understanding of lower trophic level processes that arise through biological interactions with the spatially distributed geological and physical properties of the northern GOA. This evolving understanding must take into account the flow-through nature of the northern and eastern regions—downstream from southern Southeast Alaska and northern Canada (through the ACC) and also downstream from portions of the southern oceanic Subarctic and Transition Zone domains (through the North Pacific and Alaska currents). The "open" condition places increasing importance on understanding levels of plankton imports (from the south) and exports (to the west) in the periphery of the GOA affected by the ACC (Napp et al. 1996) and shelf-break flows (Alaska Current and Alaskan Stream). It will also be necessary to understand the effects that the open ocean gyre may exert on shelf and coastal plankton stocks and their seasonal and annual production within the northern GOA. Here too the import (or export) of nutrients, organic detritus, and living plankton stocks to (or from) the shelf must be evaluated under different conditions of climate and weather.

The picture that emerges from the aggregate of previous and ongoing plankton studies describes a large oceanic ecosystem strongly forced by physical processes that are meteorologically driven. Physical processes such as deep and shallow currents, large-scale and localized upwelling and downwelling, seasonally phased precipitation, and runoff bring about changes in the ecosystem. The reproduction, growth, and death processes of the plants and animals appear to be responding primarily to marked seasonality and interannual and longer-period shifts in the intensity and location of the winter Aleutian Low. Increased upwelling in the offshore Alaska Gyre may promote higher rates of nutrient renewal in the oceanic surface waters with attendant increases in primary and secondary productivity. Elevated wind-forcing probably also accelerates the transport of upper-layer oceanic zooplankton shoreward to the shelf edge and beyond. The frequency and degree to which this ocean-derived biomass "feeds" the food webs of the continental shelf and coastal areas will depend, in part, on biological interactions with a large array of physical processes and other phenomena. Processes active in regions of horizontal and vertical currents associated with oceanographic fronts, eddies, coastal jets, shelf-break flows, and turbulence are expected to have a strong influence on the movement of ocean biomass onto the shelf and coastal areas. The actual effect of such processes and phenomena on distribution of oceanic biomass also depends on responses of plankton production to changes in levels of freshwater runoff in these regions, and on the seasonal and longer cycles in temperature and salinity. Specific mechanisms by which surface zone nutrient levels are cycled and maintained in the variety of different habitats that make up the open shelf and rugged coastal margins must be understood in much greater detail to be useful.

It seems likely that a sophisticated understanding of climate influences on the coupled nutrient and plankton production regimes that support selected consumer stocks may have to come from studies that abandon the practice of lumping taxa within broad ecologically functional units, and instead focus on "key species." Fortunately, the subarctic pelagic ecosystem (oceanic, shelf, and coastal) is dominated by a relatively small number of plankton species that serve as major conduits for matter and energy exchange to higher-level consumers each year. In the case of the zooplankton, fewer than fifty species within a handful of major taxa make up 95 percent or more of the abundance and biomass throughout the year. Because of this pattern of dominance, and further because of the different life history strategies employed by these species, a more comprehensive understanding of their ecological roles is both necessary and feasible. A decision to conduct dominant species ecology must be understood at all levels of the study so that, for instance, technicians conducting future stomach analyses of fishes, birds, or mammals will report not just "large copepods and amphipods," but rather *Neocalanus cristatus* and *Parathemisto libellula*. This nuance holds particular importance for future modelers working on numerical formulations that include "plankton." Without this degree of specificity, it is unlikely that further studies will forge the critical understanding of lower trophic level function sought in the northern GOA as necessary to inform more comprehensive studies of long-term change.

Nearshore Benthic Communities

Charles Peterson

6.1 INTRODUCTION

Because the Gulf of Alaska (GOA) covers a vast and diverse area, its benthic communities exhibit tremendous variation (Feder and Jewett 1986). As in any marine benthic system, however, the composition, functioning, and dynamics of the GOA benthic communities change predictably with certain universally important variables. The most important two environmental variables are water depth and substratum type (Rafaelli and Hawkins 1996). The following depth zones are typically distinguished:

- The intertidal zone;

- The shallow subtidal zone (bounded by depth of light penetration sufficient for photosynthesis of benthic algae);

- The continental shelf (to about 200 m); and

- The continental slope (from 200 to 4,000 m).

The most fundamental substratum distinctions are hard bottom (rocks, boulders, cobbles) and soft bottom (mobile sedimentary habitats like sands and muds). Within these two types, geomorphology varies substantially, with biological implications that often induce further habitat partitioning (Page et al. 1995, Sundberg et al. 1996).

Understanding of community composition and seasonal dynamics of GOA benthos has grown dramatically from two principal energy pulses, with two distinct pulses of research. First, in contemplation of exploration and development of the oil and gas resources of the region, the Minerals Management Service, National Oceanic and Atmospheric Administration NMFS, and Alyeska Consortium funded geographically focused benthic survey and monitoring work in the 1970s. This work provided the first windows into the quantitative benthic ecology of the region. Focus was most intense on lower Cook Inlet, the Aleutian Islands, the Alaska Peninsula, Kodiak Island, and northeast GOA, including the Valdez Arm in Prince William Sound (PWS) (Rosenberg 1972, Hood and Zimmerman 1986). The second phase

of growth in knowledge of the benthos of the GOA region was triggered by the *Exxon Valdez* oil spill (EVOS) in 1989. This work had broad geographic coverage of the rocky intertidal zone. The area receiving the most intense study was Prince William Sound (PWS), where the spill originated. Geographic coverage also included two other regions, the Kenai Peninsula–lower Cook Inlet and the Kodiak archipelago–Alaska Peninsula (Highsmith et al. 1994b; Page et al. 1995; Gilfillan et al. 1995a,b; Highsmith et al. 1996; Houghton et al. 1996a,b; Sundberg et al. 1996). Some of this benthic study following the oil spill was conducted in other habitats (soft substrata [Driskell et al. 1996]) and at other depths (shallow and deep subtidal habitats ([Houghton et al. 1993; Armstrong et al. 1995; Dean et al. 1996a,b; Dean et al. 1998, 2000; Feder and Blanchard 1998; Jewett et al. 1999]). Herring Bay on Knight Island in PWS was a site of especially intense monitoring and experimentation on rocky intertidal communities following the oil spill (van Tamelen et al. 1997).

6.2 INTERTIDAL COMMUNITIES

The intertidal habitat is the portion of the shoreline in between the high and low (0.0 m datum) tide marks. This intertidal zone occupies the unique triple interface among the land, sea, and air. The land provides substrate for occupation by intertidal organisms, the seawater the vehicle to supply necessary nutrients, and the air a medium for passage of solar energy and radiant of chemical elements (Connell 1972, Underwood and Denley 1984, Peterson 1991). Interfaces between separate systems are locations of typically high biological activity. As a triple interface, the intertidal zone is exceptionally rich and biologically productive (Ricketts and Calvin 1968, Leigh et al. 1987). Wind and tidal energy combine to subsidize the intertidal zone with planktonic foods produced in the photic (sunlit) zone of the coastal ocean. Runoff from the adjacent land mass injects new supplies of inorganic nutrients to help fuel coastal production of benthic algae, although such runoff in Alaska is typically nutrient-poor and can be very turbid (Hood and Zimmerman 1986).

The consequent abundance and diversity of life and life forms in the intertidal zone serves many important consumers, coming from land, sea, and air, and including humans. The aesthetic, economic, cultural, and recreational values of the intertidal zone and its resources augment its significance, especially in the GOA region (Peterson 2001).

The biota of intertidal habitats varies with changes in physical substrate type, wave energy regime, and atmospheric climate (Lubchenco and Gaines 1981). Substrata in the GOA intertidal zone differ as a function of size, ranging from immobile rock walls and platforms, to boulders and cobbles, to gravel, to sands, and finally to muds at the finest end of this particle-size spectrum. Rock surfaces in the intertidal zone are populated by epibiota, which are most commonly attached macro- and microalgae; sessile or immobile suspension-feeding invertebrates; and mobile grazing invertebrates including predatory sea stars and gastropods (Connell 1972, Rafaelli and Hawkins 1996). Unconsolidated (soft) substrata— the sands and muds—are occupied by large plants in low-energy environments, such as marshes, and microalgae and infaunal (buried) invertebrates in all energy regimes (Peterson 1991). Mobile scavenging and predatory invertebrates occur on both types of substratum. Intertidal communities vary with wave energy because of biomechanical constraints (especially on potentially significant predators), changing levels of food subsidy, and interdependencies between wave energy and substratum type (Leigh et al. 1987, Denny 1988). Intertidal communities tend to be most luxurious in temperate climates; ice scour and turbid freshwater limit intertidal biota at high latitudes such as those in the eastern GOA. The rocky intertidal communities of the Pacific Northwest, including the rocky shores of islands in the GOA region, are highly diverse, although less so than those in Washington. These communities are also productive, although limited by disturbance of winter storms and reduced solar insulation (Bakus 1978).

The rocky intertidal ecosystem may represent the best understood natural community of plants and animals on earth. Ecologists realized more than forty years ago that this system was uniquely well suited to experimentation because the habitat was accessible and basically two-dimensional and the organisms were manipulable and observable. Consequently, ecological science has used sophisticated experimental manipulations to produce a detailed understanding of the complex processes involved in determining patterns of distribution and abundance of rocky intertidal organisms (Paine et al. 1996, Dayton 1971, Connell 1972, Underwood and Denley 1984). Plants and animals of temperate rocky shores exhibit strong patterns of vertical zonation in the intertidal zone. Physical stresses tend to limit the upper distributions of species populations and tend to be more important higher onshore; competition for space and predation tend to limit distributions lower on the shore. Surface space for attachment is potentially limiting to both plants and animals in the rocky intertidal zone. In the absence of disturbance, space becomes limiting, and competition for that limited space results in competitive exclusion of inferior competitors and monopolization of space by a competitive dominant. Physical disturbance, biological disturbance, and recruitment limitation are all processes that can serve to maintain densities below the level at which competitive exclusion occurs (Menge and Sutherland 1987). Because of the importance of such strong biological interactions in determining the community structure and dynamics in this system, changes in abundance of certain keystone species can produce intense direct and indirect effects on other species that cascade through the ecosystem (Menge et al. 1994, Wootton 1994, Menge 1995, Paine et al. 1996).

Intertidal communities occupying unconsolidated sediments (sands and muds) are quite different from those found on rocky shores (Peterson 1991). These soft-bottom communities are composed of infaunal (buried) invertebrates, mobile microalgae, and abundant transient consumers, such as shorebirds, fishes, and crustaceans (Rafaelli and Hawkins 1996). Macroalgae are sparse, and are found attached to large shell fragments or other stable hard substrata. In very low energy environments, large plants, such as salt marsh grasses and forbs high on shore and seagrasses low on shore, occur in intertidal soft sediments (Peterson 1991). The large stretch of intertidal soft-sediment shore in between those vegetated zones has an empty appearance, which is misleading. The plants are microscopic and productive; the invertebrate animals are buried out of sight. The soft-bottom intertidal habitat represents a critically important feeding ground, especially for shorebirds, because the flat topography allows easier access than is provided by steep rocky coasts and because invertebrates without heavy protective calcium carbonate shells are common, particularly polychaetes and amphipods (Peterson 1991).

The intertidal shorelines of the GOA exhibit a wide range of habitat types. True soft-sediment shores are not common, except in Cook Inlet. Marshes, fine-grained and coarse-grained sand beaches, and exposed and sheltered tidal flats represent a small fraction of the coastline in the GOA. Sheltered and exposed rocky shores, wave-cut platforms, and beaches with varying mixtures of sand, gravel, cobble, and boulders are the dominant habitats in this region (Page et al. 1995, Sundberg et al. 1996). Abundance, biomass, productivity, and diversity of intertidal communities on the shores of the eastern GOA with nearby glaciers are depressed by proximity to sources of runoff from glacier ice melt. The islands in PWS and the Aleutian Islands, for example, have richer intertidal communities than the mainland of the northeast GOA, and the intertidal communities of Kodiak and Afognak tend to be richer than those of the Shelikof Strait mainland on the Alaska Peninsula (Bakus 1978, Highsmith et al. 1994b). Glacier ice melt depresses intertidal biotic communities by introducing turbidity and freshwater stresses.

Winter ice scour seasonally denudes epibiota along the Cook Inlet shores (Bakus 1978). Intense wave exposure can cause substratum instability on intertidal cobble and boulder shores, thereby removing intertidal epibiota directly through abrasion (Sousa 1979). Shores with well-rounded cobbles and boulders have accordingly poorer intertidal biotas than those with reduced levels of physical disturbance. Bashing from logs also represents an agent of disturbance to those rocky shores exposed to intense wave action in this region (Dayton 1971). Consequently, exposed rocky coastlines may experience more seasonal fluctuations in epibiotic coverage than communities on similar substrata in protected fjords and embayments (Bakus 1978).

The rocky intertidal shores of the spill area exhibit a typical pattern of vertical zonation, although the particular species that dominate vary in importance as a function of changing habitat conditions (Highsmith et al. 1996; Houghton et al. 1996a,b). Vertical zonation on intertidal rocky shores is a universal feature, caused by a combination of direct and indirect effects of height-specific duration of exposure to air (Paine 1966, Connell 1972).

The uppermost intertidal zone on rocky shores of the GOA is characterized by a dark band of the alga *Verruccaria*. The rockweed (*Fucus gardneri*) dominates the upper intertidal zone, which also includes two common barnacles (*Balanus glandula* and *Chthamalus dalli*), two abundant limpets (*Tectura persona* and *Lottia pelta*), and the periwinkle (*Littorina sitkana*) (SAI 1980, Hood and Zimmerman 1986, Highsmith et al. 1994b).

The middle intertidal zone commonly has even higher cover of *Fucus,* along with beds of blue mussels (*Mytilus trossulus*), the periwinkle (*Littorina scutulata*), barnacles, and the predatory drilling snail (*Nucella lamellosa* and *N. lima*) (Carroll and Highsmith 1996). In the low intertidal zone, the red alga *Rhodymenia palmata* often is dominant, although mussel beds often occupy large areas and the grazing chitons (*Katharina tunicata, Mopalia mucosa,* and *Tonicella lineata*) and predatory sea stars (*Leptasterias hexactis* and others) occur here (SAI 1980, Highsmith et al. 1994b). The blue mussel is a very significant member of this community because it is a potential competitive dominant (VanBlaricom 1987) and because its byssus and between-shell interstices provide a protected habitat for a diverse suite of smaller mobile invertebrates, including isopods, amphipods, polychaetes, gastropods, and crabs (Suchanek 1985).

Abundances of rocky intertidal plants and animals in the GOA are controlled by the same suite of factors that affect rocky shore abundances and dynamics elsewhere, especially in the Pacific Northwest. Physical factors, such as wave action from winter storms, exposure to air high on shore, ice scour, and low salinity and turbidity from glacial and land runoff, have important effects on wave-exposed areas (Dayton 1971, 1975; Bakus 1978).

Biological controls also exert significant influences. Probably the most significant of these likely controlling factors for intertidal biota are predation and recruitment limitation. Predation by sea stars is an important control of invertebrate prey population abundances and, therefore, of community composition low on intertidal rocky shores (Paine 1966, Dethier and Duggins 1988). Because blue mussels are typically the preferred prey and represent the dominant competitor for potentially limited attachment space, this predation by sea stars has important cascading effects of enhancing abundances of poorer competitors on the rock surfaces (Paine 1966). Predation by gastropods occasionally helps control mussel abundances (Carroll and Highsmith 1996) and barnacle populations higher on shore in the GOA (Ebert and Lees 1996). Shorebird predation, especially by black oystercatchers, is also known to limit abundances of limpets on horizontal rock surfaces of the Pacific Northwest intertidal zones, and this process can be readily disrupted by human interference with the shy shorebirds (Lindberg et al. 1998). The presence of numerous strong biotic interactions in this rocky intertidal community of the GOA led to many indirect effects of the EVOS in this system (Peterson 2001). Because of the influence of current flows and mortality factors such as predation in the water column, larval recruitment can also limit population abundances of marine invertebrates on intertidal rocky coasts (Gaines and Roughgarden 1987, Menge and Sutherland 1987). With a short warm season of high production in the GOA, the potential for such recruitment limitation seems high, but process studies to characterize and quantify this factor have not been conducted in the GOA. Changes in primary production, water temperature (and thus breeding season), and physical transport dynamics associated with regional climate shifts could reasonably be expected to regulate the intensity of recruitment limitation on some rocky shores in the GOA.

The consequences of change caused by various natural and human-driven factors on the structure and dynamics of the rocky intertidal communities are not well developed in the scientific literature. For example, human harvest by fisheries or subsistence users of important apex predators that exert top-down control on intertidal communities could cause substantial cascading effects through the system. But the sea stars and gastropods that are the strong predatory interactors in this community in the GOA region are not targets for harvest. The mussels that are taken in subsistence harvest provide important ecosystem services as structural habitat for small invertebrates (Suchanek 1985), as a dominant space competitor (Paine 1966), and as a widely used prey resource (Peterson 2001), but mussels do not appear limited in abundance in the GOA region.

Oceanographic processes related to climate change, either natural or human-driven through global warming, have the potential to either enhance or reduce recruitment of component invertebrate species of the rocky intertidal communities, but studies of the connections between coastal physical dynamics and shoreline communities are in their infancy (Caley et al. 1996). Perhaps the best documented driver of change in composition and dynamics of rocky intertidal communities is the impact of oil spills. The cleanup treatments after the spill, either dispersants (Southward and Southward 1978) or pressurized washes (Mearns 1996), have far more serious impacts than the oil itself. Because of the important strong interactions among species in rocky shore communities, the multiple indirect effects of oil spills on this system take about a decade to work their way out of the system (Southward and Southward 1978, Peterson 2001). Intensive sampling and experimental work on rocky intertidal communities on sheltered shores in PWS following the EVOS

make this region data-rich relative to most other Alaskan shores.

Intertidal soft sediments in the spill region of the GOA typically possess lower biomass of macroalgae and invertebrates than corresponding rocky shores at the same elevations (SAI 1980, Highsmith et al. 1994b). The taxonomic groups that dominate intertidal soft bottoms are polychaete worms, mollusks (especially bivalves), and amphipods (Driskell et al. 1996). Sandy sediments have higher representation by suspension-feeding invertebrates, whereas finer, muddy sediments are dominated by deposit-feeding species (Bakus 1978, Feder and Jewett 1986). Intertidal sandy beaches are habitat for several large suspension-feeding clams in the GOA that represent important prey resources for many valued consumers and that support commercial, recreational, and subsistence harvest (Feder and Kaiser 1980). Most important are the littleneck clam (*Protothaca staminea*), the butter clam (*Saxidomus giganteus*), the razor clam (*Siliqua patula*), the cockle (*Clinocardium nuttallii*), the pink-neck clam (*Spisula polynyma*), the gapers (*Tresus nuttallii* and *T. capax*), and others (Feder and Paul 1974). In mudflats, such as those along the shores of Cook Inlet, dense beds of a deposit-feeding clam, *Macoma balthica*, and the soft-shell clam (*Mya arenaria)* frequently occur (Feder et al. 1990). These two relatively soft-shelled clams are significant food resources for many sea ducks, and the hard-shelled clams are important prey for sea otters (Kvitek and Oliver 1992, Kvitek et al. 1992), black and brown bears (Bakus 1978), and several invertebrate consumers. Intertidal soft-bottom habitats are also important feeding grounds for shorebirds and for demersal (deep-water) fishes and crustaceans (Peterson 2001). In addition to macrofaunal invertebrates, smaller meiofaunal invertebrates are abundant on intertidal sedimentary shores. Macrofauna describes animals that are retained on a 0.5 mm mesh; meiofauna refers to animals passing through a 0.5 mm mesh but retained on 0.06 mm mesh; and microfauna are animals smaller than 0.06 mm. Nematode worms and harpacticoid copepods are the most common meiofaunal taxa in the GOA region (Feder and Paul 1980b). Harpacticoids serve an important role in the coastal food chain as prey for juvenile fishes, including salmonids (Sturdevant et al. 1996).

Little information exists on the dynamics of long-term change in structure and composition of intertidal communities in soft sediments anywhere. Some of the best understanding of important processes actually comes from the northern GOA region. The Alaska earthquake of 1964 had a tremendous influence on soft-sediment intertidal communities because of the geomorphological modifications of habitat (NRC 1971). Uplift of the shoreline around Cordova, for example, was great enough to elevate the sedimentary shelf habitat out of the depth range that could be occupied by many species of clams. Clam populations in Cordova, a town once called the clam capital of the world, have never recovered from the earthquake. The re-invasion of sea otters has similarly caused tremendous changes in clam populations in shallow soft-sediment communities of the northern GOA, mostly in subtidal areas, but also in intertidal sedimentary environments (Kvitek et al. 1992).

Human impacts can cause change in soft-sediment intertidal communities as well. Probably the most common means by which human activities modify soft-sediment communities in intertidal habitats is through alteration of sediments themselves. The application of pressurized wash after the EVOS, for example, eroded fine sediments from intertidal areas (Driskell et al. 1996) and may be responsible for long delay in recovery of clams and other invertebrates because of a slow return of sediments (Coats et al. 1999, Shigenaka et al. 1999). Addition of organic enrichment can stimulate growth, abundance, and production of opportunistic infaunal invertebrates such as several polychaetes and oligochaetes in intertidal sediments. Such responses were documented following the EVOS (Gilfillan et al. 1995a, Jewett et al. 1999), presumably because the oil itself represented organic enrichment that entered the food chain through enhanced bacterial production (Peterson 2001). Other types of organic enrichment, such as biochemical oxygen demand in treated wastewater from municipal treatment facilities or industrial discharges, can create these same responses. Deposits of toxic heavy metals from mining or other industrial activities and of toxic synthetic organic or natural organic contaminants, like polycyclic aromatic hydrocarbons in oil, can cause change in intertidal benthic communities by selectively removing sensitive taxa such as echinoderms and some crustaceans (Jewett et al. 1999).

Intertidal communities are open to use by consumers from other systems. The great extent and importance of this habitat as a feeding grounds for major marine, terrestrial, and aerial predators render the intertidal system a key to integrating understanding of the function in the entire coastal ecosystem (Peterson 2001). The intertidal habitats of the GOA are critically important feeding grounds for many important consumers:

- *Marine*—sea otters, juvenile Dungeness and other crabs, juvenile shrimps, rockfishes, cod, cutthroat trout, and Dolly Varden char in summer, and juvenile fishes of other stocks exploited commercially, recreationally, and for subsistence, including pink and chum salmon;

- *Terrestrial*—brown bears, black bears, river otters, Sitka black-tailed deer, and humans; and

- *Avian*—black oystercatchers and other shorebirds, harlequin ducks, surf scoters, goldeneyes, and other sea ducks, and bald eagles.

Intertidal gravels in anadromous streams are important spawning grounds for pink salmon, especially in PWS. Therefore, the intertidal habitat provides vital ecosystem services in the form of prey resources, spawning habitat, and nursery, as well as human services in the form of commercial, recreational, and subsistence harvest of shellfishes and aesthetic, cultural, and recreational opportunities. In short, a habitat that represents only a small fraction of the total area of the seafloor may be the most valuable for the services it provides to the coastal ecosystem and to humans.

6.3 SUBTIDAL COMMUNITIES

The subtidal habitat is the portion of the seafloor found at depths below the low tide (0.0 m datum) mark on shore. This habitat includes a relatively narrow band of shallow subtidal bottom at depths in the photic zone (the zone penetrated by light), where plants can live, and a large area of unlit seafloor, the deep subtidal bottom extending across the continental shelf and slope to depths of 4,000 m in the GOA (Feder and Jewett 1986). The depth to which sufficient light penetrates to support photosynthesis and the slope of the subtidal seafloor determine the width of the shallow subtidal zone. Along a tectonic coastline like the GOA, depth gradients are typically steep. In addition, injection of turbidity from glacier ice melt along the coast reduces light penetration through the seawater. These factors combine to produce a shallow subtidal zone supporting benthic plant production in the region of the spill that is very narrow. Consequently, the vast majority of the subtidal ecosystem, the deep subtidal area on the continental shelf and slope, depends on an energy subsidy in the form of inputs of organic matter from other marine and, to some small extent, even terrestrial habitats. These organic inputs include, most importantly, detritus from production of intertidal seaweeds and from shallow subtidal seagrasses, seaweeds, and kelps, as well as particulate inputs from phytoplankton, zooplankton, and zooplankton fecal pellets sinking down from the photic zone to settle on the seafloor. In addition, the carcasses of large animals such as whales, other marine mammals, and fishes occasionally sink to the bottom and provide large discrete packages of detritus to fuel subsequent microbial and animal production in the deep subtidal ecosystem.

Although narrow, the shallow subtidal zone in which primary production does occur is of substantial ecological significance. Many of these vegetated habitats, especially seagrass beds, macrophyte beds, and kelps, provide the following (Schiel and Foster 1986, Duggins et al. 1989):

- Nursery grounds for marine animals from other habitats;

- Unique habitat for a resident community of plant-associated animals;

- Feeding grounds for important consumers, including marine mammals, sea ducks, and many fishes and shellfishes; and

- A source of primary production for export as detritus to the deeper unlit seafloor ecosystem.

In the spill area, eelgrass (*Zostera marina)* beds are common in shallow sedimentary bottoms at the margins of protected embayments (McRoy 1970), whereas on shallow rocky subtidal habitats the kelps *Agarum, Laminaria,* and *Nereocystis* form dense beds along a large fraction of the coast (Calvin and Ellis 1978, SAI 1980, Dean et al. 1996a). Productivity estimates in wet weight for larger kelps *Nereocystis* and *Laminaria* in the northeastern GOA range up to 37 to 72 kg m^{-2}yr^{-1} (O'Clair and Zimmerman 1986). In this shallow subtidal zone, primary production also occurs in the form of single-celled algae. These microbial plants include both the phytoplankton in the water column and benthic microalgae on and in the sediments and rocks of the shallow seafloor. Both the planktonic and the benthic microalgae represent ecologically important food sources for herbivorous marine consumers. The typically high turnover rates and high food value of these microalgal foods in the shallow subtidal zone helps explain the high production of invertebrate and vertebrate consumers in this environment.

The sessile or slow-moving benthic invertebrates on the seafloor represent the bulk of the herbivore trophic level in the subtidal ecosystem. This benthic invertebrate fauna in the shallow subtidal zone differs markedly as a function of bottom type (Peterson 1991). Rocky bottoms are inhabited by epifaunal benthic invertebrates, such as sponges, bryozoans, barnacles, anthozoans, tunicates, and mussels. Sand and mud bottoms are occupied largely by infaunal (buried) invertebrates, such as polychaete worms, clams, nematodes, and amphipods. The feeding or trophic types of benthic invertebrates vary with environment, especially with current flow regime (Rhoads and Young 1970). Under more rapid flows, the benthos is dominated by suspension feeders, animals extracting particulate foods out of suspension in the water column. Under slower flows, deposit feeders dominate the benthos, feeding on organic materials deposited on or in the seafloor. The benthos also includes some predatory invertebrates, such as sea stars (e.g., leather star [*Dermasterias imbricata*] and sunflower star [*Pycnopodia helianthoides*]), crabs (e.g., helmet crab [*Telmessus cheiragonus*]) some gastropods, and some scavenging invertebrates (Dean et al. 1996b). Benthic invertebrates of soft sediments are distinguished by size, with entirely different taxa and even phyla occurring in the separate size classes. Macrofauna include the most widely recognized groups such as polychaete worms, clams, gastropods, amphipods, holothurians, and sea stars (Driskell et al. 1996; S.A. Hatch, U.S.G.S. Anchorage, pers. comm., 2001). Meiofauna include most prominently in the GOA nematodes, harpacticoid copepods, and turbellarians (Feder and Paul 1980b). Finally, microfauna include most prominently foraminifera, ciliates, and other protozoans. Because the actual species composition of the benthos changes with water depth, the shallow and deep subtidal benthic faunas in the spill zone hold few species in common. Soft-sediment communities of Alaska are best described and understood in various locations within PWS, as a result of the intense study after the oil spill.

The shallow subtidal rocky shores that are vegetated also include suites of benthic invertebrates unique to those systems. These benthic invertebrates either directly consume the large plants, such as sea urchins, or else are associated with the plant as habitat. Those species that depend upon the plant as habitat, such as several species of amphipods, crabs and other crustaceans, gastropods, and polychaetes, often are grazers as well, taking some mixture of macrophytic and epiphytic algae in their diets. Grazing by sea urchins on kelps is sufficiently intense in the absence of predation on the urchins, especially by sea otters in the spill area, to create what are known as "urchin barrens" in which the macrophytic vegetation is virtually removed from the seafloor (Estes and Palmisano 1974, Simenstad et al. 1978). In fact, this shallow subtidal community on rocky shores of the GOA represents the best example in all of marine ecology of a system controlled by top-down predation. Sea otters control abundance of the green sea urchin (*Strongylocentrotus droebachiensis*). When released from that otter predation, sea urchin abundance increases to create fronts of urchins that overgraze and denude the kelps and other macroalgae, leaving only crustose forms behind (Simenstad et al. 1978). This loss of macroalgal habitat then reduces the algal associated invertebrate populations and the fishes that use the vegetated habitat as nursery. These reductions in turn can influence productivity and abundance of piscivorous seabirds (Estes and Palmisano 1974). Recently, reduction of traditional marine mammal prey of killer whales has induced those apex consumers to switch to eating sea otters in the Aleutians, thereby extending this trophic cascade of strong interactions to yet another level (Estes et al. 1998, Estes 1999).

Consequently, the shallow subtidal community on rocky shores of the GOA is strongly influenced by predation and provision of biogenic habitat (Estes and Duggins 1995). Human disruption of the apex predators by hunting them (as historically occurred on sea otters [Simenstad et al. 1978]) or by reducing their prey (as may conceivably be occurring in the case of the Steller sea lions and harbor seals through overfishing their own prey fishes [NRC 1996]) has great potential to create tremendous cascading effects through the shallow subtidal benthic ecosystem. Furthermore, if concentration and biomagnification of organic contaminants such as PCBs, DDT, DDE, and dioxins in the tissues of apex predators, in particular in transient killer whales (C. Matkin, North Gulf Oceanic Society, Homer, Alaska, unpubl. data), causes impaired reproductive success, then human industrial pollution has great potential to modify these coastal subtidal communities on rocky shores.

The shallow subtidal community on rocky shores of the GOA is also strongly influenced by larval distribution and recruitment. Recent studies by Partnership for the Interdisciplinary Study of Coastal Oceans (PISCO) have shown that not only are the effects of competition and predation important in structuring benthic communities, but the sources and sinks of larvae are equally important. Larval abundance and behavior, where they come from, how they respond to ocean conditions, where they are retained, where they are reflected, and the dynamics regulating their recruitment are all important processes that ultimately control what lives where. Furthermore, knowledge about life histories is

insufficient to make broad generalizations about the successes and failures of recruitment events.

The shallow subtidal benthic communities in soft sediments of the GOA region function somewhat differently from their counterparts on rocky substrata. These communities are important for nutrient regeneration by microbial decomposition and for production of benthic invertebrates that serve as prey for demersal shrimps, crabs, and fishes. In some protected areas within bays, however, the shallow subtidal benthos is structured by emergent plants, specifically eelgrass in the GOA. These eelgrass beds perform ecological functions similar to those of macrophyte-dominated rocky shores, namely nursery functions, phytal habitat roles, feeding grounds, and sources of primary production (Jewett et al. 1999). In the vegetated habitats of the shallow subtidal zone, the demersal fish assemblage is typically more diverse than and quite different from the demersal fishes of the deeper subtidal zone (Hood and Zimmerman 1986). In eelgrass (*Zostera*) beds as well as in the beds of small kelps and other macrophytes (*Agarum, Nereocystis,* and *Laminaria*) in the GOA, juveniles of many species that live in deeper waters as adults use this environment as a nursery for their young because of high production of food materials and protection from predators afforded by the shielding vegetation (Dean et al. 2000). Furthermore, several fishes are associated with the plant habitat itself, including especially pickers that consume crustaceans and other invertebrates from plant surfaces, a niche that is unavailable in the absence of the vegetation. Both types of vegetated habitats in the shallow subtidal zone of the GOA contain larger predatory invertebrates, specifically sea stars and crabs. In some cases, the same species occupy both eelgrass and kelp habitats (Dean et al. 1996b).

Microbial decomposers play an extremely significant role in both shallow and deep subtidal sedimentary habitats of the sea (Braddock et al. 1996). Fungi and especially bacteria become associated with particulate organic matter and degrade the organic compounds. This decomposition process releases the nutrients such as phosphorus and nitrogen in a form that can be reused by plants when the water mass is ultimately recycled into the photic zone. In short, benthic decomposers of the subtidal seafloor play a necessary role in the nutrient cycling upon which sustained production of the sea depends. In addition, these decomposers themselves represent the foods for many deposit-feeding invertebrates of the subtidal seafloor. Much of the detritus that reaches the seafloor is composed of relatively refractive organic compounds that are not readily assimilated in the guts of animal consumers. The growth of microbial decomposers on this detritus acts to convert these materials into more utilizable nitrogen-rich biomass, namely fungi and especially bacteria. Bacteria also scavenge dissolved organic materials and repackage them into particulate bacterial biomass, which is then available for use in consumer food chains.

In the subtidal habitats, the benthic invertebrates serve as the prey for mobile epibenthic invertebrates and for demersal fishes (Jewett and Feder 1982, Hood and Zimmerman 1986). Mobile epibenthic invertebrates are distinguished from the benthos itself by their greater mobility and their only partial association with the seafloor. The vast majority of this group is composed of crustaceans, namely crabs, shrimps, tanaids, and some larger amphipods (Armstrong et al. 1995, Orensanz et al. 1998). In the GOA, this group includes Dungeness crabs; king crabs; snow crabs; Tanner crabs; both *Crangon* and *Pandalus* shrimps, such as spot shrimp, coonstriped shrimp, pink shrimp, and gray shrimp; and other shellfish resources that had great commercial importance before the climatic phase shift of the mid-1970s (Anderson and Piatt 1999; Mueter and Norcross 1999, 2000). Climate and physical oceanography have the potential to exert important influences on recruitment and year-class strength of subtidal fishery stocks in the GOA (Zheng and Kruse 2000b), but the mechanisms and processes are poorly understood. Demersal fishes are those fishes closely associated with the seafloor, including flounders, halibut, sole, rockfishes, Pacific Ocean perch, and gadids like cod and walleye pollock. They feed predominantly on the epibenthic invertebrates—the shrimps, crabs, and amphipods—but in addition prey directly on some sessile benthic invertebrates as well. Juvenile flatfish feed heavily by cropping (partial predation) on exposed siphons of clams and exposed palps of polychaetes. This role of provision of benthic invertebrate prey for demersal crustaceans and fishes is an important ecosystem service of the shallow subtidal seafloor.

The shift in the late 1970s from crabs and shrimps to dominance by demersal fishes associated with the shift in climatic regime implies a strong role for environmental forcing of community composition in this shallow subtidal system, although mechanisms of change dynamics are not understood (NRC 1996). Because of the effects of trawling on biogenic habitat, such as sponges and erect bryozoans, in subtidal soft sediments and the potential for fisheries exploitation to modify abundances of both targeted stocks

and species caught as bycatch (Dayton et al. 1995), fishery impacts to the soft-bottom benthic community are a possible driver of community change. Because the demersal fishes that are taken by trawl and other fisheries represent the prey of threatened and endangered marine mammals such as Steller sea lions, the possible implications of fishing impacts to this community are important (NRC 1996).

The benthic invertebrate community of shallow unvegetated subtidal sediments has served worldwide as an indicator system for the biological influence of marine pollution. The infaunal invertebrates that compose this bottom community are sessile or slow-moving. They are diverse, composed of many phyla and taxa with diverse responses to the suite of potential pollutants that deposit upon the sedimentary seafloor. As a result, this system is an ideal choice to monitor and test effects of marine pollution (Warwick 1993). The subtidal benthic community on the sedimentary seafloor is limited by food supply. Consequently, community abundance and biomass reflect the effects of organic enrichment. This is evident from variation in biomass among subtidal benthic communities geographically within the GOA (Feder and Jewett 1986). Therefore, changes in primary productivity in the water column above, allocation of that production between zooplanktonic herbivores and benthic invertebrates, and physical transport regimes combine to cause spatially explicit modification of soft-sediment benthic communities in unvegetated subtidal sediments that can serve to monitor ecosystem status. Furthermore, the taxonomic composition of soft-sediment benthic communities responds differentially to organic loading and toxic pollution (Warwick and Clarke 1993, Peterson et al. 1996), thereby rendering this system an excellent choice for monitoring to test among alternative drivers of ecosystem change. Among common invertebrate taxa of subtidal sedimentary habitats, the echinoderms and crustaceans (especially amphipods) are highly sensitive to toxic accumulation of heavy metals, polycyclic aromatic hydrocarbons, and synthetic organic compounds. Other taxa such as polychaetes include many opportunistic species that bloom with loading with organic pollutants, thereby allowing inferences about causation of anthropogenic responses (Peterson et al. 1996). This capability of subtidal benthic communities in soft sediments may prove useful in testing among alternative explanations for ecosystem change in the GOA.

The deeper subtidal habitats on the outer continental shelf and the continental slope are not well studied in the GOA system (Bakus 1978; SAI 1980a,b). There has been some description of the mobile epibenthic communities and the demersal fish communities of these deeper benthic habitats (Feder and Jewett 1986). Most sampling of these deeper benthic habitats involves trawling and focuses on the stocks of crabs, shrimps, and demersal fishes that are commercially exploited (Rosenberg 1972, Bakus 1978). The continental shelf as a whole (shallow to deep) represents a key fishing ground in the GOA and has correspondingly high value to humans. Because community structure of benthic systems can be modified dramatically by the physical damage done by trawls to biogenic habitat such as sponges and soft corals (Dayton et al. 1995), this human activity is the object of concern. The continental slope, on the other hand, does not experience great fishing pressure.

CHAPTER 7

Seabirds in the Gulf of Alaska

Alan Springer

7.1 OVERVIEW

The Gulf of Alaska (GOA) supports huge numbers of resident seabirds: twenty-six species nest around the periphery of the GOA, with an estimated total on the order of eight million birds (Table 7.1). Note that sea ducks are not considered seabirds for the purposes of this discussion. Most species of seabirds are colonial and aggregate during summer at about 800 colonies. A variety of habitats are used for nesting, such as cliff faces, boulder and talus fields, crevices, and burrows in soft soil. Two species, Kittlitz's and marbled murrelets, are not colonial and nest in very atypical habitats. Kittlitz's murrelets nest on scree fields in high alpine regions often many kilometers from the coast, and marbled murrelets nest mainly in mature trees in old-growth conifer forests, also often distant from the coast.

Predation by terrestrial mammals and rapacious birds undoubtedly is responsible for the nesting habitats and habits adopted by seabirds. Cliff-nesting species are free to nest on mainland sites, because mammals cannot reach them and they are large enough to defend themselves and their nests against most avian predators. Ground-nesting species do not have this option and must nest only on islands free from predatory mammals. In addition, some ground-nesting species go to and from colonies only at night, apparently to further thwart avian predators.

Foxes, rats, voles, and ground squirrels were variously introduced to most islands in the Aleutians and GOA between the late 1700s and early 1900s and severely reduced the abundances of many species of ground-nesting seabirds, such as storm-petrels, auklets, murrelets, and puffins (Bailey and Kaiser 1993, Boersma and Groom 1993, Springer et al. 1993). Today, even though foxes no longer exist on most islands, numbers of these species of ground-nesting seabirds still likely reflect the effects of introduced mammals. Moreover, predators that occur naturally occasionally have large, local effects on nesting seabirds in the GOA (Oakley and Kuletz 1996, Seiser 2000).

The distribution and abundance of nesting seabirds in the GOA is therefore governed primarily by the availability of suitable, safe nesting habitats, as well as by the availability of prey. For example, cliff-nesting species, such as murres and kittiwakes, require cliffs facing the sea. Therefore, regardless of the biomass of potential forage species in the eastern GOA, there are no murres or kittiwakes in much of the region because of the lack of sea cliffs. Where suitable nesting habitat does exist, seabirds nearly always occupy it, and fluctuations in their productivity and abundance through time are thought to be determined for the most part by fluctuations in prey populations.

Species that nest on cliff faces, such as murres and kittiwakes, are the most well studied because of their visibility. Completing censuses of cliff-nesting seabirds is comparatively easy, as is measuring several components of their breeding biology, including the study of recurring natural phenomena such as migration (phenology) and reproductive success. Consequently, precise estimates of abundance and productivity, and trends in these variables through time, are available for murres and kittiwakes at many colonies in the GOA. In addition to their visibility, murres and kittiwakes are extremely numerous and widely distributed, and more is known about them than about any other species.

In contrast, seabirds that nest underground are difficult to study. A further complication is that some of these are nocturnal as well. Despite huge numbers and broad distributions of some diurnal species, such as puffins, and nocturnal species, such as storm-petrels, much less is known about population sizes and productivity or trends in these parameters through time and space. They do have scientific value, however, because other characteristics of their biology offer valuable opportunities for obtaining information on the distribution and dynamics of prey populations important to a variety of seabirds and marine mammals.

Most seabirds in the GOA are primarily piscivorous (fish eating) during the nesting season. The principal

Table 7.1. Nesting Seabirds in the Gulf of Alaska.

English name	Scientific name	Abundance[1] (thousands)	Biomass[2] (metric tons)	Nesting habitat[3]	Foraging mode[4]
Northern fulmar	*Fulmarus glacialis*	440	268	Cliff	SF
Fork-tailed storm-petrel	*Oceanodroma furcata*	640	32	Burrow	SF
Leach's storm-petrel	*Oceanodroma leucorhoa*	1,067	53	Burrow	SF
Double-crested cormorant	*Phalacrocorax auritus*	3.3	6	Cliff	CD
Brandt's cormorant	*Phalacrocorax penicillatus*	0.086	0.2	Cliff	CD
Pelagic cormorant	*Phalacrocorax pelagicus*	21	40	Cliff	CD
Red-faced cormorant	*Phalacrocorax urile*	20	38	Cliff	CD
Unidentified cormorant	*Phalacrocorax* spp.	15	29	Cliff	CD
Mew gull	*Larus canus*	15	11	Ground	SF
Herring gull	*Larus argentatus*	1	1	Ground	SF, S
Glaucous-winged gull	*Larus glaucescens*	185	241	Ground	SF, S
Black-legged kittiwake	*Rissa tridactyla*	675	270	Cliff	SF
Arctic tern	*Sterna paradisaea*	8.9	1.2	Ground	SF
Aleutian tern	*Sterna aleutica*	9.4	1.2	Ground	SF
Unidentified tern	*Sterna* spp.	1.7	0.22	Ground	SF
Common murre	*Uria aalge*	589	589	Cliff	DD
Thick-billed murre	*Uria lomvia*	55	55	Cliff	DD
Unidentified murre[5]	*Uria* spp.	1,197	1,197	Cliff	DD
Pigeon guillemot	*Cepphus columba*	24	13	Crevice	CD
Marbled murrelet	*Brachyramphus marmoratus*	200	48	Tree	CD
Kittlitz's murrelet	*Brachyramphus brevirostris*	+	+	Scree	CD
Ancient murrelet	*Synthliboramphus antiquum*	164	38	Burrow	CD
Cassin's auklet	*Ptychoramphus aleuticus*	355	71	Burrow	DD
Parakeet auklet	*Cerorhinca monocerata*	58	17	Crevice	DD
Least auklet	*Aethia pusilla*	0.02	0.0018	Talus	DD
Crested auklet	*Aethia cristatella*	46	14	Talus	DD
Rhinoceros auklet	*Cyclorrhynchus psittacula*	170	90	Burrow	DD
Tufted puffin	*Lunda cirrhata*	1,093	874	Burrow	DD
Horned puffin	*Fratercula corniculata*	773	425	Crevice	DD
Total		**7,826**	**4,423**		

[1]From U.S. Fish and Wildlife Service (USFWS), seabird colony database: marbled murrelet in Gulf of Alaska from Piatt and Ford (1993).

[2]Based on weights of seabirds presented by DeGange and Sanger (1986).

[3]Principal type.

[4]SF = surface-feeder; CD = coastal diver; DD = deep diver; S = scavenger. From DeGange and Sanger (1986).

[5]Essentially all common murres.

exceptions include northern fulmars, storm-petrels, and thick-billed murres, which consume large amounts of squid; auklets, which specialize on zooplankton; and gulls, terns, and guillemots, which consume considerable amounts of crustaceans in addition to fish. Many species of fishes are taken, although a comparatively small number contribute the bulk of the biomass to diets of most seabirds. Overall, the three most important species of fishes are sand lance, capelin, and pollock. At certain colonies, at certain times, in certain years, or any combination of these conditions, the myctophids, Pacific cod, saffron cod, herring, sablefish, pricklebacks, prowfish, and salmon are also important to some species (Hatch 1984; Baird and Gould 1986; DeGange and Sanger 1986, 1987; Hatch and Sanger

1992; Irons 1992, Piatt and Anderson 1996; Suryan et al. 2000; V. Gill and S. Hatch, U.S. Geological Survey, Anchorage, Alaska, unpubl. data).

Resident GOA seabirds can be divided into three groups based on their foraging behavior (Table 7.1). Surface-feeders, as their name implies, obtain all of their food from about the upper 1 m of the water column and often forage over broad areas. Coastal divers can generally reach bottom and typically forage in shallow water near shore. Pelagic mid-water and deep divers are capable of exploiting prey at depths of up to nearly 200 m and of foraging over large areas (Schneider and Hunt 1982, Piatt and Nettleship 1985). Most individuals of most species forage over the continental shelf during summer. This is due primarily to the location of nesting areas, which are along the mainland coast and on nearshore islands, and the distribution of forage species, which in aggregate are more diverse and abundant on the shelf than off the shelf. Exceptions to this generalization are the fulmars and storm-petrels, which have anatomical, behavioral, and physiological adaptations that allow them to forage at great distances from their nesting areas, giving them access to resources off the shelf (Boersma and Groom 1993, Hatch 1993); and species such as kittiwakes that typically feed over the shelf, but which can efficiently exploit prey off the shelf when those prey are within foraging range from their nesting locations (Hunt et al. 1981; Springer et al. 1996; S. Hatch, U.S. Geological Survey, Anchorage, Alaska, unpubl. data).

Therefore, as a group, seabirds sample forage populations broadly in three dimensions. These characteristics, plus variations in diet between species and the sensitivity of various components of their breeding biology and population abundance to fluctuations in prey availability, make seabirds in the GOA, as elsewhere, valuable tools in the study of marine ecosystems (Cairns 1987, Aebischer et al. 1990, Furness and Nettleship 1991, Springer 1991, Hatch and Sanger 1992, Montevecchi and Myers 1996, Piatt and Anderson 1996, Springer et al. 1996).

Seabird populations in the North Pacific from California to arctic Alaska are very dynamic, waxing and waning in response to changes in prey abundance, predators, entanglement in fishing gear, and oil spills (Anderson et al. 1980, Ainley and Broekelheid 1990, Paine et al. 1990, Murphy et al. 1991, Hatch 1993, Hatch et al. 1993, Ainley et al. 1994, Byrd et al. 1998, Divoky 1998). Oil spilled from the *Exxon Valdez* killed an estimated 250,000 seabirds in the GOA, 185,000 of which were murres (Piatt and Ford 1996). Most murre mortality occurred downstream from Prince William Sound (PWS) near the Barren Islands and Alaska Peninsula and had an unknown effect on the abundance of murres at regional colonies. There is evidence that the immediate mortality and lingering effects of the spill in PWS have depressed the abundance of several other species of seabirds there throughout the 1990s (Irons et al. 2000).

A strong case also has been made for a broad-scale decline in seabird abundance in the GOA during the past two to three decades beginning before the *Exxon Valdez* oil spill (EVOS). Marine birds counted at sea in summer in PWS apparently declined by some 25 percent in aggregate between 1972 and the early 1990s (Kuletz et al. 1997). Many species contributed

to the decline, including loons, cormorants (95 percent), mergansers, Bonaparte's gulls, glaucous-winged gulls (69 percent), black-legged kittiwakes (57 percent), arctic terns, pigeon guillemots (75 percent), marbled and Kittlitz's murrelets (68 percent), parakeet auklets, tufted puffins, and horned puffins (65 percent) (Klosiewski and Laing 1994). Other census data further indicated that for the marbled murrelet, at-sea winter abundance declined by more than 50 percent throughout the GOA during this time (Beissinger 1995). Results from studies at several murre colonies in the GOA in summer tend to support this pattern. Piatt and Anderson (1996) reviewed the abundance histories of sixteen colonies and concluded that many were in decline before the EVOS. Therefore, it proved difficult to estimate the effect oil had on murre populations.

It is generally thought that alterations in forage fish abundance and community structure brought on by environmental change not associated with the oil spill, such as climate change, have been primarily responsible for falling seabird populations (Oakley and Kuletz 1996, Piatt and Anderson 1996, Hayes and Kuletz 1997, Kuletz et al. 1997, Anderson and Piatt 1999). For example, pigeon guillemot numbers in PWS in 1978 to 1980 averaged about 40 percent higher than in the early 1990s, and they declined further through 1996 (Oakley and Kuletz 1996). The decline in abundance was accompanied by a decline in the occurrence of sand lance in their diets, and it has been suggested that cause and effect relate the two. Because sand lance have a much higher fat content than the forage species guillemots switched to, such as pollock and blennies, they are nutritionally superior (Anthony and Roby 1997, Van Pelt et al. 1997). In Kachemak Bay, sand lance was particularly abundant in diets of guillemots nesting in high-density colonies in the late 1990s, and chicks fed predominantly sand lance grew faster than chicks fed lower-quality prey (Prichard 1997). Likewise, reductions in the relative use of capelin in the GOA and in diets of several species of seabirds in the 1980s compared to the 1970s also have been linked to population declines (Piatt and Anderson 1996, Anderson and Piatt 1999).

Additional evidence of possible climate-mediated population decline is the frequency and magnitude of large seabird die-offs in the past two decades. Some of these involved huge numbers of surface-feeding species in summer, particularly kittiwakes and shearwaters in the GOA and especially the Bering Sea, during years of strong El Niño events, notably 1983 and 1997 (Nysewander and Trapp 1984, Mendenhall 1997). Others involved principally murres in the GOA in winter. In 1993, on the order of 100,000 common murres starved to death, and in 1997, at least tens of thousands suffered a similar fate (Piatt and Van Pelt 1993; J. Piatt, U.S. Geological Survey, Anchorage, Alaska, unpubl. data). Such acute mortality, when added to the normal, or perhaps elevated, attrition suffered by juvenile birds in recent years, could have significant repercussions on population size. As Piatt and Anderson (1996) note, there was only one reported die-off of seabirds in the general region before 1983, and that was in the Bering Sea in 1970 (Bailey and Davenport 1972).

There is no evidence that seabirds in the GOA have been directly affected by commercial fisheries. Most of the prey of seabirds are not targeted; for example, sand lance and capelin. Adults of some prey species are fished, such as pollock, Pacific cod, and herring, but most seabirds can feed only on the small age-0 and age-1 fish of these large types and therefore do not compete with commercial fisheries for biomass. Indirect effects of commercial fishing are possible if stock sizes are affected by fishing and if stock size influences the abundance of young age classes of those species or the abundance of other forage species.

7.2 CASE STUDIES

A lot of information has been collected on seabirds in the GOA in the past three decades, although much of the data obtained in the last ten years has not yet been published or even presented. Therefore, the integration of all results into a composite picture of seabird ecology is not currently possible. Nevertheless, good information is available for some aspects of the biology of certain species at certain sites, and these examples can be used to give a general idea of the status of seabirds and their sensitivity to change in the environment. Prominent species are the black-legged kittiwake and common murre. They are among the most abundant and widely distributed seabirds, nesting at hundreds of colonies from Southeast Alaska to Unimak Pass. These attributes and their ease of study have made them the best known of all species in the GOA. Information on trends in abundance, productivity, and diets of kittiwakes and murres at several locations spans periods of one to more than four decades. Information on other species, notably fulmars and puffins, at some colonies provides additional context.

7.2.1 Middleton Island

The longest time series of reliable abundance estimates for seabirds in the GOA comes from Middleton

Island, where the first count was made in 1956 (Rausch 1958). Between 1956 and 1974, the number of kittiwakes increased by an order of magnitude, from about 14,000 to 144,000 birds (Baird and Gould 1986). That increase is thought to have been made possible by the 1964 earthquake, which uplifted large sections of Middleton Island and created extensive new nesting habitat. Numbers of kittiwakes remained high there throughout the 1970s, but began to decline steadily in the early 1980s from a peak of about 166,000 birds to about 16,000 today (Hatch et al. 1993; S. Hatch, U.S. Geological Survey, Anchorage, Alaska, unpubl. data).

The decline in abundance has been accompanied by generally low productivity since the early 1980s, averaging just 0.06 chicks per pair between 1983 and 1999 (Table 7.2). A large proportion of the decline in productivity was likely accounted for by increased predation by glaucous-winged gulls (see below). However, supplemental feeding of kittiwakes in recent years altered a wide variety of adult breeding parameters sensitive to food supply and increased survival of chicks, supporting the notion that food limitation was a contributing factor (Gill 1999; V. Gill and S. Hatch, U.S. Geological Survey, Anchorage, Alaska, unpubl. data).

The longest time series of abundance data for murres also comes from Middleton Island. As with kittiwakes, the murre population increased by about an order of magnitude following the 1964 earthquake, numbering 6,000 to 7,000 individuals by the mid-1970s. Also like kittiwakes, murre abundance at Middleton Island was in decline by the end of the decade, falling to about 4,000 individuals by 1985. The population abruptly increased the following year to nearly 8,000 birds, where it remained through 1988, rapidly declined again to about 2,000 by 1992, and has been more or less stable since (S. Hatch, U.S. Geological Survey, Anchorage, Alaska, unpubl. data). The cause of the decline is thought to have been driven by gull predation and by the growth of vegetation that hampers access of chicks to the sea once they leave the nest (S. Hatch, unpubl. data), but the sharp increases and decreases during the course of the overall decline argues for other controlling factors.

Glaucous-winged gulls also probably nested in comparatively small numbers on Middleton Island before 1964, although no counts were made in the early years. By 1973 there were fewer than 1,000 individuals and fewer than 2,000 a decade later. However, in contrast to findings for murres and kittiwakes, the population ballooned to more than

Table 7.2. Trends in Kittiwake Abundance and Productivity at Colonies in the Gulf of Alaska.

Colony	Population trajectory	Average production, 1983-2000	Number of colonies	Colony years
Increasing				
Gull Island[1]	Up	0.39	1	15
Prince William Sound[2]	Up	0.30	4	67
Barren Island[3]	Up	0.40	1	7
Stable				
Prince William Sound—Overall[2]	Level	0.18	22	372
Prince William Sound[2]	Up-Down	0.14	5	94
Prince William Sound[2]	Level	0.15	2	34
Chiniak Bay[2]	Level	0.19	1	16
Declining				
Semidi Islands[3, 4]	Down	0.05	1	11
Chisik Island[1]	Down	0.06	1	9
Prince William Sound[2]	Down	0.04	11	177
Middleton Island[4]	Down	0.06	1	?

Colonies in PWS are divided into groups of increasing, stable, and declining abundance; overall kittiwake abundance is stable in PWS.

[1]From J. Piatt, USGS, Anchorage, AK (unpublished data).
[2]From D. Irons, USFWS, Anchorage, AK (unpublished data).
[3]From USFWS, Anchorage, AK (unpublished data).
[4]From S. Hatch, USGS, Anchorage, AK (unpublished data).

12,000 birds between 1984 and 1993, and now totals about 11,000 (S. Hatch, unpubl. data). Predation by gulls on kittiwake and murre eggs and chicks may have contributed to the declines of those species (S. Hatch, U.S. Geological Survey, Anchorage, pers. comm., 2001).

The abundance of rhinoceros auklets on Middleton Island more than doubled from about 1,800 to 4,100 burrows between 1978 and 1998 (S. Hatch, unpubl. data). Although there are no hard data, it seems likely that few or no rhinoceros auklets nested there before the earthquake because of a lack of habitat (S. Hatch, unpubl. data). Therefore, the increase in rhinoceros auklet abundance might be just the result of an increase in the extent of nesting habitat as vegetation covered uplifted soils. At St. Lazaria Island in Southeast Alaska, however, rhinoceros auklet numbers nearly doubled during the 1990s (Byrd et al. 1999), indicating that other factors are possibly involved.

A lack of adequate data precludes firm conclusions about trends in abundance of tufted puffins, but it is thought that they are increasing in abundance on Middleton Island as well (S. Hatch, unpubl. data).

Pelagic cormorants are known to move between nesting areas within colonies between years; there-fore, census data are not necessarily as accurate for them as for other cliff-nesting species of seabirds. The data show that numbers of nesting pairs were comparatively stable at about 2,000 to 2,800 between the mid-1970s and mid-1980s. The number of pairs was extremely volatile from 1985 to 1993, however, rising and falling by as much as 700 percent between consecutive years. In 1993, pelagic cormorants numbered about 800 pairs, and have increased steadily since then to about 1,600 pairs (S. Hatch, unpubl. data).

Seabirds at Middleton Island feed on a variety of forage species common throughout the GOA (Hatch 1984; V. Gill and S. Hatch, U.S. Geological Survey, Anchorage, Alaska, unpubl. data). Early in the nesting season kittiwakes typically prey on extremely energy-dense myctophids, which are generally restricted in their distribution to deep-water regions off continental shelves (Willis et al. 1988, Sobolevsky et al. 1996). Later they switch to other, likely more accessible, prey and feed chicks primarily on sand lance, although capelin and sablefish are also important in some years (V. Gill and S. Hatch, U.S. Geological Survey, Anchorage, Alaska, unpubl. data).

Rhinoceros auklets feed on numerous species of fishes, but seem to be sand lance specialists (Hatch 1984, Vermeer and Westrheim 1984, Vermeer et al.

1987). At Middleton Island, sand lance contributed on average 62 percent of the biomass fed to chicks in eleven years between 1978 and 2000 (S. Hatch, U.S. Geological Survey, Anchorage, Alaska, unpubl. data). In years of apparent low abundance during the first half of the 1990s, pink salmon, capelin, greenlings, and sablefish replaced sand lance.

Tufted puffins at Middleton Island feed their chicks predominantly sand lance in years when sand lance are most abundant; sand lance make up as much as 90 percent of biomass in peak years. Tufted puffins apparently switch to other prey sooner than rhinoceros auklets when sand lance is scarce. Alternative prey of tufted puffins consists mainly of pollock and prowfish, with somewhat lesser amounts of sablefish (S. Hatch, U.S. Geological Survey, Anchorage, Alaska, unpubl. data).

7.2.2 Prince William Sound

Twenty-three kittiwake colonies in PWS were first counted in 1972, but were not counted again until 1984. These and an additional six colonies have been visited nearly each year since (Irons 1996; D. Irons, U.S. Fish and Wildlife Service, Anchorage, Alaska, unpubl. data). During this time, long-term increases and decreases have been noted at various colonies, but no obvious geographic pattern to the changes was found. Instead, four colonies have grown to large size, and eleven smaller colonies have declined, with some disappearing completely. Five other colonies first increased, then decreased, and two have not changed appreciably. At least some of these changes likely resulted from movements of adults between sites (D. Irons, unpubl. data). For example, as the Icy Bay colony declined from about 2,400 birds in 1972 to fewer than 100 by 2000, the nearby North Icy Bay colony grew from about 500 birds in 1972 to about 2,000 by the late 1990s. Overall, the total abundance of kittiwakes in PWS has remained stable, or perhaps increased slightly, despite substantial interannual variability; for example, decreasing by 45 percent between 1991 and 1993 and increasing by 35 percent between 1999 and 2000.

Overall productivity likewise has been highly variable between years, but generally has been much greater than at Middleton Island, averaging 0.18 chicks per pair since 1984 (Table 7.2). Average productivity differed considerably between colonies with different population trajectories, however (Table 7.1). The average productivity differed considerably between colonies with different population trajectories, however, with highest productivity at

colonies with increasing trends, lower productivity at colonies with stable or variable trends, and lowest productivity at colonies with declining trends (Table 7.2).

Kittiwakes in Prince William Sound prey primarily on juvenile herring and sand lance in most years (Suryan et al. 2002).

7.2.3 Lower Cook Inlet

Kittiwakes at Chisik Island in Lower Cook Inlet were first counted in 1971 (Snarski 1971), and the population appears to have fallen steadily since then. By 1978, the number of birds was down by about 40 percent and today it is just 25 percent of the 1971 total (J. Piatt, U.S. Geological Survey, Anchorage, Alaska, unpubl. data). The trend in murre abundance at Chisik Island has paralleled that of kittiwakes, but the decline has been even steeper. The population fell by more than half between 1971 and 1978, and today stands at just about 10 percent of its former abundance. Kittiwake productivity has been poor in most years, averaging just 0.06 chicks per pair (Table 7.2). Less is known about productivity of murres, which has been estimated only since 1996. In that time, it has been variable and averaged 0.56 chicks per pair (Table 7.3).

In contrast, just across Cook Inlet at Gull Island in lower Kachemak Bay, numbers of kittiwakes and murres have increased substantially since counts were first made in 1976. The abundance of kittiwakes more than doubled between the mid-1970s and mid-1980s, peaked in 1988, and has averaged about 10 percent to 15 percent lower through the 1990s (J. Piatt, unpubl. data). The growth in numbers of murres was somewhat less abrupt, but more enduring, with steady growth of about 300 percent through 1999. Productivity of kittiwakes at Gull Island has been much higher than at Chisik Island, and has been among the highest anywhere in the GOA with comparable data (Table 7.2). Productivity of murres at Gull Island has been less variable than at Chisik Island, but has averaged essentially the same, 0.52 chick per adult (Table 7.3).

Kittiwakes were first counted on the Barren Islands, at the mouth of Cook Inlet, in 1977. The next counts in 1989 to 1991 were apparently comparable. Systematic counts began in 1993 and have continued since. It is not known if the earlier (1977 to 1991) and later (1993 to 1999) groups are comparable. Within-group data indicate that there was no apparent change in kittiwake abundance during either time period. Likewise, there are two groups of

Table 7.3. Trends in Murre Abundance and Productivity at Colonies in the Gulf of Alaska.

Colony	Population trajectory	Average production, 1989-2000	Range	Colony years
Gull Island[1]	Up	0.52	0.28-0.65	4
Chisik Island[1]	Down	0.56	0.18-0.74	4
Barren Island[2]	Up	0.73	0.58-0.75	5
Semidi Islands[2,3]	Up	0.48	0.21-0.58	6

[1]From J. Piatt, USGS, Anchorage, AK (unpublished data).

[2]From USFWS, Anchorage, AK (unpublished data).

[3]From S. Hatch, USGS, Anchorage, AK (unpublished data).

counts for murres—seven counts between 1975 and 1991 and ten systematic counts between 1991 and 1999. Counts in the early part of the first interval are not comparable to later counts in that interval; therefore, it is not known whether murre numbers changed from the 1970s to the late 1980s. Since 1989, however, the population has steadily grown by about 40 percent (D.G. Roseneau, U.S. Fish and Wildlife Service, Homer, Alaska, unpubl. data). Kittiwake productivity at the Barren Islands in the 1990s was as high as at Gull Island (Table 7.2). Murre productivity since 1995 has averaged 0.73 chick per pair, which is higher than at either of the other colonies in Lower Cook Inlet.

Kittiwakes and murres at all three locations prey on a similar suite of forage fishes, but the proportion of each species in diets varies depending on their relative abundance. Sand lance, capelin, and cods are the three most important taxa of prey (J. Piatt, U.S. Geological Survey, Anchorage, Alaska, unpubl. data; D.G. Roseneau, unpubl. data). Among the cods, the proportions of pollock, Pacific cod, and saffron cod vary by location. A variety of evidence from the Lower Cook Inlet region indicates that population trends of kittiwakes and murres at the three colonies are directly related to the abundance of prey available to the birds (Kitaysky et al. 1999; Robards et al. 1999; J. Piatt, unpubl. data; D.G. Roseneau, unpubl. data).

7.2.4 Kodiak Island

Of numerous seabird colonies on Kodiak Island, only those at Chiniak Bay have received much attention. Kittiwake abundance there was stable during the latter 1970s, increased abruptly in the early 1980s, and has continued to increase since then. Kittiwake productivity at Chiniak Bay was very high for at least two years in the mid-1970s (about one chick per nest), but was poor in the 1980s, averaging just 0.11 chick per nest between 1983 and 1989. Productivity improved in the 1990s, averaging 0.24 chick per nest, and has averaged 0.19 chick per nest overall since 1983 (Table 7.2).

Kittiwakes at Chiniak Bay preyed primarily on sand lance and capelin in the 1970s, as they do today (Baird 1990; D. Kildaw, University of Alaska Fairbanks, unpubl. data). Variations in diet between years were correlated with variations in productivity (Baird 1990).

7.2.5 Semidi Islands

Approximately 2,500,000 seabirds, or about a third of all the seabirds nesting in the GOA, are found on the Semidi Islands, including about 10 percent of the kittiwakes, half of the murres and horned puffins, and nearly all of the northern fulmars (Hatch and Hatch 1983). Seabird studies on the Semidi Islands began in 1976 and have continued in most years since. Most work has occurred at Chowiet Island, which hosts on the order of 400,000 birds of at least fifteen species, with the cliff-nesting species—kittiwakes, murres, and fulmars—receiving the greatest attention.

The number of kittiwakes at Chowiet Island varied little through 1981, although the number of nests grew by 60 percent. No counts were made from 1982 to 1988. Kittiwake abundance in 1989 and 1990 had not changed, but it declined abruptly in 1991, and has averaged about 30 percent lower since. The number of kittiwake nests in 1989 had fallen back to the late 1970s level, where it has tended to remain (U.S. Fish and Wildlife Service, Anchorage, Alaska, unpubl. data). Productivity of kittiwakes at Chowiet Island was generally high between 1976 and 1981, averaging 0.43 chick per nest, with the highest level (nearly 1.2 chicks per nest) in 1981. Kittiwakes began failing to produce chicks in numbers by 1983 (no data were obtained in 1982), however, and in eleven colony years between 1983 and 1998, the average productivity was just 0.05 chick per nest (Table 7.2). Accompanying the decline in abundance and collapse of productivity was a delay of nine days in the mean laying date in the 1990s compared to the 1970s and early 1980s. Poor productivity and delayed laying are both symptomatic of food stress.

Murre abundance on Chowiet Island was stable between 1977 and 1981. Abundance was the same in 1989 when counts were next made, but in contrast to findings for kittiwakes, the population has grown steadily since, standing 30 percent higher by 1998.

As for kittiwakes, the mean laying date of murres was about ten days later in the 1990s than in the 1970s. Productivity has not varied appreciably between years, except in 1998 when it was very low. The average productivity since 1989 was 0.48 chick per pair, or about the same as at Chisik and Gull islands (Table 7.2).

Trends in fulmar abundance, productivity, and phenology through time exhibited patterns similar to those of kittiwakes and murres. As with murres, abundance has increased: numbers of fulmars grew steadily between 1976 and 1981, and generally continued that trajectory at least through the mid-1990s. As with kittiwakes, productivity of fulmars was lower in the 1980s and 1990s, averaging just 0.24 chick per nest from 1983 through 1998, compared to an average of 0.52 chick per nest from 1976 through 1981. In addition, as found for both kittiwakes and murres, the nesting phenology of fulmars was conspicuously later in the 1990s than in the 1970s.

Little is directly known about diets of kittiwakes and murres at the Semidi Islands, but based on diets of rhinoceros auklets and tufted and horned puffins there (Hatch 1984, Hatch and Sanger 1992), it can be assumed that the usual food sources—sand lance, capelin, and pollock—are most important. These prey also are significant for fulmars. In general, the diets of fulmars overlap extensively with those of kittiwakes and murres, although overall fulmar diets are much more varied (Sanger 1987, Hatch 1993). For example, fulmars are noted for eating large amounts of jellyfish and offal and for feeding jellyfish to chicks.

7.3 CONCLUSIONS

Seabird populations at colonies in the GOA are very dynamic, with numerous examples of growth and decline during the past three decades.

Murre numbers in the GOA are clearly down in such diverse habitats as Middleton Island, which lies near the edge of the continental shelf and is the most oceanic of all colonies in the GOA; at Chisik Island, which is arguably the most neritic (nearshore) colony; and apparently at several colonies along the south side of the Alaska Peninsula. Murre numbers are not uniformly down, however; they have increased dramatically at Gull Island during the past fifteen years and at the Barren Islands and the Semidi Islands during the past ten years. Although comparatively little is known about murre

productivity, it has been essentially the same in recent years at the declining colony on Chisik Island as at the growing colonies on Gull Island and the Semidi Islands. At Chisik Island, the rate of decline of the population equals the estimated adult mortality; productivity seems to be sufficient to maintain numbers if those birds were recruiting to the population. Therefore, recruitment appears to have been lacking, which could be explained by poor survival of birds raised there or by emigration to other colonies (J. Piatt, U.S. Geological Survey, Anchorage, Alaska, pers. comm.). At Gull Island, productivity and recruitment can account for only about half the rate of population growth, with immigration required to explain the other half.

There is not enough information to determine whether total kittiwake abundance in the GOA has changed one way or another. Many examples of growth, decline, and stasis in individual colonies are available, but there is no apparent broad geographic pattern to the trends. At the few colonies where both kittiwakes and murres have been monitored, abundances of the two species tend to track each other through time. Kittiwakes, along with murres, have declined at Middleton Island and Chisik Island, and apparently increased, with murres, at Gull Island. The one exception is at Chowiet Island in the Semidi Islands, where kittiwakes decreased and murres increased. Elsewhere, kittiwakes have increased at Chiniak Bay on Kodiak Island and remained stable overall in PWS.

There is a strong correlation between population trajectory and long-term average productivity of kittiwakes at many colonies. Those colonies that are increasing in size have the highest productivity; those that are declining have the lowest. Colonies that show no change have intermediate levels. There are various interpretations of such a relationship. One is that productivity and subsequent recruitment of young determines abundance. Another is that kittiwake abundance and productivity simply track changes in prey; that is, in years of high prey abundance, more adults attend colonies and produce greater numbers of chicks than in years of low prey abundance. There would not necessarily have to be any other relationship between the two.

There are conspicuous temporal patterns of kittiwake productivity at many colonies during the past seventeen years. Productivity at colonies in PWS and at Gull Island has varied in tandem, with peaks and valleys at about five-year intervals: high productivity in the mid- to late 1980s, low in the early 1990s, and higher again after 1995. For most of the record, from the early 1980s through the mid-1990s, this pattern was opposite that at Chiniak Bay on Kodiak Island, where productivity peaked in the early 1990s while it bottomed-out in PWS and at Gull Island. Productivity at the three locations tended to track together during the latter half of the 1990s.

Kittiwake productivity and population trends in PWS are well-correlated before 1991 and since 1991, but the sign (positive or negative) of the relationship differs. Before 1991, high productivity was associated with low numbers of birds at the colonies, but since 1991, the relationship has been opposite. A similar switch occurred at about the same time in the relationship between kittiwake productivity in PWS and the abundance of age-1 herring (D. Irons, U.S. Fish and Wildlife Service, Anchorage, Alaska, unpubl. data). Such differences in sign and behavior of relationships before and after the 1989-to-1990 regime shift have been pointed out for kittiwakes in the Bering Sea and for various other ecosystem components of the North Pacific. It has been suggested that the differences reflect fundamental changes in ecosystem processes (Springer 1998, Welch et al. 1998, Hare and Mantua 2000).

The peaks and valleys in kittiwake productivity in PWS have punctuated a general declining trend during the longer term. If productivity depends more on prey abundance than on predation, then it seems as though prey have tended to decline throughout PWS in the past seventeen years, notwithstanding apparent oscillations.

In many cases, local trends in the abundance of murres and kittiwakes likely reflect mesoscale or regional processes affecting prey availability. For example, differences in population trends of both species at Chisik Island and Gull Island, and differences in productivity of kittiwakes between the islands, are related to regional variations in the abundance of forage fishes (J. Piatt, U.S. Geological Survey, Anchorage, Alaska, unpubl. data). The similarity in murre productivity between colonies is likely explained by flexible time budgets, which buffers them against fluctuations in prey (Burger and Piatt 1990, Zador and Piatt 1999).

7.4 FUTURE DIRECTIONS

Seabirds in the GOA are sensitive indicators of variability in the abundance of forage fishes through time and space. How well information from particular species at particular colonies reflects broad patterns of ecosystem behavior in the GOA remains to

be seen. The problem is that nearly all of the colonies are situated in habitats with distinct mesoscale or regional properties. PWS is a prime example, where colonies are located at the heads of fjords with and without glaciers, in bays and on islands around the perimeter of the main body of the sound, and on islands in the center of the sound. The Barren Islands and Gull Island are strongly influenced by intense upwelling in Kennedy Entrance which greatly modifies local physical conditions and production processes: waters in the relatively small region are cold, nutrient-rich, and productive. Chisik Island lies in the path of the outflow of warm, nutrient-poor water from Cook Inlet. The Semidi Islands lie at the downstream end of Shelikof Strait and the center of distribution of spawning pollock in the GOA.

Thus, there are various trends in abundance of kittiwakes at the numerous colonies in PWS. Trends in abundance of kittiwakes and murres at the Barren Islands and Gull Island are opposite those at neighboring Chisik Island; and patterns of kittiwake productivity at Gull Island and Chiniak Bay are opposite of each other. Only Middleton Island, which sits isolated near the edge of the continental shelf and the Alaskan Stream, and sites on or near the coast of the Alaska Peninsula west of Kodiak Island, which lie in the flow of the Alaska Coastal Current, seem to have the potential to represent gulf-wide variability unencumbered by possibly confusing smaller-scale features.

On the other hand, there is reason for optimism that broad-scale variability is indeed expressed in seabird biology. In spite of a wide variety of local habitat characteristics and population trends of kittiwakes at the many colonies in PWS, and large differences in average long-term productivity among colonies with differing abundance trends, a common temporal pattern of productivity has been shared by almost all colonies. Concordant, clearly defined peaks and valleys have been observed at about five-year intervals. A sound-wide environmental signal has propagated through the kittiwakes regardless of their location or status.

Moreover, the signal captured by kittiwakes in PWS and expressed in patterns of productivity was also captured by kittiwakes at Gull Island, implying that they may not be as ecologically separated as one might assume considering their geographic distance and characteristics of their environments. And further expanding the spatial dimension, the temporal pattern of sand lance abundance in the vicinity of Middleton Island during the past fifteen years, as revealed by its occurrence in diets of rhinoceros auklets and tufted puffins there, matches closely the patterns of kittiwake productivity in PWS and at Gull Island. Although a long geographical stretch, it might not be such a long ecological stretch when viewed broadly, at the GOA scale, rather than in a regional geographic and ecological context. And finally, the kittiwakes at Chiniak Bay also seemed to be attuned to this same signal, notwithstanding the fact that it apparently led to opposite behavior in the local system for some of the time. One thing that is fairly certain is that the temporal and spatial patterns in various components of seabird biology exhibited in the GOA do reflect underlying patterns in food-web production and ecosystem processes. Because of the range of oceanographic situations surrounding the various colonies, detailed information from them should prove valuable in building a composite view of ecosystem behavior in the GOA.

A variety of approaches to developing a long-term monitoring program in the GOA might work, but the framework that has evolved over the past three decades already has proved useful. In-depth work is occurring or has occurred in many years since the 1970s at well-placed locations throughout the GOA. These locations include St. Lazaria Island and Forrester Island in Southeast Alaska; Middleton Island; many colonies in PWS; Chisik Island, Gull Island, and the Barren Islands in Lower Cook Inlet; Kodiak Island; the Semidi Islands; and Aiktak Island on the south side of Unimak Pass. Colonies at these locations share several well-known, tractable species that provide complementary views of the ecosystem, particularly if they are systematically exploited for their contributions. Just as information from each of these colonies will help build a composite broad view of the GOA, information from several species of seabirds at each colony will help build a composite regional view of ecosystem behavior.

Therefore, the most popular species should continue to be the main focus. These are kittiwakes and murres, the species in the GOA with the highest combined score of abundance, distribution, and ease of study. Elements of their biology are sensitive to variability in prey, as seen in the GOA and numerous places elsewhere in the North Pacific and North Atlantic.

Kittiwakes and murres do not do some things as well as second-tier species, namely the puffins. Comparatively little is known about population trends of puffins, despite the fact that they are among the most abundant and widespread of the seabirds in the GOA. This lack of knowledge results because they nest underground. However, puffins have been

used to monitor trends in forage fish abundance at numerous colonies throughout the GOA, Aleutian Islands, and British Columbia (Hatch 1984; Vermeer and Westrheim 1984; Hatch and Sanger 1992; S. Hatch, U.S. Geological Survey, Anchorage, Alaska, unpubl. data; J. Piatt, U.S. Geological Survey, Anchorage, Alaska, unpubl. data). Diets of the three species of puffins overlap extensively, but each samples the environment somewhat differently: variability in diets among the puffins, locations, and time reveals geographic patterns of forage fish community structure and fluctuations in the abundances of individual species. Puffins return whole, fresh prey to their chicks, a behavior that provides an economical, efficient means of measuring various attributes of forage fish populations, such as individual growth rates within and between years and relative year-class strength.

Third-tier species, the cormorants, guillemots, and storm-petrels, also have attributes that can provide additional useful information. Cormorant and guillemot diets overlap extensively with those of kittiwakes, murres, and puffins, but the cormorants and guillemots sample prey much nearer to colonies and sample additional species not used by the others. Storm-petrels, in contrast, range widely and sample oceanic prey not commonly consumed by any other species. In combination, the diets, abundance, and productivity of the various species of seabirds provide information on prey at multiple spatial scales around colonies. In situations when this information can be easily obtained, it should not be overlooked.

A successful strategy for seabird monitoring will balance breadth (geographic and ecological) with intensity (how much is done at each site). On the one hand, it is important to select a sufficient number of sites to adequately represent a range of environmental conditions in mesoscale and macroscale dimensions. On the other hand, studies must be thorough at each colony. Simply comparing population trends of one or two species may give uncertain, possibly misleading information on underlying conditions of the environment. Without additional information on such things as survival, emigration, recruitment, diet, and physiological condition of the birds, conclusions about causes of population change, or about what population change is saying about the environment versus what productivity is saying, are elusive.

Another need for a long-term monitoring plan is knowledge about when reliable time series begin. For example, several estimates of murre abundance at colonies in the GOA from the 1970s are likely not comparable to more recent systematic counts (Erikson

1995; D.G. Roseneau, U.S. Fish and Wildlife Service, Homer, Alaska, unpubl. data). Inappropriate comparisons could result in erroneous conclusions about population changes that might further lead to unsupported speculation concerning broader trends in ecosystem change. The consequences of inappropriate comparisons are nicely illustrated by census data from the western Alaska Peninsula. If taken at face value, the information indicates that declines in the abundance of murres have been particularly severe at colonies from the Shumagin Islands westward to Unimak Pass. However, the trend data for two of the colonies, Bird Island and Unga Island, consist of single counts made in each of two years at both colonies. The first counts in 1973 were made in mid-June, which is early in the nesting season when murre numbers are unstable at colonies and often much higher than later during the census period (Hatch and Hatch 1989). At another of the colonies, Aiktak Island, the evidence of decline is based on a single count of nearly 13,000 birds in 1980, the first year a census of the colony was performed (Byrd et al. 1999). Single counts in 1982, 1989, and 1990 ranged between 175 and about 8,000 birds. And, the lower boundary of the 90 percent confidence interval about the mean of multiple counts in 1998 was less than zero, and the upper boundary was nearly as great as the first count in 1980. One must therefore ask if the murre population has indeed changed at all over the long term at Aiktak Island, or at the other colonies in the region where similar uncertainty exists, and if so how much.

In spite of such caveats, information gained from seabirds in the past three decades reveals a great deal about the nature of variability in the GOA. We can be certain that the perpetuation and refinement of seabird studies will continue to provide insights and hypotheses useful to the broader goal of understanding the GOA ecosystem.

CHAPTER 8

Fish and Shellfish

Phillip R. Mundy and Anne Hollowed

8.1 INTRODUCTION

The Gulf of Alaska (GOA) is well known for its fish and shellfish because of its long-standing and highly valuable commercial and recreational fisheries. Less well known are the noncommercial fish and invertebrate species that compose the bulk of the animal biomass in the GOA. As a rule, status of the economically important species is fairly well known from trawl, trap, and hook catches made by research and commercial vessels (Cooney 1986a, Martin 1997a, Witherell 1999a, Kruse et al. 2000a). By the same rule, the status of many non-target fish and shellfish species is less well known, having been sampled during research investigations of limited duration (Feder and Jewett 1986, Rogers et al. 1986, Highsmith et al. 1994, Purcell et al. 2000, Rooper and Haldorson 2000, Mecklenburg et al. 2002). Species not commercially harvested are less well studied than commercially harvested species, such as Tanner crab. For example, because commercial fisheries for forage species are discouraged by regulaton, the fluctuations of their populations are not well documented. More detailed consideration of some of the less economically important, but more ecologically prominent, forage species is found in this chapter's section 8.4, Forage Species, and some of the less common shellfish species are considered in chapter 6, Nearshore Benthic Communities.

The marine fish and shellfish of the GOA fall into two major groups (Feder and Jewett 1986, Rogers et al. 1986, Cooney 1986a, Cooney 1986a, Martin 1997b, Mecklenburg et al. 2002):

1. *Fish*—bony fish, sharks, skates, and rays; and

2. *Shellfish*—the mollusks (bivalves including scallops, squid, and octopus); and crustaceans—crabs and shrimp.

Note that three other ecologically important groups, the pelagic jellyfish (Cnidaria), the bottom dwelling sea stars and urchins (Echinodermata), and the segmented worms (Annelida) are not included in the category of the fish and shellfish. All the scientific names and many common names of the species ac-cessible to trawl gear on the continental shelf and shelf break of the GOA (see shelf topography map, Figure 4.1a and b, chapter 4) are in Table 8.1.

As would be expected with high marine productivity, the fish and shellfish fisheries of the GOA have been among the world's richest in the second half of the twentieth century. Major fisheries include, or have included, halibut, groundfish (e.g., Pacific cod, pollock, sablefish, Pacific ocean perch and other rockfish, flatfish such as soles and flounders), Pacific herring, multiple species of pandalid shrimp and red king crab, five species of Pacific salmon, scallops, and other invertebrates (Cooney 1986a, Kruse et al. 2000a, Witherell and Kimball 2000). The status of major fisheries and stocks of interest are addressed in the subsections below.

8.2 OVERVIEW OF FISH

Considering collections made by all types of gear ever reported in the scientific literature, 521 species of fish are known to occur in both fresh and marine waters of Alaska (Mecklenburg et al. 2002). Alaska fish species are overwhelmingly marine (474 species) or anadromous (25 species), and the marine-anadromous species are overwhelmingly bony (471 species) with only 28 species of cartilaginous fishes such as lamprey, sharks, and sturgeons known from Alaska waters. The most common fish species are known best from commercial catches and fishery trawl surveys.

Most of the 287 GOA fish species commonly encountered in commercial harvests and marine fisheries trawl surveys are bony fish, and the largest number of species is in the sculpin family (Cottidae), followed in order of number of species by the snailfish family (Cyclopteridae), the rockfish family (Scorpaenidae), and the flatfish family (Pleuronectidae) (Tables 8.2 and 8.3). The bony fish dominate the number of species in the GOA, with less than 10 percent of species being cartilaginous fishes (Petromyzontidae to Acipenseridae, Table 8.2). Species diversity in the fish depends on the type of gear used to sample (Table 8.2). It is important to keep in mind that trawl

Table 8.1. Fish and Invertebrate Species from 1996 NMFS Trawl Surveys of the Gulf of Alaska.

Fish Species

Family	Species name	Common name
Lamnidae	*Lamna ditropis*	salmon shark
Squalidae	*Squalus acanthias*	spiny dogfish
	Somniosus pacificus	Pacific sleeper shark
Rajidae	*Bathyraja interrupta*	Bering skate
	Bathyraja trachura	black skate
	Bathyraja parmifera	Alaska skate
	Bathyraja aleutica	Aleutian skate
	Raja binoculata	big skate
	Raja rhina	longnose skate
Chimaeridae	*Hydrolagus colliei*	spotted ratfish
Bothidae	*Citharichthys sordidus*	Pacific sanddab
Pleuronectidae	*Atheresthes evermanni*	Kamchatka flounder
	Atheresthes stomias	arrowtooth flounder
	Eopsetta jordani	petrale sole
	Glyptocephalus zachirus	rex sole
	Hippoglossoides elassodon	flathead sole
	Hippoglossus stenolepis	Pacific halibut
	Isopsetta isolepis	butter sole
	Lepidopsetta bilineata	southern rock sole
	Limanda asper	yellowfin sole
	Lyopsetta exilis	slender sole
	Microstomus pacificus	Dover sole
	Parophrys vetulus	English sole
	Platichthys stellatus	starry flounder
	Pleuronectes quadrituberculatus	Alaska plaice
	Psettichthys melanostictus	sand sole
Agonidae	*Aspidophoroides bartoni*	Aleutian alligatorfish
	Bathyagonus nigripinnis	blackfin poacher
	Bathyagonus pentacanthus	bigeye poacher
	Hypsagonus quadricornis	fourhorn poacher
	Podothecus acipenserinus	sturgeon poacher
	Sarritor frenatus	sawback poacher
	Xeneretmus leiops	smootheye poacher
Ammodytidae	*Ammodytes hexapterus*	Pacific sand lance
Anarhichadidae	*Anarrhichthys ocellatus*	wolf-eel
Anoplopomatidae	*Anoplopoma fimbria*	sablefish
Argentinidae	*Nansenia candida*	bluethroat argentine
Bathylagidae	*Leuroglossus schmidti*	northern smoothtongue
Bathymasteridae	*Bathymaster caeruleofasciatus*	Alaskan ronquil
	Bathymaster signatus	searcher
Chauliodontidae	*Chauliodus macouni*	Pacific viperfish
Clupeidae	*Clupea pallasii*	Pacific herring
Macrouridae	*Albatrossia pectoralis*	giant grenadier
	Coryphaenoides cinereus	popeye grenadier
Cottidae	*Artediellus* sp.	
	Dasycottus setiger	spinyhead sculpin
	Eurymen gyrinus	smoothcheek sculpin
	Gymnocanthus galeatus	armorhead sculpin

Fish Species

Family	Species name	Common name
Cottidae (Continued)	*Gymnocanthus pistilliger*	threaded sculpin
	Hemilepidotus hemilepidotus	red Irish lord
	Hemilepidotus jordani	yellow Irish lord
	Hemilepidotus papilio	butterfly sculpin
	Hemitripterus bolini	bigmouth sculpin
	Icelinus borealis	northern sculpin
	Icelinus tenuis	spotfin sculpin
	Icelus spiniger	thorny sculpin
	Malacocottus zonurus	darkfin sculpin
	Myoxocephalus jaok	plain sculpin
	Myoxocephalus polyacanthocephalus	great sculpin
	Nautichthys oculofasciatus	sailfin sculpin
	Nautichthys pribilovius	eyeshade sculpin
	Psychrolutes paradoxus	tadpole sculpin
	Rhamphocottus richardsoni	grunt sculpin
	Thyriscus anoplus	
	Triglops forficata	scissortail sculpin
	Triglops macellus	roughspine sculpin
	Triglops pingeli	ribbed sculpin
	Triglops scepticus	spectacled sculpin
Trichodontidae	*Trichodon trichodon*	Pacific sandfish
Gadidae	*Microgadus proximus*	Pacific tomcod
	Gadus macrocephalus	Pacific cod
	Theragra chalcogramma	walleye pollock
Hexagrammidae	*Hexagrammos decagrammus*	kelp greenling
	Hexagrammos octogrammus	masked greenling
	Hexagrammos stelleri	whitespotted greenling
	Ophiodon elongatus	lingcod
	Pleurogrammus monopterygius	Atka mackerel
Cyclopteridae	*Aptocyclus ventricosus*	smooth lumpsucker
	Careproctus melanurus	blacktail snailfish
	Careproctus gilberti	smalldisk snailfish
	Eumicrotremus birulai	round lumpsucker
	Eumicrotremus orbis	Pacific spiny lumpsucker
	Paraliparis sp.	
Melamphaeidae	*Poromitra crassiceps*	crested bigscale
Melanostomiidae	*Tactostoma macropus*	longfin dragonfish
Merlucciidae	*Merluccius productus*	Pacific hake
Myctophidae	*Diaphus theta*	California headlightfish
	Lampanyctus ritteri	broadfin lanternfish
	Lampanyctus jordani	brokenline lampfish
	Stenobrachius leucopsarus	northern lampfish
Paralepidae	*Paralepis atlantica*	duckbill barracudina
Osmeridae	*Hypomesus pretiosus*	surf smelt
	Mallotus villosus	capelin
	Spirinchus thaleichthys	longfin smelt
	Thaleichthys pacificus	eulachon
Salmonidae	*Oncorhynchus gorbuscha*	pink salmon
	Oncorhynchus keta	chum salmon
	Oncorhynchus kisutch	coho salmon

Martin (1997).

The maximum depth of sampling was 500 meters.

Fish Species

Family	Species name	Common name
Salmonidae (Continued)	*Oncorhynchus nerka*	sockeye salmon
	Oncorhynchus tshawytscha	chinook salmon
	Salvelinus malma	Dolly Varden
Cryptacanthodidae	*Cryptacanthodes giganteus*	giant wrymouth
Stichaeidae	*Chirolophis decoratus*	decorated warbonnet
	Lumpenus maculatus	daubed shanny
	Lumpenus sagitta	snake prickleback
	Lumpenella longirostris	longsnout prickleback
	Poroclinus rothrocki	whitebarred prickleback
Zaproridae	*Bothrocara pusillum*	Alaska eelpout
	Lycodapus sp.	
	Lycodes palearis	wattled eelpout
	Lycodes diapterus	black eelpout
	Lycodes brevipes	shortfin eelpout
	Lycodes pacificus	blackbelly eelpout
	Zaprora silenus	prowfish
Scorpaenidae	*Sebastes aleutianus*	rougheye rockfish
	Sebastes alutus	Pacific ocean perch
	Sebastes babcocki	redbanded rockfish
	Sebastes borealis	shortraker rockfish
	Sebastes brevispinis	silvergray rockfish
	Sebastes ciliatus	dark dusky rockfish
	Sebastes crameri	darkblotched rockfish
	Sebastes elongatus	greenstriped rockfish
	Sebastes entomelas	widow rockfish
	Sebastes flavidus	yellowtail rockfish
	Sebastes helvomaculatus	rosethorn rockfish
	Sebastes maliger	quillback rockfish
	Sebastes melanops	black rockfish
	Sebastes nigrocinctus	tiger rockfish
	Sebastes paucispinis	bocaccio
	Sebastes pinniger	canary rockfish
	Sebastes polyspinis	northern rockfish
	Sebastes proriger	redstripe rockfish
	Sebastes reedi	yellowmouth rockfish
	Sebastes ruberrimus	yelloweye rockfish
	Sebastes variegatus	harlequin rockfish
	Sebastes wilsoni	pygmy rockfish
	Sebastes zacentrus	sharpchin rockfish
	Sebastolobus alascanus	shortspine thornyhead

Invertebrate Species

Phylum	Species name	Common name
Cnidaria	*Alcyonium* sp.	
	Amphilaphis sp.	
	Anthomastus sp.	
	Arthrogorgia sp.	
	Callogorgia sp.	
	Cyanea capillata	
	Cyclohelia lancellata	
	Errinopora sp.	
	Fanellia compressa	
	Gersemia sp.	sea raspberry
	Liponemis brevicornis	
	Metridium senile	
	Muriceides sp.	
	Paragorgia arborea	
	Pavonaria finmarchica	
	Plumarella sp.	
	Primnoa willeyi	
	Ptilosarcus gurneyi	
	Stylaster brochi	
	Stylatula sp.	slender seawhip
	Thouarella sp.	
Annelida	*Carcinobdella cyclostomum*	striped sea leech
	Cheilonereis cyclurus	
	Eunoe nodosa	giant scale worm
	Eunoe depressa	depressed scale worm
	Serpula vermicularis	
Arthropoda	*Acantholithodes hispidus*	fuzzy crab
	Argis dentata	Arctic argid
	Argis lar	kuro argid
	Balanus evermanni	giant barnacle
	Balanus rostratus	beaked barnacle
	Cancer gracilis	graceful rock crab
	Cancer magister	Dungeness crab
	Cancer oregonensis	Oregon rock crab
	Chionoecetes angulatus	triangle tanner crab
	Chionoecetes bairdi	bairdi tanner crab
	Chionoecetes tanneri	grooved tanner crab
	Chorilia longipes	longhorned decorator crab
	Crangon communis	twospine crangon
	Crangon dalli	ridged crangon
	Crangon septemspinosa	sevenspine bay shrimp
	Elassochirus cavimanus	purple hermit
	Elassochirus gilli	Pacific red hermit
	Elassochirus tenuimanus	widehand hermit crab
	Eualus macilenta	
	Hapalogaster grebnitzkii	
	Hyas lyratus	Pacific lyre crab
	Labidochirus splendescens	splendid hermit
	Lebbeus groenlandicus	
	Lithodes aequispinus	golden king crab
	Lopholithodes foraminatus	box crab
	Munida quadrispina	
	Oregonia gracilis	graceful decorator crab
	Pagurus aleuticus	Aleutian hermit
	Pagurus brandti	sponge hermit
	Pagurus capillatus	hairy hermit crab
	Pagurus confragosus	knobbyhand hermit

Table 8.1. Fish and Invertebrate Species from 1996 NMFS Trawl Surveys of the Gulf of Alaska (Continued).

Invertebrate Species

Phylum	Species name	Common name
Arthropoda (Continued)	*Pagurus dalli*	whiteknee hermit
	Pagurus kennerlyi	bluespine hermit
	Pagurus ochotensis	Alaskan hermit
	Pagurus rathbuni	longfinger hermit
	Pagurus tanneri	longhand hermit
	Pandalopsis dispar	sidestriped shrimp
	Pandalus borealis	northern shrimp
	Pandalus goniurus	humpy shrimp
	Pandalus hypsinotus	coonstriped shrimp
	Pandalus jordani	ocean shrimp
	Pandalus platyceros	spot shrimp
	Pandalus tridens	yellowleg pandalid
	Paralithodes camtschaticus	red king crab
	Paralithodes platypus	blue king crab
	Pasiphaea pacifica	Pacific glass shrimp
	Pasiphaea tarda	crimson pasiphaeid
	Pinnixa occidentalis	pea crab
	Placetron wosnessenskii	scaled crab
	Pugettia sp.	kelp crab
	Rhinolithodes wosnessenskii	rhinoceros crab
	Sclerocrangon boreas	sculptured shrimp
Mollusca	*Aforia circinata*	keeled aforia
	Arctomelon stearnsii	Alaska volute
	Astarte crenata	crenulate astarte
	Bathybembix bairdii	
	Beringius kennicottii	
	Beringius undatus	
	Berryteuthis magister	magistrate armhook squid
	Buccinum plectrum	sinuous whelk
	Buccinum scalariforme	ladder whelk
	Chlamylla sp.	
	Chlamys rubida	reddish scallop
	Cidarina cidaris	
	Clinocardium californiense	California cockle
	Clinocardium ciliatum	hairy cockle
	Clinocardium nuttallii	Nuttall cockle
	Colus herendeenii	thin-ribbed whelk
	Cranopsis major	
	Cyclocardia crebricostata	many-rib cyclocardia
	Cyclocardia ventricosa	stout cyclocardia
	Fusitriton oregonensis	Oregon triton
	Limopsis akutanica	Akutan limops
	Mactromeris polynyma	Arctic surfclam
	Modiolus modiolus	northern horsemussel
	Musculus discors	discordant mussel
	Musculus niger	black mussel
	Mytilus edulis	blue mussel
	Natica clausa	arctic moonsnail
	Natica russa	rusty moonsnail
	Neptunea amianta	
	Neptunea lyrata	lyre whelk
	Neptunea pribiloffensis	Pribilof whelk
	Nuculana sp.	
	Octopus dofleini	giant octopus
	Opisthoteuthis californiana	flapjack devilfish
	Patinopecten caurinus	weathervane scallop
	Plicifusus kroyeri	
	Pododesmus macroschisma	Alaska falsejingle

Invertebrate Species

Phylum	Species name	Common name
Mollusca (Continued)	*Polinices pallidus*	pale moonsnail
	Rossia pacifica	eastern Pacific bobtail
	Serripes groenlandicus	Greenland cockle
	Serripes laperousii	broad cockle
	Siliqua sp.	
	Tochuina tetraquetra	giant orange tochui
	Tridonta borealis	boreal tridonta
	Tritonia diomedea	rosy tritonia
	Volutopsius callorhinus	
	Volutopsius fragilis	fragile whelk
	Volutopsius harpa	left-hand whelk
	Yoldia scissurata	crisscrossed yoldia
	Yoldia thraciaeformis	broad yoldia
Echinodermata	*Allocentrotus fragilis*	orange-pink sea urchin
	Amphiophiura ponderosa	
	Asterias amurensis	purple-orange sea star
	Asteronyx loveni	
	Bathyplotes sp.	
	Brisaster latifrons	
	Ceramaster japonicus	red bat star
	Ceramaster patagonicus	orange bat star
	Crossaster borealis	
	Crossaster papposus	rose sea star
	Ctenodiscus crispatus	common mud star
	Cucumaria fallax	
	Diplopteraster multipes	
	Dipsacaster borealis	
	Echinarachnius parma	Parma sand dollar
	Evasterias echinosoma	
	Evasterias troschelii	
	Gephyreaster swifti	
	Gorgonocephalus caryi	
	Henricia leviuscula	
	Henricia sanguinolenta	
	Hippasteria spinosa	
	Leptasterias hylodes	
	Leptasterias polaris	
	Leptychaster pacificus	
	Lethasterias nanimensis	
	Lophaster furcilliger	
	Luidia foliata	
	Luidiaster dawsoni	
	Mediaster aequalis	
	Molpadia intermedia	
	Ophiopholis aculeata	
	Ophiura sarsi	
	Orthasterias koehleri	
	Parastichopus californicus	
	Pedicellaster magister	
	Pentamera lissoplaca	
	Poraniopsis inflata	
	Pseudarchaster parelii	
	Psolus fabricii	
	Pteraster militaris	
	Pteraster obscurus	
	Pteraster tesselatus	
	Pycnopodia helianthoides	
	Rathbunaster californicus	
	Solaster dawsoni	

Invertebrate Species

Phylum	Species name	Common name
Echinodermata (Continued)	*Solaster endeca*	
	Solaster paxillatus	
	Solaster stimpsoni	
	Stichopus japonicus	
	Strongylocentrotus droebachiensis	green sea urchin
	Strongylocentrotus franciscanus	red sea urchin
	Strongylocentrotus pallidus	white sea urchin
	Stylasterias forreri	
Porifera	*Aphrocallistes vastus*	clay pipe sponge
	Halichondria panicea	barrel sponge
	Hylonema sp.	fiberoptic sponge
	Mycale loveni	tree sponge
	Myxilla incrustans	scallop sponge
	Suberites ficus	hermit sponge
Bryozoa	*Eucratea loricata*	feathery bryozoan
	Flustra serrulata	leafy bryozoan
Brachiopoda	*Laqueus californianus*	
	Terebratalia transversa	
	Terebratulina unguicula	
Chordata	*Styela rustica*	sea potato
	Aplidium sp.	
	Boltenia sp.	
	Halocynthia aurantium	sea peach
	Molgula griffithsii	sea grape
	Molgula retortiformis	sea clod
	Synoicum sp.	

gear surveys are not designed or intended to estimate species diversity. A comparison of the known fish species composition to the species composition in the predominant types of trawl gear surveys shows that trawl gear samples underestimate the fish species diversity of the GOA (Cooney 1986b). The longest standing trawl gear surveys for the GOA are limited to the continental shelf and the shelf break (to 500 m before 1999 and to 1,000 m thereafter). The National Marine Fisheries Service (NMFS) has measured relative abundance and distribution of the principal groundfish and commercially important invertebrate species (Martin 1997b), and before 1980, the International Pacific Halibut Commission (IPHC) collected information on the abundance, distribution, and age structure of halibut. Hook and line surveys for Pacific halibut, sablefish, rockfish, and Pacific cod on the continental shelf in the GOA have been conducted by the IPHC since 1962 (Clark et al. 1999).

On the basis of the biomass available to trawl gear on the continental shelf and shelf break, flatfish and rockfish dominate the fish fauna in most areas of the GOA. As of 1996, a flatfish species, arrowtooth

flounder, dominated the overall trawl survey of the fish biomass in the GOA, followed by Pacific ocean perch (rockfish), walleye pollock (gadid), Pacific halibut (flatfish), and Pacific cod (gadid) (Martin 1997a). Biomass of the arrowtooth flounder is approaching two million metric tons, and its biomass has been steadily increasing since 1977 (Witherell 1999a). Of the next fifteen largest biomasses of species in the 1996 NMFS survey, six were flatfish and five were rockfish.

Geographic distributions of GOA fish biomass in the NMFS trawl surveys are different from the overall total. In the western GOA, Atka mackerel (Hexagrammidae) had the highest biomass in the Shumagin Islands, but this species was not among the twenty largest biomasses of species in the four other International North Pacific Fisheries Commission (INPFC) areas of the GOA. Arrowtooth flounder dominate the trawl survey biomass throughout the GOA. They are the most or second-most abundant in all five areas. Flatfish and especially soles make up a large number of high-biomass species in the western and northwestern GOA (Shumagin Islands, Chirikof, and Kodiak), and rockfish have a large number of high-biomass species in the northeastern and eastern GOA (Yakutat and Southeast). Pollock and cod are a dominant part of the biomass in the western GOA, but less so in the east. Pacific sleeper sharks are among the twenty largest biomasses of species in the north (Chirikof, Kodiak, and Yakutat), but not in the south (Shumagin Islands and Southeast). The only anadromous species, the eulachon, occurs among the twenty largest biomasses in the north, but not in the south.

With the use of a variety of gear types, including trawl net, try net, trammel net, beach seine, and tow net in waters less than 100 m, Rogers et al. (1986) provided a detailed image of the distribution of fish species and biomass with depth and by region. As was the case for the 1996 NMFS trawl surveys, species composition and relative biomass of fish species in multi-gear surveys change substantially in moving from the nearshore toward offshore areas in the GOA, as well as from one region to the next. The findings of the multiple gear surveys were consistent with the trawl survey observations in that shallow (smaller than 100 m) fish assemblages were more diverse in the north and west of the GOA than in the northeast and east (Table 8.4 in comparison to Table 8.2).

Other trends in distribution correspond to reproduction and seasonal changes in shallow waters in some

Table 8.2. Fish Families and the Approximate Number of Genera and Species Reported from the Gulf of Alaska.

Family	Quast and Hall[1]		Miscellaneous surveys[2]	
	Number of genera	Number of species	Number of genera	Number of species
Petromyzontidae	2	3	–	–
Hexanchidae	1	1	–	–
Lamnidae	2	2	1	1
Carcharhinidae	1	1	–	–
Squalidae	2	2	1	1
Rajidae	1	7	1	4
Acipenseridae	1	2	–	–
Clupeidae	2	2	1	1
Salmonidae	6	12	1	3
Osmeridae	5	6	5	6
Bathylagidae	1	4	–	–
Opisthoproctidae	1	1	–	–
Gonostomatidae	2	4	–	–
Melanostomiidae	1	1	–	–
Chauliodontidae	1	1	1	1
Alepocephalidae	1	1	–	–
Anotopteridae	1	1	–	–
Scopelarchidae	1	1	–	–
Myctophidae	7	10	1	1
Oneirodidae	1	3	–	–
Moridae	1	1	–	–
Gadidae	5	5	5	5
Ophidiidae	2	2	–	–
Zoarcidae	6	11	4	7
Macrouridae	1	3	1	1
Scomberesocidae	1	1	1	1
Melamphaidae	3	3	–	–
Zeidae	1	1	–	–
Lampridae	1	1	–	–
Trachipteridae	1	1	–	–
Gasterosteidae	2	2	–	–
Scorpaenidae	2	22	2	30
Hexagrammidae	3	6	3	5
Anoplopomatidae	2	2	1	1
Cottidae	30	54	15	24
Psychrolutidae	1	1	–	–
Agonidae	8	12	8	9
Cyclopteridae	12	38	5	7
Bramidae	1	1	–	–
Pentacerotidae	1	1	–	–
Sphyracnidae	1	1	–	–
Trichodontidae	2	2	1	1
Bathymasteridae	2	4	2	2
Anarhichadidae	1	1	1	1
Stichaidae	10	15	4	6
Ptilichthyidae	1	1	–	–
Pholididae	2	4	–	–
Scytalinidae	1	1	–	–
Zaproridae	1	1	1	1
Ammodytidae	1	1	1	1
Scombridae	2	2	–	–
Centrolophidae	1	1	–	–
Bothidae	1	1	–	–
Pleuronectidae	15	17	15	16
Cryptacanthodidae[3]	2	2	2	2
Totals	**167**	**287**	**84**	**138**

Sources: Hood and Zimmerman 1986 (after Ronholt et al. 1978).

[1]After Quast and Hall (1972).

[2]Gulf of Alaska exploratory, BCF, IPHC, and NMFS trawl survey data.

[3]Quast and Hall (1972) include these genera and species in the family Stichaeidae while Hart (1973) recognizes a separate family.

Table 8.3. Proportion of the Total Species Composition of Gulf of Alaska Fish Fauna Contributed by the 10 Dominant Fish Families in Two Different Surveys.

Family[1]	Percentage of total fish species	Family[2]	Percentage of total fish species
Cottidae	19	Scorpaenidae	10
Cyclopteridae	13	Cottidae	8
Scorpaenidae	8	Pleuronectidae	6
Pleuronectidae	6	Agonidae	3
Stichaeidae	5	Zoarcidae	2
Salmonidae	4	Cyclopteridae	2
Agonidae	4	Stichaeidae	2
Zoaricidae	4	Osmeridae	2
Myctophidae	3	Gadidae	2
Rajidae	2	Hexagrammidae	2
Total	68		39

Source: Hood and Zimmerman 1986.

[1]From Quast and Hall (1972).

[2]From GOA exploratory cruises and resource assessment surveys.

species of nearshore fishes. Estuarine bays in the Kodiak archipelago are nursery areas, with larvae and juveniles being found in nearshore and pelagic habitats within bays (Rogers et al. 1986). Blackburn (1979 in Rogers et al. 1986) found a trend of larger fish with increasing depth in studies of Ugak Bay and Alitak Bay on Kodiak Island. Most species of nearshore fish apparently move to deeper water in the winter. In Lower Cook Inlet and Southeast Alaska, juveniles and other smaller size classes of the species of local fish assemblages are found close to shore, water temperatures permitting, and larger size classes are found farther offshore at depths greater than 30 m at all times of the year.

Nearshore areas of the GOA provide rearing environments for the juveniles of many fish species. Important nursery grounds for juvenile flatfishes such as soles and Pacific halibut, are found in waters of Kachemak Bay and other waters of Lower Cook Inlet, as well as in Chiniak Bay on Kodiak Island (Norcross 1998). In Kachemak Bay, summer habitats of some juvenile flatfishes are shallower than winter habitats. Juvenile flatfish distributions in coastal waters are defined by substrate type, typically mud and mud-sand, and by depth, typically 10 to 80 m, and in the case of Chiniak Bay, by temperature. Deepwater and shallow-water assemblages were identified for the groundfish communities in both Kachemak and Chiniak bays; however, the limiting depths were different for these two localities (Norcross 1998, Mueter and Norcross 1999).

Both salmon and groundfish populations in the northeastern Pacific appear to vary annually in concert with features of climate, but the responses appear to be different (Francis et al. 1998). Patterns of year-class strength of some groundfish follow a decadal pattern of variability that may be related to shifts in large scale atmospheric forcing, while others follow a pattern more consistent with El Niño Southern Oscillation (ENSO) (Hollowed et al. 2001). The ENSO and the PDO were shown to be independent of one another (Mantua et al. 1997). The opposite responses of groundfish and salmon (positive) and crab (negative) recruitment to intensified Aleutian lows may be because different species-specific mechanisms are invoked by the same weather pattern. Because the groundfish species described by Hollowed and Wooster (1992, 1995) were mostly winter spawners, Zheng and Kruse (2000b) hypothesize that strengthened Aleutian Lows increase advection of eggs and larvae of groundfish toward onshore nursery areas, improving survival. Salmon, on the other hand, benefit from increased production of prey items under intense lows. The possible links between Aleutian lows, PDOs, and ENSO and populations of fish and other animals are discussed further below and in a recent review paper (Francis et al. 1998).

8.2.1 Salmon

The GOA is the crossroads of the world for Pacific salmon. Salmon from Japan, Russia, all of Alaska, British Columbia, and the Pacific Northwest spend part of each life cycle in the GOA (Myers et al. 2000). Five species of salmon—pink, chum, sockeye, coho, and chinook—are very common in the GOA. These species appear in the GOA as early as the first year of life (all pink, chum, and ocean type chinook and some sockeye); however, others may appear during the second (all coho and stream-type chinook and most sockeye) and rarely during the third or later years (some sockeye) (see Groot and Margolis 1991). Ecologically, the salmon species may be divided into two broad groups, marine planktivores (pink, chum, and sockeye) and marine piscivores (coho and chinook). Further ecological differentiation is apparent within planktivores. For example, the size groups of plankton consumed by chum and sockeye are inferred to be quite different, because chum use short stubby gill rakers to separate food from water, and sockeye have long feathery gill rakers as filters.

Distribution within the GOA changes with time after marine entry (Nagasawa 2000), as salmon disperse among coastal feeding grounds according to species

Table 8.4. Comparison of the Number of Fish Families and Species Found at Less Than 100 m in Different Regions of the Gulf of Alaska.

Location	Number of families	Number of species
Kodiak	22	101
Lower Cook Inlet	25	105
Prince William Sound	18	72
Southeast Alaska	NA	51

Information summarized from Rogers et al. (1986).

NA = not available.

and stock, age, size, feeding behavior, food preferences, and other factors (Myers et al. 2000). During the first year of marine life, salmon are located in estuaries, bays, and coastal areas within the Alaska Coastal Current (ACC) and continental shelf (Myers et al. 2000). With time and growth, first-year salmon move farther away from their river of origin and farther offshore. First-year salmon move out of the ACC into colder waters in fall and winter of their first year at sea.

Salmon of all ages are thought to exhibit seasonal migrations in spring and fall between onshore and offshore marine areas. In the fall, salmon of all ages move offshore to spend the winter in waters between 4°C and 8°C that are relatively poor in food, perhaps as an energy conservation strategy for surviving the winter (Nagasawa 2000). In the spring, salmon move onshore into waters that may reach 15°C where food sources are relatively abundant.

Salmon populations overall are at very high levels in Alaska, with the notable exceptions of Western Alaska chum and chinook populations originating in drainages between Norton Sound in the north and the Kuskokwim River, west of Bristol Bay (ADF&G 1998). On Norton Sound, the chum salmon populations of the Penny and Cripple rivers have exhibited very low to zero spawning stocks in the past five years. Another notable exception to the record high levels of Alaska salmon production are the Kvichak River sockeye populations of Bristol Bay, which have faltered. Some "off-peak cycle" brood years have recently failed to produce as expected (Kruse et al. 2000b).

The situation in Western Alaska notwithstanding, the 1999 commercial harvest of 404,000 t of salmon in Alaska was the second largest in recorded history behind 1995 (451,000 t) (Kruse et al. 2000b). A

large portion of the record harvests in 1999 was pink salmon from areas adjacent to the GOA, such as Prince William Sound (PWS), and Southeast Alaska. The status of salmon populations and fisheries in the following areas was recently evaluated in terms of levels of harvest and spawning escapements: areas coincident with habitats in the north central GOA of the Steller sea lion, which is listed as an endangered species under the Endangered Species Act of 1973 (ESA); Kodiak; the Alaska Peninsula; and Bristol Bay. All major commercial salmon stocks were judged to be healthy, with the exception of the Kvichak River off-cycle brood years (Kruse et al. 2000b).

Given that marine migration patterns of each stock are thought to be characteristic and somewhat unique (Myers et al. 2000), the contrast in the status of salmon stocks between Western Alaska, and Southcentral and Southeast Alaska, offers some intriguing research questions about the role of marine processes in salmon production (Cooney 1984). Understanding the processes that connect salmon production to climate, marine food production, and fishing requires understanding of the marine pathways of the salmon through time (Beamish et al. 1999b). Therefore, research approaches to understanding changes in salmon abundance on annual and decadal scales need to encompass localities that are representative of the full life cycle of the salmon and, in particular, in estuarine and marine environments. Scientific information on freshwater localities is far more common than that available for estuarine and marine areas. Given the current state of information on both hatchery and wild salmon, it is highly desirable to focus current and future efforts on estuaries and marine areas for understanding migratory pathways and other habitats, physiological indicators of individual health, trophic dynamics, and the forcing effects of weather and oceanographic processes (Brodeur et al. 2000).

8.2.2 Pacific Herring

Pacific herring populations (Funk 2001) occur in the northeastern GOA, with commercial concentrations in Southeast Alaska (Sitka), PWS, western Lower Cook Inlet, and occasionally around Kodiak. Most of the historical information on herring in the GOA comes from coastal marine fisheries that started in Alaska in 1878 (Kruse et al. 2000b); however, intensive ecological investigations at the end of the twentieth century have added information on early life history (Norcross et al. 1999). Herring deposit eggs onto vegetation in the intertidal and near subtidal waters in late spring, undergo a period of larval drift, and spend the first summer and winter nearshore in sheltered embayments. Transport of larvae by currents in relation to sites that are suitable summer feeding and overwintering grounds is likely an important factor affecting survival in the first year of life in PWS (Norcross et al. 1999), as is the nutritional status of these age-0 herring in the fall of the year (Foy and Paul 1999). Some portion of the mature herring must migrate annually between onshore spawning grounds and offshore feeding grounds; however, the geography of the life cycle between spawning and maturation is less certain.

Although the geographic scope of the herring life cycle in the Bering Sea is fairly well understood, inferences from the Bering Sea to the GOA are not direct because of apparent differences in life history strategies between the herring of the two regions (Funk 2001). Adult herring in the GOA are smaller and have shorter life spans than those in the Bering Sea. Perhaps GOA herring migrate shorter distances to food sources that are not as rich as those available to Bering Sea herring, which migrate long distances from spawning to feed among the rich food sources of the continental shelf break (Funk 2001). Genetic analyses indicate that Bering Sea and GOA herring populations are reproductively isolated (Funk 2001).

Another ecologically significant characteristic of Pacific herring is the temporal change in size at age over time (E. Brown, University of Alaska Fairbanks, pers. comm., 2000). Annual deviations from long-term (1927 to 1998) mean length at age for Sitka Sound herring indicate a decadal-scale oscillation between positive and negative deviations. This finding is consistent with the reported coincidence of size-at-age data for Pacific herring with the PDO (Ware 1991). Herring may be affected by ENSO events. Decreased catches, recruitments, and weight-at-age of herring are at times associated with ENSO events. Seabirds in the GOA that depend on herring and other pelagic forage species showed widespread mortalities and breeding failures during the ENSO events of 1983 and 1993 (Bailey et al. 1995b). The similarities between the annual patterns of abundance and the location of weather systems (annual geographically averaged sea-level atmospheric pressure) are not as clear with herring as for other fish species, such as salmon. The difference may result because herring populations tend to be dominated by the occasional strong year class, and show considerable variability in landings through the years.

The current status of herring populations may be closely related to historical fishing patterns. Long-term changes associated with commercial fishing have occurred in the apparent geographic distribution and abundance of GOA herring. Herring-reduction fisheries (oil and meal) from 1878 to 1967 reached a peak harvest of 142,000 t in 1934. That exploitation rates were high may be inferred from the fact that some locations of major herring-reduction fisheries, such as Seldovia Bay (Kenai Peninsula and Lower Cook Inlet) are now devoid of herring. It is speculated that reduction fisheries at geographic bottlenecks between herring spawning and feeding grounds, such as the entrance to Seldovia Bay and the passes of southwestern PWS, were able to apply very high exploitation rates to the adult population. Harvest management applied by the State of Alaska relies on biomass estimates, and harvests are held to a small fraction of the estimated biomass. Harvest is not allowed until the population estimate rises above a minimum or "threshold" biomass level.

Recent statewide herring harvests have averaged less than a third of the 1934 peak. Direct comparison of past and present catch statistics is problematic, however, because current rates of harvest are thought to be substantially below those applied in 1934 (Kruse et al. 2000b). Also note that recent statewide figures for herring harvests include substantial harvests from outside the GOA, and herring-reduction fisheries were located in the GOA. Populations of herring were targeted for sac roe starting in the 1970s and for sac roe and roe-on-kelp in the 1980s. Regional herring population status is variable. Population levels of herring in PWS remained at low levels in 2000, and commercial harvests were not allowed in 1994, 1995, and 1996, nor since 1998. In 1999, fishing operations were halted because of low biomass and poor recruitment. Disease is strongly suspected as a factor in keeping the population levels low. The herring fishery of Lower Cook Inlet in Kamishak Bay closed in 1999 after a very small catch in 1998 and remains closed because of low biomass levels. Catches in the Kodiak fishery for herring sac roe are declining. The bait fishery in Shelikof Strait was closed in 1999 because of its possible relation to depressed Kamishak Bay herring populations.

Significant questions remain about the geographic extent of the stocks to which the biomass estimates and fishing exploitation rates may apply in PWS (Norcross et al. 1999). The geomorphology of PWS in relation to currents plays an important role in determining the retention of larvae in nearshore areas conducive to growth and survival. The degree to which spawning aggregations of herring may represent individual stocks is a significant question, because the actual exploitation rate of herring in PWS depends on how many stocks are defined. Although it is not clear how many stocks of herring occupy PWS, conditions seem to favor more than one spawning stock (Norcross et al. 1999).

Water temperatures appear to play important roles in growth and survival of age-0 herring. Warm summer water temperatures may be conducive to growth and survival; however, the opposite seems to be true of warm water temperatures in spring and winter. Increased metabolic demands imposed by warm water on yolk-sac larvae and overwintering age-0 herring could decrease survival (Norcross et al. 1999). Availability of food before winter, and perhaps during winter, may be key to survival of age-0 herring. Input of food from the GOA may be an important key to survival for age-0 herring at some localities. Differential survival among nursery areas because of interannual variation in climate and accessibility of GOA food sources could be a key determinant of year-class strength in PWS. The sources of variability mean that geographic locality is no guarantee of any particular level of survival from year to year. Sampling whole body energy content of age-0 herring at the end of the first winter among bays could provide an indicator of year-class strength (Norcross et al. 1999).

Questions relating to the ability of disease outbreaks to control herring populations have recently been explored. Work has identified the diseases, viral hemorrhagic septicemia and a fungus, as factors potentially limiting the abundance of herring in PWS (Hostettler et al. 2000, Finney et al. 2000).

8.2.3 Pollock

Pollock are an ecologically dominant and economically important cod-like fish in the GOA. They appear to spawn at the same locations within the same marine areas each year, with location of spawning and migrations of adults linked to patterns of larval drift and locations of feeding grounds (Bailey et al. 1999). Spawning occurs at depths of 100 to 400 m, and as a result, the distributions of eggs and larvae in some areas may have been well below the depths of historical ichthyoplankton surveys. Pollock larvae feed on early developmental stages of copepods and, as juveniles, move on to feed on larger zooplankton such as euphausiids and small fishes, including

pollock. Although cannibalism is regarded as significant in the Bering Sea, it is not thought to be a significant factor in the GOA. Pollock eggs and larvae are important sources of food for other zooplankters, and year-class strength in pollock is thought to be related to abundances of marine mammals and seabirds, at least in the Bering Sea.

Pollock mature at about age 4 and may live as long as twenty years (Bailey et al. 1999). Adult walleye pollock are distributed throughout the GOA at depths above 500 m. A substantial portion (45 percent) of the total pollock biomass as well as the highest catches per unit effort (CPUEs) of the 1996 NMFS survey were found at less than 200 m in the area between Kodiak and Chirikof islands (Martin 1997). In the western GOA, the highest pollock catches and CPUEs of the 1996 NMFS trawl survey were found at less than 200 m, whereas in Yakutat and Southeast Alaska the substantial availability of pollock to trawl gear persists above 300 m. Pollock larger than 30 cm were rarely found above 200 m in the eastern GOA in 1996 (Yakutat and Southeast), although pollock of all sizes (about 10 to 70 cm) were found at all depths down to 500 m in the western GOA (Martin 1997). Although pollock are commonly found in the outer continental shelf and slope, they may also be found in nearshore areas where they may be important predators and prey; for example, in PWS (Willette et al. 2001).

Populations of pollock in the GOA are considered to be separate from those in the Bering Sea (Bailey et al. 1999). Among the most commercially important of the GOA groundfish species, exploitable biomasses of pollock populations in 1999 were estimated at 738,000 t, down from a peak of about three million t in 1982 (Witherell 1999). Annual numbers of 2-year-old pollock entering the fishable population (recruitment) from 198 to 1987 were erratic and usually lower than recruitments estimated in 1977 to 1980.

Following the climatic regime shift in 1978, pollock and other cod-like fish have dramatically increased, replacing shrimp in nearshore waters as the dominant group of organisms caught in mid-water trawls on the shelf (Piatt and Anderson 1996). Recruitment in pollock is heavily influenced by oceanographic conditions experienced by the eggs and larvae. Good conditions for juveniles of the 1976 and 1978 year class contributed to the 1982 peak in pollock biomass in the GOA (Bailey et al. 1999). Populations have gradually declined since then (Witherell 1999). Increasing mortality schedules in 1986 to 1991 may indicate increasing predation and deteriorating physical conditions for both juveniles and adults in the GOA (Bailey et al. 99). The larger-than-average year class for GOA pollock in 1988 may be related to high rates of juvenile growth coincident with warm water temperatures, lack of winds, low predator abundance, and low larval mortality rates (Bailey et al. 1996). As has been shown to be the case with other groundfish species, GOA pollock recruitments are positively correlated with ENSO events (Bailey et al. 1995b).

Issues in the management of pollock that currently remain unresolved include the geographic boundaries of stocks, their extent of migration, the effects of fishing in one geographic locale on the populations of pollock and predators in other geographic locales, and what controls the annual recruitment of young pollock to the fishable populations (Bailey et al. 1999). In relation to stock structure, spawning aggregations in PWS, the Shumagin Islands (southwest Kodiak), and Shelikof Strait (separating Kodiak from the Alaska Peninsula) may represent separate stocks. Conditions of weather and changing ocean currents and eddies in the Shelikof Strait have the capacity to alter survival of pollock larvae from year to year (Bailey et al. 1995a). In particular, the effects of shifts in the strength of the ACC on larval transport pose important questions for how year-class strength is determined. In 1996, anomalous relaxation of winds resulted in a dramatic increase in larval retention in the Shelikof basin. Increased larval retention may be favorable to survival of pollock larvae in this area, with some exceptions (Bailey et al. 1999).

8.2.4 Pacific Cod

Pacific cod is a groundfish with demersal eggs and larvae found throughout the GOA on the continental shelf and shelf break. Pacific cod of the GOA are also an economically and ecologically important species. Pacific cod had an estimated fishable population of 048,000 t in 1999, which is on the low end of the range of 600,000 to 950,000 t estimated for 1978 to 1999. Annual recruitments of GOA Pacific cod have been relatively stable since 1978, with exceptionally large numbers of 3-year-old recruits appearing in 1980 and 1998.

Pacific cod are found throughout the GOA at depths less than 500 m. They are most abundant in the western GOA (Kodiak, Chirikof, and Shumagin islands) where Pacific cod larger than 30 cm are found at all depths above 300 m, but smaller individuals are rarely found at depths less than 100 m (Martin 1997).

8.2.5 Halibut

Pacific halibut are common throughout the GOA at depths less than 400 m, and halibut are available to trawl gear at depths of 500 m (Martin 1997). In the 1996 NMFS trawl survey, the largest catches and the highest CPUE were found at depths of less than 100 m east-southeast of Kodiak on the Albatross Banks (Figure 4.1, chapter 4). In most areas of the GOA, the average weight and length of halibut caught in trawl gear increases with depth, even though the CPUE declines with depth, particularly in the western GOA (Shumagin Islands, Chirikof, and Kodiak) (Martin 1997).

The exploitable biomass of the highly prized Pacific halibut in 1999 was estimated at 258,000 t, which is above average for 1974 to 1999 (Witherell 1999). Exploitable biomass of Pacific halibut was also increasing from 1974 to 1988, after which it declined slightly.

Pacific halibut appear to undergo decadal-scale changes in recruitment, which have been correlated with both the 18.6 year cycle for lunar nodal tide (Parker et al. 1995) and the PDO.

Biomass of the dominant flatfish in the GOA, the arrowtooth flounder, is approaching two million t. Arrowtooth flounder is not heavily harvested, and their biomass has been steadily increasing since 1977.

8.3 SHELLFISH AND BENTHIC INVERTEBRATES

Shellfish are commonly found on or near the surface of the seafloor; they are epibenthic as adults, and in the water column (pelagic) for varying lengths of time as pre-adults. Exceptions to this rule abound, particularly among mollusks such as squid, which live free of the bottom as adults. Beyond the nearshore environment (at depths greater than 25 m), the shellfish and other invertebrates dominate the number of species and the biomass of the bottom, just as other assemblages of invertebrates dominate the nearshore (see chapter 6). Among the shellfish, the arthropods and mollusks often have the largest number of species. For example, of 287 species of bottom fauna identified in waters deeper than 25 m in Lower Cook Inlet, more than 67 percent were arthropods and mollusks (Feder and Jewett 1986). Many of the commercially important species of the GOA are dependent for food to a greater or lesser extent on benthic invertebrates discussed here. (Commercially important crabs and shrimp are discussed below.) Commercial crabs and shrimps, and scallops, join the fish species of Pacific cod, walleye pollock, halibut, and Pacific ocean perch as members of the subtidal benthic food web for part of each life cycle. Detritus, bacteria, and microalgae form the base for the benthic invertebrates of the GOA continental shelf, which are predominantly filter feeders (60 percent), and detritus eaters (33 percent) (Semenov 1965 in Feder and Jewett 1986). Small mollusks, small crustaceans, polychaete annelids, and other worm-like invertebrates make up the filter-feeding and detritivore component of this food web.

Regional differences are pronounced in the benthic food webs of the GOA. The eastern GOA has few filter feeders and lower average biomass relative to the northern and western GOA, in large part because of the nature of substrates and currents. In particular the benthic species composition and productivity in the GOA is determined in part by the Alaska Coastal Current (ACC), particularly in the embayments and fjords (Feder and Jewett 1986). The ACC brings freshwater to the environments containing the pelagic shellfish larvae and heavy sediment loads that define the bottom habitats of the later stages of the life cycle. Biomass of filter feeders on the continental shelf in the western GOA (138 grams per square meter [g m^{-2}]) is far higher than that found in the northeastern or eastern GOA combined (33.2 g m^{-2}). Biomasses of detritus feeders in the western (31 g m^{-2}) and eastern (12 g m^{-2}) GOA are lower than those found in the northeastern GOA (43 g m^{-2}). Biomasses of all trophic groups on the shelf break are lower than those of the adjacent shelf. The distribution of benthic invertebrates in the GOA attests to the validity of the hypothesis that the type of bottom sediment, as influenced by proximity to alluvial inputs and currents, determines the species composition, production, and productivities of benthic communities (Semenov 1965 in Feder and Jewett 1986). Sediment size is dominant among the factors controlling the distribution of benthic species (Feder and Jewett 1986).

8.3.1 Crab

The principal commercial crab species in the GOA are the king crabs (*Paralithodes* spp.), the tanner crab (*Chionoecetes bairdi*), and the Dungeness crab (*Cancer magister*). All species have benthic adults and pelagic larvae, although the life history strategies vary substantially within and among species. For example, the pelagic stages of the red king crab are herbivorous; those of the tanner crab are

carnivorous; and those of the golden king crab do not feed until they metamorphose into the benthic stages. The benthic stages of all crab species feed to a large extent on the less well known invertebrates of the benthic environments (Feder and Paul 1980a, Jewett and Feder 1983, Feder and Jewett 1986) discussed briefly above under the shellfish overview.

The status of crab populations is relatively poor in comparison to the groundfish populations (Kruse et al. 2000a). Crab catches in the GOA have shown sharp changes with time, perhaps indicative of sensitivity to climatic forcing in some species, to fishing, or to a combination of factors (Zheng and Kruse 2000b). The red king crab stock of the GOA collapsed in the early 1980s and currently shows no signs of recovery. The tanner crab populations in PWS, Cook Inlet, Kodiak, and the Alaska Peninsula have declined to low levels in the early 1990s, and harvest levels have been sharply reduced (Kruse et al. 2000b).

In a study of time-series data on recruitment for fifteen crab stocks in the Bering Sea, Aleutian Islands, and GOA, time trends in seven of fifteen crab stocks are significantly correlated with time series of the strength of Aleutian Low climate regimes (Zheng and Kruse 2000a). Time trends in recruitments among some king crab stocks were correlated over broad geographic regions, suggesting a significant role of environmental forcing in regulation of population numbers for these species. The increased ocean productivity associated with the intense Aleutian Low and warmer temperatures was inversely related to recruitment for seven of the fifteen crab stocks. The seven significantly negative correlations between ocean productivity and crab recruitment were from Bristol Bay, Cook Inlet, and the GOA. Crab stocks declined as the Aleutian Low intensified. A significant inverse relation between the brood strength of red king crab and Aleutian Low intensity was reported earlier for one of the stocks in this study, red king crab from Bristol Bay (Tyler and Kruse 1996).

Tyler and Kruse (1996, 1997) and (Zheng and Kruse 2000a) have articulated an explicit series of hypotheses linking features of physical and geological oceanography to the reproductive and developmental biology of red king and tanner crab. The hypotheses explain observed relations between climate and recruitment. Tanner and red king crab in the Bering Sea are thought to respond differently to the physical factors associated with the Aleutian Low because of the distribution of the different types of sea bottom required by the post-planktonic stage of each species.

Suitable bottom habitat for red king crabs in the Bering Sea is more generally nearshore, whereas suitable bottom habitat for tanner crab is offshore. Intense Aleutian Low conditions favor surface currents that carry or hold planktonic crab larvae onshore, whereas weak Aleutian Low conditions favor surface currents that move larvae offshore. The process may not be species specific, but stock specific, depending on the location of suitable settling habitat in relation to the prevailing currents. In the case of red king crab, Zheng and Kruse (2000b) explain the apparent paradox of lowered recruitment for red king crab during periods of increased primary productivity. Red king crab eat diatoms, and show a preference for diatoms similar to *Thalassiosira* spp., which dominate in years of weak lows and stable water columns. Strong lows contribute to well-mixed water columns and a diverse assemblage of primary producers, which may be unfavorable for red king crab larvae, but favorable for tanner crab larvae. Tanner crab larvae eat copepods, which are favored by the higher temperatures associated with intense lows.

Recently completed modeling studies (Rosenkranz 1998) support climatic variables as determinants of recruitment success in tanner crab. Predominant wind direction and temperature of bottom water were strongly related to strength of tanner crab year classes in the Bering Sea. Northeast winds are thought to set up ocean transport processes that promote year-class strength by carrying the larvae toward suitable habitat. Elevated bottom-water temperatures were expected to augment the effect of northeast wind by increasing survival of newly hatched larvae (Rosenkranz 1998).

8.3.2 Shrimp

The shrimp were once among the dominant benthic epifauna in Lower Cook Inlet and Kodiak and along the Alaska Peninsula (Feder and Jewett 1988, Anderson and Piatt 1999) and of substantial commercial importance in the GOA. Five species of pandalid shrimp dominated the commercial catches, which occurred west of 144°W longitude in PWS, Cook Inlet, Kodiak, and along the Alaska Peninsula (Kruse et al. 2000b). Shrimp fisheries in the GOA peaked at 67,000 t in 1973, reached 59,000 t in 1977, and declined thereafter to the point where shrimp fishing is virtually nonexistent in the GOA today.

Regional fisheries follow the pattern seen for the GOA as a whole. The trawl fishery for northern shrimp *(Pandalus borealis)* in Lower Cook Inlet peaked at 2,800 t in 1980 to 1981 and was closed in 1987 to 1988. The fishery for northern and sidestriped shrimp (*P. dispar*) along the outer Kenai Peninsula peaked at 888 t in 1984 to 1985 and closed in 1997 to 1998. The pot fishery for spot (*P. platyceros*) and coonstriped shrimp (*P. hypsinotus*) in PWS increased rapidly after 1978 to its peak harvest of 132 t in 1986. This pot fishery then declined to its low of 8 t in 1991 and has been closed since 1992. The trawl shrimp fishery for northern shrimp in PWS peaked at 586 t in 1984 and switched to sidestriped shrimp in 1987. The PWS trawl fishery for sidestriped shrimp peaked at 89 t in 1992, and the northern shrimp catch was virtually zero at this time. The PWS catch of sidestriped shrimp in 1999 was 29 t and falling. The Kodiak trawl fishery for northern shrimp peaked at 37,265 t in 1971, and catch thereafter declined to 3 t in 1997 to 1998. In the Aleutian Islands, shrimp catches after the 1978 season declined precipitously, and the fishery has not rebounded since.

8.4 FORAGE SPECIES

8.4.1 Definition

Forage species in the GOA include a broad suite of species that are commonly consumed by higher trophic level species (fish, seabirds, and marine mammals). Specific species included in the forage species complex vary among authors and management agencies. The North Pacific Fishery Management Council (NPFMC) groundfish fisheries management plan defines the forage species complex as a group of species that includes the following (NMFS 2001):

- Smelts (capelin, rainbow smelt, eulachon, and family Osmeridae);

- Pacific sand lance (*Ammodytes hexapterus*);

- Lanternfishes (family Myctophidae);

- Deep sea smelts (family Bathylagidae);

- Pacific sandfish (*Trichodon trichodon*);

- Euphausiids (*Thysanopoda, Euphausia, Thysanoessa,* and *Stylocheiron*);

- Gunnels (family Pholidae);

- Pricklebacks (family Stichaeidae); and

- Bristlemouths, lightfishes, and anglemouths.

Springer and Speckman (1997) extend this definition to include juvenile stages of commercially exploited species such as Pacific herring (*Clupea pallasii*), walleye pollock (*Theragra chalcogramma*), and

Pacific salmon (*Oncorhynchus* sp.). This background review focuses on a subset of species that are commonly found in coastal or oceanic regions in the *Exxon Valdez* oil spill (EVOS) GOA region. In the shelf environment, this subset includes euphausiids, capelin, eulachon, sand lance, juvenile pollock, juvenile herring, and juvenile pink salmon (*Oncorhynchus gorbuscha*). In the offshore environment, this subset includes common myctophids, such as small-finned lanternfishes (*Stenobrachius leucopsarus* and *Diaphus theta*), and bathylagids, such as the northern smoothtongue (*Leuroglossus schmidti*).

A more complete description of the life history characteristics of forage species can be found in Hart (1973) and NMFS (2001). Table 8.5 summarizes key features of the life history characteristics.

8.4.2 Resource Exploitation

Small amounts of noncommercial forage species are taken as bycatch in federal and state fisheries in the GOA (NPFMC 2000, NMFS 2001). In an attempt to discourage the development of target fisheries for forage species, the NPFMC restricts the catch of forage species to no more than 2 percent of the total landed catch of commercial fisheries in federal waters (NMFS 2001). Although the bycatch of noncommercial forage species tends to be low relative to target fisheries for commercially exploited species, the percentage of the bycatch relative to regional abundances of individual forage species is often not known because of the difficulty involved in assessing these species.

Pacific salmon fisheries off the coast of Alaska are managed by a complex system of treaties, regulations, and international agreements. State and federal agencies cooperate in managing salmon resources. The State of Alaska regulates commercial fisheries for salmon within state waters where the majority of the catch occurs. Federal agencies control the bycatch of juvenile salmon in groundfish fisheries through prohibited-species bycatch restrictions (NMFS 2001). In the EVOS GOA region, pink salmon are primarily harvested by purse seines. Most of the pink salmon taken in PWS are of hatchery origin.

State and federal agencies also cooperate in managing Pacific herring fisheries. Most of the directed herring removals occur within state waters and are regulated by ADF&G. In federal waters, the removals of Pacific herring in groundfish fisheries are regulated through prohibited-species bycatch restrictions (NMFS 2001)

State and federal agencies regulate commercial removals of walleye pollock. The majority of the catch occurs in federal waters; however, small state fisheries have started in PWS. In federal waters, the catch is regulated by federal agencies based on recommended harvest regulations provided by the NPFMC. The catch of juvenile pollock is assessed within the stock assessment and fisheries evaluation (SAFE) reports. Juvenile pollock catch is included in considerations regarding annual quotas for this species. The lack of a market for juvenile pollock less than 30 cm in length serves as an incentive to industry to minimize the bycatch of juvenile pollock. Efforts to minimize bycatch of juvenile pollock in pollock target fisheries include the voluntary adoption of alternative mesh configurations designed to reduce the retention of small pollock (Erickson et al. 1999).

8.4.3 Assessment Methods and Challenges

There are several impediments to the development of forage species assessments. The diversity of life history characteristics confound efforts to develop a multipurpose survey to assess forage species as a single complex. In addition, several forage species are small and pelagic, making them less vulnerable to the standard trawl gear used in broad-scale surveys to assess stocks conducted by Alaska Department of Fish and Game or National Marine Fisheries Service. A high priority should be placed on research designed to overcome these impediments.

Several authors have reported on possible trends in forage species abundance in the shelf and offshore environment (Hay et al. 1997, Blackburn and Anderson 1997, Anderson and Piatt 1999, Beamish et al. 1999a). These papers rely on anecdotal information from surveys that were designed to assess the abundance of another species (such as shrimp, salmon, crab, or groundfish). Indices of abundance based on these data may be subject to error because of problems with the selectivity of the gear or the limited spatial or temporal scope of the surveys.

An assessment designed for forage species is needed to develop an accurate evaluation of the distribution and abundance of this important group of species. It is unlikely that a single survey would be adequate for all forage species; therefore, a variety of survey methods should be considered. Potential survey methods for forage species are identified in Table 8.6.

Table 8.5. Summary of Key Life History Characteristics of Selected Forage Species.

Characteristics	Euphausiids: 11 species	Capelin *Mallotus villosus*	Eulachon *Thaleichthys pacificus*	Pacific sand lance *Ammodytes hexapterus*	Walleye pollock *Theragra chalcogramma*	Pacific herring *Clupea pallasii*	Pink salmon *Oncorhynchus gorbuscha*	Northern lanternfish *Stenobrachius leucopsarus*
Maximum age (years)	2	4	5	3	21	18	2	6
Maximum length (centimeters)	4	25	25	15	80	45	65	9
Prey	plankti-vorous	plankti-vorous	plankti-vorous	plankti-vorous	plankton and fish	plankti-vorous	plankton and fish	plankti-vorous
Peak spawning	spring	spring	spring	winter	winter-spring	winter-spring	summer	unknown—winter?
Spawn location	unknown	intertidal	rivers early winter	late fall,	pelagic on shelf	nearshore	rivers	unknown
Abundance trend	unknown	low stable (uncertain)	low stable (uncertain)	unknown	low stable	low	high stable	unknown
Foraging habitat	pelagic—mid-water over shelf	pelagic—mid-water over shelf	pelagic—mid-water over shelf	demersal—0-100 m	mesopelagic—demersal and over shelf	pelagic shelf	pelagic shelf and open ocean	mesopelagic—outer shelf and open ocean

8.4.4 Hypotheses about Factors Influencing Food Production for Forage Fish Production

Several hypotheses (summarized below) have been advanced to explain trends in forage fish distribution and abundance. For the most part, these hypotheses are based on research in the shelf and coastal waters of the western central GOA ecosystem, including Prince William Sound. Detailed process-oriented research has been conducted to confirm hypotheses for a small number of forage species, although these studies were often conducted in a limited geographic area representing only a fraction of the range of the species.

1. *Feeding opportunities for early feeding larvae*: Shifts in large-scale atmospheric forcing controls the structure of marine fish communities in the western central GOA ecosystem through its role in determining the timing of peak production. Species that spawn in the winter and early spring will be favored by periods of early peak production, while species that spawn in the late spring and summer will be favored by periods of delayed production (Mackas et al. 1998, Anderson and Piatt 1999).

2. *Concentration of prey for early feeding larvae*: Ocean conditions that favor concentration of forage fish and their prey will enhance production of forage species. The FOCI program identified a potential mechanism linking increased precipitation to enhanced eddy formation and reduced larval mortality. Eddies are believed

to provide a favorable environment for pollock larvae by increasing the probability of encounters between larvae and their prey (Megrey et al. 1996). Research is needed to determine whether this mechanism may be important for other forage fishes within the western and central GOA.

3. *Prey dispersal for early feeding larvae*: An inverse or dome-shaped relationship exists between the amount of wind mixing and forage fish production. Bailey and Macklin (1995b) compared hatch date distributions of larval pollock with daily wind mixing. This analysis showed that first-feeding larvae exhibited higher survival during periods of low wind mixing. Megrey et al. (1996) speculated that extremes in wind mixing would result in reduced pollock survival because low wind mixing would reduce the availability of nutrients in the mixed layer and high wind mixing would lead to reduced encounters between pollock and their prey.

4. *Competition for prey*: At finer spatial scales, prey resources for forage fish may be limited, leading to resource partitioning to minimize competition between forage fish species that occupy similar habitats. Willette et al. (1997) examined the diets of juvenile walleye pollock, Pacific herring, pink salmon, and chum salmon in PWS. Their study revealed that two species pairs (walleye pollock and Pacific herring, and pink and chum salmon) exhibited a high degree of dietary overlap. This finding suggests that in PWS, competition for food resources may occur within these pairs when food abundance is limited.

Table 8.6. Potential Surveys for Assessment of Selected Forage Species.

Type	Candidate species
Small mesh mid-water surveys	Euphausiids, capelin, eulachon, juvenile pollock (age 0 and age 1), juvenile herring, small finned lanternfishes, northern smoothtongue
High-speed near-surface trawls	Juvenile salmon
Acoustic mid-water trawl surveys	Capelin, eulachon, juvenile pollock, juvenile herring, euphausiids
Small-mesh beach seines	Sand lance
Aerial spawning surveys	Pacific herring and capelin
Light detection and ranging (LIDAR)	Useful for species within the upper 50 m
Monitoring diets of key bird predators	Juvenile pollock, capelin, and sand lance

Purcell and Sturdevant (2001) found evidence of potential competition between zooplanktivorous jellyfish and juvenile fishes in PWS. Their study showed a high rate of diet overlap in the diets of pelagic coelenterates and forage species and that these species co-occur spatially and temporally in PWS.

5. *Prey utilization*: Overwintering mortality of forage species is dependent on the amount of energy accumulated during the summer. Field and laboratory experiments suggest that the overwintering success of both age-0 Pacific herring and age-0 walleye pollock may be dependent on the amount of energy accumulated during summer (Foy and Paul 1999, Sogard and Olla 2000). However, the early life history strategy of walleye pollock may make them less susceptible to starvation during the winter period. Paul and Paul (1999) compared the growth strategies of larval and age-0 walleye pollock and Pacific herring. This comparison revealed that walleye pollock metamorphose early, allowing for an extended growth period, while Pacific herring metamorphose later and accumulate energy for overwintering. Rapid growth provides increased swimming speed leading to more successful prey capture and predator avoidance. The benefits of the pollock strategy may allow them to continue to grow through the winter (Paul et al. 1998).

8.4.4.1 Food Quality

Efforts to improve understanding of the mechanisms underlying the production of forage species would benefit from an improved understanding of the principal prey utilized by forage species. Although detailed information exists for commercial species such as juvenile pollock, salmon, and herring (Cianelli and Brodeur 1997, Willette et al. 1997), only limited information is available to describe the prey preferences of many members of the forage fish complex. In particular, information is lacking in the case of offshore species.

8.4.5 Hypotheses about Predation on Forage Fish

By definition, forage species represent an important prey resource for many higher-trophic-level consumers (fish, seabirds, and marine mammals). Top-down predation pressure on forage fish depends on several factors, including predator abundance, the abundance of alternative prey, the density of prey, and the patchiness of prey. Changes in these factors will influence the relative importance of top trophic-level forcing on forage fish production.

Evidence suggests that in some years, fish predation may exhibit a measurable effect on forage species production in the EVOS GOA region. Anderson and Piatt (1999) noted that the post regime shift increase in gadoid and pleuronectid fishes coincided with marked declines in capelin and shrimp populations. They proposed that this inverse relationship could be caused by increased predation mortality due to an increase in piscivorous (fish-eating) species. Consistent with this hypothesis, Bailey (2000) performed a retrospective analysis of factors influencing juvenile pollock survival. He provided evidence that during the 1980s, pollock populations were largely influenced by environmental conditions, and after the mid-1980s, juvenile mortality was higher, resulting from the buildup of large fish predator populations. In PWS, Cooney (1993) speculated that pollock predation could explain some of the observed trends in juvenile salmon survival. He suggested that years of high copepod abundance were associated with high juvenile salmon survival, because pollock relied on an alternative prey resource. In the open ocean, Beamish et al. (1999a) proposed that mesopelagic fishes transfer and redistribute energy through two primary trophic pathways: (1) abundant zooplankton to *Stenobrachius leucopsarsus* and then squid, and (2) *Stenobrachius leucopsarsus*, *Diaphus theta,* and *Leuroglossus schmidti* to walleye pollock, salmon, dolphin, and whales. The division of energy through these pathways is thought to influence the amount of energy reaching the seafloor.

The importance of forage fish in seabird and marine mammal diets has been demonstrated by a number of authors (Hatch and Sanger 1992, Springer et al. 1996, Kuletz et al. 1997, Ostrand et al. 1998). There is little evidence that seabird predation is sufficient to regulate the production of forage fishes in the EVOS GOA region, however. Therefore, key research elements for predation of forage species by marine mammals and seabirds should focus on the role of oceanographic features in concentrating forage species within the foraging range of seabirds and marine mammals.

While only a few studies have examined the importance of gradients (fronts) or water mass characteristics in aggregating forage species for top predators in the EVOS GOA region, the importance of these features is well known in other regions. In the Atlantic, aggregations of capelin appear to be associated with strong thermal fronts (Marchland et al. 1999). Likewise, climate impacts on the distribution and productivity of Antarctic krill (*Euphausia superba*) have been shown to produce important

impacts on higher trophic level consumers (Loeb et al. 1997, Reid and Croxall 2001). Hay et al. (1997) found that, in warm years, eulachon off the coast of British Columbia were more abundant in the offshore environment, while in cool years, eulachon were more common in the nearshore environment. Consistent with the hypothesis of Hay et al. (1997), Carscadden and Nakashima (1997) noted a marked decline in offshore capelin abundance during a cool period in the 1990s in the Atlantic.

8.4.6 Hypotheses Concerning Contamination

Because of the broad distribution and abundance of contaminants, there is little evidence to suggest that contaminants regulate the production of forage species in Alaska waters. If forage species exhibit subpopulation genetic structure, contaminants could be influential in the local mortality rate of forage fish subpopulations. The small size, short life span, and importance as a prey item for higher trophic level foragers make forage species ideal indicators of regional contaminant levels (Yeardley 2000). For example, Roger et al. (1990) noted that the high lipid content of eulachons suggests that they may be potential integrators of low-level contaminants. If forage species are to be used as a regional indicator of ecosystem conditions, research is needed to determine whether forage species bioaccumulate toxic chemicals. Studies are needed to determine whether observed accumulations of toxic chemicals are sufficient to change the mortality rate of forage species. If forage species accumulate lethal levels of toxic chemicals at the regional level, genetic studies are needed to determine whether these populations represent genetically unique subpopulation segments.

CHAPTER 9

Marine Mammals
Lloyd Lowry and James Bodkin

9.1 CHARACTERISTICS OF GOA MARINE MAMMAL FAUNA

The Gulf of Alaska (GOA) has a mostly temperate marine mammal fauna. Calkins (1986a) provided the only previously published review of GOA marine mammals, and listed 26 species as occurring in the region. Five of those (pilot whale, Risso's dolphin, right whale dolphin, white-sided dolphin, and California sea lion) are primarily southern species that occur occasionally in Southeast Alaska but rarely, if at all, in the *Exxon Valdez* oil spill (EVOS) region. He also listed the Pacific walrus, which is a subarctic species that occurs in the GOA only as occasional wanderers.

Table 9.1 provides a summary of the general characteristics of twenty marine mammal species that occur regularly in the EVOS region, including seven baleen whales, eight toothed whales and porpoises, four pinnipeds, and the sea otter. Useful reviews of information on these species can be found in Calkins (1986a), Lentfer (1988), Perry et al. (1999), Forney et al. (2000), and Ferrero et al. (2000b). Various aspects of marine mammal biology are described in detail in Reynolds and Rommel (1999).

Most of the marine mammal species shown in Table 9.1 are widely distributed in the North Pacific Ocean, and the animals that inhabit the EVOS region represent only part of the total population. Application of modern molecular genetics techniques, however, has provided much new information on population structures (Dizon et al. 1997). Researchers have found that for species such as killer whales (Hoelzel et al. 1998), beluga whales (Bickham et al. 1996, O'Corry-Crowe and Lowry 1997), harbor seals (Westlake and O'Corry-Crowe 1997), and sea otters (Scribner et al. 1997), genetic exchange among adjacent and sometimes overlapping groups of animals is so low that they need to be managed as separate stocks.

Taxonomically the GOA marine mammal fauna are in four major groups:

- Mysticete cetaceans—baleen whales;

- Odontocete cetaceans—toothed whales;

- Pinnipeds—seals, sea lions, and fur seals; and

- Mustelids—sea otters.

The baleen whales are primarily summer seasonal visitors to the GOA that come to the continental shelf and offshore waters to feed on zooplankton and small schooling fishes (Calkins 1986a, Perry et al. 1999). Breeding and calving occur in more southerly, warmer regions. The GOA is primarily a migration route for the gray whale, which breeds and calves in Baja California, Mexico, and has its primary feeding grounds in the northern Bering and Chukchi seas (Jones et al. 1984).

The large species of baleen whales were all greatly reduced by commercial over-exploitation (Perry et al. 1999). Historical information on stock structure and abundance is very limited, and, partly because of their broad distributions, accurately assessing the current abundance and population trend is generally difficult (Ferrero et al. 2000b). Humpback whales and gray whales are exceptions to that generalization. For humpbacks, estimates of population size based on individual identifications from fluke photos (Calambokidis et al. 1997) suggest that the central North Pacific stock is increasing (Ferrero et al. 2000b). For many years, systematic counts have been made of gray whales migrating along the California coast, and results indicate that starting in the 1000s the population increased by 2.5 percent per year (Breiwick 1999). Analysis of recent data suggests that the population is now stable (Paul Wade, NMFS, pers. comm., 2004).

The situation with sperm whales is much like that of the large baleen whales. Many features of their basic biology, such as stock structure, distribution, migratory patterns, and feeding ecology, are poorly known. They occur throughout the North Pacific, mostly in deep water south of 50°N latitude, but some are seen in the northern GOA at least in summer (Calkins 1986a, Perry et al. 1999). From what is known of their diet, sperm whales eat mostly deepwater fishes and squids. North Pacific sperm whales were intensely

Table 9.1. **Summary of Characteristics of Marine Mammal Species That Occur Regularly in the Gulf of Alaska *Exxon Valdez* Oil Spill Area.**

Species	Use of Gulf of Alaska by species			Population status		Management classification		
	Residence	Habitats[1]	Activities[2]	Abundance[3]	Trend	EVOS	MMPA	ESA
Mysticetes								
Blue whale	seasonal	S, D	F	small?	unknown		depleted	endangered
Fin whale	seasonal	S, D	F	medium?	unknown		depleted	endangered
Sei whale	seasonal	S, D	F	medium?	unknown		depleted	endangered
Humpback whale	seasonal	C, S, D	F	medium	increasing		depleted	endangered
Gray whale	seasonal	C, S	M, F?	large	stable			
Right whale	seasonal	S	F	small	unknown		depleted	endangered
Minke whale	resident?	C, S	F, C, B?	medium?	unknown			
Odontocetes								
Sperm whale	seasonal?	S, D	F	large?	unknown		depleted	endangered
Killer whale	resident	C, S, D	F, C, B	small	unknown	damaged		
Beluga whale	resident	C, S	F, C, B	small	stable?		depleted	
Beaked whale[4]	resident?	S, D	F, C, B	unknown	unknown			
Dall's porpoise	resident	S, D	F, C, B	large	unknown			
Harbor porpoise	resident	C, S	F, C, B	large	unknown			
Pinnipeds								
Steller sea lion	resident	T, C, S, D	F, C, B	large	declining		depleted	endangered
Northern fur seal	seasonal	S, D	M, F	large	declining		depleted	
Harbor seal	resident	T, C, S	F, C, B	large	declining	damaged		
Elephant seal	seasonal	S, D	F	large	increasing			
Mustelids								
Sea otter	resident	T, C, S	F, C, B	large	unknown	damaged		

[1]T = terrestrial; C = coastal; S = continental shelf; D = deep water.

[2]F = feeding; M = migrating; C = calving/pupping; B = breeding.

[3]small = <1,000; medium = 1,000-10,000; large = >10,000.

[4]Probably includes at least 3 species: Baird's beaked whale, Cuvier's beaked whale, and Bering Sea beaked whale.

harvested, with more than 250,000 killed during 1947 to 1987 (Perry et al. 1999). Current abundance and population trends are unknown.

In contrast to the baleen whales and sperm whale, the smaller toothed whales are primarily resident in the GOA. Very little is known about the biology of beaked whales, but the other species have been relatively well studied. Two species, killer whales and beluga whales, have been selected as focal species for research and are discussed in detail in other sections. Harbor porpoises and Dall's porpoises both have relatively large populations, and with the exception of incidental take in commercial fisheries, they are unlikely to have been significantly impacted by human activities (Ferrero et al. 2000b). Both species feed on small fishes and squids, with Dall's porpoises using mostly continental shelf and slope areas and harbor porpoises most common in coastal and continental shelf waters (Calkins 1986a).

The two resident pinniped species, Steller sea lions and harbor seals, are both focal species for research and are discussed later in this chapter.

Northern fur seals pup and breed on islands in the Bering Sea (Pribilof Islands and Bogoslof Island). A portion of the population migrates through the EVOS region on its way to and from their rookeries. Adult fur seals may feed in the GOA during migration and winter months, and nonbreeding animals may feed in the area year-round. Small fishes and squids are the primary foods of fur seals (Calkins 1986b). Historically, northern fur seals were depleted by commercial harvests, but the population, while still depleted compared to its peak number, is now large, numbering nearly one million animals. Through 1998 the population was considered stable (Ferrero et al. 2000b) but beginning in 2000 pup counts have shown a declining trend (NMFS, National Marine Mammal Laboratory, unpubl. data). Northern elephant seals pup and breed at rookeries in California and Mexico. After breeding, adult males go to the GOA to feed on deepwater fishes and cephalopods (Stewart 1997). The northern elephant seal population was greatly depleted by harvesting, but it is currently large and growing (Forney et al. 2000). The sea otter is discussed later in this chapter.

As a group, marine mammals are managed and protected by domestic legislation and international treaties that generally do not apply to other marine species (Baur et al. 1999) (see Table 9.1). Early protective efforts were in response to the need to limit commercial harvests and to reduce their impacts on declining and depleted populations. The North Pacific Fur Seal Convention, agreed to in 1911, provided protection to both fur seals and sea otters. In 1946, the International Convention for the Regulation of Whaling began to manage harvests of large whales, and it provided progressive protection to stocks as they became over-exploited. The Endangered Species Act (ESA) provides protection to marine mammals (and other species) that may be in danger of extinction because of human activities. The ESA also allows protection of "critical habitat" needed by those species. All species of marine mammals are covered by the Marine Mammal Protection Act (MMPA), which became federal law in 1972. Primary objectives of the MMPA are to "maintain the health and stability of the marine ecosystem," and for each marine mammal species to "obtain an optimum sustainable population keeping in mind the carrying capacity of the habitat." Provisions of the MMPA put a moratorium on all "taking" of marine mammals, with exceptions allowed for subsistence hunting by Alaska Natives, scientific research, public display, commercial fishing, and certain other human activities, subject to restrictions and permitting. Species determined to be below their "optimum sustainable population" level, and those listed as threatened or endangered under provisions of the ESA, are listed as depleted under the MMPA and may be given additional protection. Certain species of marine mammals were determined to have been damaged by the EVOS, and therefore have been subjects of EVOS restoration activities.

Another unique aspect of marine mammal management is the strong involvement of Alaska Natives in the process. Alaska Natives have formed a number of groups that represent their interests in research, management, conservation, and traditional subsistence uses of marine mammals. Groups especially relevant to the EVOS GOA region include the Alaska Native Harbor Seal Commission (ANHSC), the Alaska Sea Otter and Steller Sea Lion Commission, and the Cook Inlet Marine Mammal Council. The ANHSC has been particularly active in the EVOS region, and has received funds from the Trustee Council to conduct a biosampling program in Prince William Sound (PWS) and the GOA, and to contribute information about the distribution, abundance, and health of seals. Congress has recognized the benefits of involving Alaska Natives in marine mammal

management, and has included provisions for co-management programs (Alaska Native organizations working as partners with federal management agencies) in the 1994 amendments to the MMPA.

As will be discussed in detail in the following sections, some marine mammal populations have declined in the GOA (and elsewhere in Alaska) in recent years. In general, the causes of those declines are unclear, but there has been speculation that they may be in some way related to the climate regime shift that occurred in the region. The evidence supporting such a connection is the temporal coincidence of the shift to a warmer regime, which happened in the mid-1970s, and the decline of harbor seals and Steller sea lions that has occurred in the 1970s through the 1990s. Others have argued that predation by killer whales has been a cause of some declines (NRC 2003, Springer et al. 2003).

The National Research Council (NRC) reviewed evidence for a linkage between climate and marine mammal declines as part of their effort to explain changes that have occurred in recent years in the Bering Sea (NRC 1996). They found data that showed some likely negative effects of cold weather on northern fur seal pups (Trites 1990) and a strong influence of warm El Niño conditions on California sea lions (Trillmich and Ono 1991). Because most GOA marine mammals have broad ranges that include waters much warmer than the GOA, it is unlikely that a warmer regime has had any direct negative effect on their reproduction or survival. The warmer conditions, however, have resulted in changes in fish and invertebrate populations (Anderson et al. 1997) that may in turn have affected the nutrition of harbor seals and Steller sea lions (Alaska Sea Grant 1993). The NRC concluded that food limitation was likely a factor in Bering Sea pinniped population declines, but that this was due to a complex suite of biological and physical interactions and not simply the regime shift (NRC 1996).

9.2 Focal Marine Mammal Species

9.2.1 Killer Whale

Killer whales are medium-sized, toothed whales. They are a cosmopolitan species generally found throughout the world's oceans, but are most common in colder nearshore waters (Heyning and Dahlheim 1988). Sightings in Alaska show a wide distribution, mostly on the continental shelf, but also offshore (Braham and Dahlheim 1982). Because there has been no real effort to track individual killer whales, the understanding of movements is based primarily on sightings of animals that can be identified by marks and pigmentation patterns (Bigg et al. 1987). The general pattern seems to be that some killer whales may stay in areas for several months while feeding on seasonally abundant prey, but long-distance movements are not uncommon (Ferrero et al. 2000b).

In the GOA, killer whales are seen frequently in Southeast Alaska and the area between PWS and Kodiak (Matkin and Saulitis 1994). Within the EVOS GOA region, whales are seen commonly in southwestern PWS, Kenai Fiords, and southern Resurrection Bay (Matkin et al. 2000). Whales move back and forth between these areas as well as to and from Southeast Alaska (Matkin et al. 1997). Sightings from the area around Kodiak suggest that killer whales are common, but there has been little study effort devoted to that region (Matkin and Saulitis 1994).

Killer whales have been studied in detail in easily accessible areas such as Washington state, British Columbia, Southeast Alaska, and PWS. Researchers have found that killer whales have a very complex social system and population structure. Studies of association patterns (Matkin et al. 1998), vocalizations (Ford 1991, Saulitis 1993), feeding behavior (Ford et al. 1998), and molecular genetics (Hoelzel et al. 1998, Barrett-Lennard 2000) have shown that there are two primary types of killer whales. The types are termed "transient" and "resident." A primary ecological difference between the two types is that residents eat fish, while transients mostly prey on other marine mammals (Ford et al. 1998). Within each of these general types, killer whales are divided into pods that may be composed of one or more matrilineal groups. In resident whales, the pods are very stable through time, with virtually no permanent exchange of individuals between pods, but new pods may be formed by splitting off of a maternal group. A third killer whale type called "offshore" has been encountered, but little is known about them (Ford et al. 1994).

What is known of the life history and biology of killer whales in Alaska was compiled by Matkin and Saulitis (1994). Both females and males are thought to become sexually mature at about fifteen years of age. Females may produce calves until they are about forty, at intervals of two to twelve years. Mating occurs mostly during May through October, and most births happen between fall and spring. Maximum longevity has been estimated to be 80 to 90 years for females and 50 to 60 years for males. Killer whales have no natural enemies, but in some

areas, local abundance and pod structure have been affected by human activities, including live captures for public display, interactions with commercial fisheries, and the EVOS (Olesiuk et al. 1990, Dahlheim and Matkin 1994, Matkin et al. 1994, Ferrero et al. 2000b, Forney et al. 2000). Normal birth and death rates for resident killer whales are about 2 percent per year (Olesiuk et al. 1990).

Surface observations and examination of stomach contents from stranded animals have shown that as a group killer whales eat a wide array of prey, including fishes, birds, and mammals (Matkin and Saulitis 1994). More detailed studies have documented considerable prey specialization in certain pods and individuals. Resident killer whales in PWS feed mostly on coho salmon during the summer (Matkin et al. 1997) and on chinook salmon in winter and spring (C. Matkin, North Gulf Oceanic Society, Homer, Alaska, pers. comm., 2000). Transient whales in the same area eat mostly harbor seals, Dall's porpoise, and harbor porpoise (Saulitis 1993, Matkin and Saulitis 1994). Some GOA transient killer whales occasionally eat Steller sea lions (Barrett-Lennard et al. 1995).

It is difficult to come up with meaningful population estimates for killer whales, partly because they may move over great distances and partly because some groups (such as the offshore type) and areas (such as the GOA west of Resurrection Bay) have been poorly studied. Ferrero et al. (2000b) gave a minimum estimate of 717 whales in the northern resident stock of the eastern North Pacific, and Forney et al. (2000) gave a minimum number of 376 for the transient stock of the eastern North Pacific. Reliable data on trend in abundance are not available for either stock. The most recent census (1999) indicates that there are 135 killer whales in the eight pods that regularly use the Kenai Fiords–PWS region (C. Matkin, pers. comm.).

Studies of killer whales in the PWS area began in the late 1970s (von Ziegesar et al. 1986, Leatherwood et al. 1990). Because killer whales were determined to have been damaged by the EVOS, killer whale studies were intensified during 1989 to 2000 (Matkin et al. 1994, 2000). Those long-term studies allow accurate determination of numbers, because all individuals in each pod are photo-identified nearly every year. Births and deaths of individual animals are monitored, which allows the calculation of reproductive and survival rates for each pod (Matkin and Saulitis 1994, Matkin et al. 2000).

Matkin et al. (1999) used association and genealogical data to organize the resident killer whales in the

Table 9.2. Number of Whales Photographically Identified in Killer Whale Pods in the Gulf of Alaska *Exxon Valdez* Oil Spill Area, 1984 to 2000.

Pod identifier	1984	1988	1990	2000
Resident Pods				
AB	35	36	23	25
AD05	13	11	12	13
AD16	6	5	5	6
AE	13	12	13	18
AI	6	6	6	6
AJ	25	26	28	36
AK	7	8	9	11
AN10	12	13	13	20
AN20[1]	23	26	29	1
Transient Groups				
AT	22	22	13	10

Source: Matkin et al. (2000) and C. Matkin, pers comm.
[1]The entire AN20 pod has not been photographed since 1991.

EVOS GOA area into nine pods. Data on the number of whales in each of those pods for the period from 1984 to 2000 are shown in Table 9.2. All resident pods with the exception of the AB pod have either increased or stayed the same since 1984. The number of whales in the AB pod decreased by 36 percent from 1988 to 1990 and has stayed about the same since. Since 1990, the recruitment rate for the AB pod has been similar to other resident pods, but the mortality rate has been more than twice as high (Matkin et al. 2000).

Less is known about transient killer whales, and their stock structure within the eastern North Pacific is less clear. Stock assessment reports have dealt with all transient whales that occur from Alaska to California as a single stock (Forney et al. 2000). Studies have shown, however, that two groups of whales that occur in the EVOS GOA region, called AT1 transients and GOA transients, are genetically and acoustically distinct from one another and from other west coast transients (Saulitis 1993, Barrett-Lennard 2000). GOA transients range widely, but are seen only occasionally in the PWS-Kenai Fiords area. The AT1 pod occurs in the PWS-Kenai Fiords area year-round (Saulitis 1993, Matkin et al. 2000). The number of whales in the AT1 pod has declined by more than 50 percent since 1988, with only ten individuals remaining in 2000 (Table 9.2).

The declines in the AB and AT1 killer whale pods are issues of major conservation concern. Thirteen whales, mostly juveniles and adult females, disap-

peared from the AB pod from March 1989 to June 1990, the highest mortality rate ever seen in a resident killer whale pod. Although twelve calves have been born in the AB pod since then, there is no clear trend toward recovery because an additional ten animals have died. For the AT1 transients, twelve whales have died since 1988 and no calves have been recruited to the group since 1984 (C. Matkin, pers. comm.)

The causes of the declines in these two killer whale pods are not entirely clear. Killer whales are only rarely caught incidental to commercial fishing operations (Ferrero et al. 2000b). In the mid-1980s, however, the AB pod was involved in a different type of interaction with the longline fisheries for sablefish and halibut (Matkin and Saulitis 1994). Whales removed hooked fish from the lines, and fishermen attempted to deter them by shooting at them and detonating explosives. A number of whales were seen with gunshot wounds, and some of those later disappeared. In spite of eight mortalities during the previous four years, the pod numbered thirty-six animals in 1988, one more than in 1984 (Matkin et al. 1994). In March to September 1989, members of the AB pod were several times seen swimming in oil from the EVOS. Although a direct cause-effect relationship cannot be shown, there is reason to believe that the population decline is in some way due to the spill (Dahlheim and Matkin 1994, Matkin et al. 1994). Members of the AT1 transient group were also seen in oil in summer 1989, and many members of the group were missing the following year and have not been seen since (Matkin et al. 1994, 2000). An additional concern related to the potential effects of contact with oil is the consumption of harbor seals, which AT1 transients feed on to a large extent (Saulitis 1993). Because many harbor seals were coated with oil by the spill (Lowry et al. 1994b), the whales may have ingested contaminated prey. In addition, the harbor seal population has decreased. Harbor seal numbers were declining in parts of PWS before 1989, an estimated 300 seals were killed by the spill, and the seal population has continued to decline at least through 1997 (Frost et al. 1994, 1999). Therefore, the lack of recruitment into the AT1 pod may be at least partly caused by the severe reduction of harbor seal numbers in the EVOS GOA region (Matkin et al. 2000).

Other than their general status under the MMPA, Alaskan killer whales have not been afforded any special legal protection. Although the AB pod is part of a larger resident population, the AT1 group is a distinct population that is demographically and genetically isolated from other known killer whales.

9.2.2 Beluga Whale

Belugas, also called white whales or belukhas, are medium-sized, toothed whales. They have a disjunct circumpolar distribution and occur principally in arctic and subarctic waters (O'Corry-Crowe and Lowry 1997). Recent studies have shown that belugas are separated into a number of discrete genetic groups (stocks), which generally correspond to groups of animals that summer in different regions (O'Corry-Crowe et al. 1997, Brown Gladden et al. 1999). Four relatively large stocks range throughout Western and Northern Alaska, and a small stock occurs in Cook Inlet and the GOA (O'Corry-Crowe and Lowry 1997).

In the GOA, belugas are seen most commonly in Cook Inlet, but sightings have been made near Kodiak Island, in PWS, and in Yakutat Bay (Laidre et al. 2000). The fact that there have been several reports of belugas in Yakutat Bay during 1976 to 1998 suggests the possibility of a small resident group there. The other sightings have most likely been of animals from the main Cook Inlet concentration.

Because summer surveys of belugas in Cook Inlet have been conducted at irregular intervals since the 1960s and annually since 1993, beluga distribution in that region is fairly well known (Klinkhart 1966, Calkins 1984, Rugh et al. 2000). Belugas may be found throughout Cook Inlet, and in midsummer they are always most common near the mouths of large rivers in Upper Cook Inlet, especially the Beluga River, the Susitna River, and Chickaloon Bay. Other areas where they commonly have been seen include Turnagain Arm, Knik Arm, Kachemak Bay, Redoubt Bay, and Trading Bay. Rugh et al. (2000) compared the distribution of June and July sightings made in the 1990s with earlier years. They found that the proportion of sightings in Upper Cook Inlet has increased greatly in the last decade, and they conclude that the number of sightings in Lower Cook Inlet and in offshore waters has declined during those years.

In February-March 1997, aerial surveys were conducted with the specific goal of gathering information on winter distribution of the Cook Inlet beluga stock (Hansen and Hubbard 1999). The area surveyed included Cook Inlet and parts of the GOA between Kodiak Island and Yakutat Bay. Almost all beluga sightings (150 out of 160) were in the middle part of Cook Inlet, and the remaining sightings were in Yakutat Bay.

Since 1999, the National Marine Fisheries Service (NMFS) National Marine Mammal Laboratory (NMML) has gathered data on Cook Inlet beluga distribution and movements through use of satellite-linked tags. In 1999, one whale that was tagged and tracked for 110 days (from May 31 to September 17) stayed in Upper Cook Inlet (Ferrero et al. 2000a). To try to obtain information on winter distribution, two tags were attached to whales on September 13, 2000. The whales were tracked until mid-January. During that time, they moved around quite a bit in Upper Cook Inlet, but did not go south of Kalgin Island (NMML unpubl. data at http://nmml.afsc.noaa. gov/CetaceanAssessment/BelugaTagging/2000_Folder/2000_beluga_whale_tagging.htm, also 1999 and 2001 studies available by substituting year).

In many parts of Alaska, including Cook Inlet, belugas are most common in nearshore waters during the summer (Calkins 1986a, Frost and Lowry 1990). Proposed reasons for the use of nearshore habitats include the possible advantage of warm protected waters for newborn calves (Sergeant and Brodie 1969), facilitation of the epidermal molt by freshwater and rubbing on gravel (St. Aubin et al. 1990, Smith et al. 1992), and feeding on seasonally abundant coastal and anadromous fishes (Seaman et al. 1985, Frost and Lowry 1990). Although there have been no direct studies of the diet of Cook Inlet beluga whales, at least part of the reason for their congregating nearshore and near river mouths must be to feed on abundant fishes such as salmon and eulachon (Calkins 1984, Moore et al. 2000).

No life history information has been collected from Cook Inlet belugas. Biological characteristics of belugas in other areas were reported by Hazard (1988). Females become sexually mature at four to seven years of age and males at seven to nine years. Mature females give birth to calves every two to three years, mostly in late spring or summer. The maximum life span has not been well defined, but is likely to be about forty years. In the southern part of their range, belugas are preyed upon by killer whales, and in more northern areas by polar bears.

Beluga whales are difficult to enumerate for a number of reasons. Principal problems are that whales are easy to miss in muddy water or when whitecaps are present, and in all conditions some fraction of the population will be underwater where they cannot be seen. Early survey efforts largely ignored these problems and just reported the number of animals counted, which during the 1960s to 1980s was usually a few hundred. In 1994 the NMFS NMML began to produce annual estimates of population size with standardized aerial surveys of the entire Cook Inlet and a sophisticated set of methods to correct for whales that were missed by observers (R.C. Hobbs, NMFS NMML, pers. comm., 2004; Rugh et al. 2000; Hobbs et al. 2000). For each survey, they reported the number of whales counted and an estimate of the total population size (Table 9.3). Unfortunately because of problems inherent in counting whales from the air, the annual estimates are imprecise and have a relatively large coefficient of variation. Nonetheless, these data show that from 1994 to 1998 the population declined by about 45 percent and that since then it has probably been stable at about 350 animals.

Available data suggest that beluga whales in Cook Inlet rarely become entangled in fishing gear (Ferrero et al. 2000b). The largest source of mortality in recent years has been hunting by Alaska Natives. Although harvest data are imprecise, estimates of the annual number of whales killed during 1993 to 1998 ranged from 21 to 123 animals (Ferrero et al. 2000, Mahoney and Shelden 2000). This compares to a likely sustainable harvest of about twenty whales from a population of 500.

Because of the population decline and the potential for continued overharvest, several environmental groups and one individual submitted a petition to NMFS in March 1999 requesting that the Cook Inlet beluga whale be listed as an endangered species under the Endangered Species Act. Responding to the same problems, Senator Ted Stevens inserted language into federal legislation passed in May 1999 that prohibited any hunting of beluga whales by Alaska Natives, unless they had entered into a co-management agreement with NMFS to regulate the hunt. In May 2000, NMFS finalized a designation of depletion under provisions of the MMPA for the Cook Inlet beluga population, and in June 2000, the agency determined that a listing under the ESA was not warranted. There was no legal harvest of Cook Inlet belugas in either 1999 or 2000. Under terms of co-management agreements between NMFS and Alaska Native organizations, one beluga was harvested each year in 2001, 2002, and 2003.

Although overharvest by Alaska Natives in the 1990s appears to be sufficient to explain the population decline, concerns that this small isolated population may be vulnerable to other threats remain. Areas of concern that have been identified include commercial fishing, oil and gas development, municipal discharges, noise from aircraft and ships, shipping traffic, and tourism (Moore et al. 2000). The fact that the population has shown no signs of recovery after 5 years of very small harvests

Table 9.3. Counts and Population Estimates for Cook Inlet Beluga Whales, 1994 to 2003.

Year	Whale count	Abundance estimate	Coefficient of variation
1994	281	653	0.43
1995	324	491	0.44
1996	307	594	0.28
1997	264	440	0.14
1998	193	347	0.29
1999	217	367	0.14
2000	184	435	0.23
2001	211	386	0.09
2002	192	313	0.12
2003	174	357	0.11

Sources: Hobbs et al. (2000) and R.C. Hobbs and D. Rugh, NMFS NMML, pers. comm., 2004.

heightens concern that other factors are limiting population growth.

9.2.3 Steller Sea Lion

Steller sea lions are the largest species of otariid (eared seal). They are distributed around the North Pacific rim from northern Japan, the Kuril Islands and Okhotsk Sea, through the Aleutian Islands and Bering Sea, along the southern coast of Alaska, and south to California (Kenyon and Rice 1961; Loughlin et al. 1984,1992). Most large rookeries are in the GOA and Aleutian Islands. The northernmost rookery, Seal Rocks, is in the EVOS region at the entrance to PWS. Currently the largest rookery is on Lowrie Island, in the Forrester Island complex in southern Southeast Alaska.

Steller sea lions are listed as two distinct population segments under the Endangered Species Act: an eastern population that includes all animals east of Cape Suckling, Alaska, and a western population that includes all animals at and west of Cape Suckling. This distinction is based mostly on results from mitochondrial DNA genetic studies that found a distinct break in the distribution of haplotypes between locations sampled in the western part of the range and eastern locations, indicating restricted gene flow between two populations (Bickham et al. 1996, 1998). Information on distribution, population response, and phenotypic characteristics, also support the concept of two Steller sea lion stocks (Loughlin 1997).

Most adult Steller sea lions occupy rookeries during the pupping and breeding season, which extends from late May to early July (Pitcher and Calkins 1981, Gisiner 1985). Some juveniles and nonbreeding adults may summer at or near the rookeries, but most use other locations as haul-outs. During fall and winter, sea lions may be at rookery and haul-out sites that are used during the summer, and they also are seen at other locations. They do not make regular migrations, but do move considerable distances. When they reach adulthood, females generally return to the rookeries of their birth to pup and breed (Kenyon and Rice 1961, Calkins and Pitcher 1982, Loughlin et al. 1984).

Steller sea lions use a number of marine and terrestrial habitats. Adults congregate for pupping and breeding on rookeries that are usually on sand, gravel, cobble, boulder, or bedrock beaches of relatively remote islands. Haul-outs are sites used by adult sea lions during times other than the breeding season, and by nonbreeding adults and subadults throughout the year. Haul-outs may be at sites also used as rookeries, or on other rocks, reefs, beaches, jetties, breakwaters, navigational aids, floating docks, and sea ice. With the exception of sea ice, sites used for rookeries and haul-outs are traditional and the specific locations used vary little from year to year. Factors that influence the suitability of a particular area are poorly understood (Sandegren 1970, Gentry 1971, Calkins and Pitcher 1982).

When not on land, Steller sea lions are seen near shore and out to the edge of the continental shelf; in the GOA, they commonly occur near the 200 m depth contour (Kajimura and Loughlin 1988). Studies using satellite-linked telemetry have provided detailed information on at-sea movements (Merrick and Loughlin 1997). Adult females tagged at rookeries in the central GOA and Aleutian Islands in summer made short trips to sea and generally stayed on the continental shelf. In winter, adult females ranged more widely with some moving to seamounts far offshore. Pups tracked during the winter made relatively short trips to sea, but one moved 320 km from the eastern Aleutians to the Pribilof Islands.

Female Steller sea lions reach sexual maturity at three to six years of age and most breed annually during June and July (Pitcher and Calkins 1981). Males reach sexual maturity at three to seven years of age and physical maturity by age ten; they establish territories on rookeries during the breeding season, and one male may breed with several females (Thorsteinson and Lensink 1962, Sandegren 1970, Gentry 1971, Gisiner 1985). Territorial males fast for long

periods during the pupping and breeding season. Pups are born on land, normally in late May to June, and they stay on land for about two weeks, then spend an increasing amount of time in intertidal areas and swimming near shore. After giving birth, sea lion mothers attend pups constantly for about ten days, then alternate trips to sea for feeding with returns to the rookery to suckle their pup. Unlike most pinnipeds, for which weaning is predictable and abrupt, Steller sea lions may continue to nurse until they are up to three years old (Sandegren 1970, Gentry 1971, Calkins and Pitcher 1982).

Steller sea lions die from a number of causes, including disease, predation, shooting by humans, and entanglement in fishing nets or debris (Merrick et al. 1987). In addition, pups may die from drowning, starvation caused by separation from the mother, crushing by larger animals, and biting by females other than the mother (Orr and Poulter 1967, Edie 1977).

Steller sea lions are generalist predators that mostly eat a variety of fishes and invertebrates (Pitcher 1981). Seals, sea otters, and birds are also occasionally eaten (Gentry and Johnson 1981, Pitcher and Fay 1982, O'Daniel and Schneeweis 1992). Much effort has been devoted to describing the diet of sea lions in the GOA. In the mid-1970s and mid-1980s, the primary food found in sea lion stomachs was walleye pollock. Octopus, squid, herring, Pacific cod, flatfishes, capelin, and sand lance also were consumed frequently (Pitcher 1981, Calkins and Goodwin 1988). In the 1970s, walleye pollock was the most important prey in all seasons, except summer when small forage fishes (capelin, herring, and sand lance) were eaten more frequently (Merrick and Calkins 1996). Results from examination of scats collected on rookeries and haul-outs in the GOA in the 1990s confirmed that pollock has been overall the dominant prey, with Pacific cod and salmon also important in some months (Merrick et al. 1997). The diet of juvenile Steller sea lions has not been studied in detail, but it is known that they eat somewhat smaller pollock than do adults (Frost and Lowry 1986, Calkins 1998). Available data suggest that the average daily food requirement for sea lions is on the order of 5 percent to 8 percent of their body weight per day (Kastelein et al. 1990, Rosen and Trites 2000).

Satellite-linked tags attached to sea lions have provided information on the amount of time spent diving and diving depths (Merrick and Loughlin 1997). Adult females in winter spent the most time feeding and dove the deepest, and young of the year spent relatively little time diving to shallow depths. As young of the year matured, foraging effort increased from November to May.

The abundance of Steller sea lions in the western population has decreased greatly since the 1960s, to the extent that the species has been listed as endangered under the ESA. From the mid-late 1970s through 2000, index counts of adults and juveniles for the western population as a whole declined by 83 percent from 109,880 to 18,193 (Crane and Galasso 1999). Declines in the eastern GOA (Seal Rocks to Outer Island) and central GOA (Sugarloaf Island to Chowiet Island) have been of a generally similar magnitude (73 percent and 87 percent), but it appears that the decline in the eastern GOA began later than in the western GOA and other regions (Sease and Loughlin 1999, Crane and Galasso 1999) (Table 9.4). Counts of pups on rookeries have shown similar declines. Modeling and tagging studies have suggested that the proximate cause of the population decline is probably a reduction in survival of juvenile animals (York 1994, Chumbley et al. 1997). Birth rates are also comparatively low (Calkins and Goodwin 1988), which could be a contributing factor. Population viability analysis suggests that if the decline continues at its current rate some rookeries will go extinct in the next forty to fifty years, and the entire western population could be extinct within 100 to 120 years (York et al. 1996).

The multiple factors that have been suggested to affect abundance of the western Steller sea lion population in the past three to four decades (Merrick et al. 1987, NRC 2003) are represented by six related hypotheses displayed on a National Marine Fisheries Service Web page on December 27, 2001:

Brief Characterization of the Principal Hypotheses Surrounding the Steller Sea Lion Decline, http://www.fakr.noaa.gov/omi/grants/sslri/hypothesis.htm

1. *Fisheries Competition.* Commercial fisheries potentially cause or contribute to nutritional stress in the western stock of Steller sea lions by reducing either the abundance of prey at scales relevant to foraging sea lions or by disturbing prey patches so as to reduce their availability. In turn, nutritional stress is manifested in the population as increased mortality or lowered reproductive output.

2. *Environmental Change.* Environmental conditions in areas inhabited by Steller sea lions may have changed since the 1970s in ways that reduced the availability of prey for Steller sea lions and precipitated nutritional stress. The changes may have either reduced the abundance of important prey items or altered their distributions.

3. *Predation.* Predation of Steller sea lions by killer whales and sharks has increased as a function of (a) their increased population size, (b) their increased per

Table 9.4. Index Counts of Steller Sea Lions in the Eastern Gulf of Alaska (Seal Rocks to Outer Island) and Western Gulf of Alaska (Sugarloaf Island to Chowiet Island).

Survey Year	Eastern GOA	Central GOA	Western stock total
1976	7,053	24,678	109,8801
1985	–	19,002	–
1989	7,241	8,552	–
1990	5,444	7,050	30,525
1991	4,596	6,273	29,418
1992	3,738	5,721	27,286
1994	3,369	4,520	24,119
1996	2,133	3,915	22,223
1997	–	3,352	–
1998	–	3,346	20,201
1999	1,952	–	–
2000	1,894	3,177	18,193

Sources: Sease and Loughlin (1999) and NMFS (2000).

capita consumption, or (c) remained constant over time, but with increasing effects as the Steller sea lion population has diminished over time.

4. *Anthropogenic Effects.* One or more sources of anthropogenic activity, including incidental mortality (e.g. entanglement), direct mortality (e.g. shooting), commercial harvesting, subsistence harvesting, and harassment have contributed to the decline in the Steller sea lion population. Such effects would include both those over the past decades since the decline began and those which may be ongoing.

5. *Disease.* The Steller sea lion population is being reduced by diseases which may result in mortality or reduced reproductive output.

6. *Contaminants.* Contaminants from either local or distant sources have had detrimental physical impacts on Steller sea lions leading to increased mortality or reduced reproductive output.

Available data permit no definitive evaluation of any of these hypotheses at present. Loughlin (1998) concluded that there was no evidence that patterns of predation, disease, or environmental contaminants have changed sufficiently to have caused such a major decrease in abundance. In the past, many sea lions were killed in commercial harvests, by incidental entanglement in nets, and by shooting to reduce damage to fishing gear and fish depredation (Alverson 1992). That mortality may have played some part in the early stages of the decline, but such killing has been eliminated or greatly reduced and cannot explain the widespread, continuing decline.

Subsistence hunting by Alaska Natives occurs at low levels and is not judged to be an important factor overall (Ferrero et al. 2000b). One explanation for the decline is that sea lions, especially juveniles, are experiencing higher than normal mortality because they are nutritionally limited (Loughlin 1998, Crane and Galasso 1999). The nutritional limitation could be caused by environmental changes that have affected sea lion prey species, competition for prey with commercial fisheries, or some combination of the two. However, NRC (2003) concluded that at the present time nutritional stress is unlikely to be a major factor and that top-down processes, i.e., predation, appear more likely to be limiting recovery.

The decline of the western population of Steller sea lions, and the need to recover the population and protect critical habitat as required by the ESA, have been a major conservation issue in recent years (Lowry et al. 1989, Fritz et al. 1995). Actions proposed to facilitate recovery may have substantial effects on commercial fisheries and coastal communities in the GOA and elsewhere (Crane and Galasso 1999). Major research efforts have been generously funded (fiscal year 2001 $43 million, fiscal year 2002 $40 million, fiscal year 2003 $60 million) by the federal government.

9.2.4 Pacific Harbor Seal

Harbor seals are medium-sized, "earless" seals that are widespread in temperate waters of both the North Atlantic and the North Pacific. In the North Pacific, their distribution is nearly continuous from Baja California, Mexico, to the GOA and Bering Sea, through the Aleutian Islands, and to eastern Russia and northern Japan (Shaughnessy and Fay 1977, Hoover-Miller 1994).

Harbor seals are found primarily in the coastal zone where they feed and haul out to rest, give birth, care for their young, and molt. Haul-out sites include intertidal reefs, rocky shores, mud and sand bars, gravel and sand beaches, and floating glacial ice (Hoover-Miller 1994). From the results of satellite tagging studies in PWS, most adult harbor seals are known to use the same few haul-outs for most of the year (Frost et al. 1996, 1997).

Although it is relatively easy to study harbor seals while they are on haul-outs, their distribution and movements at sea are not as well understood. During 1992 to 1997, as part of Exxon Valdez oil spill restoration studies, satellite-linked depth recorders (SDRs) were attached to seals in Prince William Sound to study their at-sea behavior. Analysis of the tracking data from 49 subadult and adult harbor seals indicated that most tagged seals stayed in or near PWS, but some subadults moved 300 to 500 km east and west in the GOA (Frost et al. 2001, Lowry et al. 2001). Virtually all relocations were on the continental shelf in water less than 200 m deep. Most feeding trips for adults went 10 km or less from haul-outs, and juveniles fed mostly within 25 km. Patterns of diving (effort and depth) varied geographically and seasonally. During 1997 to 1999, SDRs were attached to 27 recently weaned harbor seal pups in PWS. Preliminary analysis of those data (Frost et al. 1998; L. Lowry and K. Frost Alaska Department of Fish and Game/University of Alaska Fairbanks, Fairbanks, unpubl. data) did not show any extraordinary movement patterns.

SDRs have also been attached to harbor seals in Southeast Alaska and the Kodiak region. Preliminary results from those tagging efforts have been reported in Small et al. (1997, 1998). The data are currently being analyzed and prepared for publication (R. Small, Alaska Dept. of Fish and Game, Juneau, pers. comm., 2001).

Overall, harbor seals are relatively sedentary and they show considerable fidelity to haul-out sites (Pitcher and McAllister 1981; Frost et al. 1996, 1997). For management purposes, the National Marine Fisheries Service (NMFS) has delineated three harbor seal stocks in Alaska:

1. The Southeast Alaska stock, including animals east and south of Cape Suckling;

2. The GOA stock, including animals from Cape Suckling to Unimak Pass and westward through the Aleutian Islands; and

3. The Bering Sea stock including animals in Bristol Bay and the Pribilof Islands (Ferrero et al. 2000b).

During the past several years, an in-depth study of Alaska harbor seal genetics has been conducted by the NMFS Southwest Fisheries Science Center. Preliminary analysis of those data indicate a number of relatively small population units with very limited dispersal among them (O'Corry-Crowe et al. 2003). Results suggest that within the EVOS area, multiple harbor seal stocks may require individual management attention. NMFS scientists are currently analyzing the molecular genetics data and preparing it for publication. NMFS managers are evaluating those results with the intention of refining stock boundaries for Alaska harbor seals.

Hoover-Miller (1994) summarized available information on Alaska harbor seal biology and life history. Both male and female harbor seals reach sexual maturity at three to seven years old. Adult females give birth to single pups once a year, on land or on glacial ice. In PWS and the GOA, most pupping occurs from mid-May through June. Newborn harbor seal pups are born with their eyes open, with an adult-like coat, and are immediately able to swim. Pups are weaned when they are three to six weeks old. Once each year in July to September, harbor seals shed their old hair and grow a new coat. During this time, the seals spend more time hauled out than they do at other times. For that reason, the molt period is a good time to count seals to estimate population sizes and trends.

Most information about the diet of harbor seals in Prince William Sound and the GOA was collected in the mid-1970s by examination of stomach contents (Pitcher 1980). The major prey overall in both PWS and adjacent parts of the GOA was pollock. Octopus, capelin, Pacific cod, and herring also are eaten frequently. Stomachs of young seals contained mostly pollock, capelin, eulachon, and herring. As part of EVOS restoration studies, blubber samples from PWS harbor seals have been analyzed for their fatty acid composition to examine their recent diets (Iverson et al. 1997; L. Lowry and K. Frost, Alaska Department of Fish and Game/University of Alaska Fairbanks, Fairbanks, unpubl. data). Initial results showed that herring, pollock, other fishes, and cephalopods (a class of squid and octopi) had been eaten. Seals sampled at the same haul-out had similar fatty acid compositions, suggesting that they had fed locally on similar prey. In contrast, seals sampled from areas as little as 80 km apart had different fatty acid compositions, indicating substantially different diets. Small et al. (1999) have examined scats from harbor seals collected near Kodiak and found mostly remains of sculpins, greenling, sand lance, and pollock.

Known predators of harbor seals include killer whales, Steller sea lions, and sharks. The impact of these predators on harbor seal populations is unknown, but may be significant. In PWS alone, killer whales may eat as many as 400 harbor seals per year (C. Matkin, North Gulf Oceanic Society, Homer, Alaska, pers. comm., 2000). The incidence of sleeper sharks caught on halibut longlines in the GOA has increased greatly in the last decade (L. Lowry and K. Frost, unpubl. data). The degree to which these sharks prey on harbor seals is unknown, but seal remains have been observed in their stomachs (C. Matkin, pers. comm.).

Before the Marine Mammal Protection Act (MMPA) was enacted, harbor seals were hunted commercially in Alaska, and they also were killed to reduce their predation on commercially important fishes (Hoover-Miller 1994). Such kills, which exceeded 10,000 animals in many years, were largely stopped in 1972. The MMPA allowed fishermen to shoot seals if they were damaging their gear or catch and could not be deterred by other means. A few hundred animals probably were killed annually for that reason during 1973 to 1993. In 1994, the MMPA was amended to require that fishermen use only nonlethal means to keep marine mammals away from their gear.

Harbor seals have been and continue to be an important food and handicraft resource for Alaska Native subsistence hunters in PWS and the GOA. The ADF&G Subsistence Division estimated the size of the harbor seal harvest annually during 1992 to 1998. The average annual kill during that period was approximately 380 seals in PWS and 360 for the Kodiak area, Cook Inlet-Kenai, and the south Alaska Peninsula combined (Wolfe and Hutchinson-Scarbrough 1999). About 88 percent of the seals shot were retrieved, and 12 percent were struck and lost. Although harvests at individual villages have varied from year to year, regional harvest levels have shown no clear trend.

Harbor seals are sometimes entangled and killed in the gear set by several commercial fisheries that operate in the EVOS GOA region. Ferrero et al. (2000b) estimated an average minimum annual mortality of 36 animals for the GOA stock. This figure was an underestimate because there have not been observer programs for several of the fisheries that are likely to interact with harbor seals.

Some harbor seals were killed by the EVOS, at least in PWS (Frost et al. 1994b). In August and September 1989, ADF&G flew aerial surveys of harbor seals in oiled and unoiled areas of central and eastern PWS. Results of those surveys were compared to earlier surveys of the same haul-outs conducted in 1983, 1984, and 1988. Before the EVOS, counts in oiled and unoiled areas of PWS were declining at a similar rate, about 12 percent per year. From 1988 to 1989, however, there was a 43 percent decline in counts of seals at oiled sites compared to 11 percent at unoiled sites. Other studies conducted as part of the EVOS damage assessment program showed that seals in oiled areas became coated with oil (Lowry et al. 1994). Many oiled seals acted sick and lethargic for the first few months after the spill. Tests of bile and tissues showed that oiled seals were metabolizing petroleum compounds (Frost et al. 1994b). Microscopic examination indicated that some oiled seals had brain damage that would likely have interfered with important functions such as breathing, swimming, diving, and feeding (Spraker et al. 1994). It was estimated that approximately 300 seals died because of the EVOS (Frost et al. 1994b). Hoover-Miller et al. (2000) disputed the mortality estimate of Frost et al. (1994b), but they admit that the spill had effects on harbor seals and do not provide an alternative estimate of mortality.

Harbor seals are one of the most common marine mammals in the EVOS GOA region. In 1973, ADF&G estimated there were about 125,000 in this region based on harvest data, observed densities of seals, and the amount of available habitat (Pitcher 1984). The most recent population estimate for the GOA harbor seal stock, derived from intensive aerial surveys conducted by NMFS, is 29,175 (Ferrero et al. 2000b). Although the methods used to derive the two estimates were very different and they are not directly comparable, the difference does suggest that a large decline in harbor seal numbers has occurred in the GOA.

Counts at individual haul-outs and along survey routes established to monitor trends confirm the decline and provide some information on the temporal pattern of changes (Table 9.5). At Tugidak Island (south of Kodiak Island), average molt period counts declined by 85 percent from 1976 to 1988 (Pitcher 1990), followed by a period of stabilization and then a modest population increase in recent years. In eastern and central PWS, the number of seals at 25 trend index sites declined by 42 percent between 1984 and 1988 (Pitcher 1989). Trend counts at index sites have shown that the decline in that part of PWS continued at least through 1997, by which time there were 63 percent fewer seals than in 1984 (Frost et al. 1999). Counts on the PWS trend route were fairly similar in 1996-2002 (Table 9.5), suggesting that the decline in that area may have slowed down or stopped. In the Kodiak trend area, harbor seal counts increased steadily during 1993-2002.

Mortality of harbor seals caused by people because of fishery interactions, the EVOS, and hunting has been fairly well documented. Each of these causes may be a contributing factor, but it seems unlikely that they could have caused such a widespread and major population decline. Other factors that could be involved in the decline include disease, food limitation, predation, contaminants, and changes in habitat availability. No strong scientific evidence has been produced, however,

Table 9.5. Counts of Harbor Seals at Index Sites in the *Exxon Valdez* Oil Spill Gulf of Alaska Area.

Year	Tugidak Island	PWS	Kodiak
1976	5,708	–	–
1977	4,618	–	–
1978	3,781	–	–
1979	3,133	–	–
1982	1,918	–	–
1984	1,469	2,488	–
1986	1,181	–	–
1988	966	1,875	–
1989	–	1,423	–
1990	882	1,058	–
1991	–	978	–
1992	820	995	–
1993	723	825	3,096
1994	800	981	3,478
1995	827	885	4,024
1996	698	791	3,415
1997	589	751	3,880
1998	852	760	4,369
1999	860	812	4,890
2000	562	651	5,066
2001	1,032	599	5,392
2002	1,182	722	5,930

Sources: Pitcher (1990), Frost et al. (1994b); G. Pendleton, pers. comm., 2004.
Figures shown for Tugidak are unadjusted mean survey counts of the southwest beach haul-outs. PWS and Kodiak counts have been adjusted to account for important covariates (Frost et al. 1999, G. Pendleton, unpubl. data).

to suggest that any of these factors has been a primary cause (Sease 1992, Hoover-Miller 1994). A Leslie matrix model for population projection showed that large changes in vital parameters (reproduction and survival) must have occurred to cause the declines in abundance seen in PWS during 1984 to 1989, and that changes in juvenile survival are likely to have the greatest effect on population growth (Frost et al. 1996).

The large decrease in harbor seal abundance in the GOA has been a major concern among scientists, resource managers, Alaska Natives, and the public. After completion of damage assessment, the Trustee Council funded restoration studies to learn about the biology and ecology of harbor seals in the spill area, and to investigate possible causes for the decline (Frost and Lowry 1994; Frost et al. 1995, 1996, 1997, 1998, 1999). At about the same time, Congress began providing funds to ADF&G to be used to investigate causes of the Alaskan harbor seal decline. Those funds were used to initiate harbor seal research programs in Southeast Alaska and the Kodiak area, and to resume long-term studies on Tugidak Island (Lewis 1996, Small et al. 1997, Small 1998, Small et al. 1999, Small and Pendleton 2001). A major part of all those studies has been live-capturing seals and attaching satellite-linked depth recorders (SDRs) to them to learn about their movements, foraging patterns, and behavior on land and at sea. As part of the field studies, researchers have weighed and measured each seal, and have taken samples for studies of blood chemistry, disease, genetics, and diet. Some parts of those studies have been completed and published, some are in the analysis and reporting stage, and others are ongoing. As discussed above, the results have added greatly to the understanding of harbor seals in this area and will continue to do so as more of the work is completed.

Any time a wildlife population declines, it is a cause for concern. For harbor seals in PWS and the GOA, however, the concern is magnified because the causes for the decline are unknown and because these seals are an important food and cultural resource of Alaska Natives. In addition, the results of genetics studies are showing very limited dispersal between seals in adjacent areas, suggesting that harbor seals should be managed as a number of relatively small units. So far GOA harbor seals have not been listed as depleted under the MMPA or as threatened or endangered under the ESA. The listing status could change if recovery doesn't happen in some genetically discrete population units.

Harbor seals may have great value as an indicator species of environmental conditions in the EVOS GOA region. They are important in the food web, both as upper level predators on commercially exploited fishes and other fishes and invertebrates, and also as a food resource for killer whales and Alaska Native hunters. Because they are non-migratory and have low dispersal rates, changes in their abundance and behavior should be reflective of changes in local environmental conditions in the areas they inhabit. Further, they are relatively easy to study, and during the past 30 years a considerable amount of baseline data has been collected on their abundance, distribution, and other aspects of their biology and ecology.

9.2.5 Sea Otter

Sea otters are the only completely marine species of the aquatic Lutrinae, or otter subfamily, of the family Mustelidae. They occur only in coastal waters around the North Pacific rim, from central Baja California, Mexico, to the northern islands of Japan.

The northern distribution of sea otters is limited by the southern extent of winter sea ice that limits access to foraging habitat (Kenyon 1969, Riedman and Estes 1990). Southern range limits are less well understood, but are likely related to reduced marine productivity at lower latitudes, increasing water temperatures, and thermoregulatory constraints imposed by the sea otter's dense fur.

Three subspecies of sea otters are recognized: *Enhydra lutris lutris* from Asia to the Commander Islands of Russia, *Enhydra lutris kenyoni* from the western Aleutians to northern California, and *Enhydra lutris nereis*, south of the Oregon (Wilson et al. 1991). The subspecific taxonomy suggested by morphological analyses is largely supported by subsequent molecular genetic data (Cronin et al. 1996, Scribner et al. 1997). The distribution of mitochondrial DNA haplotypes suggests little or no recent female-mediated gene flow among populations. Populations separated by large geographic distances, however, share some haplotypes (for example, in the Kuril and Kodiak islands), suggestive of common ancestry and some level of historical gene flow. The differences in genetic markers among contemporary sea otter populations likely reflect the following:

- Periods of habitat fragmentation and consolidation during Pleistocene glacial advance and retreat;

- Some effect of reproductive isolation over large spatial scale; and

- The recent history of harvest-related reductions and subsequent recolonization (Cronin et al. 1996, Scribner et al. 1997).

Sea otters occupy and use only coastal marine habitats. The seaward limit of their feeding habitat, which is about the 100 m depth contour, is defined by their ability to dive to the seafloor. Although sea otters may be found at the surface in deeper water, either resting or swimming, they must maintain relatively frequent access to shallower depths where they can feed. In PWS, 98 percent of the sea otters are found in water with depths less than 200 m and sea otter abundance is inversely correlated with water depth, with about 80 percent of the animals observed in water less than 40 m deep (Bodkin and Udevitz 1999). Sea otters forage in diverse bottom types, from fine mud and sand to rocky reefs. Although they may haul out on intertidal or supratidal shores, no aspect of their life history requires leaving the ocean. Where present, surface-canopy kelps provide preferred resting habitat. In areas lacking kelp canopies, sea otters rest in groups or alone in open water, but may select areas protected from large waves where available. Sea otters generally feed alone and often rest in groups of ten or fewer, but also occur in groups numbering in the hundreds (Riedman and Estes 1990).

Relatively few data are available to describe relations between sea otter densities and habitat characteristics. Maximum sea otter densities of about twelve per square kilometer (km^{-2}) have been reported from the Aleutian and Commander islands (Kenyon 1969, Bodkin et al. 2000) where habitats are largely rocky. Maximum densities in Orca Inlet of PWS, a shallow soft-sediment habitat, are about 16 km^{-2}. Equilibrium, or sustainable densities, likely vary among habitats, with reported values of about 5 to 8 km^{-2}. In PWS, sea otter densities vary among areas, averaging about 1.5 km^{-2} and ranging from fewer than one to about 6 km^{-2} (Bodkin and Udevitz 1999; U.S. Geological Survey, Anchorage, Alaska, unpubl. data).

The sea otter is the largest mustelid, with males considerably larger than females. Adult males attain weights of 45 kg and total lengths of 148 cm. Adult females attain weights of 36 kg and total lengths of 140 cm. At birth, pups weigh about 1.7 to 2.3 kg and are about 60 cm in total length.

Adult male sea otters gain access to estrous females by establishing and maintaining territories from which other males are excluded (Kenyon 1969, Garshelis et al. 1984, Jameson 1989). Male territories vary in size from about 20 to 80 hectares. Territories may be located in or adjacent to female resting or feeding areas or along travel corridors between those areas, and are occupied continuously or intermittently through time (Loughlin 1981, Garshelis et al. 1984, Jameson 1989). Female sea otters attain sexual maturity as early as age 2, and by age 3 most females are sexually mature. Where food resources may be limiting population growth, sexual maturation may be delayed to four to five years of age.

Adult female reproductive rates range from 0.80 to 0.94 (Siniff and Ralls 1991, Bodkin et al. 1993, Jameson and Johnson 1993, Riedman et al. 1994, Monson and DeGange 1995, Monson et al. 2000a). Among areas where sea otter reproduction has been studied, reproductive rates appear to be similar despite differences in resource availability. Although copulation and subsequent pupping can take place at any time of year, there appears to be a positive relation between increasing latitude and reproductive synchrony. In California, pupping is weakly synchronous to nearly uniform across months; while

in PWS, a distinct peak in pupping occurs in late spring.

Reproductive output remains relatively constant across a broad range of ecological conditions, and pup survival appears to be influenced by resource availability, primarily food. At Amchitka Island, a population at or near equilibrium density, dependent pup survival ranged from 22 percent to 40 percent, compared to nearly 85 percent at Kodiak Island, where food was not limiting and the population was increasing (Monson et al. 2000a). Post-weaning annual survival is variable among populations and years, ranging from 18 percent to nearly 60 percent (Monson et al. 2000a). Factors affecting survival of young sea otters, rather than reproductive rates, may be important in ultimately regulating sea otter population size. Survival of sea otters more than two years of age is generally high, approaching 90 percent, but gradually declines through time (Bodkin and Jameson 1991, Monson et al. 2000a). Most mortality, other than human related, occurs during late winter and spring (Kenyon 1969, Bodkin and Jameson 1991, Bodkin et al. 2000). Maximum ages, based on tooth annuli, are about 22 years for females and 15 years for males.

Although the sex ratio before birth (fetal sex ratio) is one to one (Kenyon 1982, Bodkin et al. 1993), sea otter populations generally consist of more females than males. Age-specific survival of sea otters is generally lower among males (Kenyon 1969, Kenyon 1982, Siniff and Ralls 1991, Monson and DeGange 1995, Bodkin et al. 2000), resulting in a female-biased adult population

The sea otter relies on air trapped in the fur for insulation and an elevated metabolic rate to generate internal body heat. To maintain the elevated metabolic rate, energy intake must be high, requiring consumption of prey equal to about 20 percent to 33 percent of their body weight per day (Kenyon 1969, Costa 1982).

The sea otter is a generalist predator, known to consume more than 150 different prey species (Kenyon 1969, Riedman and Estes 1990, Estes and Bodkin 2001). With few exceptions, their prey generally consist of sessile or slow moving benthic invertebrates such as mollusks, crustaceans, and echinoderms. Preferred foraging habitat is generally in depths less than 40 m (Riedman and Estes 1990), although studies in Southeast Alaska have found that some animals forage mostly at depths from 40 to 80 m (Bodkin et al. 2004). A sea otter may forage several times daily, with feeding bouts averaging about three hours, separated by periods of rest that also average about three hours. Generally, the amount of time a sea otter allocates toward foraging is positively related to sea otter density and inversely related to prey availability. Time spent foraging may be a meaningful measure of sea otter population status (Estes et al. 1982, Garshelis et al. 1986).

Although the sea otter is known to prey on a large number of species, only a few tend to predominate in the diet, depending on location, habitat type, season, length of occupation, and the individual sea otter (Estes et al. 2003). The predominately soft-sediment habitats of Southeast Alaska, PWS, and Kodiak Island support populations of clams that are the primary prey of sea otters. Throughout most of Southeast Alaska, burrowing bivalve clams (species of *Saxidomus*, *Protothaca*, *Macoma*, and *Mya*) predominate in the sea otter's diet (Kvitek et al. 1993). They account for more than 50 percent of the identified prey, although urchins (*S. droebachiensis*) and mussels (*Modiolis modiolis*, *Musculus* spp.) can also be important. In PWS and at Kodiak Island, clams account for 34 percent to 100 percent of the otter's prey (Calkins 1978, Doroff and Bodkin 1994, Doroff and DeGange 1994). Mussels (*Mytilus trossulus*) apparently become more important as the length of occupation by sea otters increases, ranging from 0 percent at newly occupied sites at Kodiak to 22 percent in long-occupied areas (Doroff and DeGange 1994). Crabs (*Cancer magister*) were once important sea otter prey in eastern PWS, but apparently have been depleted by otter foraging and are no longer eaten in large numbers (Garshelis et al. 1986). Sea urchins are minor components of the sea otter diet in PWS and the Kodiak archipelago. In contrast, the sea otter diet in the Aleutian, Commander, and Kuril islands is dominated by sea urchins and a variety of finfish (including hexagrammids, gadids, cottids, perciformes, cyclopterids, and scorpaenids) (Kenyon 1969, Estes et al. 1982). Sea urchins tend to dominate the diet of low-density sea otter populations, whereas fishes are consumed in populations near equilibrium density (Estes et al. 1982). For unknown reasons, sea otters in regions east of the Aleutian Islands rarely consume fish.

Sea otters also exploit episodically abundant prey such as squid (*Loligo* spp.) and pelagic red crabs (*Pleuroncodes planipes*) in California and smooth lumpsuckers (*Aptocyclus ventricosus)* in the Aleutian Islands. On occasion, sea otters attack and consume seabirds, including teal (*Anas crecca*), scoters (*Melanitta perspicillata*), loons (*Gavia immer*), gulls (*Larus* spp.), grebes (*Aechmophorus occidentalis*),

and cormorants (*Phalacrocorax* spp.) (Kenyon 1969, Riedman and Estes 1990).

Sea otters are known for the effects their foraging has on the structure and function of nearshore marine communities. They provide an important example of the ecological "keystone species" concept (Power et al. 1996). In the absence of sea otter foraging during the twentieth century, populations of several species of urchins (*Strongylocentrotus* spp.) became extremely abundant. Grazing activities of urchins effectively limited kelp populations, resulting in deforested areas known as "urchin barrens" (Lawrence 1975, Estes and Harrold 1988). Because sea urchins are a preferred prey item, as otters recovered they dramatically reduced the sizes and densities of urchins, as well as other prey such as mussels, *Mytilus* spp. Released from the effects of urchin-related herbivory, populations of macroalgae responded, resulting in diverse and abundant populations of understory and canopy-forming kelp forests. Although other factors, both non-living (abiotic) and living (biotic), can also limit sea urchin populations (Foster and Schiel 1988, Foster 1990), the generality of the sea otter effect in reducing urchins and increasing kelp forests is widely recognized (reviewed in Estes and Duggins 1995). Further cascading effects of sea otters in coastal rocky subtidal communities may stem from the proliferation of kelp forests. Following sea otter recovery, kelp forests provide food and habitat for other species, including finfish (Simenstad et al. 1978, Ebeling and Laur 1998), which provide forage for other fishes, birds, and mammals. Furthermore, where present, kelps provide the primary source of organic carbon to the nearshore marine community (Duggins et al. 1989).

Effects of sea otter foraging are also documented in rocky intertidal and soft-sediment marine communities. The size-class distribution of mussels was strongly skewed toward animals with shell lengths smaller than 40 mm where otters were present; however, mussels with shell lengths larger than 40 mm comprised a large component of the population where sea otters were absent (VanBlaricom 1988). In soft-sediment coastal communities, sea otters forage on epifauna (crustaceans, echinoderms, and mollusks) and infauna (primarily clams). They generally select the largest individuals. These foraging characteristics cause declines in prey abundance and reductions in size-class distributions, although the deepest burrowing clams (such as *Tresus nuttallii* and *Panopea generosa*) may attain refuge from some sea otter predation (Kvitek and Oliver 1988, Kvitek et al.

1992). Community level responses to reoccupation by sea otters are much less studied in soft-sediment habitats that dominate much of the North Pacific, and additional research is needed in this area.

A century ago, sea otters were nearly extinct, having been reduced from several hundred thousand individuals, by a multinational commercial fur harvest. They persisted largely because they became so rare that, despite exhaustive efforts, they were only seldom found (Lensink 1962). Probably less than a few dozen individuals remained in each of thirteen remote populations scattered between California and Russia (Kenyon 1969, Bodkin and Udevitz 1999). By about 1950, it was clear that several of those isolated populations were recovering. Today, about 90,000 sea otters occur throughout much of their historic range (Table 9.6), although suitable unoccupied habitat remains in Asia and North America (Bodkin 2003).

Trends in sea otter populations today vary widely from rapidly increasing in Canada, Washington, and Southeast Alaska, to stable or changing slightly in PWS, the Commander Islands, and California, to declining rapidly throughout the entire Aleutian archipelago (Estes et al. 1998, Estes and Bodkin 2001). Rapidly increasing population sizes are easily explained by abundant food and space resources, and increases are anticipated until those resources become limiting. Relatively stable populations can be generally characterized by food limitation and birth rates that approximate death rates. The recent large-scale declines in the Aleutian archipelago are unprecedented in recent times and demonstrate complex relations between coastal and oceanic marine ecosystems (Estes et al. 1998). The magnitude and geographic extent of the Aleutian decline into the GOA are unknown, but the PWS population appears relatively stable. The view of sea otter populations has been largely influenced by events in the past century when food and space were generally unlimited. As food and space become limiting, however, it is likely that other mechanisms, such as predation, contamination, human take, or disease will play increasingly important roles in structuring sea otter populations.

A number of predators include sea otters in their diet, most notably the white shark (*Carcharadon charcharias*) and the killer whale (*Orcinus orca*). Bald eagles (*Haliaeetus leucocephalus*) may be a significant source of very young pup mortality. Terrestrial predators, including wolves (*Canis lupus*), bears (*Ursus arctos*), and wolverine (*Gulo gulo*) may kill sea otters when they come ashore, although such instances are likely rare. Before the work of Estes et al. (1998) predation was thought to play a minor role in regulating sea otters (Kenyon 1969).

Pathological disorders related to enteritis and pneumonia are common among beach-cast carcasses and may be related to inadequate food resources, although such mortalities generally coincide with late winter periods of inclement weather (Kenyon 1969, Bodkin and Jameson 1991, Bodkin et al. 2000). Nonlethal gastrointestinal parasites are common, and lethal infestations are occasionally observed. Among older animals, tooth wear can lead to abscesses and systemic infection, eventually contributing to death.

Contaminants are of increasing concern in the conservation and management of sea otter populations throughout the North Pacific. Concentrations of organochlorines, similar to levels causing reproductive failure in captive mink (*Mustela vison*), occurred in the Aleutian Islands and California, whereas otters from Southeast Alaska were relatively uncontaminated (Estes et al. 1997, Bacon et al. 1998). Elevated levels of butyltin residues and organochlorine compounds have been associated with sea otter mortality caused by infectious disease in California (Kannan et al. 1998, Nakata et al. 1998). Changes in stable lead isotope compositions from pre-industrial and modern sea otters in the Aleutians reflect changes in the sources of lead in coastal marine food webs. In pre-industrial samples, lead was from natural deposits; in contemporary sea otters, lead is primarily from Asian and North American industrial sources (Smith et al. 1990).

Susceptibility of sea otters to oil spills, largely because of the reliance on their fur for thermoregulation, has long been recognized (Kenyon 1969, Siniff et al. 1982) and this was confirmed by EVOS. Accurate estimates of acute mortality resulting from EVOS are not available, but nearly 1,000 sea otter carcasses were recovered in the months following the spill (Ballachey et al. 1994). Estimates of carcass recovery rates ranged from 20 percent to 59 percent (DeGange et al. 1994, Garshelis 1997), indicating mortality of up to several thousand animals (Ballachey et al. 1994). Sea otter mortality in areas where oil deposition was heaviest and persistent was nearly complete, and through at least 1997, sea otter numbers had not completely recovered in those heavily oiled areas (Bodkin and Udevitz 1994, Dean et al. 2000). Long-term effects include reduced sea otter survival for at least a decade following the spill (Monson et al. 2000b), likely a result of sublethal oiling in 1989, chronic exposure to residual oil in the years following

Table 9.6.   Recent Counts or Estimates of Sea Otter (*Enhydra lutris*) Abundance in the North Pacific.

Subspecies	Area	Year	Number	Status
E.l. lutris	Russia	1995-1997	17,000	Stable in Kurils and Commander Islands, increasing in Kamchatka
E.l. kenyoni	Alaska, USA	1994-2002	70,700	Declining in Aleutians, uncertain in GOA, and increasing in Southeast
	British Columbia, Canada	1998	2,500	Increasing
	Washington, USA	1997	500	Increasing
E.l. nereis	California, USA	2003	2,500	Uncertain
Total			93,200	

Source: Bodkin (2003).

the spill, and spill-related effects on invertebrate prey populations (Ballachey et al. 1994, Fukuyama et al. 2000, Peterson 2001). As human populations increase, exposure to acute and chronic environmental contaminants will likely increase. Improved understanding of the effects of contaminants on keystone species, such as sea otters, may be valuable in understanding how and why ecosystems change.

Human activities contribute to sea otter mortality throughout the Pacific Rim. Incidental mortality occurs in the course of several commercial fisheries. In California, an estimated annual take of eighty sea otters in gill and trammel nets, out of a population numbering about 2,000, likely contributed to a lack of population growth during the 1980s (Wendell et al. 1986). Developing fisheries and changing fishing techniques continue to present potential problems to recovering sea otter populations. In Alaska, sea otters are taken incidentally in gillnet, seine, and crab trap fisheries throughout the state, but total mortality has not been estimated (Rotterman and Simon-Jackson 1988). Alaska Natives are permitted to harvest sea otters for subsistence and handicraft purposes. The harvest is largely unregulated and exceeded 1,200 in 1993, with most of that from a few, relatively small areas. In addition, an illegal harvest of unknown magnitude continues throughout much of the geographic range of sea otters.

Sea otters occupy an important and well documented position as an upper-level predator in nearshore communities of the North Pacific. In contrast to most marine mammals that are part of a plankton and fish trophic web, sea otters rely almost exclusively on nearshore benthic invertebrates, which are supported at least in part by the kelps and other algae present in shallow benthic habitats.

Relatively little work has been conducted in investigating relations between those physical and biological attributes that contribute to variation in productivity of nearshore marine invertebrates, such as the clams, mussels, and crabs that sea otters consume, and how that variability in productivity translates into variation in annual sea otter survival. Given the observed variation in sea otter survival, and the recognized role of food in regulating sea otter populations, understanding these relations would provide some empirical measure of the relative contributions of predation and primary production as controlling factors in structuring nearshore marine communities. Due to the small size of their home ranges, sea otters integrate physical and biological attributes of the ecosystem over small spatial scales. Further, both sea otters and their prey occur nearshore, allowing accurate and efficient monitoring of sea otters, their prey, and physical and biological ecosystem attributes. This suite of factors offers a strong foundation for understanding mechanisms, and interactions among factors that regulate long-lived mammalian populations. Given that many populations of large carnivorous mammals are severely depleted worldwide, such an understanding would likely be broadly applicable to conservation and management.

CHAPTER 10

Economics of Human Uses and Activities in the Northern Gulf of Alaska

James Richardson and Gregg Erickson

10.1 INTRODUCTION

Human uses have likely affected the productivity of Gulf of Alaska (GOA) marine and surrounding terrestrial environments during the 4,000 or more years of human presence in the GOA region.

Trends since the 1989 *Exxon Valdez* oil spill suggest that the pace of change in human-caused effects may have accelerated. The spill itself changed attitudes toward acceptable risks of human-caused disruption, while economic trends have brought about more intense use of some resources and diminishing use of others. Understanding these trends will sharpen strategies for long-term monitoring and extend our understanding of how human uses may affect ecosystem productivity.

In the period before contact with Europeans, Kodiak, Prince William Sound, and most other areas affected by the oil spill were populated by Alutiiq peoples, linguistically related to the Yupik Eskimos of the Bering Sea coast and the Aleut cultures of the western Alaska Peninsula and Aleutian Islands. All of these cultures were "ocean-facing," deriving most of their livelihood from the sea, with relatively little economic dependence on upland resources (Dumond 1983).

The cultural values and economic systems of these communities appear to have been very stable. The central role of marine mammal and fish resources in the Alutiiq subsistence economies profoundly influenced the social organization of pre-contact societies and shaped their spiritual and cultural values. In the face of environmental variability, rituals and other cultural observances focused on assuring predictable marine resource abundance. Failure of a prime resource such as a salmon run could threaten the extinction of an entire community.

While the Alutiiq had highly developed technologies for exploiting fishery resources with minimum expenditures of time and labor, strongly conservative values and attitudes toward environmental change

and resource use tended to limit overharvesting. Property rights to resources such as salmon streams or sea otter hunting areas were vested in clans and villages, who were responsible for stewardship of the resource and its spiritual embodiments (Cooley 1963). Elements of these values remain strong in some GOA communities.

Notwithstanding the high value attributed to environmental stability and sustainability, human activity was a significant factor in pre-contact changes in resource abundance in other parts of the Pacific littoral (Jackson et al. 2001). Human-caused effects might have extended to the salmon resources exploited by the Alutiiq. And certainly sea otters were extirpated from the interior waters of Prince William Sound before the arrival of Europeans in the middle of the eighteenth century (Lensink 1964, Simenstad et al. 1978).

The hundred years following contact brought an end to the relative cultural and economic stability. European traders and fur hunters possessed weapon technologies and an organizational infrastructure that allowed them to quickly dominate the small, fragmented Alutiiq communities. Europeans also brought upland-facing cultural attitudes that reflected diminished concern for the sustainability and stability of ocean resources. Whatever constraints against overexploitation may have been afforded by the sophisticated system of Alutiiq property rights and clan-based institutional systems, all were quickly brushed aside. For resources that attracted European commercial attention, the results were invariably disastrous.

The sea otter was the first resource to attract commercial attention. Though the trade in pelts was fabulously profitable at the outset, the resource base that made the trade possible quickly shrunk in the face of unremitting harvest pressure to supply Asian and European markets. By the time of the transfer of Alaska to the United States, only remnant populations remained (Rogers 1962).

Improved transportation and food preservation technologies in the late nineteenth century opened the region's salmon resources to markets thousands to tens of thousands of kilometers distant. Canned salmon production grew from 1.3 million cases in 1900 to a peak of 8.5 million in 1936, and then collapsed from overexploitation to 1.6 million cases in 1959, the year Alaska became a state. Not until the late 1970s did the institutional development of fishery entry limitations make it possible to meet the biological requirements of sustained salmon harvests without dissipating most of the potential economic gains in excess costs.

Despite its long and rich history of human occupation and use, the GOA marine environment remains relatively unsullied, at least in the popular understanding. The closing years of the twentieth century saw significant declines in commercial fishing, marine transportation of oil, and logging. Subsistence use of GOA resources partially rebounded after the 1989 oil spill, while tourism and recreational uses of the GOA resources and environment grew.

Many of the benefits of the GOA environment are largely non-market, non-use, existence values with heavy emphasis on the future. Future existence of endangered populations of wild salmon stocks, future protection of charismatic megafauna such as killer whales and sea otters, and the global marine commons are examples (Brown 2000). Contingent valuation studies conducted in 1990 provided an immediate post-spill benchmark of the economic existence value of GOA resources directly affected by the oil spill (NOAA 1993). No follow-up work has been done to confirm subsequent changes in GOA existence values. Other economic studies, however, suggest that the public continues to assign high values to the existence of healthy environments, and apply increasingly sophisticated and stringent criteria for evaluating environmental health, particularly in relation to environments viewed as relatively pristine (Whitehead and Hoban 1999). The mission of sustaining a healthy ecosystem and its focus on long- term monitoring have been shaped by the need for a long-term understanding of how human activity shapes the environment, and how human- and non-human-caused environmental change can be distinguished.

10.2 SOCIOECONOMIC PROFILE OF THE REGION

The bulk of the land area draining into the *Exxon Valdez* oil spill–affected parts of the GOA is found in five boroughs (a county-level governmental unit unique to Alaska), a portion of a sixth borough, and one unorganized census area. According to the 2000 census, just under 400,000 people, 63 percent of Alaska's population, live in this physiographic GOA region; about 71,000 of those people live in the Prince William Sound, lower Cook Inlet, Kodiak Island, and Alaska Peninsula areas that were directly affected by the oil spill. Two to three times that number use the area seasonally for work and recreation. An estimated 700,000 out-of-state tourists visit the region each year (ADCED 2002, Northern Economics Inc. 2002). Although this area is larger in geographic scope than the EVOS GOA region, it reflects the scope of the potential human impacts on the region.

The GOA region has grown rapidly throughout the twentieth century, but that growth has recently decelerated. During the 1990s, the population grew by 19 percent and non-agricultural jobs by 26 percent, the slowest decadal rates since the 1930s (G.J. Williams, Alaska Dept. of Labor, Juneau, pers. comm., 2000).

Most growth in the 1990s has occurred in three urbanized areas: Anchorage, the bedroom communities of the southern Matanuska and Susitna valleys, and the urbanized west-central Kenai Peninsula around the cities of Kenai and Soldotna. In the remainder of the region, including almost all the areas immediately impacted by the spill, growth has been slower. Table 10.1 shows how boundaries of the overall region and the subregion directly affected by the spill are defined. During the 1990s, the population in the directly affected subregion grew by seven percent, less than half as fast as the population of the GOA region as a whole. The 2000 census found 35,470 people residing in the directly affected subregion (U.S. Bureau of the Census 2001).

Migration to and from the GOA region has been highly volatile. High wages and low unemployment in Alaska relative to the Pacific Northwest have generally stimulated net immigration to the region, while the reverse condition has led to a net population exodus. Over the last half century economic cycles in Alaska have tended to be out of phase with those in the Pacific Northwest, amplifying the migratory swings.

Demographic data for the 1989-1999 interval and preliminary information for 1999-2000 suggest that the 1990s were the first decade since the 1930s in which newcomers to Alaska failed to replace all of those who left. The GOA region is likely to have experienced similar net outmigration over the decade of the 1990s (G.J. Williams, pers. comm., 2002).

Table 10.1. Representation of Boroughs and Census Areas in Gulf of Alaska and Oil Spill Regions.

Borough or census area	GOA economic region	Oil spill region
Anchorage Borough	All	None
Aleutians East Borough	All	None
Kenai Peninsula Borough	All	South and southeast portion: Homer, Seldovia, Port Graham, Seward
Kodiak Island Borough	All	All
Lake and Peninsula Borough	Southern portion only: Chignik, Chignik Lagoon, Chignik Lake, Ivanof Bay, Perryville	Southern portion only: Chignik, Chignik Lagoon, Chignik Lake, Ivanof Bay, Perryville
Matanuska-Susitna Borough	All	None
Valdez-Cordova Census Area	All	Prince William Sound and Cordova census subareas

The major reason for the recent net outmigration was the attraction created by the fast-growing economy in the Pacific Northwest and the rest of the nation, and the relatively torpid rate of economic growth in Alaska.

Over the long term, net migration has been less important to Alaska population growth than the state's chronic excess of births over deaths. Average annual net migration in the twenty years between 1979 and 1999 was +1,487 persons, while the average excess of births over deaths during the same period was +8,928 (G.J. Williams, pers. comm., 2000).

This persistent excess has been a consequence of three longstanding features of the state's demographics—fertility rates well above the national averages in all racial groups, an unusually large percentage of residents of child-bearing age, and an unusually small share of the population in the older age groups where natural mortality is highest.

As is described in subsequent sections, commercial fishing, marine transportation of oil, and the wood products industries in the GOA region have all declined in recent years, while tourism and recreation-related industries have grown, as has federal spending. Money transfers to households have also grown, most notably from the state's permanent fund dividend, an annual payment to all residents from earnings on the state's $25 billion oil-money savings account (U.S. Bureau of Economic Analysis 2002). Deepening of local economies through support sector growth also has played a role, with Alaska

businesses and households now buying more goods and services locally and importing fewer goods and services from outside the state. Continuation of these trends would suggest a continuation of slow economic and population growth (Goldsmith 2001).

The fundamentals of Alaska's economy are likely to remain rooted for some time in the state's natural resources, including the indirect effects of oil revenue recycled through state government. As the world's population grows, the demand for access to Alaska's scenic beauty and open spaces of the state is likely to increase as well. Beyond the economic effects of increased tourism, the intangible quality of Alaska as a place of wilderness, beauty, and a special way of life will continue to attract migrants to the last frontier, increasing pressures of human uses and activities on the GOA environment.

10.2.1 Prince William Sound–Southeast Kenai

The Prince William Sound–Southeast Kenai (PWS-SEK) region is a coastal belt extending from the mouth of the Copper River on the east, in an arc around Prince William Sound, southwest along the GOA coast, and around the southern tip of the Kenai Peninsula to just past Port Graham and Nanwalek. It includes numerous offshore islands. The region is mountainous throughout, and three of its four largest communities are located at the heads of deep fiords. All of the PWS-SEK region is within the Chugach or Kenai mountains, and the region's boundaries are roughly the same as those of the

Chugach Regional Native Corporation. Most of its land area is in or adjacent to the Chugach National Forest.

Between 1990 and 2000, the population of the PWS-SEK region grew less than six percent, well below the rates in the GOA region or the state. In 2000, 12,211 people lived in PWS-SEK, 80 percent of whom live in seven communities. The three largest communities—Cordova (population 2,454), greater Seward (3,430), and Valdez (4,036)—are predominantly non-Native, although Valdez and Cordova are home to Alaska Native village corporations and tribes. Of the five other communities, Chenega Bay (86), Port Graham (171), Nanwalek (177), and Tatitlek (107) are Alaska Native villages, and Whittier (182) is mostly non-Native (U.S. Bureau of the Census 2001).

Of the seven communities, only Valdez, Whittier, and Seward have highway access to the state's main road system. Whittier and Seward have Alaska Railroad passenger and freight service. Cordova, Valdez, Whittier, Tatitlek, Chenega Bay, and Seward are served by the Alaska Marine Highway System. Except for Valdez, all of the communities grew during the 1990s, although at rates well below the average of the state or GOA region. The population of Valdez declined by one percent.

The economic base of the seven communities in PWS-SEK is almost entirely resource dependent (Fried and Windisch-Cole 1999a). The Cordova economy is based on commercial fishing, primarily for pink and red salmon. Recent declines in the value of landings have been a hardship to the community and to the Prince William Sound Aquaculture Corporation that operates hatcheries in the sound. Some biologists have expressed concern that the 600 million or more smolt that hatcheries annually release into the sound and adjacent waters have had a deleterious effect on wild salmon (Hilborn 1992).

In recent years formerly important herring fisheries have been closed due to inadequate stocks. However, Cordova has recently benefited from an increase in small-scale tourism, and some cruise ships have visited the port, but the community remains in economic distress.

Valdez, as the terminus of the trans-Alaska pipeline, depends on the oil industry, but did not suffer seriously from the downsizing that occurred in the industry during the 1990s. This is due to additional labor required in Valdez to implement safety and pollution prevention measures adopted in the wake of the 1989 spill. The state's official oil production forecast suggests that crude shipments will roughly maintain their current level over the next decade.

Notwithstanding its dependence on oil, the Valdez economy is more diversified than any other community in PWS. Valdez has used revenue from its large oil-related tax base in ways designed to stimulate economic diversification. The city invested $48 million in cargo and port facilities in an attempt to become the major entry port for cargo headed to the Alaska Interior. The scheme has yielded some success. Other investments in seafood processing have also resulted in additional jobs, but their cost-effectiveness remains uncertain. Although the population of Valdez declined slightly in the 1990s, jobs do not appear to have experienced a similar decline (Alaska Department of Labor 2001).

The major growth industry in Valdez is tourism and recreation. The number of fishing charter boats operating out of the local small boat harbor doubled between 1997 and 1999. Although cruise ship visits have become an important part of the summer economy, cruise ship visitation in 2002 is anticipated to be around twenty-six cruise ships, down from forty-five in 2001 (Valdez Convention and Visitor's Bureau, pers. comm.). As cruise ship operators redeploy vessels away from foreign waters, the number of visits is expected to increase.

Seward, more than any other community in the GOA region, has transitioned from an economic dependence on fluctuating seafood and timber markets to a visitor and recreation-based economy. Most economic growth since 1990 has been driven by the visitor industry, with employment in trade, services, and transportation growing at a 5.9 percent annual rate. The community has capitalized on its road and railroad access, to market itself as the major jumping-off point for visits to the Kenai Fjords National Park and Alaska Maritime National Wildlife Refuge. Seward's Alaska SeaLife Center has created another visitor attraction. More than 260,000 cruise ship passengers disembarked at Seward in 2000 (Goldsmith and Martin 2001).

Commercial fishing has trended downward in importance throughout the 1990s, but it remains a significant part of the Seward economy. The nearby state prison and other government facilities, including the headquarters for the Kenai Fjords National Park, are also important year-round employers. Although a major sawmill was opened in 1993, it never became competitive, and has remained closed since 1994.

Although its growing dependence on the seasonal visitor industry has been a concern, in the 1990s Seward developed a diverse and dynamic economy: "Over the last decade, it has successfully exploited its location beyond people's expectations." (Fried and Windisch-Cole 1999b).

Whittier depends on transportation and visitor-related businesses. The other four small communities in the PWS-SWK region augment commercial fishing, logging, aquaculture, and other cash-based activities with subsistence fishing, hunting, and gathering.

10.2.2 Western Kenai Peninsula Borough

The western Kenai Peninsula (WKP) region encompasses all the drainages to the northwest of the crest of the Kenai Mountains except those at the southern tip of the peninsula around Port Graham and Nanwalek. In addition, it includes the relatively sparsely populated area on the west side of Cook Inlet.

In terms of its physiography the area faces Cook Inlet (Barnes 1958); its economy has been closely linked since the 1960s with the oil and gas developments in the inlet and on the nearby uplands.

The WKP region is connected to Alaska's main road system, and is only a few hours by car from Anchorage, the state's largest metropolitan area. Homer and Kenai have scheduled air service from Anchorage.

The region grew 23 percent in the 1990s, making it second only to the Matanuska-Susitna Borough as the fastest growing area in the GOA region (G.J. Williams, Alaska Dept. of Labor, Juneau, pers. comm., 2000). In addition to oil and gas, the WKP economy depends on commercial fishing, sportfishing, and other outdoor recreation. About 46,500 people live in the WKP region, with over two-thirds living in or near the cities of Kenai and Soldotna. Soldotna is the headquarters of the Kenai Peninsula Borough and the Kenai Borough School District, the fourth and first-largest employers in the borough, respectively. Government at all levels accounts for 23 percent of the non-agricultural jobs in the borough, slightly less than the 26 percent statewide (Fried and Windisch-Cole 1999).

The southern Kenai Peninsula has Seldovia (286 persons) and Homer (3,946). Homer, on the north side of Kachemak Bay, lies at the southern terminus of the state's main road system, and has been popularized in the colorful writings of author Tom Bodett as "the end of the road."

Homer has attracted a significant number of retirees. According to the 2000 census, 10.1 percent of Homer residents are older than 64, the highest percentage of any community in the state. The percentage of over-64 residents in the borough as a whole is 7.3 percent, the highest in the GOA region. The statewide percentage of residents over age 64 is 5.7 percent (G.J. Williams, pers. comm., 2000).

10.2.3 Kodiak Island Borough

The Kodiak Island Borough occupies the Kodiak archipelago west of the GOA, and a largely uninhabited strip of the Alaska Peninsula coastline across the stormy Shelikof Strait. The borough population in 2000 was 13,913, of which 64 percent (8,864) lived in the City of Kodiak, the adjacent Coast Guard station, or on the road system nearby. The borough population grew six percent between 1990 and 2000, about one-third as fast as growth in the GOA region as a whole (U.S. Bureau of the Census 2001).

There are six outlying communities: the Alaska Native villages of Port Lions, Ouzinkie, Larsen Bay, Karluk, Old Harbor, and Akhiok, none of which have road connections to each other or the city of Kodiak.

The region's only scheduled jet service is to the Kodiak municipal airport, co-located at the U.S. Coast Guard air station. The Alaska Marine Highway System serves Kodiak and Port Lions. Other communities depend exclusively on air taxis or unscheduled private vessels for access.

The economy of the archipelago depends heavily on commercial fishing and seafood processing, with the borough's population swelling in the fishing season (Alaska Department of Labor 2001). Kodiak is one of the world's major centers of seafood production and has long been among the largest ports in the nation for seafood volume and value of landings.

Village residents largely depend on subsistence hunting and fishing. Kodiak Island also has a growing recreation and tourism economy and is home to a state-owned commercial rocket launch facility that held its first successful launch in 1999. The U.S. Coast Guard Station, with 1,840 permanent residents in 2000, is a major employer.

10.2.4 Alaska Peninsula

The Alaska Peninsula is on the western edge of the northern GOA, and encompasses the Aleutians East Borough and the southern part of the Lake and

Peninsula Borough. The total population of the region is 3,153. Sand Point, with 952 residents, and King Cove, with 792, are the largest communities (U.S. Bureau of the Census 2001). Aside from government spending, the cash economy of the area depends on the success of the fishing fleets.

Five smaller communities on the south side of the Alaska Peninsula lie within the area directly affected by the *Exxon Valdez* oil spill: Chignik, Chignik Lagoon, Chignik Lake, Ivanof Bay, and Perryville. The population of this area is 456, but may double during the fishing season. All five of these communities are in the Lake and Peninsula Borough and served by scheduled air taxi service. Chignik is also served by the Alaska Marine Highway ferries on a seasonal basis.

Sand Point, Chignik, Chignik Lagoon, and King Cove serve as regional salmon fishing centers. In addition to salmon and salmon roe, fish processing plants in Chignik produce herring roe, halibut, cod, and crab. About half the permanent population of these communities is Alaska Native.

Chignik Lake, Ivanof Bay, and Perryville are predominantly Alaska Native villages and maintain a subsistence lifestyle, relying on salmon, trout, marine fish and shellfish, crab, clams, moose, caribou, and bear. Commercial fishing provides cash income. Many residents leave during the summer months to fish or work for fish processors elsewhere in the region.

10.2.5 Anchorage/Mat-Su Urban Area

Anchorage, located at the head of Cook Inlet, and the Matanuska-Susitna (Mat-Su) Borough just to the north of Anchorage, constitute the economic, financial, and industrial capital of the state. Although outsiders often conceive of Alaska as sparsely populated, the state is also highly urban, and becoming more so. In 2000, 51 percent of Alaska's population lived in the Anchorage/Mat-Su metropolitan area, up from 48 percent a decade earlier. Between 1990 and 2000, Anchorage/Mat-Su added 53,584 residents, more than the 2000 population of Juneau and Ketchikan combined, the state's third and fourth largest urban areas (U.S. Bureau of the Census 2001). Although Anchorage/Mat-Su is situated outside the oil spill subregion, its geographic proximity suggests that growth there will—as it has in the past—produce environmental impacts in the area directly affected by the oil spill. This is likely to be particularly true where the surface transportation connections already exist, as they do to Seward, Whittier, and Valdez.

No economic development is likely to occur anywhere in the state without links to Anchorage. It serves as headquarters for the state's major financial institutions, its oil companies, major media outlets, largest labor unions, religious organizations, and most of its federal military and civilian government bureaucracy. The Anchorage airport is the major funnel through which most of the state's visitor traffic and a significant share of its seafood harvest pass.

Many Anchorage/Mat-Su residents work in other parts of the state, especially construction workers, oil workers, and fishermen (Fried 2000). These workers provide Anchorage with a direct source of income earned in other parts of the state. With the most diversified economy in the state, Anchorage is better positioned than any other community in the state to maintain growth in the face of economic hardship.

10.3 ECONOMICS AND ECOLOGICAL IMPACTS

At first glance, Prince William Sound presents an aspect of pristine and untrammeled wilderness, and this is one of her major delights. Anchored in a secluded cove or ascending a trackless ridge, it is easy to imagine oneself as the first explorer. Yet, a closer examination of the shoreline quickly reveals subtle signs of former habitation. Decayed, sawed off stumps line the shores—witness to former hand-logging operations. The logs were used for cabins, firewood, fishtraps, cannery pilings, mining timbers, railroad ties, fox farm pens and even ship building. If one rummages around the moss, alder and devils club along the shores, virtually every bay reveals the rotted foundations of some old cabin or fox pen. Abandoned, frail human structures do not last long in this damp climate and under such heavy winter snow-loads. And perhaps this is as it should be.

This quote from a book about sailing in Prince William Sound (Lethcoe and Lethecoe, 1985) is a fitting introduction to a section on human use activities in the northern GOA. At least a portion of the public has a perception that, prior to the Exxon Valdez oil spill, the region had little human impact. To the contrary, there has been a succession of different types of human habitation and economic activities in the northern GOA. Many of these activities had a high level of impact on both the environment and other users and residents of the region.

The earliest inhabitants of the region were nomadic Asian explorers crossing the Bering Land Bridge and spreading southward. The dates of first human occupation in Prince William Sound are not known, but radio carbon dating estimates go as far back as 205 AD.

Beginning in the 1700s, the northern GOA was used by a succession of explorers and developers. Russian and English fur traders in the 1700s were followed by development of fish canneries in the late 1880s. The first fox farms were developed in 1894 at Seal Island. Mining activity in the region also developed in the latter part of the 1890s. In 1897, Klondike gold was discovered, opening up the region as a gateway to Alaska's Interior. Mining began in the northern GOA in 1896. The communities of Ellamar and Latouche were built to develop copper mines. The Kennicott copper mine was developed around 1905 and resulted in the Valdez to Copper River and Northwestern Railway in 1911.

Mining and fox farming gradually declined, and military activity during World War II added a new type of activity to the region. Whittier remained an active military port until 1960. Commercial fisheries were developed and expanded in the 1950s, 1960s, and 1970s. The late 1970s were dominated by development of the trans-Alaska pipeline and the terminal at Valdez. The 1980s and 1990s have shown a large expansion in recreation and tourism.

10.3.1 Commercial Fishing

Commercial fishing is by far the predominant human activity in the northern GOA and is thought at this time to have the potential for the most significant impacts on the GOA ecosystem. Within the GOA, the major commercial fisheries are salmon, Pacific herring, pollock, cod, halibut, and shellfish. Tens of thousands of individuals participate in these fisheries.

The period before the 1989 oil spill was a time of relative prosperity for many commercial fishermen. Since 1989, commercial fishing in the northern GOA has undergone dramatic changes as a result of changes in salmon markets, declining abundance of other fish stocks, institutional changes associated with fishery "rationalization," harvest limitations designed to protect endangered species, and other factors.

Communities within the EVOS GOA region have varying levels of dependence on commercial fishing. The communities most dependent on commercial fishing are Cordova, Kodiak (and the outlying six villages within the Kodiak Island Borough), Chignik, Chignik Lagoon, Sand Point, and King Cove. Commercial fishing is an important but less dominant economic sector in the road-accessible communities of Valdez, Whittier, Seward, and Homer.

10.3.1.1 Salmon

Commercial fishing for pink, sockeye, sockeye, chum, coho, and chinook salmon has long been a mainstay of the northern GOA commercial fishing industry. Salmon are harvested by seine, drift gillnet, and set gillnet gear. Pink salmon are the dominant species in PWS, contributing over eight percent of total salmon landings by volume and contributing the largest share of ex-vessel value. In Cook Inlet, Kodiak, and the Alaska Peninsula, sockeye are by far the dominant species.

PWS exhibits a pattern of odd-even run strength for pink salmon that persists even with the influence of hatchery production. The very low catch levels in 1992 and 1993 were due to closures associated with the *Exxon Valdez* oil spill. Harvests since then have increased, but unlike most other Alaska fisheries, are now highly dependent on hatchery returns.

Nonprofit hatcheries have operated in Prince William Sound since the mid 1970s. The Prince William Sound Aquaculture Corporation (PWSAC) began operations in 1976 and operates five hatcheries: the W.F. Noerenberg, Armin F. Koernig, Cannery Creek, Main Bay, and Gulkana facilities. The Valdez Fisheries Development Association has operated the Solomon Gulch hatchery since 1979 (Kron 1993). Much smaller salmon enhancement programs operate in Cook Inlet and Kodiak.

Returns of both wild and hatchery salmon fluctuate greatly from year to year. During the period 1960-1976, when the pink salmon fishery was supported wholly by wild stocks, the average pink salmon catch in Prince William Sound was 3.3 million fish (Eggers et al. 1991). The pink salmon harvest during this period fluctuated from 0.1 to 7.3 million fish. Since hatchery releases were begun, the average pink salmon catch has been 19.7 million.

In 2001, 76 percent of the total pink salmon return was harvested by PWSAC to cover the costs of hatchery operations. In 2002, the percentage was reduced to 54 percent in an attempt to make more of the salmon resource available to commercial fishermen. PWSAC has significant long-term financial obligations, with over $30 million in outstanding state loans.

Salmon prices and market demand for salmon produced in the northern GOA as well as other parts of Alaska are at relatively depressed levels. The primary reason for the market trend has been a huge increase in world production of farmed salmon. Alaska salmon face both price and quality competition from salmon originating in Chile, Norway, Canada, and other farmed salmon-producing countries.

10.3.1.2 Herring

Herring are harvested predominantly for sac roe for export to foreign markets. Quotas are established for each discrete stock. Herring fisheries in the region are currently at low levels. In the 2000 season, Prince William Sound and Cook Inlet were both closed due to low abundance. Limited herring fisheries occurred in Kodiak and the Alaska Peninsula.

10.3.1.3 Shellfish

Most of the shellfish fisheries in the northern GOA are closed to commercial fishing due to inadequate stocks. Within PWS, no crab harvests have been permitted for several years, and there is no evidence of recovery. The decline of PWS crab is thought to be associated with the growth of the sea otter population, which preys heavily on shellfish (Trowbridge 1995).

Miscellaneous fisheries for PWS scallops, Cook Inlet scallops and hard shell clams, and Kodiak sea cucumbers and Dungeness crab offer limited opportunities for fishermen.

10.3.1.4 Groundfish

GOA groundfish catches have ranged from a low of 135,400 metric tons (t) in 1978 to a high of 352,800 t in 1984. The 2001 groundfish harvest was 181,400 t (NPFMC 2001). Pollock has been the dominant species in the overall catch, followed by Pacific cod and sablefish. Groundfish abundance in the GOA has been relatively stable, rising slowly since the mid-1980s. The estimated long-term annual yield for GOA groundfish is about 450,000 t. The recent five-year average yield has been about 230,000 t per year. The wide disparity between the potential and recent yield is due to fishing restrictions imposed by the North Pacific Fishery Management Council to reduce incidental catches of Pacific halibut. A major portion of the GOA groundfish biomass consists of arrowtooth flounder, with little or no current commercial value. A 1989 National Marine Fisheries Service trawl survey estimated that arrowtooth flounder made up the greatest proportion of total biomass at nearly every site surveyed (NPFMC 2001).

A specific Prince William Sound pollock quota has been established since 1995. The sound's pollock harvest has averaged 1,800 t since 1995. This harvest occurs mostly during the winter months and is processed in Cordova and Seward.

10.3.1.5 Halibut

The Gulf of Alaska is managed by the International Pacific Halibut Commission as Area 3B. The 2001 harvest quote for Area 3B was 16.4 million pounds.

Halibut harvested in the central and western Gulf are delivered to the ports of Cordova, Homer, Seward, Valdez, and Whittier. In 2001, 12.2 million pounds of halibut were landed in Homer, making it the number one port in landings among the entire west coast. Most of the halibut landed in Homer is iced, loaded into refrigerator vans, and trucked to the Pacific Northwest for distribution to markets.

10.3.1.6 Future Resource Outlook and Issues for Commercial Fisheries

Commercial fisheries in the EVOS GOA area have been in a state of dynamic flux for the past several years. Among the ongoing issues affecting commercial fishermen are the following:

Environmental and oceanographic conditions. Ocean survival is a key factor in regulating the magnitude of returning salmon and the level of harvest. Since the 1970s, the ocean environment has been favorable off Alaska, and salmon runs increased. However, there are indications that North Pacific circulation patterns may be shifting away from conditions favorable for Alaska salmon production (Mantua et al. 1997). If the warm water regime off Alaska reverses to a cold regime, natural salmon production will decrease throughout Alaska to levels observed in the 1960s. Hatchery production and other salmon enhancement efforts may aid in maintaining harvests if natural production declines, but the outlook remains uncertain. GOA pollock and cod stocks are likely to decrease over the next several years, while most other GOA groundfish remain stable.

A major ecological concern with all types of removals by fishing activities is the sustainability of fish stocks, which could be affected by directed fisheries or as a result of discarded bycatch in other fisheries and high seas interception. This concern drives responsible fishery management. The predominant fishery stocks historically fluctuate because of natural variability and climate cycles, and for that reason, harvest rates are set at sustainable fractions of the available biomass. However, concern still exists that setting harvest rates without a complete understanding of those fluctuations could lead to unintentional overharvest, resulting in population declines that could take years to rebound.

In addition, bycatch may have unintended consequences on non-targeted fish populations. In many fisheries, observers monitor the bycatch. In addition, bycatch is often only a small fraction of the overall mortality. However, bycatch is not monitored in all fisheries, and may be significant in some.

Another ecological concern with all types of fishing is the removal of marine nutrients (nitrates, phosphates, iron) that are key to sustaining the long-term productivity of watersheds (Finney et al. 2000). Fishing for a dominant anadromous species such as salmon may lower the productive capacity of a watershed not only for salmon, but also for a wide range of plants, fish, and mammals that are known to depend on marine nutrients. When combined with the loss of nutrients associated with development of riparian (river and other waterfront) habitats and wetlands, the loss of marine nutrients may contribute to oligotrophy or "starvation" of the watershed. Unfortunately, not enough monitoring data on marine nutrients in tributaries of the GOA are available to understand the degree to which oligotrophication is occurring.

A third ecological concern with fishing is the potential for unintentional degradation of habitats and attendant losses of plant and animal species. Sportfishing activities in watersheds have substantially degraded some riparian habitats in Southcentral Alaska, resulting in lost vegetation, lost fish habitat, and siltation, and necessitating walkways and management restrictions. Various types of marine fishing methods and gear, such as pots and bottom trawls (very large bag-shaped nets), also have the potential for degrading sea-bottom habitat and reducing populations of sedentary species such as corals and seaweeds.

Protection has already been afforded to marine habitats in some sensitive areas by excluding gear types that are thought to be injurious to habitat. For example most state waters are closed to bottom trawling. In the eastern GOA, both state and federal waters are now closed to trawling and dredging in part to protect coral habitats from possible trawling impacts. There are numerous trawl-and-dredge closure areas near Kodiak Island, the Alaska Peninsula, and the Aleutian Islands. But not all areas of the Bering Sea and GOA (especially those that have sandy and sediment bottom types) are vulnerable to trawling impacts. Given the amount of marine habitats already subject to closure, more information on how to define

critical marine habitats is essential to balancing fishing opportunities and protection of habitat.

Commercial fishing also has the potential to affect other elements of the marine ecosystem, such as bird and marine mammal populations. Effects result either directly, through entanglement in fishing nets or disturbance to haul-outs and rookeries, or indirectly, through impacts on food supplies. Areas where marine mammals feed and that are adjacent to their haul-out areas have been closed to commercial fishing in parts of the Bering Sea, Aleutian Islands, and GOA. A recent National Marine Fisheries Service (NMFS) Biological Opinion (NMFS 2000) concludes that lack of food is the reason that the endangered Steller sea lion is not recovering from serious declines in the GOA and Bering Sea. On the basis of this opinion, NMFS has severely limited fixed-gear and trawl fishing for several groundfish species, a major food source for the Steller sea lion. However, this opinion has been extremely controversial, and several independent teams of science reviewers have concluded that there is no evidence that sea lions are nutritionally limited and no evidence that fisheries are causing prey depletion.

Salmon fisheries in the GOA are notable because hatcheries produce the majority of some salmon species in some areas and, in specific fisheries, the majority of salmon harvested. Billions of juvenile salmon are released annually from hatcheries in three areas within the northern GOA: Cook Inlet, Kodiak, and PWS. Within this region, 56% of the salmon in the traditional commercial harvest were of hatchery origin in 1999. The percentage is higher if cost-recovery fisheries are also included. In PWS in particular, hatchery production provides a majority of the pink and chum salmon harvested and a substantial fraction of the sockeye and coho salmon harvested. In 1999, hatchery pink salmon contributed 84% of the number of pink salmon harvested by commercial fisheries in PWS.

Ecological concerns related to hatcheries include reduced production of wild fish because of competition between hatchery and wild salmon during all stages of the life cycle, loss of genetic diversity in wild salmon, and overharvest of wild salmon during harvest operations targeting hatchery salmon. Information on the interactions between hatchery and wild fish in specific locations, as well as on the impact of salmon produced in hatcheries in both Asia and North America on food webs in the GOA, appears to be essential to long-term fishery management programs.

Resource and legal issues. Actions taken under the Endangered Species Act (ESA) as a result of depressed levels of Steller sea lions have created economic hardship for commercial groundfish fishermen from several communities, particularly Kodiak, King Cove, and Sand Point. The National Marine Fisheries Service developed a biological opinion that pointed to commercial fishing as one of the factors in declining numbers of Steller sea lions. Regulations designed to protect the species by limiting groundfish fishing were put in place in 2002. The status of harbor seals and sea otters is also uncertain, and ESA actions in relation to these species could create additional difficulties for fishermen and marine resource–dependent communities.

Regulatory actions. The North Pacific Fishery Management Council (NPFMC) is considering a groundfish "rationalization" program for the GOA groundfish fisheries. A similar program covering Bering Sea fisheries established individual fisheries quotas (IFQs), and made other major changes to fisheries management. The fishing interests in the northern GOA will be profoundly affected by the decisions of the NPFMC on these issues.

Since its implementation several years ago, the NPFMC's IFQ share system has spread halibut and sablefish landings over a longer period of time, and as a result, the fresh market has largely displaced frozen production. Road-accessible Homer is now the largest halibut landing port on the West Coast, with over 10 million pounds delivered per year. Most of the halibut landed there are placed in iced totes and delivered to processing and distribution companies in the Pacific Northwest via refrigerated van.

Commercial Fishing Summary

Reasons for monitoring: Many commercial fisheries in the northern GOA are at very depressed levels or are currently closed. Interactions with protected species or species that have a subsistence priority may create new problems for commercial fishing in the future. Future activities can have significant ecological impacts.

Type of impacts: Commercial fishing activities create resource conflicts and impact other user groups through gear loss and discard, and oil and fuel spills. Resource competition can affect other fish, bird, and marine mammal populations. Removal of marine nutrients can affect productivity of watersheds. Fishing

gear and techniques may degrade habitat. Hatchery production and salmon farms can have negative environmental effects.

Who is monitoring: Alaska Department of Fish and Game (ADF&G) is the primary agency for monitoring commercial fishing effort and harvests in state waters. The National Marine Fisheries Service has primary responsibility for monitoring fishing effort and harvests in offshore marine waters (three to 200 miles offshore). The International Pacific Halibut Commission has primary responsibility for monitoring effort and harvests for halibut.

Regulatory authority: The Alaska Board of Fisheries has regulatory authority for fisheries that occur in state waters. The North Pacific Fishery Management Council has regulatory authority for fisheries that occur in offshore marine waters. Recommendations from the NPFMC require action by the Secretary of Commerce to take effect.

10.3.2 Recreation/Tourism

Recreation and tourism are the fastest growing economic activities and human uses in the northern GOA, but incomplete data leave many uncertainties regarding the characteristics of use and rates of growth.

10.3.2.1 Commercial Recreation on Excursion Vessels

Commercial excursion boats operating out of Valdez, Whittier, Seward, Homer and, to a lesser extent, Kodiak provide sightseeing trips for visitors. This group is composed of several large companies that take most of the passengers, with smaller companies providing services to a much smaller sector of the market. According to a 1990 survey of excursion boat passengers visiting the Kenai Fjords National Park itself, most boat passengers (77 percent) were from other states (72 percent) or other countries (5 percent) (Littlejohn 1990). The 5-year data series includes only passengers traveling into Kenai Fjords National Park, and excludes excursion boat passengers that stay within Resurrection Bay.

Excursion boat visitation appears to have declined slightly in 2000 and 2001, but this may reflect a trend toward more Resurrection Bay trips as excursion operators attempted to accommodate the demand for shorter trips typically sought by cruise ship passengers.

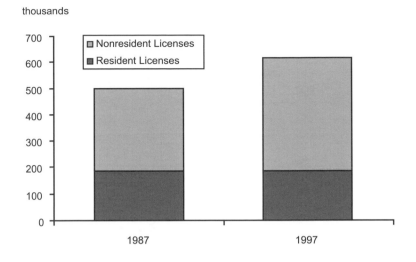

Figure 10.1. Alaska sport fishing licenses, 1987 and 1997.

As limited as the Kenai Fjords' data may be, they are superior to the situation for other areas in the northern GOA, where data are completely lacking.

10.3.2.2 Trends in Sportfishing Effort

Data on sportfishing effort are also limited. ADF&G data show the use of private boats for fishing out of Seward and Valdez increased steadily from 1988 through 1995, dropped sharply in 1996, and has increased slowly since that time (ADF&G various years). Because ADF&G changed the way these data were compiled for the years after 1995, they are of only limited usefulness for long-term trend analysis.

Overall sportfishing effort within the northern GOA is centered on the road-accessible areas. Cordova, Seward, and Homer are the most popular ports for marine fishing. Whittier and Kodiak are less popular ports for marine fishing. Freshwater angling is concentrated along the road-accessible areas of Cook Inlet and the Susitna River watershed. The number of resident sport anglers in Southcentral Alaska has been on a slightly decreasing trend since 1992, but the total number of anglers has increased due to the growth in the numbers of nonresident anglers. Nonresident licenses sold in Alaska increased 46 percent between 1987 and 1997 (see Figure 10.1). ADF&G has a study under way to investigate the reasons for the declining number of resident anglers (ADF&G various years).

10.3.2.3 Cruise Ships

Cruise ships dock at five ports in the greater GOA region: Anchorage, Homer, Seward, Valdez, and Whittier. Seward dominates in cruise ship dockings. Cruise ship patrons typically take passage on either a northbound or southbound run, choosing to fly to or from Anchorage on the reverse leg of their trip. Seward has the important features of proximity to Anchorage as well as access to the Kenai Fjords National Park and the ease of combining a rail or scenic bus ride segment. Seward also offers considerable time savings for cruise ships traveling to or from the Pacific Northwest, compared with travel to the Port of Anchorage. Cruise ship docking in Seward can offer passengers a one-week turnaround schedule via return air. The growth of cruise ship use in the oil spill region has been well documented (Figure 10.2).

Cruise ship visitors are non-consumptive users of resources within the northern GOA as they move from port to port, but may become consumptive users when in port. Short-duration sportfishing trips are a popular activity for passengers while in port. Recreation and tourist users, including cruise ship users, can be compatible or incompatible with other uses and groups of users, based on their use characteristics. For example, cruise ship passengers are probably not affected by seeing groups of boaters or kayakers. However, boaters and kayakers may

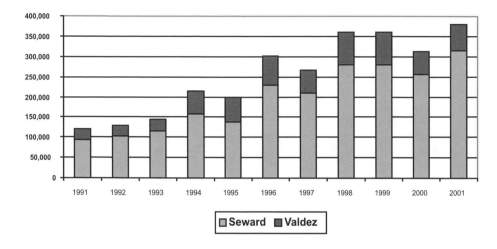

Figure 10.2. Cruise ship visitors to Seward and Valdez, 1991-2001. Source: Seward Chamber of Commerce, Valdez Convention and Visitors Bureau, McDowell Group 2001.

have their experience adversely affected by too many contacts with cruise ships.

Cruise ships often carry more people than populate many Alaska towns. One well known impact of cruise ships is air and water pollution. Cruise ships also affect other user groups by their presence in the northern GOA and, in some areas, by competing with local residents for sportfish harvests. In July 2001, Alaska enacted a law to regulate cruise ship and ferry wastewater discharges in marine waters. The new law sets discharge limits for greywater (sink, shower, and galley water) and blackwater (treated sewage) for fecal coliform and suspended solids. It limits discharge to areas at least one mile offshore and requires vessels to be moving at least six knots during discharge. Sampling of discharges is required, and the Alaska Department of Environmental Conservation (ADEC) has independent authority to perform additional sampling. Finally, the new law requires improved record keeping and reporting of vessel disposal of wastewater, hazardous waste, and garbage.

Seward will continue to be the major Southcentral Alaska port for cruise ship passengers to embark and disembark. Valdez anticipated a sharp decline in cruise ship passengers in 2002 due to Holland America ending its port calls in that community. The cruise ship visitation in Valdez in 2002 was anticipated to be around 26 cruise ships, down from 45 in 2001 (Valdez Convention & Visitors bureau, pers. comm.).

10.3.2.4 Recreation/Tourism Issues

Sportfishing within the northern GOA has created local environmental damage in some areas by concentrating activity in fragile areas. One area of major concern is the Kenai River, famous for its king and sockeye sportfishing. ADF&G evaluated these impacts along the Kenai River in 1994 (ADF&G 1994) to provide a baseline for future assessments. Sportfishing can also contribute to localized depletion of fish stocks.

Increased hiking and camping on coastal areas and riverbanks can lead to trampling erosion and related impacts on local water quality. The Chugach National Forest is currently completing an analysis of remote recreation carrying capacity in areas around Prince William Sound that may provide information on use impacts and appropriate levels of use. The Alaska Division of Parks completed an analysis of carrying capacity for the Kenai River in 1991 which identified areas of the river where crowding was diminishing user satisfaction for fishing and other recreational experiences (Alaska State Parks 1993).

In October 2001, the North Pacific Fishery Management Council recommended an individual fisheries quota (IFQ) program for commercial charter operators fishing for halibut. Requiring new charter operators to purchase halibut shares to take out sport charters may tend to shift sportfishing effort toward currently non-limited species, such as Pacific cod, ling cod, and rockfish, creating localized depletions and potential resource concerns. If commercial halibut charter prices increase as a result of the IFQ program, use of the resource by non-charter private boats may increase in reaction. Impacts on the resource base could be significant.

The growing use of jet skis for recreational use and their potential for disturbing nesting waterfowl has led ADF&G to ban jet ski use in Kachemak Bay.

Some residents of Prince William Sound communities expressed concern with a potential huge flood of new recreational users to the region as a result of completion of the Whittier tunnel, providing road access to the sound and potential impacts to shorelines, tidelands, and nearshore waters, as well as the fish and wildlife populations that rely on these habitats. The tunnel opened on June 7, 2000, and had a total of 88,000 vehicles for the remainder of that year. In 2001, the Whittier tunnel vehicle traffic totaled 85,772 through December 17 (G. Burton, Alaska Dept. of Transportation, pers. comm., 2001). The initial level of traffic through the Whittier tunnel is much lower than anticipated by the Alaska Department of Transportation and Public Facilities. Local residents speculate that the use tolls imposed after the first year of operation have discouraged users.

Recreation/Tourism Summary

Reasons for monitoring: Immediate impacts of high use levels on habitat as well as localized depletion of fisheries resources. Although recreational users may impact other user groups, areas of conflict are largely unstudied.

Type of impacts: Potential for resource depletion, damage to fragile habitat, disturbance to wildlife on rookeries and haul-outs, competition among user groups, water quality degradation from discharges and spills.

Agencies managing for a subsistence priority can create impacts on other user groups using resources within the northern GOA.

Who is monitoring: ADF&G is the primary agency for monitoring sportfishing effort and harvests. The U.S. Forest Service monitors uses within Chugach National Forest. The National Park Service monitors use levels within the Kenai Fjords National Park.

Regulatory authority: The Alaska Board of Fisheries and Board of Game have regula-

---

tory authority over sportfishing and hunting within state lands and waters.

The North Pacific Fishery Management Council has made a recommendation for new regulations dealing with halibut charter vessels.

The U.S. Coast Guard has enforcement authority for vessel operations in marine waters.

10.3.3 Oil and Gas Development

The oil and gas industry is a major economic force in Prince William Sound (PWS) and Cook Inlet. Crude oil from the Alaska North Slope is transported by pipeline to Valdez, where it is loaded onto tankers and shipped to the contiguous United States, abroad, and to a refinery on Cook Inlet, near Kenai. Whatever their destination, tankers carrying this oil traverse PWS and the GOA on their journey (Fried and Windisch-Cole 1999).

The number of tanker voyages from the Port of Valdez has declined from 640 in 1995 to 411 in 1999, partly due to a four percent increase in the average load per vessel, but mostly as the result of reduced North Slope production (ADEC 2000).

Annual shipments through PWS peaked at 705 million barrels in 1988 and have declined in every year since. Shipments in 2001 are estimated at 366 million barrels, almost exactly one-half of what they were at the peak. The annual rate of change in shipments varied from −10 percent in 1998-99, when oil prices were low, to −1 percent in 2000-2001, when prices were high. The state of Alaska's official oil production forecast issued in December 2001 predicted that North Slope production would increase nine percent in 2002, and then remain relatively constant through 2009 (see Figure 10.3). The forecasters acknowledge, however, that unexpected changes in oil prices could shift the trajectory up or down (Alaska Department of Revenue Tax Div., unpubl. data, 2001).

Commercialization of North Slope natural gas reserves—estimated at more than 90 trillion cubic feet—could cause PWS tanker traffic to increase. Under one concept, proposed more than 30 years ago and still popular in Alaska, a gas pipeline would be built parallel to the oil line, terminating at a liquefied natural gas (LNG) facility near Valdez. LNG from the plant would be exported in specially built tank ships to the Far East, Mexico, or the U.S. West Coast. A similar, but much smaller, LNG plant has operated in Cook Inlet since 1966.

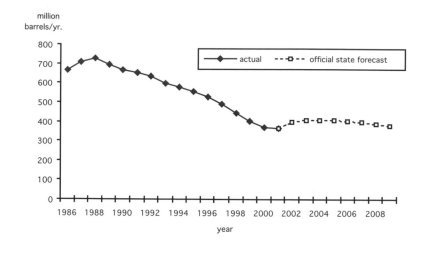

Figure 10.3. Prince William Sound oil shipments.

A separate gas-to-liquid (GTL) commercialization proposal would transform the gas to methanol liquid or a chemically related product that would be shipped to Valdez in the existing trans-Alaska oil pipeline (Alaska Highway Natural Gas Policy Council 2001).

Three recent studies, sponsored separately by the North Slope gas owners, the state, and an independent energy consulting firm, concluded that the GTL and LNG proposals (including a pipeline project terminating at an LNG plant in northern Cook Inlet) are likely to be less feasible than alternatives in which the gas is shipped by pipeline through Canada to markets in the contiguous United States (Alaska Highway Natural Gas Policy Council 2001; Purvin & Gertz, Ltd. 2000; Brown 2002). Volumes of gas to be shipped under the various commercialization proposals range up to 2.2 trillion cubic feet per year, equivalent in energy content to roughly 350 million barrels of oil (Purvin & Gertz, Ltd. 2000). In most applications, substitution of gas for oil reduces greenhouse gas emissions by about 15 percent. No project for commercializing North Slope gas has yet attracted commitments for the $7 billion to $20 billion in investment expected to be required.

Megaprojects do not have an exclusive franchise on potential petroleum developments in the GOA area. The first producing oil wells in Alaska were at Katalla, southeast of Cordova. Small-scale production continued there from 1902, until destruction of the local refinery by fire in 1933. The Chugach Alaska Corporation, owner of much of the Katalla oil and gas acreage, believes that modern technology may make

the Katalla oil resource economical to redevelop (Chugach Alaska Corporation, unpubl. data, 2001).

Modern oil development in Alaska began in 1957 in the Cook Inlet basin, with discovery of oil at the Swanson River field in the Kenai National Wildlife Refuge. In 2001, the basin produced eleven million barrels of oil, about three percent of the volume coming from the North Slope (Alaska Oil and Gas Conservation Commission 2001).

Most of the oil and much of the natural gas produced from the Cook Inlet comes from offshore platforms. Underwater pipelines transport oil and gas to terminals on both sides of Cook Inlet. Much of Cook Inlet oil production is delivered to a local refinery in Nikiski, north of Kenai, for processing.

State forecasters expected oil production from the Cook Inlet basin to increase, reaching fifteen million barrels per year in state fiscal year 2003-2004. An aggressive state leasing program initiated in 1999, together with planned increases in federal offshore lease offerings, could stimulate additional new production thereafter (Alaska Department of Revenue 2001).

Much of the new exploration in Cook Inlet, however, has been targeted toward natural gas. Cook Inlet gas has provided low cost energy to the Anchorage metropolitan area since 1962, and since the late 1960s has provided energy and feedstock to an LNG plant and a large fertilizer manufacturing facility at Nikiski. The bulk of the region's electricity comes from gas-fired generation.

In recent years Cook Inlet gas sales have ranged close to a quarter trillion cubic feet. The region's utilities and major industrial users believe that additional discoveries or imports from the North Slope will be needed in the next decade to sustain current industrial gas uses and meet the growing demand for utility gas and electric generation (ADNR 2002).

Major concerns about oil and gas development in the northern GOA include the potential for oil spills from vessel traffic, such as the 1987 T/S *Glacier Bay* spill in Cook Inlet and the 1989 EVOS. Small chronic spills, pipeline corrosion and subsequent leaks, disposal of drilling wastes and potential impacts on water quality, and the introduction of exotic species from ballast waters are other major concerns. Only 6,000 gallons of crude oil were reported spilled in the region from 1998 to 1999 (ADEC 2001).

Oil producers, shippers, and refiners are required to have contingency plans detailing response capabilities and specific response actions in the event of a spill. In addition, the Oil Pollution Act of 1990 authorized regional citizen advisory groups in PWS and Cook Inlet to oversee oil and gas activities. These groups, along with state and federal agencies, maintain oversight of oil industry operations in their respective regions.

Oil and Gas Development Summary

Reasons for monitoring: Increased North Slope development could result in increased tanker traffic and more underwater pipelines. Cook Inlet production is mostly offshore or near the shore and could have impacts on marine system.

Type of impacts: Potential for oil spills from vessel traffic, small chronic spills, pipeline corrosion and subsequent leaks, disposal of drilling wastes, introduction of exotic species in ballast waters.

Who is monitoring: ADEC and the U.S. Coast Guard require oil producers, shippers, and refiners to have contingency plans detailing capabilities and planned actions in response to spills. Regional citizen advisory councils in Prince William Sound and Cook Inlet provide citizen oversight and conduct some monitoring activities.

Regulatory authority: U.S. Coast Guard regulates tanker traffic. U.S. EPA and ADEC are primary agencies regulating activities because of potential impacts on water quality.

10.3.4 Subsistence

Subsistence is an important traditional activity practiced by residents of northern GOA communities to provide food and cultural enrichment. Fifteen predominantly Alaska Native communities in the EVOS GOA region, with a total population of about 2,200 people, rely heavily on harvests of subsistence resources such as fish, shellfish, seals, deer, and waterfowl. Subsistence harvests in 1998 varied among communities from 250 to 500 pounds per person, indicating strong dependence on subsistence resources. Subsistence activities also support the culture and traditions of these communities. Many families in other communities also rely on the subsistence resources of the spill area.

In addition to the cultural aspects of subsistence, its economic importance comes from import substitution. Rural residents are able to rely on wild foods rather than food imported into the region. Dependence on subsistence production is typically higher in remote areas and lower near population centers, although there are exceptions to this general trend.

Knowledge of subsistence patterns and consumption largely relies on focused household surveys conducted by the ADF&G Subsistence Division. The division's analysis and monitoring focuses on subsistence production, consumption, sharing patterns, and species of concern. Subsistence studies are typically conducted at irregular intervals, often oriented toward a specific management issue or need, such as the *Exxon Valdez* oil spill. The household studies provide a cross-sectional profile of use patterns at a particular time. Due to the focus on oil spill impacts and the availability of funding, several subsistence studies conducted in communities across the oil spill region over the past ten years have provided a wealth of data and information. The declining frequency of subsistence studies suggests that future changes in use patterns within northern GOA communities may not be as well documented.

ADF&G researchers have developed village contacts who provide accurate tracking of subsistence harvests of salmon, seals, sea lions, marine mammals, and halibut. It is more difficult for ADF&G to track subsistence harvests of marine invertebrates and marine fish, so there is a much lower level of confidence in the estimated use levels for these species.

In a recent report funded jointly by the Minerals Management Service (MMS) and ADF&G, researchers analyzed subsistence patterns for communities within the area affected by the *Exxon Valdez* oil spill (Fall et al. 2001). The communities analyzed were Chenega Bay, Cordova, Tatitlek, Valdez, Kenai, Nanwalek, Port Graham, Seldovia, Akhiok, Karluk, Kodiak City, Larsen Bay, Old Harbor, Ouzinkie, Port Lions, Chignik, Chignik Lagoon, Chignik Lake, Ivanof Bay, and Perryville.

The study tracked wild food harvests measured in pounds per capita before and after the *Exxon Valdez* oil spill, producing the following findings:

• Subsistence production averages over 300 pounds per person per year throughout the region. In predominantly Native communities, subsistence production averages 352 pounds annually per person. In Cordova subsistence production averages 200 pounds per person annually, and in Kodiak it averages 148 pounds per person.

• Subsistence production uses nearly seventeen different types of resources per household.

• The studies show a very high participation rate in subsistence harvests and use, particularly in predominantly Native communities where 99 percent of residents used subsistence resources.

• Subsistence production is often distributed through an extensive network of sharing. In predominantly Native communities, 87.5 percent of households received resources and 78.3 percent of households gave away resources.

• Following the *Exxon Valdez* oil spill, there was an immediate decline of over fifty percent in subsistence harvests. Equally important as the decline in production was the reduction in the range of resources used. At first the reduction was due to fear of oil contamination, and later due to the scarcity of resources.

• The impacts of the oil spill caused a disruption in sharing and teaching of children and a temporary increase in household income associated with spill cleanup activities during the year following the spill.

• In the years from 1990 to the present, there has been a gradual rebound in subsistence production from the EVOS communities. But communities in Prince William Sound have been slower to rebound than areas outside the sound.

• Since the EVOS, several communities have increased their dependence on fish and reduced their dependence on marine mammals and shellfish.

In addition to the ADF&G Subsistence Division and the Federal Subsistence Board, others monitoring subsistence uses and harvests of certain species include the Alaska Board of Fisheries and the North Pacific Fishery Management Council. The Council recently completed an analysis of impacts relating to subsistence halibut and has recommended new regulations for that species.

The National Marine Fisheries Service (NMFS) follows the status of the beluga whale population and funds operation of the Alaska Beluga Committee. The Committee has attempted to understand beluga whale subsistence harvests through an informal network of contacts. The Cook Inlet Marine Mammal Council, composed of Cook Inlet beluga whale subsistence hunters, works independently of the Alaska Beluga Committee to focus on beluga whales in Cook Inlet.

The Alaska Native Harbor Seal Commission partners with the ADF&G Subsistence Division in a harvest assessment project to interview hunters and collect data on the subsistence harvest of seals. This effort is currently funded by the National Marine Fisheries Service. The U.S. Fish & Wildlife Service has a program to monitor the harvests of sea otters. USFWS also monitors waterfowl.

The ADF&G Subsistence Division has been working to coordinate and report on the various monitoring efforts. However, their efforts have been funded through special research funding, such as EVOS. Although another round of surveys is anticipated in 2004, future funding is uncertain for the ADF&G Subsistence Division to continue coordination of subsistence monitoring as well as periodic household surveys within northern GOA communities.

The impact of subsistence harvests on injured resources, particularly marine mammals, has not been determined. In some cases, it may become necessary to address the impact of subsistence on recovery, as was necessary for Cook Inlet beluga whales. ADF&G and NMFS are working cooperatively to combine research efforts on harbor seals. The results of this research program may improve understanding of the status of harbor seals and reasons for population declines within the northern GOA. However, the program will not address the effects of subsistence harvests on this resource.

10.3.4.1 Current and Potential Issues on Subsistence

Subsistence activities and production are related to many factors, such as population growth within villages and communities and changes in the abundance and distribution of fish and wildlife resources. The criminal settlement subsistence restoration program, using money from the *Exxon Valdez* settlement, has funded thirty-two projects totaling $5.6 million in support of subsistence restoration (Fall et al. 2001). These included fish enhancement projects, development of infrastructure for subsistence activities, cultural education, and mariculture. The *Exxon Valdez* Trustee Council's Habitat Protection Program has protected over 650,000 acres within the northern GOA through outright purchase of lands or conservation easements. This program ensures that the lands protected will remain part of the productive ecosystem, thus aiding support of the resource base for subsistence production.

Increasing use within Prince William Sound by boaters, fishermen, hunters, and other recreational users may affect future subsistence opportunities through direct competition or the indirect effects of increased traffic in areas where subsistence harvests occur. In 1995, a consulting firm evaluated the impact of completion of the Whittier tunnel on subsistence uses within six communities: Chenega Bay, Tatitlek, Cordova, Whittier, Hope, and Cooper Landing (Stephen R. Braund & Associates 1995).

The study found that subsistence users from the GOA communities identified increased boat traffic within Prince William Sound and the potential increased direct competition for fish and wildlife resources from increased numbers of visitors as their greatest concerns related to the opening of the Whittier tunnel. Although use of the Whittier tunnel has been much lower than forecast, the overall trend in increasing recreation use in the region may create conflicts with subsistence activities.

Recent changes in subsistence regulation and management may affect other user groups, including sport and commercial fishermen, hunters, and others.

Some future issues may include:

- Definitions of federally recognized subsistence users could greatly increase the number of subsistence users from outside the GOA region. For example, the Federal Subsistence Board currently plans to allow all recognized subsistence users from anywhere in Alaska to participate in subsistence harvests on the Kenai Peninsula. The Board earlier moved to restrict subsistence salmon fishing within the Copper River watershed to those living in the region.

- The Federal Subsistence Board has received proposals to extend its jurisdiction to include marine waters and species.

- In two decisions in Southeast Alaska, the Federal Subsistence Board has preemptively closed state fisheries in freshwater to make sure that there would be enough fish for subsistence in federal harvest areas. During the 2001 fishing season, the Federal Subsistence Board preemptively closed all the commercial, sport, and state subsistence fisheries operating within federal waters in both the Kuskokwim and Yukon drainages to ensure that the federal subsistence users would have access to salmon resources.

- In a recent decision, the Federal Subsistence Board increased the limits for subsistence harvests in the Copper River by fish wheels, with no upper limit on king salmon. If the subsistence harvest of king salmon is substantially increased in Copper River fisheries, sport and commercial users could face restrictions.

- The North Pacific Fishery Management Council took final action in April 2002 to define subsistence halibut fishing in Alaska waters. Subsistence management actions include a limit on the number of hooks, a 30-fish annual limit, a system to permit temporary transfer of subsistence rights, and a gear stacking allowance for multiple subsistence fishermen on a single vessel.

- The decline of the beluga whale in Cook Inlet provides an example of a resource problem alleged to be caused by subsistence harvests. Under the Marine Mammal Protection Act, state and federal agencies were unable to take any action to address the declining resource until the population reached the point where it could be classified as depleted under the Endangered Species Act. If the beluga whales fail to recover, many commercial activities within Cook Inlet could face restriction.

Subsistence Summary

Reasons for monitoring: Subsistence uses have not yet recovered and are a priority use under state and federal law.

Type of impacts: Subsistence harvests of recovering species have the potential for causing at least localized depletion of some species.

Agencies managing for a subsistence priority can create impacts on other user groups using resources within the northern GOA.

Who is monitoring: ADF&G is the primary agency for monitoring subsistence uses and harvests.

Regulatory authority: The U.S. Fish and Wildlife Federal Subsistence Board has regulatory and allocation authority within federal lands in Alaska.

The Alaska Board of Fisheries and Board of Game have regulatory authority over subsistence within state lands and waters.

The North Pacific Fishery Management Council has made a recommendation for new regulations dealing with subsistence halibut.

Federal laws, such as the Marine Mammal Protection Act and the Migratory Bird Treaty Act regulate subsistence uses in both state and federal waters.

10.3.5 Timber and Forest Products

Ancestors of the Alutiiq peoples who occupied most of the GOA area are believed to have migrated into the region from treeless areas to the west and north. In the late eighteenth century, at the time of the first contacts with Europeans, the Alutiiq made relatively little use of timber resources except for heat (Dumond 1983).

Many small logging and sawmill operations grew up in the nineteenth century to support local fish processing and mining operations. In the early twentieth century, most of the sawlog timber resources of the Prince William Sound area, the Kenai Peninsula, and the Kodiak archipelago came under the control of the U.S. Forest Service. In addition to supporting local fish processing and mining, GOA forests also supplied railroad ties and timber for bridges to the Alaska Railroad and the Copper River & Northwestern Railway.

Throughout most of the 20th century, the timber industry remained small. From 1910 through 1986,

total commercial harvests from government land in the GOA region averaged less than four million board feet (MMBF) per year, and never exceeded 12 MMBF per year. As part of a policy to encourage timber-based manufacturing within the national forest and nearby communities, the U.S. Forest Service largely prohibited the export from Alaska of unprocessed timber (Rogers 1962). Until 1987, there were essentially no forest products exported from the region to anywhere outside Alaska.

That all changed in the 1980s, when regional and village Native corporations, established under the Alaska Native Claims Settlement Act (ANCSA) began receiving lands selected by them in accordance with the act. For the first time in the history of the GOA region, significant timber resources moved under the control of private, profit-seeking corporations. Most of the high-quality timber has since been logged in an effort to monetize the timber assets as rapidly as possible. Annual harvest volumes from the region grew from less than ten MMBF in 1986, to a peak of about 235 MMBF in 1995, and then quickly declined (USDA Forest Service 2000b). Although a major sawmill was opened in Seward in 1993, it never became competitive, and has remained closed since 1994. As allowed under federal law, almost all of the private timber was exported from the state, most being sold abroad as unprocessed logs (Fried and Windisch-Cole 1999).

Since 1996, a dwindling supply of high-quality timber and a depressed world market for softwood have caused a dramatic decline in harvest from the GOA region. No major timber operations are currently operating in PWS. Some logging continues in the Kodiak archipelago, and small-scale timber operations are planned for parts of the Kenai Peninsula. Improving market conditions and rising softwood prices could significantly increase the market for significant volumes of currently marginal timber, especially on Afognak Island.

A significant factor affecting forest planning in the GOA area is a major spruce bark beetle infestation. A series of timber sales of beetle-damaged stands on state lands have been proposed (USDA Forest Service 2000a). Harvest from the state's proposed sales would encompass an estimated 115 MMBF over a maximum of five years, but adverse market conditions have caused commercial interest in the offerings to wane, and some recent sales have received no bids. In 2000 the state offered almost 12 MMBF, but the amount cut was less than three MMBF (ADNR 2000).

Concerns about logging include long-term effects on the marine ecosystem of bark detritus at log transfer sites, impacts on anadromous streams from siltation, and upland habitat destruction. The Alaska Department of Environmental Conservation reported in 2000 that twenty-four percent of the water bodies on the state's list of polluted sites are listed due to some aspect of logging (ADEC 2000). A significant issue related to logging is the increased access to previously remote lands provided by logging roads. Logging operations on the Kenai Peninsula alone have added more than 3,000 miles of roads in the region. This increased access has encouraged all-terrain vehicle use in sensitive habitats, such as the headwaters of salmon streams.

Timber and Forest Products Summary

Reasons for monitoring: Immediate impacts of logging on anadromous fish and riparian habitat. Point source impacts of wood processing facilities on air and water quality. Long-term habitat and water quality degradation from past logging and pollution of uplands and marine sediments.

Type of impacts: Erosion, wide swings in water temperature, loss of habitat, changes in carbon cycle, increased human pressure due to access. Industrial air and water quality impacts from wood processing.

Who is monitoring: USFS on federal land, ADNR on state and private land. ADF&G monitors impacts on economically important sport, commercial, and subsistence species. ADEC and EPA monitor effects of bark deposition on the marine environment. EPA and ADEC monitor point source industrial effects on air and water quality.

Regulatory authority: State and federal laws have established regulatory authority over most aspects of logging and wood processing. Federal laws include the Clean Water Act, the Endangered Species Act, the Wilderness Act, the Federal Land Planning and Management Act, the National Forest Management Act, the Forest and Rangeland Renewable Resources Planning Act and others; state authorities in Alaska Statutes include Title 16 (ADF&G), Title 47 (ADEC), and the Forest Practices Act.

10.3.6 Urbanization and Road Building

Urban areas are likely to continue to grow from natural population growth and from immigration from smaller communities within Alaska and from outside the state. Increasing urbanization diminishes some basic environmental qualities, even when development is planned and regulated with care. Along with greater numbers and density of residents comes additional air pollution, water pollution, use of lands for solid waste disposal, increased levels of noise, and other effects. Continued expansion of urban areas and increasing density of development of suburban zones inevitably degrade the habitat. Changes in land surfaces can change entire hydrologic systems and cause water pollution problems. Urban growth leads to increasing disposal of human waste. Most metropolitan communities in the country are required to complete secondary treatment of sewage effluent, but Anchorage, operating under a 301 Clean Water Act Section (H) waiver, only completes primary treatment of the sewage effluent piped into Cook Inlet. The inherent turbidity of Cook Inlet water was a significant factor in EPA's grant of the waiver.

Treated waste or street runoff may lead to changes in species composition and productivity of watersheds within the region. A 1998 study of the Kenai River showed a decreased diversity of benthic invertebrates in areas of the river below storm drain outfalls (Litchfield and Milner 1998). What was important in this study was the discovery that even though the benthic invertebrate community was still in place, certain species were missing from the surveyed areas. Based on this study, it appears as if some key indicator species could be used to measure at least some of the effects of storm runoff pollution.

As part of its stormwater discharge permit through ADEC, the Municipality of Anchorage is mapping the impervious surfaces within its area and studying the response of stream macroinvertebrates. Under a U.S. Environmental Protection Agency (EPA) Clean Water Act Section 319 grant from ADEC, the U.S. States Department of Agriculture Cooperative Extension Service is also studying the effects of impervious surfaces. A pilot project is planned for the Anchorage area, and if successful, the methodology may be applied to other areas in the future.

Diminished environmental quality from increased population density is not limited strictly to urban areas. As population density increases in previously rural areas—for example along the Kenai River—there has been a documented loss of environmental quality. In 1994, ADF&G published a study evaluating the cumulative impacts of development and human uses on fish habitat on the Kenai River (Liepitz 1994). Factors diminishing water quality include wetlands loss, point source pollution from outhouses or faulty septic systems, and household spills of oils and other contaminants.

Wetlands play an important ecological role in filtration for water quality and stormwater protection. The Municipality of Anchorage has a wetlands plan, with high- and low-value wetlands identified. There is no plan delineating the extent of wetlands and analyzing their function and values for the rest of the region, however.

The ADEC is responsible for monitoring and regulating state water. However, due to staff and funding limitations, the agency does not attempt to track down and resolve household or small commercial violations. The U.S. Geological Survey operates a National Water Quality Assessment (NAWQA) program tracking water quality and non-point pollution sources in urban watersheds. The goals of the NAWQA Program are to describe current water quality conditions for a large part of the nation's freshwater streams and aquifers; describe how water quality is changing over time; and improve our understanding of the primary natural and human factors affecting water quality (USGS 2001). The Cook Inlet Basin is part of the NAWQA program. The Cook Inlet study will provide increased understanding of water quality in the streams and ground water of the Cook Inlet Basin and identify factors that influence water quality.

Roads are an important factor in habitat damage and water quality degradation. A 2001 study (Western Native Trout Campaign 2001) evaluated the relationship between public roadless lands and existing native trout populations in western states. This report evaluates the diminished status of wild trout and the habitat damage associated with development of road systems. The report concludes that roadless areas are essential to persistence and rebuilding of native salmonid populations.

Human access to streams increases as the number of miles of road increases. Trampling of stream banks, changes in stream configuration created by culverting of roads, reduction in riparian zone vegetation, and a multitude of other problems created by road building and access lead to aquatic habitat degra-

dation and loss of basic productivity. Increased human access to small rivers and streams containing relatively large animals such as salmon and river otters also usually leads to loss of aquatic species through illegal taking, despite the best efforts of law enforcement. Indeed, limitations in budgets usually lead resource management and protection agencies to focus scarce resources on sensitive areas during critical seasons, leaving degradation to take its course in less sensitive locations.

Within the northern GOA, road building and urbanization are of most concern within the Cook Inlet area. There are no agencies monitoring or evaluating the effects of roads on habitat and water quality.

Urbanization and Road Building Summary

Reasons for monitoring: Direct impacts to fish and wildlife species. Immediate loss of wetlands and water quality.

Type of impacts: Erosion, wide swings in water temperature, erratic water flow and diminished water quality, loss of habitat, changes in carbon cycle, increased human pressure due to access.

Who is monitoring: The Municipality of Anchorage has a wetlands plan but little ongoing involvement. ADF&G and private research groups (such as the Western Native Trout Campaign) study the cumulative effects of road-building and development. The USGS NAWQA program monitors water quality within the Cook Inlet Basin.

Regulatory authority: ADF&G has Title 16 authority over anadromous fish streams. The ADEC and the U.S. EPA have regulatory authority over water quality. The Army Corps of Engineers has regulatory authority over development on wetlands.

10.3.7 Other Industrial Activity

Large oil spills like the *Exxon Valdez* oil spill are rare occurrences. More common are smaller discharges of refined oil products, crude oil, and a variety of hazardous substances. These occur frequently in the commercial fishing, petroleum, and timber industries and in a wide variety of commercial establishments such as gas stations and dry cleaners. One of the worst spills near the Kenai River was due to repeated discharges of dry cleaning fluid over many years (Alaska Dept. of Environmental Conservation, River Terrace Spill, unpubl. data, 2002).

Under state law, the release of hazardous substances and oil must be reported to the Alaska Department of Environmental Conservation (ADEC). In 2000, a total of 604 spills were reported in the EVOS GOA region (Table 10.2), resulting in a total discharge of 39,744 gallons of refined oil products, crude oil, and hazardous substances. Although small spills were reported throughout this region, the largest number of spills (497) and the greatest volume of discharge (24,340 gallons) occurred in Cook Inlet. Most spills (90 percent) involved refined oil products, accounting for about 88 percent of the total volume discharged. Only 3,000 gallons of crude oil were reported spilled in the EVOS GOA region during 2000 (ADEC, unpubl. data, 2002).

Spills reported to ADEC include spills onshore as well as discharges into the marine environment. The effects of these small spills depend on such variable factors as the volume of the discharge, its toxicity and persistence in the environment, the time of year the spill occurred, and the significance of the affected environment in the life history of species of concern.

Other Industrial Activity Summary

Reasons for monitoring: Direct contamination of water quality. Danger of loss of fish and wildlife.

Type of impacts: Erosion, wide swings in water temperature, loss of habitat, changes in carbon cycle, increased human pressure due to access. Industrial air and water quality impacts.

Who is monitoring: The ADEC and U.S. EPA do some limited monitoring.

Regulatory authority: The ADEC and U.S. EPA have regulatory authority over water quality.

10.3.8 Contaminants and Food Safety

The presence of industrial and agricultural contaminants in aquatic environments has generated worldwide concerns about potential effects on marine organisms and human consumers. The remoteness of the northern GOA from centers of industry and human population does not necessarily offer protection. Industrial and agricultural contaminants can be transported great distances by atmospheric and marine mechanisms, and evidence of persistent organochlorines (DDT), polychlorinated biphenyls (PCBs), dichlorodiphenyldichloroethylene (DDE), other organic pollutants, and heavy metals has been found in the Arctic, subarctic, and areas adjacent to the GOA (Crane and Galasso 1999). For example, measurable amounts of organochlorines have been found in precipitation and fishes of the Copper River Delta, a tributary of the GOA that forms the eastern boundary of Prince William Sound (Ewald et al. 1998).

In the case of mercury and other metals, such as inorganic arsenic, cadmium, and selenium, low concentrations of the contaminants may be present in the natural environment, with industrial and agricultural sources contributing additional quantities. In many cases there is no known local or regional environmental, industrial, or agricultural source.

A variety of geophysical pathways bring these materials into the GOA, including ocean currents and prevailing winds. In particular, the prevailing atmospheric circulation patterns transfer various materials as aerosols from Asia to the east across the North Pacific (Pahlow and Riebsell 2000) where they enter the marine environment in the form of rain or snow. PCBs and DDT can bioaccumulate in living marine organisms. For example, sampling of transient killer whales that eat marine mammals indicated concentrations of PCBs and DDT derivatives that are many times higher than in resident fish-eating whales. The sources of these contaminants are not known.

There is also concern about the potential effects of contaminants on people, especially those who consume fish and shellfish, waterfowl, and marine mammals. At higher levels of exposure, many of the chemicals noted above can cause adverse effects in people, such as the suppression of the immune system caused by PCBs.

The government of Alaska does not monitor environmental pollutants in the marine environment or marine organisms on a regular basis, although a small fish-testing program was begun in summer 2002. There is no ongoing program for sampling food safety in subsistence resources in coastal communities, although the oil spill provided the opportunity to sample subsistence resources for hydrocarbons in the affected areas from 1989 through 1994. Federal funding for a joint federal-state-Alaska Native initiative has been requested from Congress. The National Oceanic and Atmospheric Administration (NOAA) annually has measured chemicals in mollusks and sediments since 1984, as well as in the livers of bottom-dwelling groundfish and in sediments at the sites of fish capture. The Prince William Sound Regional Citizens' Advisory Council has measured hydrocarbon concentrations and sources within areas of PWS and the GOA. This program focuses on sampling of intertidal mussels and nearby sediments.

Contaminants and Food Safety Summary

Reasons for monitoring: Industrial and agricultural contaminants are concentrated in fish and wildlife species. This can cause mortality in affected fish and wildlife as well as danger to humans consuming contaminated fish and wildlife.

Type of impacts: Persistence within the environment and potentially spreading to fish, wildlife, and humans.

Who is monitoring: NOAA monitors chemicals in mollusks, sediments, and bottom-dwelling groundfish.

Regulatory authority: The U.S. EPA has regulatory authority over contaminants in aquatic environments.

10.3.9 Global Warming

Although driven by forces outside the control of Alaska's natural resource managers, global warming is an essential consideration for development and implementation of research programs. The earth's climate is predicted to change because human activities, such as the combustion of fossil fuels and increased agriculture, deforestation, landfills, industrial production, and mining, are altering the chemical composition of the atmosphere through the buildup of greenhouse gases. These gases are primarily carbon dioxide, methane, nitrous oxide, and chlorofluorocarbons. Their heat-trapping property is undisputed, as is the fact that global temperatures are rising. Observations collected during the last century suggest that the average land surface temperature has risen 0.45° to 0.6°C. Precipitation has increased by about one percent over the world's continents in the last century, with high-latitude areas tending to see more significant increases in rainfall and rising sea levels. This increase is consistent with observations that indicate the northern GOA sea surface temperature has increased by 0.5°C

since 1940, and that precipitation in Alaska (excluding Southeast Alaska) increased eleven percent from 1950 through 1990.

Increasing concentrations of greenhouse gases are likely to accelerate the rate of climate change. The changes seen in the northern GOA and their relationship to other warming and cooling cycles in the North Pacific and the combined effects on global climate are important for understanding how humans affect biological production. Some populations of fish and marine mammals that show longtime trends, up or down, or sharp rapid changes in abundance, are actively managed through harvest restraints. The extent to which harvest restraints may be effective in establishing or altering trends in abundance of exploited species can be understood only within the context of climate change.

A rise in sea level is an anticipated change from global warming, leading to flooding of low-lying property, loss of coastal wetlands, erosion of beaches, salt water intrusion into fresh water wells and increased costs for maintenance and/or replacement of roads and bridges (U.S. EPA 1998). An increase in ocean level may have profound impacts on salmon production. The loss of estuarine wetlands from the 1964 earthquake resulted in major losses of pink salmon habitat in Prince William Sound.

Global warming may also have a negative effect on use of water resources throughout Alaska by leading to earlier and more concentrated spring runoff periods. There could be detrimental effects on forests within the northern GOA, for species that are adapted to a cooler temperature regime.

Global Warming Summary

Reasons for monitoring: Danger of losses to fish and wildlife. Salt water intrusion into freshwater supplies.

Type of impacts: Flooding of low-lying property, loss of coastal wetlands, erosion of beaches, salt water intrusion into freshwater wells, increase in public costs for maintenance, and replacement of roads and bridges.

Who is monitoring: U.S. EPA.

Regulatory authority: U.S. EPA has regulatory authority over activities that add to global warming. Many sources are international and not subject to regulation.

Modeling

Gretchen Oosterhout

Modeling, as well as observing systems designed to support modeling efforts, have been established in the Gulf of Alaska (GOA) and North Pacific. Regional monitoring and research programs should build on the strengths of past and existing programs. In this chapter, modeling strategies of established programs are reviewed, followed by discussion of the purposes of modeling, a hierarchical framework for organizing different types of models, options available in modeling strategies and methods, and the means of evaluating modeling proposals.

The chapter concludes with a section on North Pacific models.

11.1 SURVEY OF MODELING

11.1.1 Modeling Strategies of Established Programs

This subsection provides statements summarizing modeling strategies.

GOOS (Global Ocean Observing System)

Linking user needs to measurements requires a managed, interactive flow of data and information among three essential subsystems of the IOOS (Integrated Ocean Observing System): (1) the observing subsystem (measurement of core variables and the transmission of data), (2) the communications network and data management subsystem (organizing, cataloging, and disseminating data), and (3) the modeling and applications subsystem (translating data into products in response to user needs). Thus, the observing system consists of the infrastructure and expertise required for each of these subsystems as well as that needed to insure the continued and routine flow of data and information among them. (U.S. GOOS 2000)

PICES (North Pacific Marine Science Organization)/NEMURO (North Pacific Ecosystem Model for Understanding Regional Oceanography)

Models serve to extrapolate retrospective and new observations through space and time, assist with the design of observational programs, and test our understanding of the integration and functioning of ecosystem components. Clear differences were identified in the level of advancement of the various disciplinary models. Atmosphere-ocean and physical circulation models are the most advanced, to the extent that existing models are generally useful now for CCCC (climate change and carrying capacity) objectives, at least on the Basin scale. Circulation models in territorial and regional seas are presently more varied in their level of development, and may need some coordination from PICES. Lower trophic level models are advancing, and examples of their application coupled with large-scale circulation models are beginning to appear. There is a need for comparisons of specific physiological models, and for grafting of detailed mixed layer models into the general circulation models. With upper trophic level models, there are several well-developed models for specific applications, but workshop participants felt there were as yet no leading models available for general use within the CCCC program. This is an area that needs particular attention and encouragement from PICES. (Perry et al. 1997)

GLOBEC (Global Ocean Ecosystems Dynamics)

The physical models . . . can be coupled with a suite of biological, biophysical and ecosystems models. Development of biological models should occur concurrently with development of the physical model. Four types of biological or biophysical models are recommended. . . . Linking outputs from each of these models will allow the examination of ecosystem level questions regarding top down or bottom up controls in determining pelagic production in the Bering Sea. (U.S. GLOBEC, No date)

11.1.2 Core Variables for Modeling

Table 11.1 shows spatial domains, currencies, inputs, and outputs for several of the most relevant North Pacific models.

11.2 PURPOSES OF MODELING

The ultimate goal of both gathering data and developing models is to increase understanding. Pickett et al. (1994, cited in Pace 2001, p. 69) define this goal, in the realm of science, as "an objectively determined, empirical match between some set of confirmable, observable phenomena in the natural world and a conceptual construct."

Table 11.1. Model Spatial Domains, Currencies, Inputs, and Outputs.

Model name/ Model region	Model spatial domain	Inputs	Outputs/currency
Single-species stock assessment models that include predation	Across EBS and GOA pollock distributions	Fisheries data and predator biomass	Pollock population and mortality trends— number at age (and biomass at age)
Bering Sea MSVPA	The modeled region is the EBS shelf and slope north to about 61°N	Fisheries, predator biomass, and food habits data. This model requires estimates of other food abundance supplied by species outside the model.	Age-structured population dynamics for key species—numbers at age
BORMICON for the Eastern Bering Sea	The model is spatially explicit with 7 defined geographic regions that have pollock abundance and size distribution information.	Temperature is included and influences growth and consumption.	Spatial size distribution of pollock
Evaluating alternative fishing strategies	U.S. Exclusive Economic Zone	Gear-specific fishing effort, including bycatch	Biomass of managed fish species
Advection on larval pollock recruitment	Southeast Bering Sea shelf	OSCURS surface currents (wind-driven)	Index of pollock recruitment
Shelikof Pollock IBM	Western GOA from just southwest of Kodiak Island to the Shumagin Islands shelf, water column to 100 m	From physical model: Water velocities, wind field, mixed-layer depth, water temperature, and salinity; *Pseudocalanus* field (from NPZ model)	Individual larval characteristics such as age, size, weight, location, life stage, hatch date, consumption, respiration
GLOBEC NPZ 1-D and 3-D Models	Water column (0-100 m), coastal GOA from Dixon Entrance to Unimak Pass, 100 m of water column over depths <2,000 m, 5 m depth bins × 20 km horizontal grid	Irradiance, MLD Temperature, diffusivity, bottom depths, water velocities (u, v, w)	Diffusivity, ammonium, nitrate, detritus, small and large phytoplankton, dinoflagellates, tintinnids, small coastal copepods, *Neocalanus*, and euphausiids Nitrate and ammonium: mmol m^{-3} All else: mg carbon m^{-3}
Steller Sea Lion IBM	Should be applicable to a specific sea lion rookery or any domain surrounding haul-out in the Bering Sea, Aleutian Islands, or GOA	The main input will be a 3-D field of prey (fish) distribution, derived either from hypothetical scenarios or (later) modeled based on acoustic data.	Individual sea lion characteristics such as age, location, life stage, and birth date are recorded. Caloric balance is the main variable followed for each individual.
Shelikof NPZ Model, 1-D and 3-D Versions	Water column (0-100 m), GOA from southwest of Kodiak Island to Shumagin Islands. 1 m depth bins for 1-D version; 1 m depth × 20 km for 3-D version	Irradiance, MLD, temperature, bottom depths, water velocities (u, v, w)	Nitrogen, phytoplankton, *Neocalanus* densities, *Pseudocalanus* numbers m^{-3} for each of the 13 stages (egg, 6 naupliar, 6 copepodites)

Table 11.1. Model Spatial Domains, Currencies, Inputs, and Outputs (Continued).

Model name/ Model region	Model spatial domain	Inputs	Outputs/currency
GOA Pollock Stochastic Switch Model	Shelikof Strait, Gulf of Alaska	Number of eggs to seed the model. Base mortality, additive and multiplicative mortality. Adjustment parameters for each mortality factor.	Number of 90-day-old pollock larvae through time
NEMURO	Ocean Station P (50°N 145°W), Bering Sea (57.5°N 175°W), and Station A7 off the east of Hokkaido Island, Japan (41.3°N 145.3°W)	15 state variables and parameters, including 2 phytoplankton, 3 zooplankton, and multiple nutrient groups	Ecosystem fluxes are tracked in units of nitrogen and silicon.
Eastern Bering Sea Shelf Model 1 Ecopath	500,000 km^2 in EBS south of 61°N	Biomass, production, consumption, and diet composition for all major species in each ecosystem	Balance between produced and consumed per area biomass (t km^{-2}). Future work will explore energy (kcal km^{-2}) and nutrient dynamics.
Eastern Bering Sea Ecopath Shelf Model 2	500,000 km^2 in eastern Bering Sea south of 61°N		
Western Bering Sea Shelf Ecopath	300,000 km^2 on western Bering Sea shelf		
Gulf of Alaska Shelf Ecopath	NPFMC management areas 610, 620, 630, and part of 640		
Aleutian Islands, Pribilof Islands Ecopath	Not determined		
Prince William Sound Ecopath	Whole Prince William Sound		

Source: Kerim Aydin, NMFS, Seattle, WA.
BORMICON = Boreal Migration and Consumption Model
EBS = Eastern Bering Sea
GLOBEC = Global Ocean Ecosystem Dynamics
GOA = Gulf of Alaska
km = kilometer
kcal = kilocalorie
m = meter
MLD = mixed layer depth
mmol = millimolar
MSVPA = Multispecies Virtual Population Analysis
NEMURO = North Pacific Ecosystem Model for Understanding Regional Oceanography
NPFMC = North Pacific Fishery Management Council
NPZ = nutrient-phytoplankton-zooplankton
OSCURS = Ocean Surface Current Simulations
t = metric ton
YD = days of year

A model—Pickett's "conceptual construct"—is useful if it helps people represent, examine, and use hypothetical relationships. Data—Pickett's "confirmable, observable phenomena in the natural world"—can be analyzed with statistical tools such as the following:

- Analyses of the variance, regressions, and classification and regression trees (CARTs);

- Mathematical tools such as Fourier transforms or differential equations; and

- Qualitative models such as engineering "free body" diagrams, network diagrams, or loop models.

Fundamental goals of statistical or mathematical analyses are to develop correlative, and perhaps even causal, relationships and an understanding of patterns and trends. In particular, there is a need to distinguish between random variability, noise, and patterns or trends that can be used to explain and predict.

In other words, the goal of gathering and analyzing data is to improve our conceptual and analytical models of the world, and the goal of developing models is to represent and examine hypothetical relationships that can be tested with data.

One of the most useful applications of even relatively simple statistical and conceptual models is in experimental design that permits investigating the possible roles of various parameters and their interactions, ranking the relative importance of uncertainties that may need to be resolved (Fahrig 1991, Oosterhout 1998), and estimating impacts of sample size and observational error (Carpenter et al. 1994, Ludwig 1999, Botkin et al. 2000, Meir and Fagan 2000). Statistical models assess how the variability in one or more kinds of data relates to variability of others. To answer the "why" and "how" questions, however, mechanistic models can be used to develop and test hypotheses about causes and effects (Gargett et al. 2001). (Mechanistic in this use is intended to describe the philosophy of mechanism, especially explaining phenomena through reference to physical or biological causes.) For monitoring and modeling to be useful for solving problems, they must contribute to improving decision-making (Holling and Clark 1975, Holling 1978, Hilborn 1997, Botkin et al. 2000, Ralls and Taylor 2000).

Toward this end, one goal of GOA research programs is to use models predictively to assist managers in solving problems. It is important that expectations be realistic, however. The mechanisms that drive ecological systems, particularly those related to cli-mate and human activities, are not currently well enough understood for predictions about natural systems to be reliably successful. It is not unreasonable to expect that predictive models that managers will be able to use to produce at least short-term reliable forecasts will eventually be developed, but advances in decision-support models will require a long-term commitment to advancing understanding on which those decision-support models will ultimately have to be based.

Prediction is, however, an important goal of a modeling program even in the short run, because science advances with the development and testing of predictive hypotheses. Mechanistic studies are essential to advancing understanding, but carrying out these studies requires defining cause-effect or predictive hypotheses, and then testing those predictions against subsequent data or events with analytical models.

The fundamental goal of GOA research programs is to identify and better understand the natural and human forces that cause changes in GOA ecosystems. This research goal has a pragmatic purpose that can only be served, in the end, by linking correlative and mechanistic studies with the predictive needs of decision makers. Decision-making, prediction, and understanding are inevitably linked, and maintaining that link can help keep a research program focused on its ultimate objectives, and help it to avoid narrow inquiry and the distractions of small temporary problems (Pace 2001).

An often-overlooked benefit provided by the process of developing a model is that it can, and probably should, facilitate communication among researchers, managers, and the public.

To summarize, in GOA research programs, the specific purposes of modeling are to

- Inform, communicate, and provide common problem definition;

- Identify key variables and relationships;

- Set priorities;

- Improve and develop experimental designs to attain monitoring objectives; and

- Improve decision-making and risk assessment.

11.3 HIERARCHICAL FRAMEWORK

It is critical that GOA research programs develop a hierarchical modeling strategy to ensure that short-term, smaller-scale decisions about monitoring and modeling studies will be consistent with the conceptual foundation. Smaller-scope research studies to test particular hypotheses and develop correlative relationships must fit within a larger synthesis framework connecting the more narrowly focused research disciplines. Deductive studies to relate empirical data to synthetic constructs are just as important as inductive studies to elucidate general principles, and it is important that researchers keep straight whether they are investigating the meaning of the data, given the theory, or the validity of the theory, given the data. Neither can be done unless modeling, monitoring, and data management strategies are developed together.

Models may be verbal, visual, statistical, or numerical. Statistical models are also known as "correlative" and "stochastic," and numerical models are also known as "deterministic" and "mechanistic." Note that "prediction," "analysis," and "simulation" are terms that describe the use of models, and not necessarily their type. The modeling hierarchy provides links between observations and explanations, development of theory and design of experiments, and advancement of science and the practice of management. The "top" of this hierarchy, the conceptual foundation, is the source of questions and hypotheses to be explored. Statistical, analytical, and simulation models will be developed explicitly to link the "confirmable, observable phenomena in the natural world" to the "conceptual construct," as Pickett et al. put it (1994, cited in Pace 2001, p. 69).

For example, a visual model of the conceptual foundation is shown in an influence diagram in Figure 11.1, which shows the forces of change on the left and the objects of ultimate interest that are subject to change on the right. In between the two are the intervening elements and relationships on which the human and natural forces act. It is the nature of the connections among these physical and ecological elements that is hypothesized to bring about the changes that GOA research programs seek to understand. Therefore, these connections should provide the overall modeling structure.

This conceptual model is linked to the monitoring plan through the variables defined as "essential to monitor" in the conceptual foundation, illustrated in a network diagram in Figure 1.3 (Chapter 1). The analytical relationships between the monitored variables of Figure 1.3 and the conceptual foundation represented by Figure 1.4 (Chapter 1), are developed and investigated with statistical and analytical tools, called models.

The ultimate goal of GLOBEC's Northeast Pacific modeling appears to be a suite of computer models that represents an entire conceptual foundation. The way this is framed in programs like GLOBEC, the North Pacific Marine Science Organization (called PICES), and Global Ocean Observing System (GOOS) (see section 11.2 of this chapter) is as linked physical and biological models representing the physical and biological worlds over time and space (marine as well as terrestrial).

The National Research Council describes this idealized goal as follows (NRC 2000, p. 16): develop a whole-ecosystem fishery model as a guide to think about what needs to be monitored. Such a model would use current and historical data to relate yields to climate data and contaminant levels and might stress biological and physical endpoints (zooplankton/phytoplankton blooms, macrofauna populations) and climate and physical oceanography endpoints, in conjunction with modeling.

Such a conceptual framework can stimulate heated arguments, creative debate, and perhaps synthesis among researchers who have tended to work in somewhat independent fields with different theoretical foundations and languages (Zacharias and Roff 2000). On a pragmatic level, however, it is too general to help decision makers choose to fund one proposal over another.

A feasible way to proceed from what can be done now is through an iterative process framed by the conceptual foundation (Figure 11.1). The conceptual foundation should be the explicit source of hypothetical correlative and cause-and-effect relationships. Those relationships should be stated as hypotheses, and should be used to determine what needs to be measured and when, where, and how. If the monitoring and modeling plans are developed within this framework, the measurements can be compared to model predictions, the results can be used to update the scientific background and the monitoring plan, and the iteration can continue.

11.4 DEFINING AND EVALUATING MODELING STRATEGIES

Modeling efforts for the short term should be developed as part of a long-term strategy defined by goals of research programs. The modeling strategy must be consistent with research implementation tools and strategies and mission goals. Research modeling should accomplish the following:

- Focus on filling gaps, thus avoiding duplication of efforts or "reinventing the wheel";

- Emphasize synthesis;

- Depend as much as possible on already existing programs;

- Maintain focus on the research questions; and

- Emphasize efficiency.

In developing a specific management strategy, it is often useful to think of it as a decision framework (Keeney 1992), and to start by defining an ideal. For example, an ideal model would arguably require input data that are relatively easy to measure, readily available, and reliable indicators of change. The cause-effect theory that drives the modeled system or species behavior would be based not only on statistically valid correlative studies, but also on plausible and well-developed mechanistic studies and their resulting theoretical constructs. The model would produce credible predictions under plausible scenarios, and would help answer questions and raise new ones.

This ideal model would be easy for other scientists and managers to comprehend, and it would be readily available for others to deconstruct, test, and critique. The overarching conceptual model would be modularized so that components of it could be developed and tested relatively quickly by experts from multiple disciplines. Ideally, data already available could be used to test and validate the components and their interactions, and could allow quick learning that could be used to redirect the modeling and monitoring strategies. Sensitivity analysis of the components, and the interactions between the components, would be a highly productive source for subsequent model and monitoring plan development. Model structure would be flexible and have robust mechanisms for assimilating new data and revising model structure. As a result, short-term progress toward the long-term goals could be achieved and documented.

A modeling strategy is the roadmap that provides the means for achieving the ultimate modeling goals. An idealized model like the one described above is a useful step toward defining the attributes of an efficient, workable strategy. Development of such an idealized model can produce a useful communication tool. Table 11.2 identifies preliminary objectives and attributes derived from this idealized model that could be used to evaluate modeling strategies.

11.5 MODELING METHODS

The modeling "niche" of GOA research will be defined in part by a gap analysis, particularly focused on where it fits with established major regional programs, especially those of GLOBEC, GOOS, and PICES.

The relationship between monitoring, modeling, and decision-making described here is consistent with the relationships of these programs. A useful context is provided by a table compiled for GLOBEC by K. Aydin of the National Oceanic and Atmospheric Administration (Seattle), which summarizes North Pacific models of the Alaska Fisheries Science Center and others (Table 11.2). Correctly defining the GOA research niche is important to avoid duplication of effort and to make best use of work already being done by others.

Developing a model should be perfectly analogous to designing a controlled experiment. A useful model structure will be driven by the questions it needs to help people answer, not by the computer technology and programming expertise of model developers (although technology and expertise may impose constraints). As a general rule, useful models do not tend to be complex, in part because they must be comprehensible to be believed and used by decision makers. That said, models based on laws of physics, which can be validated against those laws and either data or scale physical models, have advanced further than ecological models in their ability to provide useful output from highly complex models.

11.5.1 Links among Models and among Modelers

One of the most important challenges confronting modelers will be to develop common languages and modeling frameworks that will allow them to resolve the temporal, mathematical, ecological, physical, and spatial sources of disconnects among the various academic paradigms. This challenge will require significant commitment to improving communication skills, developing qualitative verbal or visual models, and using intuitive problem-structuring tools that combine different modeling techniques, such as network, systems, or loop models. An additional benefit of this kind of approach is that these types of visual, qualitative models should be comprehensible to researchers from any scientific discipline, managers, and the public. The attribute of being widely comprehensible will help facilitate the support of stakeholders.

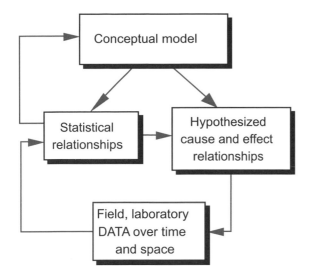

Figure 11.1. Feedback control system linking the conceptual foundation, monitoring, and modeling efforts.

The feasibility of managing research programs depends in large part on the communication skills of experts in the components and linkages that make up the conceptual foundation. Establishing effective communication among experts from different organizations is a widespread problem facing systems modelers (Caddy 1995). Experts in these fields should bring substantial background capabilities to their work from their common language of mathematics and science learned in graduate school. The modelers also should be required to demonstrate the ability to work with counterparts to develop a shared systems view and conceptual models.

11.5.2 Deterministic Versus Stochastic Models

Detecting and understanding change requires that uncertainty and variability play a central role in the analyses (Ralls and Taylor 2000). Two key questions that must be addressed by anyone trying to detect and understand change are the problems of Type I and Type II error. Type I error is "seeing" something that is not really there; and Type II error is concluding something is not there, when it really is. Dealing with these types of error in decision-making requires weighing the evidence that suspected change is caused by a (theoretically) definable pattern or trend or is "normal" process error, observation error, or some combination. Equally important, and often overlooked, is how real indicators of change may be hidden by process or observation error or by incorrect assumptions about how things work.

Dealing with uncertainty and variability in models requires at a minimum carrying out sensitivity analysis on simple deterministic models, with particular emphasis on model structure (Hilborn and Mangel 1997). But it is often more efficient and more useful to incorporate stochasticity into simple models. Stochastic models need not necessarily be more data intensive than deterministic models. Overlooking the assumptions required in choosing a mean (or median) or geometric mean, as a representative value for a deterministic parameter is one of the most widespread, but overlooked, sources of modeling error (Vose 2000). At least stochastic modeling requires that probability distributions be explicitly defined.

Simplistic deterministic models can be every bit as misleading and improper as stochastic models (Schnute and Richards 2001), but because they are more familiar, and their single-number inputs and outputs are easier to think about than uncertainties and ranges, they may lead to false confidence on the part of decision makers. Risk assessment in most fields requires analyzing probability distributions and uncertainties, not mean trajectories (Glickman and Gough 1990, Burgman et al. 1993, Vose 2000).

One fundamental issue of interest to decision makers is often how best to prioritize research efforts. A key part of such an issue is ranking the relative impacts of uncertainties on a decision. In this case, it is possible that thoughtful sensitivity analysis carried out on a simple, deterministic model (or multiple models) may be adequate for the job, particularly as a first step in "weeding out" variables that are likely to be extraneous. But developing a stochastic version of relatively simple models may be more efficient (Vose 2000). If care is taken to distinguish between environmental or process variation and observational or functional uncertainty, then statistical tools such as analysis of variance or regression can be used to investigate the relative impacts of uncertainties (Meyer et al. 1986, Mode and Jacobson 1987a,b Fahrig 1991, Law and Kelton 1991, Oosterhout 1996, Ruckelshaus et al. 1997, Oosterhout 1998, Vose 2000). This approach can be very helpful in developing analytical structures as well as modeling plans. It also lends itself well to decision analysis and risk assessment because it is similar to the "value of imperfect information" analyses widely used in risk assessment and decision analysis (von Winterfeldt

Table 11.2. Potential Objectives and Attributes for Use in Evaluation of Modeling Strategies.

Objective or Attribute	Supported by models that help . . .
Relevance to research	Identify variables and relationships.
	Characterize uncertainty and noise, impacts of process and observation error.
	Elucidate general principles rather than narrow, unique focus driven by short-term perceived crisis.
Contribution to future	Inform, communicate, develop common problem definitions.
	Set priorities, clarify relative impacts of variables and relationships.
	Improve and develop experimental (monitoring) designs.
	Prioritize and elucidate impacts of uncertainties in data and in model structure and assumptions.
	Increase utility of using simpler models to identify key variables and relationships to use in future models.
	Advance the state of the art; for example, increase available methodologies by borrowing from other fields, particularly engineering and medicine, tools such as neural nets, genetic algorithms, CARTs, other kinds of regression (Jackson et al. 2001).
Efficiency of approach	Synthesize, exploit, and integrate existing data and existing programs whenever possible; for example, from oceanographic programs such as NOAA, OCSEAP, GLOBEC, and GOOS.
	Elucidate links between things that are easy to measure and key indicators of change, whatever they might be.
	Elucidate links between correlations (which are usually easier to develop) and explanatory mechanisms (which are usually more difficult).
Maintenance and development	Accessibility of models to end users, other modelers.
	Contribution to data management, data assimilation effort.
	Contribution to solving problems for resource managers and regulators.

and Edwards 1986, Keeney 1992, Hilborn 1997, Punt and Hilborn 1997).

11.5.3 Correlative Versus Mechanistic Models

The use of statistics-based tools such as regressions to make deterministic or probabilistic predictions will generally be easier than developing deterministic or stochastic biological models, because of a dearth of predictive "laws" of biology, let alone ecology. Because statistics-based models are correlative, cause-and-effect explanations will eventually be needed if change is to be understood and predicted reliably. Because some things are easier and more reliable to measure than others, simple models that can help develop correlative relationships between hard-to-measure parameters and easy-to-measure parameters may be of particular interest.

11.5.4 Modeling and Monitoring Interaction

Models should be developed to use and synthesize readily available data whenever possible. This approach will also help identify data needs. Similarly, whenever possible, monitoring plans should be developed to fit the models that will be used to analyze and interpret them. Data management, assimilation, and synthesis should be key considerations for both monitoring and modeling.

One useful way to incorporate data into improving an existing statistical or simulation model is with the Bayesian revision methods (Marmorek et al. 1996, Punt and Hilborn 1997, Hilborn 1997). Bayesian methods might be useful to consider with respect to the question about how much emphasis should be put on annual forecasts, because Bayesian methods lend themselves well to incorporating incoming data into previous forecasts. This entire approach also lends itself well to decision-analysis techniques.

Models are tools for assimilating data and optimizing data collection as expressed for the GOOS program (IOC 2000, p. 36):

A validated assimilation model can be most useful in optimizing the design of the observing subsystem upon which it depends. This underscores the mutual dependence of observing and modeling the ocean, i.e., observations should not be conducted independently of modeling and vice versa. For example the so-called "adjoint method" of assimilation can be used to gauge the sensitivity of model controls (e.g., open boundary and initial conditions, mixing parameters) to the addition or deletion of observations at arbitrary locations within the model domain. In this regard, "observation system simulation experiments" are becoming increasingly popular in oceanography as a way of assessing various sampling strategies. The model is first run with realistic forcing and model parameters. The output is then subsampled at times and locations at which the observations were sampled. These simulated observations are then assimilated into the model and the inferred field compared against the original field from which the "observations" were taken. This allows the efficacy of the assimilation scheme and sampling strategy to be evaluated (at least to the extent that the model is believed to be a reasonable representation of reality).

11.6 EVALUATING MODEL PROPOSALS

The following guidelines were proposed for evaluating research model proposals for the GOA. They are presented here for their utility in the GOA as well as other locations.

Model proposals should be evaluated within a decision-structured framework such as that outlined above and detailed in Table 11.2. As a starting point, successful model proposals can provide the following:

- Define who will use the model and for what. If the proposal is to continue or expand an existing model, it should describe who is currently using it and for what. If relevant, the proposal should also identify who could be using it, for what, and why they are not able to use it now.

- Define the questions the model is supposed to answer, and directly link those questions to the key questions and hypotheses for research.

- Argue convincingly that the model structure is adequate for the purpose, and that no better (cheaper, faster, more comprehensible, more direct) way exists to answer these questions.

- Show a schematic (flowchart) that is clear, complete, and concise.

- Explain how uncertainty and variability will be represented and analyzed.

- Describe the system characteristics that will be left out or simplified and how the analysis will evaluate the impacts.

- Define data needs and show how the modeling effort will be coordinated with data assimilation and data management efforts.

- Define validation approach.

- Define how the modeling efforts will be communicated to other scientists, managers, and the public; and how input from model stakeholders will be incorporated into the effort, if appropriate.

11.7 SUMMARY

Feasibility and pragmatism in research programs dictate that walking will have to come before running and that focused, simpler models will have to come before large-scale, multidisciplinary models. Walking first means developing verbal and statistical models where numerical models cannot be developed because of a lack of data and understanding. Learning to run requires developing coupled numerical biophysical models that accurately portray the ecosystem. Running means using the biophysical models in a predictive sense. The models must adapt to changes in the conceptual foundation, because the conceptual foundation is designed to change as new information is incorporated. Nonetheless, no matter how many improvements are made, it is probably not reasonable to expect consensus on how that conceptual foundation should be used to develop a strategic modeling policy.

In a constrained world, "consensus" in practice usually means accepting a strategy that enough decision makers find no more offensive than they can accept; optimization, on the other hand, means figuring out the tradeoffs necessary to achieve as many objectives as reasonably possible. Adopting a decision-structured approach for the modeling strategy will help ensure that it is driven by the fundamental objectives of research programs, that the modeling questions are defined by the conceptual foundation, and the tradeoffs can be defined, weighed, and justified.

11.8 NORTH PACIFIC MODELS

The following summary of physical and biological modeling in the North Pacific was prepared by K. Aydin, National Marine Fisheries Service (NMFS), Seattle (Kerim.Aydin@noaa.gov). Descriptions of the hypotheses embodied by each model are followed by details of model features and development in tables for ease of reference and comparison of models. Geographic areas, time periods addressed, status of development, and person to contact for more information is included in Table 11.3.

11.8.1 Predation

The NMFS Alaska Fisheries Science Center has developed two single-species stock assessment models that include predation: one for Eastern Bering Sea pollock (Livingston and Methot 1998) and one for Gulf of Alaska pollock (Hollowed et al. 2000). One for Aleutian Islands Atka mackerel may be developed in the future. The purpose of these models is to better understand the sources and time trends of natural mortality for pollock by explicitly incorporating predation mortality induced by their major predators into an age-structured fish stock assessment model. We have learned that not only is natural mortality for younger fish much higher than that for adults, but also that it varies across time, depending on time trends in predator stocks. This finding about mortality has given us better ideas of what influences predation has on fish recruitment through time and helps us to separate predation and climate-related effects on recruitment. We can better show the demands of other predators such as marine mammals for a commercially fished stock and how it might influence the dynamics of that stock (although we still need to make progress in understanding the effects on the marine mammals).

11.8.2 Bering Sea MSVPA

We now have a multispecies virtual population analysis (MSVPA) model for the Bering Sea (Livingston and Jurado-Molina 2000). This model includes predation interactions among several commercially important groundfish stocks and also predation by arrowtooth flounder and northern fur seal on these stocks. This model can give us a better idea of the predation interactions among several stocks. We can use outputs from this type of model to help us understand what the possible multispecies implications are of our single-species-oriented fishing strategies. Results from these forecasting exercises show that a particular fishing strategy may have the opposite of the intended effect if multispecies interactions are taken into consideration. We have also done multispecies forecasting with this model by using different hypotheses about regime shifts and associated fish recruitment patterns.

11.8.3 Eastern Bering Sea BORMICON

We have an initial version of a spatially explicit model of pollock movement and cannibalism in the Eastern Bering Sea. We hope to better understand the differences in spatial overlap of predators and prey and how that affects the population dynamics of each. The model we have modified for the Bering Sea, BORMICON (boreal migration and consumption model), is being used in other boreal ecosystems. Migrations are prescribed currently, with the hope that we can prescribe movement based on physical factors in the future. The influence of spatial overlap of cannibalistic adult pollock with juveniles on the population dynamics of pollock is being investigated. Hypotheses about larval drift positions and the resulting overlap and cannibalism are also being explored. This model could be linked in the future to an individual-based larval pollock model and to a nutrient-phytoplankton-zooplankton model that could prescribe zooplankton abundance by area as alternate food for adults and as the primary food for juveniles.

11.8.4 Multiple Gear Types

Analytical approaches to evaluating alternative fishing strategies with multiple gear types have been employed. The analytical approach for simulating current groundfish management in the North Pacific U.S. Exclusive Economic Zone involves considering interactions among a large number of species (including target, nontarget, and prohibited) areas and gear types. To evaluate the consequences of alternative management regimes, modeling was used to predict the likely outcome of management decisions by using statistics on historical catch of different species by gear types and areas. Management of the Alaska groundfish fisheries is complex, given the large numbers of species, areas, and gear types. The managers schedule fisheries openings and closures to maximize catch subject to catch limits and other constraints. These management actions are based on expectations about the array of species likely to be captured by different gear types and the cumulative effect that each fishery has on the allowable catch of each individual target species and other species groups. Management decisions were simulated by an in-season management model that predicts capture

Table 11.3. Model Areas, Time Period, Contact Person, and Model Status.

Model name/Model region	Time period	Contact
Single-species stock assessment models that include predation	EBS: 1964-95 GOA: 1964-97 (Annual)	Patricia Livingston[1]
Bering Sea MSVPA	1979-98 3 months (Quarterly)	Patricia Livingston Jesus Jurado-Molina[1]
BORMICON for the Eastern Bering Sea	1979-97 1 month	Patricia Livingston
Evaluating Alternative Fishing Strategies	Current	Jim Ianelli[1]
Advection on Larval Pollock Recruitment	90 days of larval drift 1970s-present	Jim Ianelli
Shelikof Pollock IBM	YD 60-270 (Daily)	Sarah Hinckley[1]
GLOBEC NPZ 1-D and 3-D Models	YD 60-270 (eventually year-round). (Daily)	Sarah Hinckley
Steller Sea Lion IBM	Summer or winter, minutes to days	Sarah Hinckley
Shelikof NPZ Model, 1-D and 3-D Versions	YD 60-270 (eventually year-round). (Daily)	Sarah Hinckley
GOA Pollock Stochastic Switch Model	32 years (replicates) (Daily)	Bern Megrey[1]
NEMURO	1 full year, (Daily)	Bern Megrey
Eastern Bering Sea Shelf Model 1 Ecopath	1950s and early 1980s (Annual)	Patricia Livingston
Eastern Bering Sea Shelf Model 2 Ecopath	1979-1998 (Annual)	Kerim Aydin[1]
Western Bering Sea Shelf Ecopath	Early 1980s (Annual)	Kerim Aydin Victor Lapko[2]
Gulf of Alaska Shelf Ecopath	1990-99 (Annual)	Sarah Gaiches[1]
Aleutian Islands, Pribilof Islands Ecopath	1990s-2000s (Annual)	Patricia Livingston Lorenzo Ciannelli[1]
Prince William Sound Ecopath	Pre- and post 1989 oil spill (Annual)	Tom Okey[3]

[1]NMFS, Seattle, WA.
[2]TINRO-Centre.
[3]University of British Columbia, Vancouver.
BORMICON = Boreal Migration and Consumption Model
EBS = Eastern Bering Sea
GLOBEC = Global Ocean Ecosystem Dynamics
GOA = Gulf of Alaska
MSVPA = Multispecies Virtual Population Analysis
NEMURO = North Pacific Ecosystem Model for Understanding Regional Oceanography
NPZ = nutrient-phytoplankton-zooplankton
YD = days of the year

of target and nontarget species by different fisheries based on historical catch data by area and gear type. The groundfish population abundance for each alternative regime was forecast for a 5-year period beginning from the present. This approach provides a reasonable representation of the current fisheries management practice for dealing with the multispecies nature of catch in target fisheries.

In addition to the model and its projected results, agency analysts also used the scientific literature, ongoing research, and professional opinion of fishery experts in their respective fields to perform qualitative assessments.

11.8.5 Larval Pollock Recruitment

A model involving the influence of advection on larval pollock recruitment investigates the environmental relationship between surface advection during the post-spawning period (pollock egg and larval stages) and pollock survival. Wespestad et al. (1997) found that during years when the surface currents tended north-northwestward along the shelf, class strength was improved compared to years when currents were more easterly. They used the ocean surface current simulations (OSCURS) surface advection model to simulate drift. Subsequently (Ianelli et al. 1998), their analysis was extended to apply within a stock assessment model. The model uses surface advection during a 90-day period to determine the "goodness" of the advective field for juvenile pollock.

11.8.6 Shelikof Pollock IBM

A pollock individual-based model (IBM) was designed to run in conjunction with the 3-D physical model (SPEM) and the Shelikof nutrient-phytoplankton-zooplankton model. Its purpose is to examine, at a mechanistic level, hypotheses about recruitment of pollock in Shelikof Strait, especially as they refer to transport, growth, and (somewhat) mortality of pollock from spawning through the fall of the 0-age year.

11.8.7 GLOBEC and NPZ

A Global Ocean Ecosystem Dynamics (GLOBEC) nutrient-phytoplankton-zooplankton (NPZ) 1-D and 3-D modeling effort (the 3-D NPZ model coupled with a physical model of the circulation of the region) is designed to test hypotheses about the effect of climate change/regime shifts on production in the coastal region of the GOA, including effects on cross-

shelf transport, upstream effects, local production, and suitability of the region as habitat for juvenile salmon.

11.8.8 Steller Sea Lion IBM

This sea lion individual-based model (IBM) will be designed to examine how sea lion energy reserves change, through foraging and bioenergetics, depending on the distribution, density, patchiness, and species composition of a dynamic prey field (as influenced by factors such as potential local depletion by fishing). It should be applicable to any domain surrounding a specific sea lion rookery or haul-out in the Bering Sea, Aleutian Islands, or Gulf of Alaska. Sea lion characteristics such as age, location, life stage, and birth date are recorded. Caloric balance is the main variable followed for each individual.

11.8.9 Shelikof NPZ

Shelikof nutrient-phytoplankton-zooplankton models, 1-D and 3-D versions, were designed to produce a temporally and spatially explicit food source (*Pseudocalanus* stages) for larval pollock, as input to the pollock IBM model. This set of coupled (biological and physical) models was designed to be used to examine hypotheses about pollock recruitment in the Shelikof Strait region.

11.8.10 GOA Pollock Stochastic Switch

A GOA walleye pollock stochastic switch model was designed as a mathematical representation of a conceptual model, presented in Megrey et al. 1996. It is a numerical simulation model of the recruitment process. A generalized description of stochastic mortality is formulated as a function of three specific mortality components considered important in controlling survival (random, caused by wind mixing events, and caused by prevalence of oceanic eddies). The sum total of these components, under some conditional dependencies, determines the overall survival experienced by the recruits.

11.8.11 NEMURO

A North Pacific ecosystem model for understanding regional oceanography (NEMURO) represents the minimum state variables needed to represent a generic nutrient-phytoplankton-zooplankton (NPZ) marine ecosystem model for the North Pacific. Ecosystem fluxes are tracked in both units of nitrogen and silicon. Carbon flux process equations recently have been added. The purpose of the model is to examine the effects of climate variability on the marine ecosystem through regional comparisons using the same ecosystem model structure and process equations.

11.8.12 Ecopath

Several mass-balance ecosystem models (Ecopath) for North Pacific regions have been generated. Mass-balance food web models provide a way for evaluating the importance of predator-prey relationships, the roles of top-down and bottom-up forcing in modeled ecosystems, and the changes in ecosystem structure resulting from environmental perturbations (natural or anthropogenic). In addition, the models may provide a way to compare natural predation mortality with respect to predator biomass and fishing levels, and determine the quality of data available for a given system.

Eastern Bering Sea Shelf Ecopath Model 1. Although many of these models were done in the past for the Alaska region, the most up-to-date published model is the effort by Trites et al. (1999) for the Eastern Bering Sea. These models are highly aggregated across age groups and species groups and best highlight our gaps in understanding of how ecosystems function and our lack of data on certain ecosystem components. Walleye pollock is divided into two biomass groups: pollock ages 0 to 1 and pollock age 2 and older. This model is useful for testing ecosystem hypotheses about bottom-up and top-down forcing and to examine system level properties and energy flow among trophic levels. The Eastern Bering Sea model extent includes the main shelf and slope areas north to about 61°N and excludes nearshore processes and ecosystem groups.

Eastern Bering Sea Shelf Model 2 and Western Bering Sea Shelf Ecopath Model. The second Eastern Bering Sea Shelf model breaks down the earlier model into more detailed species groupings to tease apart the dynamics of individual species, especially in the commercially important groundfish. Spatial extensions to the model include subdividing into inner, middle, and outer biophysical domains. The model will be calibrated with respect to top-down and bottom-up forcing with the use of "checkpoint" food webs for several years in the 1990s, the 1979-1998 time series of trawl data, and Multispecies Virtual Population Analysis (MSVPA)/other assessment analyses. The primary purpose of this model is to investigate the relative role of natural and anthropogenic disturbances on the food web as a whole. A Western Bering Sea Shelf model, built as a joint U.S.-Russian project, is currently being completed.

Gulf of Alaska, Continental Shelf, and Slope (Excluding Fjord, Estuarine, and Intertidal Areas) Ecopath Model. Throughout the 1990s there were extensive commercial fisheries in the GOA for groundfish, as well as crab, herring, halibut, and salmon. Removals of both target species and bycatch by these (and historical) fisheries have been suggested as a possible cause for the decline of the western stock of Steller sea lions, which are now listed as endangered species. An Ecopath/Ecosim model for the GOA could test the hypothesis that fishery removals of groundfish and bycatch during the 1990s has contributed to the continued decline of Steller sea lions.

In addition, a community restructuring, in which shrimp populations declined dramatically and commercial fish populations increased between the 1960s and the 1990s, may have taken place, according to small mesh trawl surveys conducted by the National Marine Fisheries Service and Alaska Department of Fish and Game. An additional hypothesis, which could be tested with this model, is that this trophic reorganization has had a negative impact on marine mammal and bird populations in the GOA. Finally, the effects of an apparent increase in shark populations on their prey and the relative importance of these effects in the whole system could be evaluated with an Ecopath model.

The Aleutian Island and Pribilof Islands Ecopath Models. While the Eastern Bering Sea and GOA model may capture broad-scale dynamics of widespread fish stocks, their scale is too large to address local depletion. This issue may be important for island-based fish such as Atka mackerel, and may be critical for determining the effect that changes in the food web may have on the endangered Steller sea lion. This smaller-scale Ecopath model will be used in conjunction with larger-scale models to examine the possibility of linking the models across scales.

Prince William Sound Ecopath Models. An Ecopath model of Prince William Sound was constructed by a collaboration of experts from the region during 1998-1999 (Okey and Pauly 1999). The *Exxon Valdez* Oil Spill Trustee Council funded this effort for the purpose of "ecosystem synthesis." The project was coordinated by the University of British Columbia Fisheries Centre and overseen by the National Marine Fisheries Service Office of Oil Spill Damage Assessment and Restoration. Prince William Sound is well defined geographically; spatial definition of the system consisted of drawing lines across Hinchinbrook Entrance, Montague Strait, and smaller entrances. The time period represented by the model,

1994-1996, is the post-spill period with the broadest and most complete set of ecosystem information. This food web model consists of 48 functional groups ranging from single ontogenetic stages of special-interest species to highly aggregated groupings. A variety of hypotheses are being addressed with the PWS model—most relate to the 1989 *Exxon Valdez* oil spill and the fisheries in the area.

References

ADCED. 2002. Alaska Visitor Statistics, Alaska Department of Community and Economic Development. Program IV Fact sheet.

ADEC. 2000. Strategy document. Alaska's nonpoint source pollution strategy. Alaska Department of Environmental Conservation, Juneau.

ADEC. 2001. Spills database. Alaska Department of Environmental Conservation, Juneau.

ADEC, ADNR, ADF&G, and Alaska Office of the Governor. 2001. Alaska's clean water actions: Protecting our waters. Alaska Department of Environmental Conservation, Juneau.

ADF&G. Various years. Harvest, catch and participation in Alaska sport fisheries. Fishery data series. Alaska Department of Fish and Game, Juneau.

ADF&G. 1998. Report on the failure of western Alaska salmon runs and the link to ocean and climate changes. Alaska Department of Fish and Game, Juneau.

ADF&G. 2002. Draft Aquatic Nuisance Species Management Plan. Alaska Department of Fish and Game.

ADNR. 2000. Five-year schedule of timber sales in the Kenai-Kodiak area, FY-01 through FY-05. Alaska Department of Natural Resources.

ADNR. 2002. Alaska natural gas in-state demand study. Alaska Department of Natural Resources, Anchorage.

Aebischer, N.J., J.C. Coulson, and J.M. Colebrook. 1990. Parallel long-term trends across four marine trophic levels and weather. Nature 347:753-755.

Ahlnäes, K., T.C. Royer, and T.H. George. 1987. Multipole dipole eddies in the Alaska coastal current detected with Landsat thematic mapper data. Journal of Geophysical Research 92:13041-13047.

Ainley, D.G., and R.J.E. Broekelheid. 1990. Seabirds of the Farallon Islands. Stanford University Press, Stanford.

Ainley, D.G., W.J. Sydeman, S.A. Hatch, and U.W. Wilson. 1994. Seabird population trends along the west coast of North America: Causes and extent of regional concordance. Studies in Avian Biology 15:119-133.

Alaska Department of Labor. 2001. 1999 Alaska employment and earnings summary report by census area. Alaska Department of Labor.

Alaska Highway Natural Gas Policy Council. 2001. Report to the Governor. Alaska Department of Community and Economic Development, Anchorage.

Alaska Oil and Gas Conservation Commission. 2001. Annual report 2000. Alaska Department of Administration, Anchorage.

Alaska Sea Grant College Program. 1993. Is it food? Addressing marine mammal and seabird declines: Workshop summary. Alaska Sea Grant College Program, University of Alaska Fairbanks.

Alaska State Parks. 1993. The Kenai River carrying capacity study: Final report by the Division of Parks and Outdoor Recreation with assistance from the National Park Service Rivers, Trails and Conservation Assistance Program and Shelby Research Associates.

Allen, M.R., P.A. Stott, J.F.B. Mitchell, R. Schnur, and T.L. Delworth. 2000. Quantifying the uncertainty in forecasts of anthropogenic climate change. Nature 407:617-620.

Allen, S.E. 1996. Topographically generated, subinertial flows within a finite length canyon. Journal of Physical Oceanography 26:1608-1632.

Allen, S.E. 2000. On subinertial flow in submarine canyons: Effects of geometry. Journal of Geophysical Research 105:1285-1298.

Alverson, D.L. 1992. A review of commercial fisheries and the Steller sea lion (*Eumetopias jubatus*): The conflict arena. Reviews in Aquatic Sciences 6:203-256.

Anderson, D.W., F. Gress, K.F. Mais, and P.R. Kelly. 1980. Brown pelicans as anchovy stock indicators and their relationships to commercial fishing. California Cooperative Oceanic Fisheries Investigations Reports (CalCOFI) 21:54-61.

Anderson, G.C., and R.E. Munson. 1972. Primary productivity studies using merchant vessels in the North Pacific Ocean. In: A.Y. Takenoti (ed.), Biological oceanography of the northern North Pacific Ocean. Idemitsu Shoten, Tokyo, pp. 245-251.

Anderson, P.J., and J.F. Piatt. 1999. Community reorganization in the Gulf of Alaska following ocean climate regime shift. Marine Ecology Progress Series 189:117-123.

Anderson, P.J., J.E. Blackburn, and B.A. Johnson. 1997. Declines of forage species in the Gulf of Alaska, 1972-1995, as an indicator of regime shift. In: Forage fishes in marine ecosystems: Proceedings of the International Symposium on the Role of Forage Fishes in Marine Ecosystems. Alaska Sea Grant College Program, University of Alaska Fairbanks, pp. 531-543.

Anthony, J.A., and D.D. Roby. 1997. Variation in lipid content of forage fishes and its effect on energy provisioning rates to seabird nestlings. In: Forage fishes in marine ecosystems: Proceedings of the International Symposium on the Role of Forage Fishes in Marine Ecosystems. Alaska Sea Grant College Program, University of Alaska Fairbanks, pp. 725-729.

Armstrong, D.A., P.A. Dinnel, J.M. Orensanz, J.L. Armstrong, T.L. McDonald, R.F. Cusimano, R.S. Nemeth, M.L. Landolt, M.L. Skalski, R.F. Lee, and R.J. Huggett. 1995. Status of selected bottom fish and crustacean species in Prince William Sound following the *Exxon Valdez* oil spill. In: P.G. Wells, J.N. Butler, and J.S. Hughes (eds.), *Exxon Valdez* oil spill: Fate and effects in Alaskan waters. American Society for Testing and Materials, Philadelphia, pp. 485-547.

Bacon, C.E., W.M. Jarman, J.A. Estes, M. Simon, and R.J. Norstrom. 1998. Comparison of organochlorine contaminants among sea otter (*Enhydra lutris*) populations in California and Alaska. Environmental Toxicology and Chemistry 18:452-458.

Bailey, E.P., and G.H. Davenport. 1972. Die-off of common murres on the Alaska Peninsula and Unimak Island. Condor 74:215-219.

Bailey, E.P., and G.W. Kaiser. 1993. Impacts of introduced predators on nesting seabirds in the northeast Pacific. In: K. Vermeer, K.T. Briggs, K.H. Morgan, and D. Siegel-Causey (eds.), The status, ecology, and conservation of marine birds of the North Pacific. Canadian Wildlife Service, Ottawa, pp. 218-226.

Bailey, K.M. 2000. Shifting control of recruitment of walleye pollock *Theragra chalcogramma* after a major climatic and ecosystem change. Marine Ecology Progress Series 198:215-224.

Bailey, K.M., N.A. Bond, and P.J. Stabeno. 1999a. Anomalous transport of walleye pollock larvae linked to ocean and atmospheric patterns in May 1996. Fisheries Oceanography 8:264-273.

Bailey, K.M., A.L. Brown, M.M. Yoklavich, and K.L. Mier. 1996. Interannual variability in growth of larval and juvenile walleye pollock *Theragra chalcogramma* in the western Gulf of Alaska, 1983-91. Fisheries Oceanography 6:137-147.

Bailey, K.M., T.J. Quinn II, P. Bentzen, and W.S. Grant. 1999b. Population structure and dynamics of walleye pollock, *Theragra chalcogramma*. Advances in Marine Biology 37:179-255.

Bailey, K.M., M.F. Canino, J.M. Napp, S.M. Spring, and A.L. Brown. 1995a. Contrasting years of prey levels, feeding conditions and mortality of larval walleye pollock *Theragra chalcogramma* in the western Gulf of Alaska. Marine Ecology Progress Series 119:11-23.

Bailey, K.M., S.A. Macklin, R.K. Reed, R.D. Brodeur, W.J. Ingraham, J.F. Piatt, M. Shima, R.C. Francis, P.J. Anderson, T.C. Royer, A.B. Hollowed, D.A. Somerton, and W.S. Wooster. 1995b. ENSO events in the northern Gulf of Alaska, and effects on selected marine fisheries. California Cooperative Oceanic Fisheries Investigations Reports (CalCOFI) 36:78-96.

Baird, P.A., and P.J. Gould. 1986. The breeding biology and feeding ecology of marine birds in the Gulf of Alaska. MMS/NOAA OCSEAP Final Report 45:121-503.

Baird, P.H. 1990. Influence of abiotic factors and prey distribution on diet and reproductive success of three seabird species in Alaska. Ornis Scandinavica 21:224-235.

Bakus, G.J. 1978. Benthic ecology in the Gulf of Alaska. Energy/Environment '78. Society of Petroleum Industry Biologists, Los Angeles, pp. 169-192.

Ballachey, B.E., J.L. Bodkin, and A.R. DeGange. 1994. An overview of sea otter studies. In: T.R. Loughlin (ed.), Marine mammals and the *Exxon Valdez*. Academic Press, San Diego, pp. 47-59.

Banse, K. 1982. Cell volumes, maximal growth rates of unicellular algae and ciliates, and the role of ciliates in the marine pelagial. Limnology and Oceanography 27:1059-1071.

Barnes, F.F. 1958. Cook Inlet Susitna Lowland. National Park Service, U.S. DOI. Landscapes of Alaska. University of California Press, Berkeley.

Barrett-Lennard, L.G. 2000. Population structure and mating patterns of killer whales (*Orcinus orca*) as revealed by DNA analysis. Ph.D. thesis, University of British Columbia, Vancouver.

Barrett-Lennard, L.G., K. Heise, E. Saulitis, G. Ellis, and C. Matkin. 1995. The impact of killer whale predation on Steller sea lion populations in British Columbia and Alaska. Unpublished Report. North Pacific Universities Marine Mammal Research Consortium, Vancouver.

Baumgartner, A., and E. Reichel. 1975. The world water balance. Elsevier, New York.

Baur, D.C., M.J. Bean, and M.L. Gosliner. 1999. The laws governing marine mammal conservation in the United States. In: J.R. Twiss Jr. and R.R. Reeves (eds.), Conservation and management of marine mammals. Smithsonian Institution Press, Washington, D.C., pp. 48-86.

Beamish, R.J., K.D. Leask, O.A. Ianov, A.A. Balanov, A.M. Orlov, and B. Sinclair. 1999a. The ecology, distribution, and abundance of mid-water fishes of the subarctic Pacific gyres. Progress in Oceanography 43:399-442.

Beamish, R.J., D.J. Noakes, G.A. McFarlane, L. Klyashtorin, V.V. Ivanov, and V. Kurashov. 1999b. The regime concept and natural trends in the production of Pacific salmon. Canadian Journal of Fisheries and Aquatic Sciences 56:516-526.

Beissinger, S.R. 1995. Population trends of the marbled murrelet projected from demographic analyses. In: C.J. Ralph, G.L. Hunt Jr., M.G. Raphael, and J.F. Piatt (eds.), Ecology and conservation of the marbled murrelet. Pacific Southwest Research Station, U.S. Forest Service, Berkeley, pp. 385-393.

Ben-David, M., R.W. Flynn, and D.M. Schell. 1997a. Annual and seasonal changes in diets of martens: Evidence from stable isotope analysis. Oecologia 111(2):280-291.

Ben-David, M., T.A. Hanley, and D.M. Schell. 1998a. Fertilization of terrestrial vegetation by spawning Pacific salmon: The role of flooding and predator activity. Oikos 83:47-55.

Ben-David, M., T.A. Hanley, D.R. Klein, and D.M. Schell. 1997b. Seasonal changes in diets of coastal and riverine mink: The role of spawning Pacific salmon. Canadian Journal of Zoology 75:803-811.

Ben-David, M., R.T. Bowyer, L.K. Duffy, D.D. Roby, and D.M. Schell. 1998b. Social behavior and ecosystem processes: River otter latrines and nutrient dynamics of terrestrial vegetation. Ecology 79:2567-2571.

Berger, A., J. Imbrie, J. Hays, G. Kukla, and B. Saltzman. 1984. Milankovitch and climate. Reidel, Boston.

Bickham, J.W., J.C. Patton, and T.R. Loughlin. 1996. High variability for control-region sequences in a marine mammal: Implications for conservation and biogeography of Steller sea lions (*Eumetopias jubatus*). Journal of Mammalogy 77:95-108.

Bickham, J.W., T.R. Loughlin, J.K. Wickliffe, and V.N. Burkanov. 1998. Genetic variation in the mitochondrial DNA of Steller sea lions: Haplotype diversity and endemism in the Kuril Islands. Biosphere Conservation 1:107-117.

Bigg, M.A., G.E. Ellis, J.K.B. Ford, and K.C. Balcomb. 1987. Killer whales: A study of their identification, genealogy, and natural history in British Columbia and Washington State. Phantom Press, Nanaimo.

Bilby, R.E., B.R. Fransen, and P.A. Bisson. 1996. Incorporation of nitrogen and carbon from spawning coho salmon into the trophic system of small streams: Evidence from stable isotopes. Canadian Journal of Fisheries and Aquatic Sciences 53:164-173.

Blackburn, J.E., and P.J. Anderson. 1997. Pacific sand lance growth, seasonal availability, movements, catch variability, and food in the Kodiak–Cook Inlet area of Alaska. In: Forage fishes in marine ecosystems: Proceedings of the International Symposium on the Role of Forage Fishes in Marine Ecosystems. Alaska Sea Grant College Program, University of Alaska Fairbanks, pp. 409-426.

Bodkin, J.L. 2003. Sea otters. In: G.A. Feldhamer, B.C. Thompson, and J.A. Chapman (eds.), Wild mammals of North America, 2nd edn. Johns Hopkins University Press, Baltimore, pp. 735-743.

Bodkin, J.L., and R. Jameson. 1991. Patterns of seabird and marine mammal carcass deposition along the central California coast, 1980-1986. Canadian Journal of Zoology 69:1149-1155.

Bodkin, J.L., and M.S. Udevitz. 1994. An intersection model for estimating sea otter mortality along the Kenai Peninsula. In: T.R. Loughlin (ed.), Marine mammals and the *Exxon Valdez*. Academic Press, San Diego, pp. 81-95.

Bodkin, J.L., and M.S. Udevitz. 1999. An aerial survey method to estimate sea otter abundance. In: G.W. Garner, S.C. Amstrup, J.L. Laake, B.F.J. Manly, L.L. McDonald, and D.G. Robertson (eds.), Marine mammal survey and assessment methods. Balkema Press, Netherlands, pp. 13-29.

Bodkin, J.L., A.M. Burdin, and D.A. Ryzanov. 2000. Age and sex specific mortality and population structure in sea otters. Marine Mammal Science 16:201-219.

Bodkin, J.L., G.G. Eslinger, and D.H. Monson. 2004. Foraging depths of sea otters and implications to coastal marine communities. Marine Mammal Science 20(2):305-321

Bodkin, J.L., D. Mulcahy, and C.J. Lensink. 1993. Age specific reproduction in the sea otter (*Enhydra lutris*): An analysis of reproductive tracts. Canadian Journal of Zoology 71:1811-1815.

Boersma, P.D., and M.J. Groom. 1993. Conservation of storm petrels in the North Pacific. In: K. Vermeer, K.T. Briggs, and D. Siegel-Causey (eds.), Status and ecology of temperate North Pacific seabirds. Canadian Wildlife Service, Ottawa, pp. 110-121.

Bogard, S.J., P.J. Stabeno, and J.D. Schumacher. 1994. A census of mesoscale eddies in Shelikof Strait, Alaska during 1989. Journal of Geophysical Research 99:18243-18254.

Booth, B.C. 1988. Size classes and major taxonomic groups of phytoplankton at two locations in the subarctic Pacific Ocean in May and August, 1984. Marine Biology 97:275-286.

Booth, B.C., J. Lewin, and J.R. Postel. 1993. Temporal variation in the structure of autotrophic and heterotrophic communities in the subarctic Pacific. Progress in Oceanography 32:57-99.

Botkin, D.B., D.L. Peterson, and J.M. Calhoun. 2000. The scientific basis for validation monitoring of salmon for conservation and restoration plans. University of Washington, Olympic Natural Resources Center, Forks.

Bower, A. 1991. A simple kinematic mechanism for mixing fluid parcels across a meandering jet. Journal of Physical Oceanography 21:173-180.

Boyd, P.W., A.J. Watson, C.S. Law, E.R. Abraham, T. Trull, R. Murdoch, D.C.E. Bakker, A.R. Bowie, K.O. Buesseler, H. Chang, et al. 2000. A mesoscale phytoplankton bloom in the polar Southern Ocean stimulated by iron fertilization. Nature 407:695-702.

Braddock, J.F., J.E. Lindstrom, T.R. Yeager, B.T. Rasley, and E.J. Brown. 1996. Patterns of microbial activity in oiled and unoiled sediments in Prince William Sound. American Fisheries Society Symposium 18:94-108.

Braham, H.W., and M.E. Dahlheim. 1982. Killer whales in Alaska documented in the Platforms of Opportunity Program. Report to the International Whale Commission 32:643-646.

Breiwick, J.W. 1999. Gray whale abundance estimates, 1967/68-1997/98: ROI, RY, and K. In: D.J. Rugh, M.M. Muto, S.E. Moore, and D.P. DeMaster (eds.), Status review of the Eastern North Pacific stock of gray whales. NOAA Technical Memorandum NMFS-AFSC-103, pp. 62.

Brodeur, R.D., and D.M. Ware. 1992. Long-term variability in zooplankton biomass in the subarctic Pacific Ocean. Fisheries Oceanography 1:32-38.

Brodeur, R.D., and D.M. Ware. 1995. Interdecadal variability in distribution and catch rates of epipelagic nekton in the Northeast Pacific Ocean. In: R.J. Beamish (ed.), Climate change and northern fish populations. Canadian Special Publication of Fisheries and Aquatic Sciences 121:329-356.

Brodeur, R.D., B.W. Frost, S.R. Hare, R.C. Francis, and W.J. Ingraham Jr. 1996. Interannual variations in zooplankton biomass in the Gulf of Alaska and covariation with California current zooplankton biomass. California Cooperative Oceanic Fisheries Investigations Reports (CalCOFI) 37:80-100.

Brodeur, R.D., G.W. Boehlert, E. Casillas, M.B. Eldridge, J.H. Helle, W.T. Peterson, W.R. Heard, S.T. Lindley, and M.H. Schiewe. 2000. A coordinated research plan for estuarine and ocean research on Pacific salmon. Fisheries 25:7-16.

Broecker, W.S. 1982. Glacial to interglacial changes in ocean chemistry. Progress in Oceanography 11:151-197.

Brower Jr., W.A., R.G. Baldwin, C.N. Williams Jr., J.L. Wise, and L.D. Leslie. 1988. Climate atlas of the outer continental shelf waters and coastal regions of Alaska. Vol. I, Gulf of Alaska. National Climatic Data Center, Asheville, North Carolina.

Brown, G. 2000. Renewable natural resources management and use without markets. Journal of Economic Literature 38:875-914.

Brown, J. 2002. Remarks to the Resource Development Council for Alaska. Alaska Support Industry Alliance and Anchorage Chamber of Commerce, June 28, 2002, Anchorage, Alaska.

Brown Gladden, J.G., M.M. Ferguson, M.K. Freisen, and J.W. Clayton. 1999. Population structure of North American beluga whales (*Delphinapterus leucas*) based on nuclear DNA microsatellite variation and contrasted with the population structure revealed by mitochondrial DNA variation. Molecular Ecology 8:347-363.

Burger, A.E., and J.F. Piatt. 1990. Flexible time budgets in breeding common murres: Buffers against variable prey abundance. Studies in Avian Biology 14:71-83.

Burgman, M.A., S. Ferson, and H.R. Akcakaya. 1993. Risk assessment in conservation biology. Chapman and Hall, United Kingdom.

Burrell, D.C. 1986. Interaction between silled fjords and coastal regions. In: D.W. Hood and S.T. Zimmerman (eds.), The Gulf of Alaska physical environment and biological resources. NOAA Ocean Assessments Division, Alaska Office, Washington, D.C., pp. 187-220.

Byrd, G.V., D.E. Dragoo, and D.B. Irons. 1998. Breeding status and population trends of seabirds in Alaska in 1997. U.S. Fish and Wildlife Service, Homer, Alaska.

Byrd, G.V., D.E. Dragoo, and D.B. Irons. 1999. Breeding status and population trends of seabirds in Alaska in 1998. U.S. Fish and Wildlife Service, Homer, Alaska.

Caddy, J.F. 1995. Comment—Fisheries management science: A plea for conceptual change. Canadian Journal of Fisheries and Aquatic Sciences 52:2057-2058.

Cairns, D.K. 1987. Seabirds as indicators of marine food supplies. Biological Oceanography 5:261-271.

Calambokidis, J., G.H. Steiger, J.M. Straley, T. Quinn, L.M. Herman, S. Cerchio, R. Salden, M. Yamaguchi, F. Sato, J.R. Urban, et al. 1997. Abundance and population structure of humpback whales in the North Pacific basin. NOAA/NMFS, Southwest Fisheries Science Center, LaJolla.

Caley, K.J., M.H. Carr, M.A. Hixon, T.P. Hughes, J.P. Jones, and B.A. Menge. 1996. Recruitment and the local dynamics of open marine populations. Annual Review of Ecology and Systematics 27:477-500.

Calkins, D.G. 1978. Feeding behavior and major prey species of the sea otter, *Enhydra lutris*, in Montague Strait, Prince William Sound, Alaska. Fishery Bulletin U.S. 76:125-131.

Calkins, D.G. 1984. Susitna hydroelectric project phase II annual report: Big game studies. Vol. IX, belukha whale. Alaska Department of Fish and Game, Anchorage.

Calkins, D. 1986a. Marine mammals. In: D.W. Hood and S.T. Zimmerman (eds.), The Gulf of Alaska physical environment and biological resources. NOAA Ocean Assessments Division, Alaska Office, Washington, D.C., pp. 527-558.

Calkins, D.G. 1986b. Sea lion investigations in southern Alaska. In: Final report to the National Marine Fisheries Service, Alaska Region. Alaska Department of Fish and Game, Anchorage, p. 23.

Calkins, D.G. 1998. Prey of Steller sea lions in the Bering Sea. Biosphere Conservation 1:33-44.

Calkins, D.G., and E. Goodwin. 1988. Investigation of the declining sea lion population in the Gulf of Alaska. Unpublished Report. Alaska Department of Fish and Game, Anchorage.

Calkins, D.G., and K.W. Pitcher. 1982. Population assessment, ecology and trophic relationships of Steller sea lions in the Gulf of Alaska. In: Environmental assessment of the Alaskan continental shelf. U.S. Department of Commerce and U.S. Department of the Interior, pp. 447-546.

Calvin, N.I., and R.J. Ellis. 1978. Quantitative and qualitative observations on *Laminaria digitata* and other subtidal kelps of southern Kodiak Island, Alaska. Marine Biology 47:331-336.

Canino, M.F., K.M. Bailey, and L.S. Incze. 1991. Temporal and geographic differences in feeding and nutritional condition of walleye pollock larvae *Theragra chalcogramma* in Shelikof Strait, Gulf of Alaska. Marine Ecology Progress Series 79:27-35.

Carlson, P.R., T.R. Burns, B.F. Molnia, and W.C. Schwab. 1982. Submarine valleys in the northeast Gulf of Alaska: Characteristics and probable origin. Marine Geology 47:217-242.

Carpenter, S.R., K.L. Cottingham, and C.A. Stow. 1994. Fitting predator-prey models to time series with observation errors. Ecology 75:1254-1264.

Carroll, M.L., and R.C. Highsmith. 1996. Role of catastrophic disturbance in mediating *Nucella-Mytilus* interactions in the Alaskan rocky intertidal. Marine Ecology Progress Series 138:125-133.

Carscadden, J., and B.S. Nakashima. 1997. Abundance and changes in distribution, biology and behavior of capelin in response to cooler waters of the 1990s. In: Forage fishes in marine ecosystems: Proceedings of the International Symposium on the Role of Forage Fishes in Marine Ecosystems. Alaska Sea Grant College Program, University of Alaska Fairbanks, pp. 457-468.

Chapman, D.C. 2000. A numerical study of the adjustment of a narrow stratified current over a sloping bottom. Journal of Physical Oceanography 30:2927-2940.

Chapman, D.C., and S.J. Lentz. 1994. Trapping of a coastal density front by the bottom boundary layer. Journal of Physical Oceanography 24:1464-1479.

Chisholm, S.W. 2000. Stirring times in the Southern Ocean. Nature 407:685-687.

Chumbley, K., J. Sease, M. Strick, and R. Towell. 1997. Field studies of Steller sea lions (*Eumetopias jubatus*) at Marmot Island, Alaska 1979 through 1994. NOAA Technical Memorandum NMFS-AFSC-77.

Cianelli, L., and R. Brodeur. 1997. Bioenergetics estimation of juvenile pollock food consumption in the Gulf of Alaska. In: Forage fishes in marine ecosystems: Proceedings of the International Symposium on the Role of Forage Fishes in Marine Ecosystems. Alaska Sea Grant College Program, University of Alaska Fairbanks, pp. 71-76.

Clark, W.G., S.R. Hare, A.M. Parma, P.J. Sullivan, and R.J. Trumble. 1999. Decadal changes in growth and recruitment of Pacific halibut (*Hippoglossus stenolepis*). Canadian Journal of Fisheries and Aquatic Sciences 56:242-252.

Coats, D.A., E. Imamura, A.K. Fukuyama, J.R. Skalski, S. Kimura, and J. Steinbeck. 1999. Monitoring of biological recovery of Prince William Sound intertidal sites impacted by the *Exxon Valdez* oil spill: 1997 biological monitoring survey. NOAA Technical Memorandum NOS OR&R I. NOAA Hazardous Materials Response Division, Seattle.

Connell, J.H. 1972. Community interactions on marine rocky intertidal shores. Annual Review of Ecology and Systematics 3:169-192.

Cooley, R.A. 1963. Politics and conservation: The decline of the Alaska salmon. Harper and Rowe, New York.

Cooney, R.T. 1983. Some thoughts on the Alaska Coastal Current as a feeding habitat for juvenile salmon. In: W.G. Pearcy (ed.), The influence of ocean conditions on the production of salmonids in the North Pacific. Sea Grant College Program, Oregon State University, pp. 256-268.

Cooney, R.T. 1986. The seasonal occurrence of *Neocalanus cristatus*, *Neocalanus plumchrus*, and *Eucalanus bungii* over the shelf of the northern Gulf of Alaska. Continental Shelf Research 5:541-553.

Cooney, R.T. 1988. Distribution and ecology of zooplankton in the Gulf of Alaska. Bulletin of the Ocean Research Institute of Tokyo 26:27-41.

Cooney, R.T. 1989. Acoustic evidence for the vertical partitioning of biomass in the epipelagic zone of the Gulf of Alaska. Deep-Sea Research 36:1177-1189.

Cooney, R.T. 1993. A theoretical evaluation of the carrying capacity of Prince William Sound, Alaska, for juvenile Pacific salmon. Fisheries Research 18:77-87.

Cooney, R.T., and K.O. Coyle. 1982. Trophic implications of cross-shelf copepod distributions in the southeastern Bering Sea. Marine Biology 70:187-196.

Cooney, R.T., K.O. Coyle, E. Stockmar, and C. Stark. 2001. Seasonality in surface-layer net zooplankton communities in Prince William Sound, Alaska. Fisheries Oceanography 10(Suppl. 1):97-109.

Cooney, R.T., J.R. Allen, M.A. Bishop, D.L. Eslinger, T. Kline, B.L. Norcross, C.P. McRoy, J. Milton, E.V. Patrick, A.J. Paul, D. Salmon, D. Scheel, G.L. Thomas, S.L. Vaughan, and T.M. Willette. 2001. Ecosystem control of pink salmon (*Oncorhynchus gorbuscha*) and Pacific herring (*Clupea pallasi*) populations in Prince William Sound, Alaska. Fisheries Oceanography 10(Suppl. 1):1-13.

Costa, D.P. 1982. Energy, nitrogen and electrolyte flux and sea-water drinking in the sea otter, *Enhydra lutris*. Physiological Zoology 55:34-44.

Coyle, K.O. 1997. Distribution of large calanoid copepods in relation to physical oceanographic conditions and foraging auklets in the western Aleutian Islands. Ph.D. thesis, University of Alaska Fairbanks. 172 pp.

Crane, K., and J.L. Galasso. 1999. Arctic environmental atlas. U.S. Naval Research Laboratory, Office of Naval Research, Washington, D.C.

Crawford, W.R. 1984. Energy flux and generation of diurnal shelf waves along Vancouver Island. Journal of Physical Oceanography 14:1600-1607.

Crawford, W.R., and R.E. Thomson. 1984. Diurnal period shelf waves along Vancouver Island: A comparison of observations with theoretical models. Journal of Physical Oceanography 14:1629-1646.

Crawford, W.R., and F.A. Whitney. 1999. Mesoscale eddies in the Gulf of Alaska. EOS, Transactions of the American Geophysical Union 80:365-370.

Cronin, M.A., J. Bodkin, B. Ballachey, J. Estes, and J.C. Patton. 1996. Mitochondrial-DNA variation among subspecies and populations of sea otters (*Enhydra lutris*). Journal of Mammalogy 72:546-557.

Cummins, P.F., and L.-Y. Oey. 2000. Simulation of barotropic and baroclinic tides off northern British Columbia. Journal of Physical Oceanography 27:762-781.

Dagg, M. 1993. Grazing by the copepod community does not control phytoplankton production in the open subarctic Pacific Ocean. Progress in Oceanography 32:163-184.

Dagg, M.J., and E.W. Walser Jr. 1987. Ingestion, gut passage, and egestion by the copepod *Neocalanus plumchrus* in the laboratory and in the subarctic Pacific Ocean. Limnology and Oceanography 32:178-188.

Dahlheim, M.E., and C.O. Matkin. 1994. Assessment of injuries to Prince William Sound killer whales. In: T.R. Loughlin (ed.), Marine mammals and the *Exxon Valdez*. Academic Press, San Diego, pp. 163-171.

Dayton, P.K. 1971. Competition, disturbance, and community organization: The provision and subsequent utilization of space in a rocky intertidal community. Ecological Monographs 41:351-389.

Dayton, P.K. 1975. Experimental studies of algal canopy interactions in a sea otter–dominated kelp community at Amchitka Island, Alaska. Fishery Bulletin U.S. 73:230-237.

Dayton, P.K., S.F. Thrush, M.T. Agardy, and R.J. Hoffman. 1995. Environmental effects of marine fishing. Aquatic Conservation of Marine and Freshwater Ecosystems 5:205-232.

Dean, T.A., M.S. Stekoll, and R.O. Smith. 1996a. Kelps and oil: The effects of the *Exxon Valdez* oil spill on subtidal algae. American Fisheries Society Symposium 18:412-423.

Dean, T.A., S.C. Jewett, D.R. Laur, and R.O. Smith. 1996b. Injury to epibenthic invertebrates resulting from the *Exxon Valdez* oil spill. American Fisheries Society Symposium 18:424-439.

Dean, T.A., J.L. Bodkin, S.C. Jewett, D.H. Monson, and D. Jung. 2000. Changes in sea urchins and kelp following a reduction in sea otter density as a result of the *Exxon Valdez* oil spill. Marine Ecology Progress Series 199:281-291.

Dean, T.A., M.S. Stekoll, S.C. Jewett, R.O. Smith, and J.E. Hose. 1998. Eelgrass (*Zostera marina* L.) in Prince William Sound, Alaska: Effects of the *Exxon Valdez* oil spill. Marine Pollution Bulletin 36:201-210.

DeGange, A.R., and G.A. Sanger. 1986. Marine birds. In: D.W. Hood and S.T. Zimmerman (eds.), The Gulf of Alaska physical environment and biological resources. NOAA Ocean Assessments Division, Alaska Office, Washington, D.C., pp. 479-526.

DeGange, A.R., A.M. Doroff, and D.H. Monson. 1994. Experimental recovery of sea otter carcasses at Kodiak Island, Alaska, following the *Exxon Valdez* oil spill. Marine Mammal Science 10:492-496.

Denman, K.L., H.J. Freeland, and D.L. Mackas. 1989. Comparison of time scales for biomass transfer up the marine food web and coastal transport processes. Canadian Special Publication of Fisheries and Aquatic Sciences 108:255-264.

Denny, M.W. 1988. Biology and mechanics of the waveswept environment. Princeton University Press, Princeton.

Dethier, M.N., and D.O. Duggins. 1988. Variations in strong interactions in the intertidal zone along a geographic gradient: A Washington-Alaska comparison. Marine Ecology Progress Series 50:97-105.

Dewailly, E., P. Ayotte, S. Bruneau, C. Laliberte, D.C.G. Muir, and R.J. Norstrom. 1993. Inuit exposure to organochlorines through the aquatic food chain in Arctic Quebec. Environmental Health Perspectives 101:618-620.

Divoky, G.J. 1998. Factors affecting the growth of a black guillemot colony in northern Alaska. Ph.D. thesis, University of Alaska Fairbanks.

Dizon, A.E., S.J. Chivers, and W.F. Perrin. 1997. Molecular genetics of marine mammals. Society for Marine Mammalogy Special Publication 3:388.

Dodimead, A.J., F. Favorite, and T. Hirano. 1963. Salmon of the North Pacific Ocean. Part II. Review of oceanography of the subarctic Pacific region. International North Pacific Fisheries Commission Bulletin 13:1-195.

Doroff, A.M., and J.L. Bodkin. 1994. Sea otter foraging behavior and hydrocarbon levels in prey. In:, T.R. Loughlin (ed.), Marine mammals and the *Exxon Valdez*. Academic Press, San Diego, pp. 193-208.

Doroff, A.M., and A.R. DeGange. 1994. Sea otter, *Enhydra lutris*, prey composition and foraging success in the northern Kodiak archipelago. Fishery Bulletin U.S. 92:704-710.

Driskell, W.B., A.K. Fukuyama, J.P. Houghton, D.C. Lees, A.J. Mearns, and G. Shigenaka. 1996. Recovery of Prince William Sound intertidal infauna from *Exxon Valdez* oiling and shoreline treatments, 1989 through 1992. American Fisheries Society Symposium 18:362-378.

Duggins, D.O., C.A. Simenstad, and J.A. Estes. 1989. Magnification of secondary production by kelp detritus in coastal marine ecosystems. Science 245:170-173.

Dumond, D.E. 1983. Alaska and the northeast coast. In: J.D. Jennings (ed.), Ancient North Americans. W.H. Freeman and Company, New York.

Ebeling, A.W., and D.R. Laur. 1998. Fish populations in kelp forests without sea otters: Effects of severe storm damage and destructive sea urchin grazing. In: G.R. VanBlaricom and J.A. Estes (eds.), The community ecology of sea otters. Springer Verlag, Berlin, pp. 169-191.

Ebert, T.A., and D.C. Lees. 1996. Growth and loss of tagged individuals of the predatory snail *Nucella lamellosa* in areas within the influence of the *Exxon Valdez* oil spill in Prince William Sound. American Fisheries Society Symposium 18:349-361.

Edie, A.G. 1977. Distribution and movements of Steller sea lion cows (*Eumetopias jubatus*) on a pupping colony. University of British Columbia, Vancouver.

Egbert, G.D., and R.D. Ray. 2000. Significant dissipation of tidal energy in the deep ocean inferred from satellite altimeter data. Nature 405:775-778.

Eggers, D.M., L.R. Peltz, B.G. Bue, and T.M. Willette. 1991. Trends in abundance of hatchery and wild stocks of pink salmon in Cook Inlet, Prince William Sound, and Kodiak, Alaska. In: Proceedings of the International Symposium on Biological Interactions of Wild and Enhanced Salmonids, June 1991. Nanaimo, British Columbia.

Emery, W.J., and K. Hamilton. 1985. Atmospheric forcing of interannual variability in the northeast Pacific Ocean: Connections with El Niño. Journal of Geophysical Research 90:857-868.

Enfield, D. 1997. Multi-scale climate variability: Besides ENSO, what else? In: Colloquium on El Niño-Southern Oscillation (ENSO): Atmospheric, Oceanic, Societal, Environmental and Policy Perspectives. July 20-August 1, 1997. National Center for Atmospheric Research, Boulder, Colorado.

Erickson, D., E. Pikitch, P. Suuronen, E. Lehtonen, C. Bublitz, C. Klinkert, and C. Mitchell. 1999. Selectivity and mortality of walleye pollock escaping from the codend and intermediate (extension) selection of a pelagic trawl. Final Report to NMFS by Alaska Fishery Development Foundation, Anchorage.

Erikson, D.E. 1995. Surveys of murre colony attendance in the northern Gulf of Alaska following the *Exxon Valdez* oil spill. In: P.G. Wells, J.N. Butler, and J.S. Hughes (eds.), *Exxon Valdez* oil spill: Fate and effects in Alaskan waters. American Society for Testing and Materials, Philadelphia, pp. 780-819.

Eslinger, D., R.T. Cooney, C.P. McRoy, A. Ward, T. Kline, E.P. Simpson, J. Wang, and J.P. Allen. 2001. Plankton dynamics: Observed and modeled responses to physical factors in Prince William Sound, Alaska. Fisheries Oceanography 10(Suppl. 1):81-96.

Estes, J.A. 1999. Response to Garshelis and Johnson. Science 283:175.

Estes, J.A., and J.L. Bodkin. 2001. Marine otters. In: W.F. Perrin, B. Wursig, H.G.M. Thewissen, and C.R. Crumly (eds.), Encyclopedia of marine mammals. Academic Press, San Diego.

Estes, J.A., and D.O. Duggins. 1995. Sea otters and kelp forests in Alaska: Generality and variation in a community ecological paradigm. Ecological Monographs 65:75-100.

Estes, J.A., and C. Harrold. 1988. Sea otters, sea urchins, and kelp beds: Some questions of scale. In: G.R. VanBlaricom and J.A. Estes (eds.), The community ecology of sea otters. Springer Verlag, Berlin, pp. 116-142.

Estes, J.A., and J.F. Palmisano. 1974. Sea otters: Their role in structuring nearshore communities. Science 185:1058-1060.

Estes, J.A., R.J. Jameson, and E.B. Rhode. 1982. Activity and prey selection in the sea otter: Influence of population status on community structure. American Naturalist 120:242-258.

Estes, J.A., M.T. Tinker, T.M. Williams, and D.F. Doak. 1998. Killer whale predation on sea otters linking oceanic and nearshore ecosystems. Science 282:473-476.

Estes, J.A., C.E. Bacon, W.M. Jarman, R.J. Norstrom, R.G. Anthony, and A.K. Miles. 1997. Organochlorines in sea otters and bald eagles from the Aleutian archipelago. Marine Pollution Bulletin 34:486-490.

Estes, J.A., M.L. Riedman, M.M. Staedler, and M.T. Tinker. 2003. Individual variation in prey selection by sea otters: Patterns, causes, and implications. Journal of Animal Ecology 72:144-155.

EVOSTC. 2000. Gulf Ecosystem Monitoring: A sentinel monitoring program for the conservation of the natural resources of the northern Gulf of Alaska. GEM Science Program NRC review draft. *Exxon Valdez* Oil Spill Trustee Council, Anchorage.

Ewald, G., P. Larsson, H. Linge, L. Okla, and N. Szarzi. 1998. Biotransport of organic pollutants to an inland Alaska lake by migrating sockeye salmon (*Oncorhynchus nerka*). Arctic 51:40-47.

Fahrig, L. 1991. Simulation methods for developing general landscape-level hypotheses of single-species dynamics. In: M.G. Turner and R.H. Gardner (eds.), Quantitative methods in landscape ecology: The analysis and interpretation of landscape heterogeneity. Springer-Verlag, New York, pp. 417-442.

Fall, J., R. Miraglia, W. Simeone, C.J. Utermohle, and R.J. Wolfe. 2001. Long term consequences of the *Exxon Valdez* oil spill for coastal communities of Southcentral Alaska. OCS Study, Minerals Management Service (MMS) 2001-032, Technical Report 163.

Farmer, D.M., and J.D. Smith. 1980. Generation of lee waves over the sill in Knight Inlet, in fjord oceanography. In: H.J. Freeland, D.M. Farmer, and C.D. Levings (eds.), NATO Conference on Fjord Oceanography, Victoria, B.C., 1979. Plenum Press, New York, pp. 259-270.

Favorite, F. 1974. Flow into the Bering Sea through Aleutian Island passes. In: D.W. Hood and E.J. Kelley (eds.), Oceanography of the Bering Sea with emphasis on renewable resources: Proceeding of an international symposium. Institute of Marine Science, University of Alaska, Fairbanks, pp. 3-38.

Favorite, F., A.J. Dodimead, and K. Nasu. 1976. Oceanography of the subarctic Pacific region, 1960-71. International North Pacific Fisheries Commission Bulletin 33:1-187.

Feder, H.M., and A. Blanchard. 1998. The deep benthos of Prince William Sound, Alaska, 16 months after the *Exxon Valdez* oil spill. Marine Pollution Bulletin 36:118-130.

Feder, H.M., and S.C. Jewett. 1986. The subtidal benthos. In: D.W. Hood and S.T. Zimmerman (eds.), The Gulf of Alaska physical environment and biological resources. NOAA Ocean Assessments Division, Alaska Office, Washington, D.C., pp. 347-398.

Feder, H.M., and G.E. Kaiser. 1980. Intertidal biology. In: J.M. Colonell (ed.), Port Valdez, Alaska: Environmental studies 1976-1979. University of Alaska, Institute of Marine Science, Fairbanks.

Feder, H.M., and A.J. Paul. 1974. Age, growth and size-weight relationships of the soft-shell clam, *Mya arenaria*, in Prince William Sound, Alaska. Proceedings of the National Shellfisheries Association 64:45-52.

Feder, H.M., and A.J. Paul. 1980a. Food of the king crab, *Paralithodes camtschatica* and the Dungeness crab, *Cancer magister* in Cook Inlet, Alaska. Proceedings of the National Shellfisheries Association 70(2):240-246.

Feder, H.M., and A.J. Paul. 1980b. Seasonal trends in meiofaunal abundance on two beaches in Port Valdez, Alaska. Syesis 13:27-36.

Feder, H.M., A.S. Naidu, and A.J. Paul. 1990. Trace-element and biotic changes following a simulated oil-spill on a mudflat in Port Valdez, Alaska. Marine Pollution Bulletin 21:131-137.

Ferrero, R.C., S.E. Moore, and R.C. Hobbs. 2000. Development of beluga, *Delphinapterus leucas,* capture and satellite tagging protocol in Cook Inlet, Alaska. Marine Fisheries Review Special Issue 62(3):112-123.

Ferrero, R.C., D.P. DeMaster, P.S. Hill, M. Muto, and A.L. Lopez. 2000. Alaska marine mammal stock assessments, 2000. National Marine Fisheries Service, National Marine Mammal Laboratory. NOAA Technical Memorandum NMFS-AFSC-119.

Finney, B.P. 1998. Long-term variability of Alaska sockeye salmon abundance determined by analysis of sediment cores. North Pacific Anadromous Fish Commission Bulletin 1:388-395.

Finney, B.P., I. Gregory-Eaves, M.S.V. Douglas, and J.P. Smol. 2002. Fisheries productivity in the northeastern Pacific Ocean over the past 2,200 years. Nature 416:729-733.

Finney, B.P., I. Gregory-Eaves, J. Sweetman, M.S.V. Douglas, and J.P. Smol. 2000. Impacts of climatic change and fishing on Pacific salmon abundance over the past 300 years. Science 290:795-799.

Flather, R.A. 1988. A numerical investigation of tides and diurnal-period continental shelf waves along Vancouver Island. Journal of Physical Oceanography 18:115-139.

Ford, J.K.B. 1991. Vocal traditions among resident killer whales (*Orcinus orca*) in coastal waters of British Columbia. Canadian Journal of Zoology 69:1454-1483.

Ford, J.K.B., G. Ellis, and K.C. Balcomb. 1994. Killer whales: The natural history and genealogy of *Orcinus orca* in British Columbia and Washington state. University of British Columbia Press, Vancouver, and University of Washington Press, Seattle.

Ford, J.K.B., G.M. Ellis, L.G. Barrett-Lennard, A.B. Morton, and K.C. Balcomb III. 1998. Dietary specialization in two sympatric populations of killer whales (*Orcinus orca*) in coastal British Columbia and adjacent waters. Canadian Journal of Zoology 76:1456-1471.

Foreman, M.G.G., and R.E. Thomson. 1997. Three-dimensional model simulations of tides and buoyancy currents along the west coast of Vancouver Island. Journal of Physical Oceanography 27:1300-1325.

Foreman, M.G.G., W.R. Crawford, J.Y. Cherniawsky, R.F. Henry, and M.R. Tarbotton. 2000. A high-resolution assimilating tidal model for the northeast Pacific Ocean. Journal of Geophysical Research 105:28629-28651.

Forney, K.A., J. Barlow, M.M. Muto, M. Lowry, J. Baker, G. Cameron, J. Mobley, C. Stinchcomb, and J.V. Caretta. 2000. U.S. Pacific marine mammal stock assessments, 2000. NOAA Technical Memorandum NOAA-TM-NMFS-SWFSC-305. 276 pp.

Foster, M.S. 1990. Organization of macroalgal assemblages in the Northeast Pacific: The assumption of homogeneity and the illusion of generality. Hydrobiologia 192:21-33.

Foster, M.S., and D.R. Schiel. 1988. Kelp communities and sea otters: Keystone species or just another brick in the wall. In: G.R. VanBlaricom and J.A. Estes (eds.), The community ecology of sea otters. Springer Verlag, Berlin, pp. 92-108.

Foy, R.J., and A.J. Paul. 1999. Winter feeding and changes in somatic energy content for age 0 Pacific herring in Prince William Sound, Alaska. Transactions of the American Fisheries Society 128:1193-1200.

Francis, R.C., and S.R. Hare. 1994. Decadal-scale regime shifts in the large marine ecosystems of the northeast Pacific: A case for historical science. Fisheries Oceanography 3:279-291.

Francis, R.C., S.R. Hare, A.B. Hollowed, and W.S. Wooster. 1998. Effects of interdecadal climate variability on the oceanic ecosystems of the northeast Pacific. Fisheries Oceanography 7:1-21.

Freeland, H.J., and K.L. Denman. 1982. A topographically controlled upwelling center off southern Vancouver Island. Journal of Marine Research 40:1069-1093.

Freeland, H.J., and D.M. Farmer. 1980. Circulation and energetics of a deep, strongly stratified inlet. Canadian Journal of Aquatic Science 37:1398-1410.

Freeland, H.J., K.L. Denman, C.S. Wong, F. Whitney, and R. Jacques. 1997. Evidence of change in the winter mixed layer in the northeast Pacific Ocean. Deep-Sea Research 44:2117-2129.

Fried, N. 2000. The Matanuska-Susitna Borough. Alaska Department of Labor and Workforce Development, Alaska Economic Trends 20.

Fried, N., and B. Windisch-Cole. 1999a. Prince William Sound. Alaska Department of Labor and Workforce Development, Alaska Economic Trends 10(9).

Fried, N., and B. Windisch-Cole. 1999b. An economic profile: The Kenai Peninsula. Alaska Department of Labor and Workforce Development, Alaska Economic Trends 19(10):3-15.

Fritz, L.W., R.C. Ferrero, and R.J. Berg. 1995. The threatened status of Steller sea lions, *Eumetopias jubatus*, under the Endangered Species Act: Effects on Alaska groundfish fisheries management. Marine Fisheries Review 57:14-27.

Frost, B.W. 1983. Interannual variation of zooplankton standing stock in the open Gulf of Alaska. In: W.S. Wooster (ed.), From year to year: Interannual variability of the environment and fisheries of the Gulf of Alaska and eastern Bering Sea. Washington Sea Grant Program, University of Washington, Seattle, pp. 146-157.

Frost, B.W. 1991. The role of grazing in nutrient rich areas of the open sea. Limnology and Oceanography 36:1616-1630.

Frost, B.W. 1993. A modeling study of processes regulating plankton standing stock and production in the open subarctic Pacific Ocean. Progress in Oceanography 32:17-56.

Frost, K.J., and L.F. Lowry. 1986. Sizes of walleye pollock, *Theragra chalcogramma,* consumed by marine mammals in the Bering Sea. Fishery Bulletin U.S. 84:192-197.

Frost, K.J., and L.F. Lowry. 1990. Distribution, abundance, and movements of beluga whales, *Delphinapterus leucas*, in coastal waters of western Alaska. In: T.G. Smith, D.J. St. Aubin, and J.R. Geraci (eds.), Advances in research on the beluga whale, *Delphinapterus leucas*. Canadian Bulletin of Fisheries and Aquatic Sciences 224:39-57.

Frost, K.J., and L.F. Lowry. 1994. Habitat use, behavior, and monitoring of harbor seals in Prince William Sound, Alaska, *Exxon Valdez* oil spill restoration project annual report (Restoration Project 93046). Alaska Department of Fish and Game, Wildlife Conservation Division, Fairbanks.

Frost, K.J., L.F. Lowry, and J. ver Hoef. 1995. Habitat use, behavior, and monitoring of harbor seals in Prince William Sound, Alaska, *Exxon Valdez* oil spill restoration project annual report (Restoration Project 94064 and 94320F). Alaska Department of Fish and Game, Wildlife Conservation Division, Anchorage.

Frost, K.J., L.F. Lowry, and J.M. ver Hoef. 1999. Monitoring the trend of harbor seals in Prince William Sound, Alaska, after the *Exxon Valdez* oil spill. Marine Mammal Science 15:494-506.

Frost, K.J., C.A. Manen, and T.L. Wade. 1994a. Petroleum hydrocarbons in tissues of harbor seals from Prince William Sound and the Gulf of Alaska. In: T.R. Loughlin (ed.), Marine mammals and the *Exxon Valdez*. Academic Press, San Diego, pp. 331-358.

Frost, K.J., M.A. Simpkins, and L.F. Lowry. 2001. Diving behavior of sub-adult and adult harbor seals in Prince William Sound, Alaska. Marine Mammal Science 17(4):813-834.

Frost, K.J., L.F. Lowry, J. Small, and S.J. Iverson. 1996. Monitoring, habitat use, and trophic interactions of harbor seals in Prince William Sound, *Exxon Valdez* oil spill restoration project annual report (Restoration Project 95064). Alaska Department of Fish and Game, Division of Wildlife Conservation, Fairbanks.

Frost, K.J., L.F. Lowry, J.M. ver Hoef, and S.J. Iverson. 1997. Monitoring, habitat use, and trophic interactions of harbor seals in Prince William Sound, *Exxon Valdez* oil spill restoration project annual report (Restoration Project 96064). Alaska Department of Fish and Game, Division of Wildlife Conservation, Fairbanks.

Frost, K.J., L.F. Lowry, E.H. Sinclair, J. ver Hoef, and D.C. McAllister. 1994b. Impacts on distribution, abundance, and productivity of harbor seals. In: T.R. Loughlin (ed.), Marine mammals and the *Exxon Valdez*. Academic Press, San Diego, pp. 97-118.

Frost, K.J., L.F. Lowry, J.M. ver Hoef, S.J. Iverson, and T. Gotthardt. 1998. Monitoring, habitat use, and trophic interactions of harbor seals in Prince William Sound, Alaska, *Exxon Valdez* oil spill restoration project annual report (Restoration Project 97064). Alaska Department of Fish and Game, Division of Wildlife Conservation, Fairbanks.

Fukuyama, A.K., G. Shigenaka, and R.Z. Hoff. 2000. Effects of residual *Exxon Valdez* oil on intertidal *Protothaca staminea*: Mortality, growth, and bioaccumulation of hydrocarbons in transplanted clams. Marine Pollution Bulletin 40:1042-1050.

Fulton, J.D. 1983. Seasonal and annual variations of net zooplankton at Ocean Station "P", 1956-1980. Canadian Data Report of Fisheries and Aquatic Sciences 374:65.

Funk, F. 2001. Abundance, biology, and historical trends of Pacific herring, *Clupea pallasi*, in Alaskan waters. REX workshop: Trends in herring populations and trophodynamics. In: G.A. McFarlane, B.A. Megrey, and B.A. Taft (eds.), PICES-GLOBEC International Program on Climatic Change and Carrying Capacity, Report of the 2001 BASS/MODEL Workshop. PICES Scientific Report 17:86-93.

Furness, R.W., and D.N.C. Nettleship. 1991. Seabirds as monitors of changing marine environments. Proceedings of the International Ornithological Congress 20:2237-2280.

Gaines, S.D., and J. Roughgarden. 1987. Fish and offshore kelp forests affect recruitment to intertidal barnacle populations. Science 235:479-481.

Ganopolski, A., and S. Rahmstorf. 2001. Rapid changes of glacial climate simulated in a coupled climate model. Nature 409:153-158.

Gargett, A. 1997. Optimal stability window: A mechanism underlying decadal fluctuations in north Pacific salmon stocks. Fisheries Oceanography 6(2):109-117.

Gargett, A.E., M. Li, and R. Brown. 2001. Testing mechanistic explanations of observed correlations between environmental factors and marine fisheries. Canadian Journal of Fisheries and Aquatic Sciences 58:208-219.

Garrett, C.J.R., and J.W. Loder. 1981. Dynamical aspects of shallow sea fronts. Philosophical Transactions of the Royal Society of London A302:563-581.

Garshelis, D.L. 1997. Sea otter mortality estimated from carcasses collected after the *Exxon Valdez* oil spill. Conservation Biology 11:905-916.

Garshelis, D.L., J.A. Garshelis, and A.T. Kimker. 1986. Sea otter time budgets and prey relationships in Alaska. Journal of Wildlife Management 50:637-647.

Garshelis, D.L., A.M. Johnson, and J.A. Garshelis. 1984. Social organization of sea otters in Prince William Sound, Alaska. Canadian Journal of Zoology 62:2648-2658.

Gawarkiewicz, G. 1991. Linear stability models of shelf-break fronts. Journal of Physical Oceanography 21:471-488.

Gawarkiewicz, G., and D.C. Chapman. 1992. The role of stratification in the formation and maintenance of shelf-break fronts. Journal of Physical Oceanography 22:753-772.

Gay III, S.M., and S.L. Vaughan. 2001. Seasonal hydrography and tidal currents of bays and fjords in Prince William Sound, Alaska. Fisheries Oceanography 10(Suppl. 1):159-193.

Gentry, R.L. 1971. Social behavior of the Steller sea lion. Ph.D. thesis, University of California, Santa Cruz.

Gentry, R.L., and J.H. Johnson. 1981. Predation by sea lions on northern fur seal neonates. Mammalia: Journal de morphologie, biologie, systematique des mammiferes 45:423-430.

Gilfillan, E.S., D.S. Page, E.J. Harner, and P.D. Boehm. 1995a. Shoreline ecology program for Prince William Sound, Alaska, following the *Exxon Valdez* oil spill: Part 3–biology. In: P.G. Wells, J.N. Butler, and J.S. Hughes (eds.), *Exxon Valdez* oil spill: Fate and effects in Alaskan waters. American Society for Testing and Materials, Philadelphia, pp. 398-443.

Gilfillan, E.S., T.H. Suchanek, P.D. Boehm, E.J. Harner, D.S. Page, and N.A. Sloan. 1995b. Shoreline impacts in the Gulf of Alaska region following the *Exxon Valdez* oil spill. In: P.G. Wells, J.N. Butler, and J.S. Hughes (eds.), *Exxon Valdez* oil spill: Fate and effects in Alaskan waters. American Society for Testing and Materials, Philadelphia, pp. 444-487

Gill, V.A. 1999. Breeding performance of black-legged kittiwakes (*Rissa tridactyla*) in relation to food availability: A controlled feeding experiment. Master's thesis, University of Alaska Anchorage.

Gisiner, R.C. 1985. Male territorial and reproductive behavior in the Steller sea lion, *Eumetopias jubatus*. Ph.D. thesis, University of California, Santa Cruz.

Glickman, T.S., and M. Gough. 1990. Readings in risk. Resources for the future, Washington D.C. Johns Hopkins University Press, Baltimore.

Goering, J.J., W.E. Shiels, and C.J. Patton. 1973. Primary production. In: D.W. Hood. W.E. Shiels, and E.J. Kelley (eds.), Environmental studies of Port Valdez. University of Alaska, Institute of Marine Science, Fairbanks, pp. 253-279.

Goldsmith, S. 2001. Economic projections: Alaska and the Southern Railbelt 2000-2025. Prepared for Chugach Electric Association by Institute of Social and Economic Research, University of Alaska Anchorage.

Goldsmith, S., and S. Martin. 2001. ANILCA and the Seward economy. Prepared for Alaska State Office, National Audubon Society, by Institute of Social and Economic Research, University of Alaska Anchorage.

Gresh, T., J. Lichatowich, and P. Schoonmaker. 2000. An estimation of historic and current levels of salmon production in the Northeast Pacific ecosystem: Evidence of a nutrient deficit in the freshwater systems of the Pacific Northwest. Fisheries 25:15-21.

Groot, C., and L. Margolis. 1991. Pacific salmon life histories. University of British Columbia Press, Vancouver.

Hampton, M.A., P.R. Carlson, and H.J. Lee. 1986. Geomorphology, sediment and sedimentary processes. In: D.W. Hood and S.T. Zimmerman (eds.), The Gulf of Alaska physical environment and biological resources. NOAA Ocean Assessments Division, Alaska Office, Washington, D.C., pp. 93-143.

Hansen, D.J., and J.D. Hubbard. 1999. Distribution of Cook Inlet beluga whales (*Delphinapterus leucas*) in winter. U.S. Department of the Interior, Minerals Management Service, Anchorage.

Hare, S.R., and N.J. Mantua. 2000. Empirical evidence for North Pacific regime shifts in 1977 and 1989. Progress in Oceanography 47:103-146.

Hare, S.R., N.J. Mantua, and R.C. Francis. 1999. Inverse production regimes: Alaska and west coast Pacific salmon. Fisheries 24:6-14.

Hart, J.L. 1973. Pacific fishes of Canada. Bulletin of the Fisheries Research Board of Canada 180:740.

Hatch, S.A. 1984. Nestling diet and feeding rates of rhinoceros auklets in Alaska. In: D.N. Nettleship, G.A. Sanger, and P.F. Springer (eds.), Marine birds: Their feeding ecology and commercial fisheries relationships. Canadian Wildlife Service, Ottawa, pp. 106-115.

Hatch, S.A. 1993. Ecology and population status of northern fulmars (*Fulmarus glacialis*) of the North Pacific. In: K. Vermeer, K.T. Briggs, K.H. Morgan, and D. Siegel-Causey (eds.), Status, ecology, and conservation of marine birds of the North Pacific. Canadian Wildlife Service, Ottawa, pp. 82-92.

Hatch, S.A., and M.A. Hatch. 1983. Populations and habitat use of marine birds in the Semidi Islands. Murrelet 64:39-46.

Hatch, S.A., and M.A. Hatch. 1989. Attendance patterns of murres at breeding sites: Implications for monitoring. Journal of Wildlife Management 53:483-493.

Hatch, S.A., and G.A. Sanger. 1992. Puffins as samplers of juvenile pollock and other forage fish in the Gulf of Alaska. Marine Ecology Progress Series 80:1-14.

Hatch, S.A., G.V. Byrd, D.B. Irons, and G.L. Hunt. 1993. Status and ecology of kittiwakes (*Rissa tridactyla* and *R. brevirostris*) in the North Pacific. In: K. Vermeer, K.T. Briggs, K.H. Morgan, and D. Siegel-Causey (eds.), Status, ecology, and conservation of marine birds of the North Pacific. Canadian Wildlife Service, Ottawa, pp. 140-153.

Hay, D.E., J. Boutillier, M. Joyce, and G. Langford. 1997. The eulachon (*Thaleichthys pacificus*) as an indicator species in the North Pacific. In: Forage fishes in marine ecosystems: Proceedings of the International Symposium on the Role of Forage Fishes in Marine Ecosystems. Alaska Sea Grant College Program, University of Alaska Fairbanks, pp. 509-530.

Hayes, D.L., and K.J. Kuletz. 1997. Decline of pigeon guillemot populations in Prince William Sound, Alaska, and apparent changes in distribution and abundance of their prey. In: Forage fishes in marine ecosystems: Proceedings of the International Symposium on the Role of Forage Fishes in Marine Ecosystems. Alaska Sea Grant College Program, University of Alaska Fairbanks, pp. 699-702.

Hays, J.D., J. Imbrie, and N.J. Skackleton. 1976. Variations in the Earth's orbit: Pacemaker of the ice ages. Science 194:1121-1132.

Hazard, K. 1988. Beluga whale, *Delphinapterus leucas*. In: J.W. Lentfer (ed.), Selected marine mammals of Alaska: Species accounts with research and management recommendations. U.S. Marine Mammal Commission, Washington, D.C., pp. 195-235.

Heggie, D.T., and D.C. Burrell. 1981. Deepwater renewals and oxygen consumption in an Alaskan fjord. Estuarine, Coastal and Shelf Science 13:83-99.

Heinrich, A.K. 1962. The life history of plankton animals and seasonal cycles of plankton communities in the oceans. Journal du Conseil Conseil International pour l'Exploration de la Mer 27:15-24.

Heyning, J.E., and M.E. Dahlheim. 1988. *Orcinus orca*. Mammalian Species 304:1-9.

Hickey, B.M. 1997. The response of a steep-sided narrow canyon to strong wind forcing. Journal of Physical Oceanography 27:697-726.

Highsmith, R.C., T.L. Rucker, M.S. Stekoll, S.M. Saupe, M.R. Lindeberg, R.N. Jenne, and W.P. Erickson. 1996. Impact of the *Exxon Valdez* oil spill on intertidal biota. American Fisheries Society Symposium 18:212-237.

Highsmith, R.C., M.S. Stekoll, W.E. Barber, L. Deysher, L. McDonald, D. Strickland, and W.P. Erickson. 1994. Comprehensive assessment of coastal habitat, *Exxon Valdez* Oil Spill. State/Federal Natural Resource Damage Assessment Final Report (Coastal Habitat Study Number 1A). University of Alaska Fairbanks, School of Fisheries and Ocean Sciences, Fairbanks.

Hilborn, R. 1992. Hatcheries and the future of salmon in Northwest. Fisheries 17(1):5-8.

Hilborn, R. 1997. Statistical hypothesis testing and decision theory in fisheries science. Fisheries 22:19-20.

Hilborn, R., and M. Mangel. 1997. The ecological detective: Confronting models with data. Princeton University Press, Princeton.

Hobbs, R.C., D.J. Rugh, and D.P. DeMaster. 2000. Abundance of belugas, *Delphinapterus leucas,* in Cook Inlet, Alaska, 1994-1998. Marine Fisheries Review 62(3):37-45.

Hoelzel, A.R., M.E. Dahlheim, and S.J. Stern. 1998. Low genetic variation among killer whales (*Orcinus orca*) in the eastern North Pacific, and genetic differentiation between foraging specialists. Journal of Heredity 89(2):121-128.

Holling, C.S. 1978. Adaptive environmental assessment and management. John Wiley and Sons, Chichester.

Holling, C.S., and W.C. Clark. 1975. Notes towards a science of ecological management. In: W.H. van Dobben and R.H. Lowe-McConnell (eds.), First International Congress of Ecology. Dr W. Junk B.V. Publishers, The Hague, Netherlands, pp. 247-251.

Hollowed, A.B., and W.S. Wooster. 1992. Variability of winter ocean conditions and strong year classes of northeast Pacific groundfish. ICES Marine Science Symposium 195:433-444.

Hollowed, A.B., and W.S. Wooster. 1995. Decadal-scale variations in the eastern subarctic Pacific: II. Response of northeast Pacific fish stocks. In: R.J Beamish (ed.), Climate change and northern fish populations. National Research Council of Canada, Ottawa, pp. 373-385.

Hollowed, A., J.N. Ianelli, and P. Livingston. 2000. Including predation mortality in stock assessments: A case study for Gulf of Alaska pollock. ICES Journal of Marine Science 57:279-293.

Hood, D.W., and S.T. Zimmerman. 1986. The Gulf of Alaska, physical environment and biological resources. NOAA Ocean Assessments Division, Alaska Office, Washington, D.C.

Hoover-Miller, A.A. 1994. Harbor seal (*Phoca vitulina*) biology and management in Alaska. Pacific Rim Research, Washington, D.C.

Hoover-Miller, A., K.R. Parker, and J.J. Burns. 2000. A reassessment of the impact of the *Exxon Valdez* oil spill on harbor seals (*Phoca vitulina richardsi*) in Prince William Sound, Alaska. Marine Mammal Science 17:111-135.

Hostettler, F.D., R.J. Rosenbauer, and K.A. Kvenholden. 2000. Reply: Response to comment by Bence et al. Organic Geochemistry 31:939-943.

Houghton, R.W., D.B. Olson, and P.J. Celone. 1986. Observation of an anticyclonic eddy near the continental shelf break south of New England. Journal of Physical Oceanography 16:60-71.

Houghton, J.P., D.C. Lees, W.B. Driskell, and S.C. Lindstrom. 1996a. Evaluation of the condition of Prince William Sound shorelines following the *Exxon Valdez* oil spill and subsequent shoreline treatment: Vol. I, 1994 biological monitoring survey. NOAA, Hazardous Materials Response and Assessment Division. NOAA Technical Memorandum NOS ORCA 91.

Houghton, J.P., D.C. Lees, W.B. Driskell, S.C. Lindstrom, and A.J. Mearns. 1996b. Recovery of Prince William Sound epibiota from *Exxon Valdez* oiling and shoreline treatments, 1989 through 1992. American Fisheries Society Symposium 18:379-411.

Houghton, J.P., A.K. Fukuyama, D.C. Lees, H. Teas III, H.L. Cumberland, P.M. Harper, T.A. Ebert, and W.B. Driskell. 1993. Evaluation of the 1991 condition of Prince William Sound shorelines following the *Exxon Valdez* oil spill and subsequent shoreline treatment: Vol. II, 1991 biological monitoring survey. NOAA, Hazardous Materials Response and Assessment Division, Seattle.

Hunt Jr., G.L., B. Burgesson, and G.A. Sanger. 1981. Feeding ecology of seabirds of the eastern Bering Sea. In: D.W. Hood and J.A. Calder (eds.), The eastern Bering Sea shelf: Oceanography and resources. NOAA, Juneau, vol. 2, pp. 629-648.

Hunt Jr., G.L., C.L. Baduini, R.D. Brodeur, K.O. Coyle, N.B. Kachel, J.M. Napp, S.A. Salo, J.D. Schumacher, P.J. Stabeno, D.A. Stockwell, T. Whitledge, and S. Zeeman. 1999. The Bering Sea in 1998: A second consecutive year of weather forced anomalies. EOS, Transactions of the American Geophysical Union 89:561-566.

Ianelli, J.N., L. Fritz, T. Honkalehto, N. Williamson, and G. Walters. 1998. Bering Sea–Aleutian Islands walleye pollock assessment for 1999. In: Stock assessment and fishery evaluation report for the groundfish resources of the Bering Sea/Aleutian Islands regions. Section 1. North Pacific Fishery Management Council, Anchorage, Alaska, pp. 1-79.

Incze, L.S., D.W. Siefert, and J.M. Napp. 1997. Mesozooplankton of Shelikof Strait, Alaska: Abundance and community composition. Continental Shelf Research 17:287-305.

Incze, L.S., A.W. Kendall, J.D. Schumacher Jr., and R.K. Reed. 1989. Interactions of a mesoscale patch of larval fish (*Theragra chalcogramma*) with the Alaska Coastal Current. Continental Shelf Research 9:269-284.

IOC. 2000. Strategic design plan for the coastal component of the Global Ocean Observing System (GOOS). Intergovernmental Oceanographic Commission, UNESCO, Paris.

Irons, D.B. 1992. Aspects of foraging behavior and reproductive biology of the black-legged kittiwake. Ph.D. thesis, University of California, Irvine.

Irons, D.B. 1996. Size and productivity of black-legged kittiwake colonies in Prince William Sound before and after the *Exxon Valdez* oil spill. In: S.D. Rice, R.B. Spies, D.A. Wolf, and B.A. Wright (eds.), Proceedings of the *Exxon Valdez* Oil Spill Symposium. American Fisheries Society Symposium 18:738-747.

Irons, D.B., S.J. Kendall, W.P. Erickson, L.L. McDonald, and B.K. Lance. 2000. Nine years of *Exxon Valdez* oil spill: Effects on marine birds in Prince William Sound, Alaska. Condor 102:723-737.

Iverson, S.J., K.J. Frost, and L.F. Lowry. 1997. Fatty acid signatures reveal fine scale structure of foraging distribution of harbor seals and their prey in Prince William Sound, Alaska. Marine Ecology Progress Series 151:255-271.

Jackson, D.A., P.R. Peres-Neto, and J.D. Olden. 2001. What controls who is where in freshwater fish communities: The roles of biotic, abiotic, and spatial factors. Canadian Journal of Fisheries and Aquatic Sciences 58:157-170.

Jackson, J.B., M.X. Kirby, W.H. Berger, K.A. Bjorndal, L.W. Botsford, B.J. Bourque, R.H. Bradbury, R. Cooke, J. Erlandson, J.A. Estes, et al. 2001. Historical overfishing and the recent collapse of coastal ecosystems. Science 293:629-638.

Jacob, K.H. 1986. Seismicity, tectonics, and geohazards of the Gulf of Alaska regions. In: D.W. Hood and S.T. Zimmerman (eds.), The Gulf of Alaska physical environment and biological resources. NOAA Ocean Assessments Division, Alaska Office, Washington, D.C., pp. 45-186.

Jameson, R.J. 1989. Movements, home ranges, and territories of male sea otters off central California. Marine Mammal Science 5:159-172.

Jameson, R.J., and A.M. Johnson. 1993. Reproductive characteristics of female sea otters. Marine Mammal Science 9:156-167.

Jewett, S.C., and H.M. Feder. 1982. Food and feeding habits of the king crab *Paralithodes camtschatica* near Kodiak Island, Alaska. Marine Biology 66:243-250.

Jewett, S.C., and H.M. Feder. 1983. Food of the Tanner crab *Chionoecetes bairdi* near Kodiak Island, Alaska. Journal of Crustacean Biology 3:196-207.

Jewett, S.C., T.A. Dean, R.O. Smith, and A. Blanchard. 1999. *Exxon Valdez* oil spill: Impacts and recovery in the soft-bottom benthic community in and adjacent to eelgrass beds. Marine Ecology Progress Series 185:59-83.

Johnson, W.R., T.C. Royer, and J.L. Luick. 1988. On the seasonal variability of the Alaska Coastal Current. Journal of Geophysical Research 93:12423-12437.

Jones, M.L., S.L. Swartz, and S. Leatherwood. 1984. The gray whale *Eschrichtius robustus*. Academic Press, London.

Joyce, T.M., J.K.B. Bishop, and O.B. Brown. 1992. Observations of offshore shelf water transport induced by a warm core ring. Deep-Sea Research 39:97-113.

Kajimura, H., and T.R. Loughlin. 1988. Marine mammals in the oceanic food web of the eastern subarctic Pacific. Bulletin of the Ocean Research Institute of Tokyo 26:187-223.

Kannan, K., K.S. Guruge, N.J. Thomas, S. Tanabe, and J.P. Giesy. 1998. Butyltin residues in southern sea otters (*Enhydra lutris nereis*) found dead along California coastal waters. Environmental Science and Technology 32:1169-1175.

Kastelein, R.A., N. Vaughan, and P.R. Wiepkema. 1990. The food consumption of Steller sea lions (*Eumetopias jubatus*). Aquatic Mammals 15:137-144.

Kawamura, A. 1988. Characteristics of the zooplankton biomass distribution in the standard Norpac net catches in the North Pacific region. Bulletin of Plankton Society of Japan 35:175-177.

Keeney, R. 1992. Value-focused thinking. Harvard University Press, London.

Kendall, A.W., R.I. Perry, and S. Kim. 1996. Fisheries oceanography of walleye pollock in Shelikof Strait, Alaska. Fisheries Oceanography 5:203.

Kenyon, K.W. 1969. The sea otter in the eastern Pacific Ocean. North American Fauna 68:352.

Kenyon, K.W. 1982. Sea otter, *Enhydra lutris*. In: J.A. Chapman and G.A. Feldhamer (eds.), Wild mammals of North America. Johns Hopkins University Press, Baltimore, pp. 704-410.

Kenyon, K.W., and D.W. Rice. 1961. Abundance and distribution of the Steller sea lion. Journal of Mammalogy 42:223-234.

Kirsch, J., G.L. Thomas, and R.T. Cooney. 2000. Acoustic estimates of zooplankton distributions in Prince William Sound, spring 1996. Fisheries Research 47:245-260.

Kitaysky, A.S., J.C. Wingfield, and J.F. Piatt. 1999. Dynamics of food availability, body condition and physiological stress response in breeding kittiwakes. Functional Ecology 13:577-584.

Klein, W.H. 1957. Principal tracks and mean frequencies of cyclones and anti-cyclones in the Northern Hemisphere. U.S. Weather Bureau, Research Paper Number 40. U.S. Government Printing Office, Washington, D.C.

Klinck, J.M. 1996. Circulation near submarine canyons: A modeling study. Journal of Geophysical Research 101:1211-1223.

Kline Jr., T.C. 1999. Temporal and spatial variability of $^{13}C/^{12}C$ and $^{15}N/^{14}N$ in pelagic biota of Prince William Sound, Alaska. Canadian Journal of Fisheries and Aquatic Sciences 56(Suppl. 1):94-117.

Kline, T.C., J.J. Goering, O.A. Mathisen, P.H. Poe, and P.L. Parker. 1990. Recycling of elements transported upstream by runs of Pacific salmon: I. ^{15}N and ^{13}C evidence in Sashin Creek, Southeastern Alaska. Canadian Journal of Fisheries and Aquatic Sciences 47:136-144.

Kline, T.C., J.J. Goering, O.A. Mathisen, P.H. Poe, P.L. Parker, and R.S. Scalan. 1993. Recycling of elements transported upstream by runs of Pacific salmon: II. ^{15}N and ^{13}C evidence in the Kvichak River watershed, Bristol Bay, Southwestern Alaska. Canadian Journal of Fisheries and Aquatic Sciences 50:2350-2365.

Klinkhart, E.G. 1966. The beluga whale in Alaska. Alaska Department of Fish and Game, Federal Aid in Wildlife Restoration Project Report Vol. VII.

Klosiewski, S.P., and K.K. Laing. 1994. Marine bird populations of Prince William Sound, Alaska, before and after the *Exxon Valdez* oil spill. U.S. Fish and Wildlife Service, Anchorage.

Koblinsky, C.J., P.P. Niiler, and W.J. Schmitz Jr. 1989. Observations of wind-forced deep ocean currents in the North Pacific. Journal of Geophysical Research 94:10773-10790.

Kron, T. 1995. Prince William Sound salmon enhancement programs and considerations relative to wild stocks. In: M.R. Collie and J.P. McVey (eds.), Interactions between cultured species and naturally occurring species in the environment. U.S.-Japan Coop. Prog. Nat. Res. Tech. Rep. 22. Alaska Sea Grant College Program 95-03, University of Alaska Fairbanks, pp. 49-52.

Kruse, G.H., F.C. Funk, H.J. Geiger, K.R. Mabry, H.M. Savikko, and S.M. Siddeek. 2000. Overview of state-managed marine fisheries in the central and western Gulf of Alaska, Aleutian Islands, and southeastern Bering Sea, with reference to Steller sea lions. Alaska Department of Fish and Game, Regional Information Report 5J00-10, Juneau.

Kuletz, K.J., D.B. Irons, B.A. Agler, and J.F. Piatt. 1997. Long-term changes in diets of populations of piscivorous birds and mammals in Prince William Sound, Alaska. In: Forage fishes in marine ecosystems: Proceedings of the International Symposium on the Role of Forage Fishes in Marine Ecosystems. Alaska Sea Grant College Program, University of Alaska Fairbanks, pp. 703-706.

Kvitek, R.G., and J.S. Oliver. 1988. Sea otter foraging habits and effects on prey populations and communities in soft-bottom environments. In: G.R. VanBlaricom and J.A. Estes (eds.), The community ecology of sea otters. Springer Verlag, Berlin, pp. 22-47.

Kvitek, R.G., and J.S. Oliver. 1992. Influence of sea otters on soft-bottom prey communities in Southeast Alaska. Marine Ecology Progress Series 82:103-113.

Kvitek, R.G., C.E. Bowlby, and M. Staedler. 1993. Diet and foraging behavior of sea otters in southeast Alaska. Marine Mammal Science 9:168-181.

Kvitek, R.G., J.S. Oliver, A.R. DeGange, and B.S. Anderson. 1992. Changes in Alaskan soft-bottom prey communities along a gradient in sea otter predation. Ecology 73:413-428.

Lagerloef, G. 1983. Topographically controlled flow around a deep trough transecting the shelf off Kodiak Island, Alaska. Journal of Physical Oceanography 13:139-146.

Laidre, K., K.E.W. Shelden, B.A. Mahoney, and D.J. Rugh. 2000. Distribution of beluga whales, *Delphinapterus leucas*, and survey effort in the Gulf of Alaska. Marine Fisheries Review 62(3):27-36.

Lambeck, K. 1980. The Earth's variable rotation: Geophysical causes and consequences. Cambridge University Press, London.

Larkin, G.A., and P.A. Slaney. 1997. Implications of trends in marine-derived nutrient influx to south coastal British Columbia salmonid production. Fisheries 22(11):16-24.

Law, A.M., and W.D. Kelton. 1991. Simulation modeling and analysis. McGraw-Hill, New York.

Lawrence, J.M. 1975. On the relationship between marine plants and sea urchins. Oceanography and Marine Biology Annual Review 13:213-286.

Leatherwood, S., C.O. Matkin, J.D. Hall, and G.M. Ellis. 1990. Killer whales, *Orcinus orca*, photo-identified in Prince William Sound, Alaska 1976-1987. Canadian Field-Naturalist 104:362-371.

LeBrasseur, R.J. 1965. Biomass atlas of net-zooplankton in the northeastern Pacific Ocean, 1956-1964. Fisheries Research Board of Canada Manuscript Report Series (Oceanography and Limnological) 201:1-60.

Leigh Jr., E.G., R.T. Paine, J.F. Quinn, and T.H. Suchanek. 1987. Wave energy and intertidal productivity. Proceedings of the National Academy of Sciences USA 84:1314-1318.

Lensink, C. 1959. Distribution and status of sea otters in Alaska. Tenth Alaskan Science Conference, August 25-28, 1959.

Lensink, C.J. 1962. The history and status of sea otters in Alaska. Ph.D. thesis, Purdue University, West Lafayette, Indiana.

Lentfer, J. 1988. Selected marine mammals of Alaska: Species accounts with research and management recommendations. Marine Mammal Commission, Washington, D.C.

Lethcoe, J., and N. Lethcoe. 1985. Cruising guide to Prince William Sound, Alaska. Vol. II: Eastern part Prince William Sound. Prince William Sound Books, Valdez, Alaska. 181 pp.

Lewis, J.P. 1996. Harbor seal investigations in Alaska. National Marine Fisheries Service Annual Report Award NA57FX0367, Juneau.

Liepitz, G.S. 1994. An assessment of the cumulative impacts of development and human uses on fish habitat on the Kenai River. Alaska Department of Fish and Game Technical Report 94-6.

Lindberg, D.R., J.A. Estes, and K.I. Warheit. 1998. Human influences on trophic cascades along rocky shores. Ecological Applications 8:880-890.

Lindeman, R.L. 1942. The trophodynamic aspect of ecology. Ecology 23:399-418.

Litchfield, V., and A. Milner. 1998. Kenai River bioassessment: Effects of storm drain outfall on the benthic invertebrate community. Alaska Department of Fish and Game Report 2A98-26.

Littlejohn, M. 1990. Kenai Fjords National Park Visitor Services Project, report 31. National Park Service, Cooperative Park Studies Unit, University of Idaho, Moscow.

Livingston, P.A., and J-J. Jurado-Molina. 2000. A multispecies virtual population analysis of the eastern Bering Sea. ICES Journal of Marine Science 57:294-299.

Livingston, P.A., and R.D. Methot. 1998. Incorporation of predation into a population assessment model of eastern Bering Sea walleye pollock. In: F. Funk, T.J. Quinn II, J. Heifetz, J.N. Ianelli, J.E. Powers, J.F. Schweigert, P.J. Sullivan, and C.-I. Zhang (eds.), Fishery stock assessment models. Alaska Sea Grant College Program, University of Alaska Fairbanks, pp. 663-678.

Livingstone, D., and T.C. Royer. 1980. Observed surface winds at Middleton Island, Gulf of Alaska, and their influence on ocean circulation. Journal of Physical Oceanography 10:753-764.

Loeb, V., V. Siegel, O. Holm-Hansen, R. Hewitt, R. Fraser, W. Trivelpiece, and S. Trivelpiece. 1997. Effects of sea-ice extent and krill or salp dominance on the antarctic food web. Nature 387:897-900.

Longhurst, A.L. 1976. Vertical migration. In: D.H. Cushing and J.J. Walsh (eds.), The ecology of the seas. W.B. Sanders Co., Philadelphia, pp. 116-137.

Loughlin, T.R. 1981. Home range and territoriality of sea otters near Monterey, California. Journal of Wildlife Management 44:576-582.

Loughlin, T.R. 1997. Using the phylogeographic method to identify Steller sea lion stocks. In: A.E. Dizon, S.J. Chivers, and W.F. Perrin (eds.), Molecular genetics of marine mammals. Society for Marine Mammalogy Special Publication 3:159-171.

Loughlin, T.R. 1998. The Steller sea lion: A declining species. Biosphere Conservation 1:91-98.

Loughlin, T.R., A.S. Perlov, and V.A. Vladimirov. 1992. Range-wide survey and estimation of total number of Steller sea lions in 1989. Marine Mammal Science 8:220-239.

Loughlin, T.R., D.J. Rugh, and C.H. Fiscus. 1984. Northern sea lion distribution and abundance: 1956-80. Journal of Wildlife Management 48:729-740.

Lowry, L.F., K.J. Frost, and T.R. Loughlin. 1989. Importance of walleye pollock in the diets of marine mammals in the Gulf of Alaska and Bering Sea, and implications for fishery management. In: Proceedings of the International Symposium on the Biology and Management of Walleye Pollock. Alaska Sea Grant College Program, University of Alaska Fairbanks, pp. 701-726.

Lowry, L.F., K.J. Frost, J.M. ver Hoef, and R.A. DeLong. 2001. Movements of satellite-tagged sub-adult and adult harbor seals in Prince William Sound, Alaska. Marine Mammal Science 17:835-861.

Lowry, L.F., K.J. Frost, R. Davis, R.S. Suydam, and D.P. DeMaster. 1994. Movements and behavior of satellite-tagged spotted seals (*Phoca largha*) in the Bering and Chukchi seas. NOAA Technical Memorandum NMFS-AFSC-38. 71 pp.

Lubchenco, J., and S.D. Gaines. 1981. A unified approach to marine plant-herbivore interactions. I. Populations and communities. Annual Review of Ecology and Systematics 12:405-437.

Ludwig, D. 1999. Is it meaningful to estimate a probability of extinction? Ecology 80:298-310.

Luick, J.L., T.C. Royer, and W.P. Johnson. 1987. Coastal atmospheric forcing in the northern Gulf of Alaska. Journal of Geophysical Research 92:3841-3848.

Lynch-Stieglitz, J., W.B. Curry, and N. Slowey. 1999. Weaker Gulf Stream in the Florida Straits during the last glacial maximum. Nature 402:644-648.

Lynde, M.V. 1986. The historical annotated landing (HAL) database: Documentation of annual harvest of groundfish from the northeast Pacific and eastern Bering Sea from 1956-1980. Master's thesis, University of Washington, Seattle. 202 pp.

Mackas, D.L., and B.W. Frost. 1993. Distributions and seasonal/interannual variations in the phytoplankton and zooplankton biomass. PICES Scientific Report 1:51-56.

Mackas, D.L., R. Goldblatt, and A.G. Lewis. 1998. Interdecadal variation in developmental timing of *Neocalanus plumchrus* populations at Ocean Station P in the subarctic North Pacific. Canadian Journal of Fisheries and Aquatic Sciences 55:1878-1893.

Mackas, D.L., H. Sefton, C.B. Miller, and A. Raich. 1993. Vertical habitat partitioning by large calanoid copepods in the oceanic subarctic Pacific during spring. Progress in Oceanography 32:259-294.

Macklin, S.A., G.M. Lackmann, and J. Gray. 1988. Offshore directed winds in the vicinity of Prince William Sound, Alaska. Monthly Weather Review 116:1289-1301.

Mahoney, B.A., and K.E.W. Shelden. 2000. Harvest history of belugas, *Delphinapterus leucas*, in Cook Inlet, Alaska. Marine Fisheries Review Special Issue 62(3):124-133.

Malloy, R.J., and G.F. Merrill. 1972. Vertical crustal movement on the sea floor. The great Alaska earthquake of 1964, Vol. 6: Oceanography and coastal engineering. National Research Council, National Academy of Sciences, Washington, D.C.

Malthus, T. 1798. An essay on the principle of population, as it affects the future improvement of society, with remarks on the speculations of Mr. Godwin, M. Condorcet, and other writers. Printed for J. Johnson, London. 396 pp.

Mangel, J., L.M. Talbot, G.K. Meffe, M.T. Agardy, D.L. Alverson, J. Barlow, D.B. Botkin, G. Budowski, T. Clark, J. Cooke, et al. 1996. Principles for the conservation of wild living resources. Ecological Applications 6:338-362.

Mann, K.H., and J.R.N. Lazier. 1996. Dynamics of marine ecosystems, biological-physical interactions in the oceans, 2nd edn. Blackwell Science, Inc., Cambridge.

Mantua, N.J., S.R. Hare, Y. Zhang, J.M. Wallace, and R.C. Francis. 1997. A Pacific interdecadal climate oscillation with impacts on salmon production. Bulletin of the American Meteorological Society 78:1069-1079.

Mantyla, A.W., and J.L. Reid. 1983. Abyssal characteristics of the world ocean waters. Deep-Sea Research 30:805-833.

Marchland, C., Y. Simrad, and Y. Gratton. 1999. Concentration of capelin (*Mallotus villosus*) in tidal upwelling fronts at the head of the Laurentian Channel in the St. Lawrence estuary. Canadian Journal of Fisheries and Aquatic Sciences 56:1832-1848.

Marmorek, D.R., J.J. Anderson, L. Bashan, D. Bouillon, T. Cooney, R. Derison, P. Dygert, L. Garrett, A. Giorgi, O.P. Langness, et al. 1996. Plan for analyzing and testing hypotheses (PATH): Final report on retrospective analyses for fiscal year 1996. ESSA Technologies, Vancouver.

Martin, J.H. 1990. Glacial-interglacial CO_2 change: The iron hypothesis. Paleoceanography 5:1-13.

Martin, J.H. 1991. Iron, Leibig's law, and the greenhouse. Oceanography 4:52-55.

Martin, J.H., and R.M. Gordon. 1988. Northeast Pacific iron distributions in relation to primary productivity. Deep-Sea Research 35:177-196.

Martin, M.H. 1997. Data report: 1996 Gulf of Alaska bottom trawl survey. NOAA Technical Memorandum NMFS-AFSC-82. 235 pp.

Mathisen, O.A. 1972. Biogenic enrichment of sockeye salmon lakes and stock productivity. Verhandlungen der Internationalen Vereinigung für Theoretische and Angewandte Limnologie 18:1089-1095.

Mathisen, O.A., J.J. Goering, and E.V. Farley. 2000. Nitrogen and carbon isotope ratios in sockeye salmon smolts. Verhandlungen der Internationalen Vereinigung für Theoretische and Angewandte Limnologie 27:3121-3124.

Matkin, C.O., and E.L. Saulitis. 1994. Killer whale (*Orcinus orca*) biology and management in Alaska. Marine Mammal Commission report no. T75135023, Washington, D.C.

Matkin, C.O., G.M. Ellis, M.E. Dahlheim, and J. Zeh. 1994. Status of killer whales in Prince William Sound, 1985-1992. In: T.R. Loughlin (ed.), Marine mammals and the *Exxon Valdez*. Academic Press, San Diego, pp. 141-162.

Matkin, C.O., G. Ellis, L. Barrett-Lennard, H. Jurk, and E. Saulitis. 2000. Photographic and acoustic monitoring of killer whales in Prince William Sound and Kenai Fjords, Alaska. North Gulf Oceanic Society, Restoration Project 99012 Annual Report, Homer, Alaska.

Matkin, C.O., D.R. Matkin, G.M. Ellis, E. Saulitis, and D. McSweeney. 1997. Movements of resident killer whales in southeastern Alaska and Prince William Sound, Alaska. Marine Mammal Science 13:469-475.

Matkin, C.O., G. Ellis, L. Barrett-Lennard, H. Jurk, D. Sheel, and E. Saulitis. 1999. Comprehensive killer whale investigation. North Gulf Oceanic Society, Restoration Project 98012 Annual Report, Homer, Alaska.

Matkin, C.O., D. Scheel, G. Ellis, L. Barrett-Lennard, H. Jurk, and E. Saulitis. 1998. Comprehensive killer whale investigation, *Exxon Valdez* oil spill restoration project. North Gulf Oceanic Society, Restoration Project 97012, Homer, Alaska.

May, R.M. (ed.). 1973. Stability and complexity in model ecosystems. Princeton University Press, Princeton.

McAllister, C.D. 1969. Aspects of estimating zooplankton production from phytoplankton production. Journal of the Fisheries Research Board of Canada 26:199-220.

McDowell Group. 2001. The economic impacts of the cruise industry in Anchorage, 1999. Anchorage. 36 pp.

McElroy, M.P. 1983. Marine biological controls on atmospheric CO_2 and climate. Nature 302:328-329.

McRoy, C.P. 1970. Standing stocks and other features of eelgrass (*Zostera marina*) populations on the coast of Alaska. Journal of the Fisheries Research Board of Canada 27:1811-1821.

McRoy, C.P., and J.J. Goering. 1974. Coastal ecosystems of Alaska. In: H.T. Odum, B.J. Copeland, and E.H. McMahan (eds.), Coastal ecological systems of the United States, Vol. 3. The Conservation Foundation, Washington, D.C., pp. 124-145.

Mearns, A.J. 1996. *Exxon Valdez* shoreline treatment and operations: Implications for response, assessment, monitoring, and research. American Fisheries Society Symposium 18:309-328.

Mecklenburg, C.W., T.A. Mecklenburg, and L.K. Thorsteinson. 2002. Fishes of Alaska. American Fisheries Society, Bethesda. 1037 pp.

Megrey, B.A., A.B. Hollowed, S.R. Hare, S.A. Macklin, and P.J. Stabeno. 1996. Contributions of FOCI research to forecasts of year-class strength of walleye pollock in Shelikof Strait, Alaska. Fisheries Oceanography 5(Suppl. 1):189-203.

Meier, M.F. 1984. Contribution of small glaciers in global sea level. Science 226:1418-1421.

Meir, E., and W.F. Fagan. 2000. Will observation error and biases ruin the use of simple extinction models? Conservation Biology 14:148-154.

Melsom, A., S.D. Meyers, H.E. Hurlburt, E.J. Metzger, and J.J. O'Brien. 1999. ENSO effects on the Gulf of Alaska eddies. Earth Interactions 3, http://EarthInteractions.org.

Mendenhall, V.M. 1997. Preliminary report on the 1997 Alaska seabird die-off. U.S. Fish and Wildlife Service, Anchorage, Alaska.

Menge, B.A. 1995. Indirect effects in marine rocky intertidal interaction webs: Patterns and importance. Ecological Monographs 65:21-74.

Menge, B.A., and E.D. Sutherland. 1987. Community regulation: Variation in disturbance, competition, and predation in relation to gradients of environmental stress and recruitment. American Naturalist 130:730-757.

Menge, B.A., E.L. Berlow, C.A. Blanchette, S.A. Navarette, and S.B. Yamada. 1994. The keystone species concept: Variation in interaction strength in a rocky intertidal habitat. Ecological Monographs 64:249-287.

Merrick, R.L., and D.G. Calkins. 1996. Importance of juvenile walleye pollock, *Theragra chalcogramma*, in the diet of Gulf of Alaska Steller sea lions, *Eumetopias jubatus*. In: R.D. Brodeur, P.A. Livingston, T.R. Loughlin, and A.B. Hollowed (eds.), Ecology of juvenile walleye pollock, *Theragra chalcogramma*. NOAA Technical Report NMFS 126:153-166.

Merrick, R.L., and T.R. Loughlin. 1997. Foraging behavior of adult female and young-of-the-year Steller sea lions in Alaskan waters. Canadian Journal of Zoology 75:776-786.

Merrick, R.L., M.K. Chumbley, and G.V. Byrd. 1997. Diet diversity of Steller sea lions (*Eumetopias jubatus*) and their population decline in Alaska: A potential relationship. Canadian Journal of Zoology 54:1342-1348.

Merrick, R.L., T.R. Loughlin, and D.G. Calkins. 1987. Decline in abundance of the northern sea lion, *Eumetopias jubatus*, in Alaska, 1956-86. Fishery Bulletin U.S. 85:351-365.

Meyer, J.S., C.G. Ingersoll, L.L. McDonald, and M.S. Boyce. 1986. Estimating uncertainty in population growth rates: Jackknife vs. bootstrap techniques. Ecology 67:1156-1166.

Meyers, S.D., and S. Basu. 1999. Eddies in the eastern Gulf of Alaska from TOPEX/POSEIDON altimetry. Journal of Geophysical Research 104:13333-13343.

Miller, C.B. 1988. *Neocalanus flemingeri*, a new species of Calanidae (Copepoda: Calanoida) from the subarctic Pacific Ocean, with a comparative redescription of *Neocalanus plumchrus* (Marukawa) 1921. Progress in Oceanography 20:223-274.

Miller, C.B. 1993. Pelagic production processes in the subarctic Pacific. Progress in Oceanography 32:1-15.

Miller, C.B., and M.J. Clemons. 1988. Revised life history analysis of the large grazing copepods in the subarctic Pacific Ocean. Progress in Oceanography 20:293-313.

Miller, C.B., and R.D. Nielsen. 1988. Development and growth of large calanoid copepods in the subarctic Pacific, May 1984. Progress in Oceanography 20:275-292.

Miller, C.B., B.W. Frost, B. Booth, P.A. Wheeler, M.R. Landry, and N. Welschmeyer. 1991a. Ecological processes in the subarctic Pacific: Iron limitation cannot be the whole story. Oceanography 4:71-78.

Miller, C.B., B.W. Frost, P.A. Wheeler, M.R. Landry, N. Welschmeyer, and T.M. Powell. 1991b. Ecological dynamics in the subarctic Pacific, possibly iron limited system. Limnology and Oceanography 36:1600-1615.

Minobe, S. 1997. A 50-70 year climatic oscillation over the North Pacific and North America. Geophysical Research Letters 24:683-686.

Minobe, S. 1999. Resonance in bidecadal and pentadecadal climate oscillations over the North Pacific: Role in climatic regime shifts. Geophysical Research Letters 26:855-858.

Mode, C.J., and M.E. Jacobson. 1987a. A study of the impact of environmental stochasticity on extinction probabilities by Monte Carlo integration. Mathematical BioSciences 83:105-125.

Mode, C.J., and M.E. Jacobson. 1987b. On estimating critical population size for an endangered species in the presence of environmental stochasticity. Mathematical BioSciences 85:185-209.

Molnia, B.F. 1981. Distribution of continental shelf surface sedimentary units between Yakutat and Cross Sound, northeastern Gulf of Alaska. Journal of the Alaska Geological Society 1:60-66.

Monson, D.H., and A.R. DeGange. 1995. Reproduction, preweaning survival, and survival of adult sea otters at Kodiak Island, Alaska. Canadian Journal of Zoology 73:1161-1169.

Monson, D.H., J.A. Estes, J.L. Bodkin, and D.B. Siniff. 2000a. Life history plasticity and population regulation in sea otters. Oikos 90:457-468.

Monson, D.H., D.F. Doak, B.E. Ballachey, A.M. Johnson, and J.L. Bodkin. 2000b. Long-term impacts of the *Exxon Valdez* oil spill on sea otters, assessed through age-dependent mortality patterns. Proceedings of the National Academy of Sciences, Washington, D.C., pp. 6562-6567.

Montevecchi, W.A., and R.A. Myers. 1996. Dietary changes of seabirds indicate shifts in pelagic food webs. Sarsia 80:313-322.

Moore, S.E., K.E.W. Shelden, L.K. Litzky, B.A. Mahone, and D.J. Rugh. 2000. Beluga, *Delphinapterus leucas*, habitat associations in Cook Inlet, Alaska. Marine Fisheries Review Special Issue 62(3):60-80.

Muench, R.D., and D.T. Heggie. 1978. Deep water exchange in Alaskan subarctic fjords. In: B. Kjerfve (ed.), Estuarine transport processes. B. Baruch Institute for Marine Biology and Coastal Research, University of South Carolina Press, Columbia, pp. 239-267.

Muench, R.D., H.O. Mofjeld, and R.L. Charnell. 1978. Oceanographic conditions in lower Cook Inlet: Spring and summer 1973. Journal of Geophysical Research 83:5090-5098.

Mueter, F.J., and B.L. Norcross. 1999. Linking community structure of small demersal fishes around Kodiak Island, Alaska, to environmental variables. Marine Ecology Progress Series 190:37-51.

Mueter, F.J., and B.L. Norcross. 2000. Species composition and abundance of juvenile groundfish around Steller sea lion *Eumetopias jubatus* rookeries in the Gulf of Alaska. Alaska Fishery Research Bulletin 7:33-43.

Mundy, P.R. 1996. The role of harvest management in the future of Pacific salmon populations: Shaping human behavior to enable the persistence of salmon. In: R.J. Naiman and D. Stouder (eds.), Chapman Hall, New York, pp. 315-330.

Murphy, E.C., A.M. Springer, D.G. Roseneau, and B.A. Cooper. 1991. High annual variability in reproductive success of kittiwakes (*Rissa tridactyla*) at a colony in western Alaska. Journal of Animal Ecology 60:515-534.

Musgrave, D., T. Weingartner, and T.C. Royer. 1992. Circulation and hydrography in the northwestern Gulf of Alaska. Deep-Sea Research 39:1499-1519.

Myers, K.W., R.V. Walker, H.R. Carlson, and J.H. Helle. 2000. Synthesis and review of U.S. research on the physical and biological factors affecting ocean production of salmon. In: J.H. Helle, Y. Ishida, D. Noakes, and V. Radchenko (eds.), Recent changes in ocean production of Pacific salmon. North Pacific Anadromous Fish Commission Bulletin, Vancouver, pp. 1-9.

Mysak, L., R.D. Muench, and J.D. Schumacher. 1981. Baroclinic instability in a downstream varying channel: Shelikof Strait, Alaska. Journal of Physical Oceanography 11:950-969.

Nagasawa, K. 2000. Winter zooplankton biomass in the subarctic North Pacific, with a discussion on the overwintering survival strategy of Pacific Salmon (*Oncorhynchus* spp.). In: J.H. Helle, Y. Ishido, D. Noakes, and V. Radchenko (eds.), Recent changes in ocean production of Pacific salmon. North Pacific Anadromous Fish Commission Bulletin, Vancouver, pp. 21-32.

Nakata, H., K. Kannan, L. Jing, N.J. Thomas, S. Tanabe, and J.P. Giesey. 1998. Accumulation pattern of organochlorine pesticides and polychlorinated biphenyls in southern sea otters (*Enhydra lutris nereis*) found stranded along coastal California, USA. Environmental Pollution 103:45-53.

Napp, J.M., L.S. Incze, P.B. Ortner, D.L. Siefert, and L. Britt. 1996. The plankton on Shelikof Strait, Alaska: Standing stock, production, mesoscale variability and their relevance to larval fish survival. Fisheries Oceanography 5:19-35.

Niebauer, H.J., J. Roberts, and T.C. Royer. 1981. Shelf break circulation in the northern Gulf of Alaska. Journal of Geophysical Research 86:13041-13047.

Niebauer, H.J., T.C. Royer, and T.J. Weingartner. 1994. Circulation of Prince William Sound, Alaska. Journal of Geophysical Research 99:14113-14126.

NMFS. 2000. Endangered Species Act: Section 7. Consultation, biological opinion and incidental take statement. NMFS Office of Protected Resources, Silver Spring, Maryland.

NMFS. 2001. Alaska groundfish fisheries draft programmatic supplemental environmental impact statement. NOAA/NMFS, Alaska Region.

NMFS. 2002. Principal hypotheses surrounding the Steller sea lion decline (SSLI). http://www.afsc.noaa.gov/Stellers/hypotheses.htm. Accessed June 15, 2004.

NOAA. 1993. Report of the NOAA panel on contingent valuation. Federal Register 58:10.

Norcross, B.L. 1998. Defining habitats for juvenile groundfishes in southcentral Alaska with emphasis on flatfishes. Vol. 1, final report, Coastal Marine Institute, University of Alaska Fairbanks.

Norcross, B.L., E.D. Brown, R.J. Foy, M. Frandsen, S. Gay, T.C. Kline Jr., D.M. Mason, E.V. Patrick, A.J. Paul, and K.D.E. Stokesbury. 2001. A synthesis of the early life history and ecology of juvenile Pacific herring in Prince William Sound, Alaska. Fisheries Oceanography 10(Suppl. 1):42-57.

Northern Economics Inc. 2002. Alaska visitors' expenditures and options fall/winter 2000-01. Prepared for Alaska Department of Community and Economic Development.

NPFMC. 2000. Stock assessment and fishery evaluation report for groundfish resources of the Gulf of Alaska. North Pacific Fishery Management Council, Anchorage, Alaska.

NRC. 1971. The great Alaska earthquake of 1964. National Research Council, National Academy Press, Washington, D.C.

NRC. 1996. The Bering Sea ecosystem. National Research Council, National Academy Press. Washington, D.C.

NRC. 1999. Sustaining marine fisheries. National Research Council, National Academy Press, Washington, D.C.

NRC. 2000. Ecological indicators for the nation. National Research Council, National Academy Press, Washington, D.C.

NRC. 2002. A century of ecosystem science: Planning long-term research in the Gulf of Alaska. National Research Council, National Academy Press, Washington, D.C.

NRC. 2003. Decline of the Steller sea lion in Alaskan waters. National Research Council, National Academies Press, Washington, D.C. 204 pp.

Nysewander, D.R., and J.L. Trapp. 1984. Widespread mortality of adult seabirds in Alaska, August-September 1983. U.S. Fish and Wildlife Service, Anchorage.

Oakley, K.L., and K.J. Kuletz. 1996. Population, reproduction, and foraging of pigeon guillemots at Naked Island, Alaska, before and after the *Exxon Valdez* oil spill. In: S.D. Rice, R.B. Spies, D.A. Wolfe, and B.A. Wright (eds.), American Fisheries Society Symposium 18:759-769.

O'Clair, C., and S.T. Zimmerman. 1986. Biogeography and ecology of the intertidal and shallow subtidal communities. In: D.W. Hood and S.T. Zimmerman (eds.), The Gulf of Alaska physical environment and biological resources. NOAA Ocean Assessments Division, Alaska Office, Washington, D.C., pp. 305-346.

O'Corry-Crowe, G.M., and L.F. Lowry. 1997. Genetic ecology and management concerns for the beluga whale (*Delphinapterus leucas*). In: A.E. Dizon, S.J. Chivers, and W.F. Perrin (eds.), Molecular genetics of marine mammals. Society for Marine Mammalogy Special Publication 3:249-274.

O'Corry-Crowe, G.M., K.K. Martien, and B.L. Taylor. 2003. The analysis of population genetic structure in Alaskan harbor seals, *Phoca vitulina*, as a framework for the identification of management stocks. NOAA Administrative Report LJ-03-08. 64 pp.

O'Corry-Crowe, G.M., A.E. Dizon, R.S. Suydam, and L.F. Lowry. 2002. Molecular genetic studies of population structure and movement patterns in a migratory species: The beluga whale (*Delphinapterus leucas*) in the western Nearctic. In: C.J. Pfeiffer (ed.), Molecular and cell biology of marine mammals. Krieger Publishing Company, Malabar, Florida, pp. 50-61.

O'Corry-Crowe, G.M., R.S. Suydam, A. Rosenberg, K.J. Frost, and A.E. Dizon. 1997. Phylogeography, population structure and dispersal patterns of the beluga whale *Delphinus leucas* in the western Nearctic revealed by mitochondrial DNA. Molecular Ecology 6:955-970.

O'Daniel, D., and J.C. Schneeweis. 1992. Steller sea lion, *Eumetopias jubatus*, predation on glaucous-winged gulls, *Larus glaucescens*. Canadian Field-Naturalist 106:268.

Okey, T.A., and D. Pauly. 1999a. A mass-balanced model of trophic flows in Prince William Sound: De-compartmentalizing ecosystem knowledge. In: Ecosystem approaches for fisheries management. Alaska Sea Grant College Program, University of Alaska Fairbanks, pp. 621-635.

Okey, T.A., and D. Pauly. 1999b. Trophic mass balance model of Alaska's Prince William Sound ecosystem, for the post-spill period 1994-1996. EVOS Restoration Project 98330-1 Annual Report. Fisheries Centre, University of British Columbia, Vancouver.

Okkonen, S.R. 1992. The shedding of an anticyclonic eddy from the Alaskan Steam as observed by the GEOSAT altimeter. Geophysical Research Letters 19:2397-2400.

Olesiuk, P.F., M.A. Bigg, G.M. Ellis, S.J. Crockford, and R.J. Wigen. 1990. An assessment of the feeding habits of harbour seals (*Phoca vitulina*) in the Strait of Georgia, British Columbia, based on scat analysis. Canadian Technical Report of Fisheries and Aquatic Sciences 1730.

Omori, M. 1969. Weight and chemical composition of some important oceanic zooplankton in the North Pacific Ocean. Marine Biology 3:4-10.

Oosterhout, G.R. 1996. An evolutionary simulation of the tragedy of the commons. Ph.D. thesis, Portland State University, Portland, Oregon.

Oosterhout, G. 1998. PasRAS: A stochastic simulation of chinook and sockeye life histories. Decision Matrix, Inc., Eagle Point, Oregon.

Orensanz, J.M.L., J. Armstrong, D. Armstrong, and R. Hilborn. 1998. Crustacean resources are vulnerable to serial depletion: The multifaceted decline of crab and shrimp fisheries in the Greater Gulf of Alaska. Reviews in Fish Biology and Fisheries 8:117-176.

Orr, R.T., and T.C. Poulter. 1967. Some observations on reproduction, growth, and social behavior in the Steller sea lion. Proceedings of the California Academy of Sciences 35:193-226.

Ostrand, W.D., K.O. Coyle, G.S. Drew, J.M. Maniscalco, and D.B. Irons. 1998. Selection of forage-fish schools by murrelets and tufted puffins in Prince William Sound, Alaska. Condor 100:286-297.

Overland, J.E. 1990. Prediction of vessel icing at near-freezing sea surface temperatures. Weather and Forecasting 5:62-77.

Pace, M.L. 2001. Prediction and the aquatic sciences. Canadian Journal of Fisheries and Aquatic Sciences 58:63-72.

Page, D.S., E.S. Gilfillan, P.D. Boehm, and E.J. Horner. 1995. Shoreline ecology program for Prince William Sound, Alaska, following the *Exxon Valdez* oil spill: Part 1, Study design and methods. In: P.G. Wells, J.N. Butler, and J.S. Hughes (eds.), *Exxon Valdez* oil spill: Fate and effects in Alaskan waters. American Society for Testing and Materials, Philadelphia, pp. 263-295.

Paine, R.T. 1966. Food web complexity and species diversity. American Naturalist 100:65-75.

Paine, R.T., J.T. Wootton, and P.D. Boersma. 1990. Direct and indirect effects of Peregrine Falcon predation on seabird abundance. Auk 107:1-9.

Paine, R.T., J.L. Ruesink, A. Sun, E.L. Soulanille, M.J. Wonham, C.D.G. Harley, D.R. Brumbaugh, and D.L. Secord. 1996. Trouble on oiled waters: Lessons from the *Exxon Valdez* oil spill. Annual Review of Ecology and Systematics 27:197-235.

Parker, K.S., T.C. Royer, and R.B. Deriso. 1995. High-latitude climate forcing and tidal mixing by the 18.6-year lunar nodal cycle and low-frequency recruitment trends in Pacific halibut (*Hippoglossus stenolepis*), in climate change and northern fish populations. In: R.J. Beamish (ed.), Canadian Special Publication of Fisheries and Aquatic Sciences 121:447-458.

Parsons, T.R. 1986. Ecological relations. In: D.W. Hood and S.T. Zimmerman (eds.), The Gulf of Alaska physical environment and biological resources. NOAA Ocean Assessments Division, Alaska Office, Washington, D.C., pp. 561-570.

Parsons, T.R., and C.M. Lalli. 1988. Comparative oceanic ecology of the plankton communities of the subarctic Atlantic and Pacific oceans. Oceanography and Marine Biology Annual Review 26:317-359.

Parsons, T.R., M. Takahashi, and B. Hargrave. 1984. Biological oceanographic processes, 3rd edn. Pergamon Press, New York.

Paul, A.J., and J.M. Paul. 1999. First-year energy storage patterns of Pacific herring and walleye pollock: Insight into competitor strategies. In: Ecosystem approaches for fisheries management. Alaska Sea Grant College Program, University of Alaska Fairbanks, pp. 117-127.

Paul, A.J., and R. Smith. 1993. Seasonal changes in somatic energy content of yellowfin sole *Pleuronectes asper* Pallas 1814. Journal of Fish Biology 43:131-138.

Paul, A.J., J.M. Paul, and R.L. Smith. 1998. Seasonal changes in whole-body energy content and estimated consumption rates of age 0 walleye pollock from Prince William Sound, Alaska. Estuarine, Coastal and Shelf Science 47:251-259.

Peixoto, J.P., and A.H. Oort. 1992. Physics of climate. American Institute of Physics, New York.

Perry, R.I., S. Yoo, and M. Terazaki. 1997. MODEL task team report, workshop on conceptual/theoretical studies and model development. North Pacific Marine Science Organization (PICES), Sidney, British Columbia.

Perry, S.L., D.P. DeMaster, and G.K. Silber. 1999. The great whales: History and status of six species listed as endangered under the U.S. Endangered Species Act of 1973. Marine Fisheries Review 61:1-74.

Peterson, C.H. 1991. Intertidal zonation of marine invertebrates in sand and mud. American Scientist 79:236-249.

Peterson, C.H. 2001. The *Exxon Valdez* oil spill in Alaska: Acute, indirect and chronic effects on the ecosystem. Advances in Marine Biology 39:1-103.

Peterson, C.H., M.C. Kennicutt II, R.H. Green, P. Montagna, D.E. Harper Jr., E.N. Powell, and P.F. Rosigno. 1996. Ecological consequences of environmental perturbations associated with offshore hydrocarbon production: A perspective on long-term exposures in the Gulf of Mexico. Canadian Journal of Fisheries and Aquatic Sciences 53:2637-2654.

Piatt, J.F. 2000. Survival of adult murres and kittiwakes in relation to forage fish abundance. EVOS Restoration Project 99338 Annual Report. U.S. Geological Survey, Alaska Biological Science Center, Anchorage.

Piatt, J.F., and P. Anderson. 1996. Response of common murres to the *Exxon Valdez* oil spill and long-term changes in the Gulf of Alaska marine ecosystem. In: S.D. Rice, R.B. Spies, D.A. Wolf, and B.A. Wright (eds.), Proceedings of the *Exxon Valdez* Oil Spill Symposium. American Fisheries Society Symposium 18:720-737.

Piatt, J.F., and R.G. Ford. 1993. Distribution and abundance of marbled murrelets in Alaska. Condor 95:662-669.

Piatt, J.F., and R.G. Ford. 1996. How many birds were killed by the *Exxon Valdez* oil spill? In: S.D. Rice, R.B. Spies, D.A. Wolfe, and B.A. Wright (eds.), Proceedings of the *Exxon Valdez* Oil Spill Symposium. American Fisheries Society Symposium 18:712-719.

Piatt, J.F., and D.N. Nettleship. 1985. Diving depths of four alcids. Auk 102:293-297.

Piatt, J.F., and T.I. van Pelt. 1993. A wreck of common murres (*Uria aalge*) in the northern Gulf of Alaska during February and March of 1993. U.S. Fish and Wildlife Service, Anchorage, Alaska.

Piatt, J.F., and T.I. van Pelt. 1998. Survival of adult murres and kittiwakes in relation to forage fish abundance. EVOS Restoration Project 99338 Annual Report. U.S. Geological Survey, Anchorage.

Pickart, R.S. 2000. Bottom boundary layer structure and detachment in the shelfbreak jet of the Middle Atlantic Bight. Journal of Physical Oceanography 30:2668-2686.

Pickett, S.T.A., J. Kolasa, and C.G. Jones. 1994. Ecological understanding. Academic Press, San Diego.

Piorkowski, R.J. 1995. Ecological effects of spawning salmon on several southcentral Alaskan streams. Ph.D. thesis, University of Alaska Fairbanks.

Pitcher, K.W. 1980. Food of the harbor seal, *Phoca vitulina richardsi*, in the Gulf of Alaska. Fishery Bulletin U.S. 78:544-549.

Pitcher, K.W. 1981. Prey of the Steller sea lion, *Eumetopias jubatus*, in the Gulf of Alaska. Fishery Bulletin U.S. 79:467-472.

Pitcher, K.W. 1984. The harbor seal (*Phoca vitulina richardsi*). In: J.J. Burns, K.J. Frost, and L.F. Lowry (eds.), Marine mammals species accounts. Alaska Department of Fish and Game, Juneau. Wildlife Technical Bulletin 7:65-70.

Pitcher, K.W. 1989. Harbor seal trend count surveys in southern Alaska, 1988. U.S. Marine Mammal Commission, Washington, D.C.

Pitcher, K.W. 1990. Major decline in the number of harbor seals, *Phoca vitulina richardsi*, on Tugidak Island, Gulf of Alaska. Marine Mammal Science 6:121-134.

Pitcher, K.W., and D.G. Calkins. 1981. Reproductive biology of Steller sea lions in the Gulf of Alaska. Journal of Mammalogy 62:599-605.

Pitcher, K.W., and F.H. Fay. 1982. Feeding by Steller sea lions on harbor seals. Murrelet 63:70-71.

Pitcher, K.W., and D.C. McAllister. 1981. Movements and haul out behavior of radio-tagged harbor seals, *Phoca vitulina*. Canadian Field-Naturalist 95:292-297.

Plafker, G. 1972. Tectonics. In: The great Alaska earthquake of 1964, Vol. 6: Oceanography and coastal engineering. National Academy of Sciences, National Research Council, Washington, D.C., pp. 47-122.

Plakhotnik, A.F. 1964. Hydrological description of the Gulf of Alaska. In: P.A. Moiseev (ed.), Soviet fisheries investigations in the Northeast Pacific, part II. Israel Program for Scientific Translations for the U.S. Department of the Interior and the National Science Foundation, Jerusalem, p. 289.

Polovina, J.J., G.T. Mitchum, and G.T. Evans. 1995. Decadal and basin-scale variation in mixed layer depth and impact on biological production in the Central and North Pacific, 1960-88. Deep-Sea Research 42:1701-1716.

Power, M.E., D. Tilman, J.A. Estes, B.A. Menge, W.J. Bond, L.S. Mills, G. Daily, J.C. Castilla, J. Lubchenco, and R.T. Paine. 1996. Challenges in the quest for keystones. Bioscience 46:609-620.

Prichard, A.K. 1997. Evaluation of pigeon guillemots as bioindicators of nearshore ecosystem health. Master's thesis, University of Alaska Fairbanks.

Punt, A.E., and R. Hilborn. 1997. Fisheries stock assessment and decision analysis: The Bayesian approach. Reviews in Fish Biology and Fisheries 7:35-63.

Purcell, J.E., and M.V. Sturdevant. 2001. Prey selection and dietary overlap among zooplanktivorous jellyfish and juvenile fishes in Prince William Sound, Alaska. Marine Ecology Progress Series 210:67-83.

Purvin & Gertz, Ltd. 2000. Alaskan gas development strategies. Purvin & Gertz, Ltd., Calgary, Alberta.

Quast, J.C., and E.L. Hall. 1972. List of fishes of Alaska and adjacent waters with a guide to some of their literature. NOAA Technical Memorandum NMFS-SSRF-658.

Quinn, T.J., and R.B. Deriso. 1999. Quantitative fish dynamics. Oxford University Press.

Rafaelli, D., and S. Hawkins. 1996. Intertidal ecology. Chapman and Hall, London.

Ralls, K., and B.L. Taylor. 2000. Introduction to special section: Better policy and management decisions through explicit analysis of uncertainty: New approaches from marine conservation. Conservation Biology 14:1240-1242.

Ramp, S.R. 1986. The interaction of warm core rings with the shelf water and the shelf/slope front south of New England. Ph.D. thesis, University of Rhode Island.

Rausch, R. 1958. The occurrence and distribution of birds on Middleton Island, Alaska. Condor 60:227-242.

Reeburgh, W.S., and G.W. Kipphut. 1986. Chemical distributions and signals in the Gulf of Alaska, its coastal margins and estuaries. In: D.W. Hood and S.T. Zimmerman (eds.), The Gulf of Alaska physical environment and biological resources. NOAA Ocean Assessments Division, Alaska Office, Washington, D.C., pp. 77-91.

Reed, R.K., and J.D. Schumacher. 1986. Physical oceanography. In: D.W. Hood and S.T. Zimmerman (eds.), The Gulf of Alaska physical environment and biological resources. NOAA Ocean Assessments Division, Alaska Office, Washington, D.C., pp. 57-75.

Reid Jr., J.L. 1965. Intermediate waters of the Pacific Ocean. Johns Hopkins Oceanographic Studies. Johns Hopkins University Press, Baltimore. 85 pp.

Reid, J.L. 1981. On the mid-depth circulation of the world ocean. In: B.A. Warren and C. Wunsch (eds.), Evolution of physical oceanography scientific surveys in honor of Henry Stommel. MIT Press, Cambridge, pp. 70-111.

Reid, K., and J.P. Croxall. 2001. Environmental response of upper trophic-level predators reveals a system change in an antarctic marine ecosystem. Proceedings of the Royal Society of London B Biological Sciences 268:377-384.

Reynolds Jr., J.E., and S.A. Rommel. 1999. Biology of marine mammals. Smithsonian Institution Press, Washington, D.C.

Rhoads, D.C., and D.K. Young. 1970. The influence of deposit-feeding organisms on sediment stability and community trophic structure. Journal of Marine Research 28:150-178.

Richardson, R.W. 1936. Winter air-mass convergence over the North Pacific. Monthly Weather Review 64:199-203.

Ricker, W.E. 1975. Computation and interpretation of biological statistics of fish populations. Bulletin of the Fisheries Research Board of Canada 191:1-382.

Ricketts, E.F., and J. Calvin. 1968. Between Pacific tides, 4th edn. Stanford University Press, Stanford.

Ricklefs, R.E. 1990. Scaling patterns and process in marine ecosystems. In: K. Sherman, L.M. Alexander, and B.D. Gold (eds.), Large marine ecosystems: Patterns, processes and yields. American Association for the Advancement of Science, Washington, D.C., pp. 169-178.

Riedman, M.L., and J.A. Estes. 1990. The sea otter (*Enhydra lutris*): Behavior, ecology and natural history. U.S. Fish and Wildlife Service Biological Report 90-14, Washington, D.C. 126 pp.

Riedman, M.L., J.A. Estes, M.M. Staedler, A.A. Giles, and D.R. Carlson. 1994. Breeding patterns and reproductive success of California sea otters. Journal of Wildlife Management 58:391-399.

Robards, M., J.F. Piatt, A. Kettle, and A. Abookire. 1999. Temporal and geographic variation in fish populations in nearshore and shelf areas of lower Cook Inlet. Fishery Bulletin U.S. 97(4):962-977.

Roden, G. 1970. Aspects of the mid-Pacific transition zone. Journal of Geophysical Research 75:1097-1109.

Rogers, D.E., B.J. Rogers, and R.J. Rosenthal. 1986. The nearshore fishes. In: D.W. Hood and S.T. Zimmerman (eds.), The Gulf of Alaska physical environment and biological resources. NOAA Ocean Assessments Division, Alaska Office, Washington, D.C., pp. 399-415

Rogers, G. 1962. The future of Alaska: The economic consequences of statehood. Johns Hopkins University Press, Baltimore.

Rogers, I.H., I.K. Birtwell, and G.M. Kurzynski. 1990. The Pacific eulachon (*Thaleichthys pacificus*) as a pollution indicator organism in the Fraser River estuary, Vancouver, British Columbia. The Science of the Total Environment 97/98:713-727.

Rogers, J.C. 1981. The North Pacific oscillation. Journal of Climatology 1:39-57.

Romano, M.D., D.D. Roby, J.F. Piatt, and A. Kitaysky. 2000. Effects of diet on growth and body composition of nestling seabirds. EVOS Restoration Project 98163N Annual Report. U.S. Geological Survey, Oregon Cooperative Fish and Wildlife Research Unit, and Oregon State University, Corvallis, Oregon.

Ronholt, L.L., H.H. Shippen, and E.S. Brown. 1978. Demersal fish and shellfish resources of the Gulf of Alaska from Cape Spencer to Unimak Pass 1948-1976: A historical view. Vol. I. Environmental Assessment of the Alaskan Continental Shelf, Final Reports of Principal Investigators 2 (Biological Studies) 1-304.

Rosen, D.A.S., and A.W. Trites. 2000. Pollock and the decline of Steller sea lions: Testing the junk-food hypothesis. Canadian Journal of Zoology 78:1243-1250.

Rosenberg, D.H. 1972. A review of the oceanography and renewable resources of the northern Gulf of Alaska. Alaska Sea Grant Report 73-3, and Institute of Marine Science IMS Report R72-23, University of Alaska, Fairbanks.

Rosenkranz, G. 1998. Statistical modeling of Tanner crab recruitment. Master's thesis, University of Alaska Fairbanks.

Rotterman, L.M., and T. Simon-Jackson. 1988. Sea otter. In: J.W. Lentfer (ed.), Selected marine mammals of Alaska. U.S. Marine Mammal Commission, Washington, D.C., pp. 237-275.

Royer, T.C. 1975. Seasonal variations of waters in the northern Gulf of Alaska. Deep-Sea Research 22:403-416.

Royer, T.C. 1981a. Baroclinic transport in the Gulf of Alaska. Part I, Seasonal variations of the Alaska current. Journal of Marine Research 39:239-250.

Royer, T.C. 1981b. Baroclinic transport in the Gulf of Alaska. Part II, A freshwater-driven coastal current. Journal of Marine Research 39:251-266.

Royer, T.C. 1982. Coastal freshwater discharge in the northeast Pacific. Journal of Geophysical Research 87:2017-2021.

Royer, T.C. 1993. High-latitude oceanic variability associated with the 18.6 year nodal tide. Journal of Geophysical Research 98:4639-4644.

Royer, T.C. 1998. Coastal processes in the northern North Pacific. In: A.R. Robinson and K.H. Brink (eds.), The sea. John Wiley and Sons, New York, pp. 395-414.

Royer, T.C., D.V. Hansen, and D.J. Pashinski. 1979. Coastal flow in the northern Gulf of Alaska as observed by dynamic topography and satellite-tracked drogued drift buoys. Journal of Physical Oceanography 9:785-801.

Ruckelshaus, M., C. Hartway, and P. Jareuva. 1997. Assessing the data requirements of spatially explicit dispersal models. Conservation Biology 11:1298-1306.

Rugh, D.J., K.E.W. Shelden, and B.A. Mahoney. 2000. Distribution of beluga whales, *Delphinapterus leucas*, in Cook Inlet, Alaska, during June/July 1993-2000. Marine Fisheries Review 62(3):6-21.

Rutherford, S., and S. D'Hondt. 2000. Early onset and tropical forcing of 100,000-year Pleistocene glacial cycles. Nature 408:72-75.

SAI. 1980a. Environmental assessment of the Alaskan Continental Shelf. Kodiak interim synthesis report, 1980. Science Applications, Inc., Boulder

SAI. 1980b. Environmental assessment of the Alaskan Continental Shelf. Northeast Gulf of Alaska interim synthesis report. Science Applications, Inc., Boulder.

Sambrotto, R.N., and C.J. Lorenzen. 1986. Phytoplankton and primary production. In: D.W. Hood and S.T. Zimmerman (eds.), The Gulf of Alaska physical environment and biological resources. NOAA Ocean Assessments Division, Alaska Office, Washington, D.C., pp. 249-282.

Sandegren, F.E. 1970. Breeding and maternal behavior of the Steller sea lion (*Eumetopias jubatus*) in Alaska. Master's thesis, University of Alaska, Fairbanks.

Sanger, G.A. 1987. Trophic levels and trophic relationships of seabirds in the Gulf of Alaska. In: J.P. Croxall (ed.), Seabirds: Feeding ecology and role in marine ecosystems. Cambridge University Press, Cambridge, pp. 229-257.

Saulitis, E.L. 1993. The vocalizations and behavior of the "AT"-group of killer whales (*Orcinus orca*) in Prince William Sound, Alaska. Master's thesis, University of Alaska Fairbanks.

Schiel, D.R., and M.S. Foster. 1986. The structure of subtidal algal stands in temperate waters. Oceanography and Marine Biology Annual Review 24:265-307.

Schlitz, R. 1999. The interaction of shelf water with warm core rings. U.S. Department of Commerce, NOAA Technical Report.

Schmidt, G.M. 1977. The exchange of water between Prince William Sound and the Gulf of Alaska. Master's thesis, University of Alaska, Fairbanks.

Schneider, D., and G.L. Hunt Jr. 1982. A comparison of seabird diets and foraging distribution around the Pribilof Islands, Alaska. In: D.N. Nettleship, G.A. Sanger, and P.F. Springer (eds.), Marine birds: Their feeding ecology and commercial fisheries relationships. Minister of Supply and Services, Canada, pp. 86-95.

Schnute, J.T., and L.J. Richards. 2001. Use and abuse of fishery models. Canadian Journal of Fisheries and Aquatic Sciences 58:10-17.

Schumacher, J.D., and A.W. Kendall Jr. 1991. Some interactions between young walleye pollock and their environment in the western Gulf of Alaska. California Cooperative Oceanic Fisheries Investigations (CalCOFI) 32:22-40

Schumacher, J.D., and T. Royer. 1993. Review of the physics of the subarctic gyre. PICES Scientific Report No. 1:37-40.

Schumacher, J.D., C.A. Pearson, and R.K. Reed. 1982. An exchange of water between the Gulf of Alaska and the Bering Sea through Unimak Pass. Journal of Geophysical Research 87:5785-5795.

Schumacher, J.D., P.J. Stabeno, and S.J. Bogard. 1993. Characteristics of an eddy over the continental shelf: Shelikof Strait, Alaska. Journal of Geophysical Research 98:8395-8404.

Schumacher, J.D., P.J. Stabeno, and A.T. Roach. 1990. Volume transport in the Alaska Coastal Current. Continental Shelf Research 9:1071-1083.

Scribner, K.T., J. Bodkin, B. Ballachey, S.R. Fain, M.A. Cronin, and M. Sanchez. 1997. Population genetic studies of the sea otter (*Enhydra lutris*): A review and interpretation of available data. In: A.E. Dizon,, S.J. Chivers, and W.F. Perrin (eds.), Molecular genetics of marine mammals. Society for Marine Mammalogy Special Publication 3:197-208.

Seaman, G.A., K.J. Frost, and L.F. Lowry. 1985. Investigations of belukha whales in coastal waters of western and northern Alaska. Part I. Distribution, abundance and movements. National Oceanic and Atmospheric Administration and Alaska Department of Fish and Game. 60 pp.

Sease, J.L. 1992. Status review, harbor seals (*Phoca vitulina*) in Alaska. NOAA/NMFS, AFSC, Seattle, Washington. 74 pp.

Sease, J.L., and T.R. Loughlin. 1999. Aerial and land-based surveys of Steller sea lions (*Eumetopias jubatus*) in Alaska, June and July 1997 and 1998. NOAA Technical Memorandum NMFS-AFSC-100. 61 pp.

Seiser, P.E. 2000. Mechanism of impact and potential recovery of pigeon guillemots (*Cepphus columba*) after the *Exxon Valdez* oil spill. Master's thesis, University of Alaska Fairbanks.

Sergeant, D.E., and P.F. Brodie. 1969. Body size in white whales, *Delphinapterus leucas*. Journal of the Fisheries Research Board of Canada 26:2561-2580.

Shaughnessy, P.D., and F.H. Fay. 1977. A review of the taxonomy and nomenclature of North Pacific harbour seals. Journal of Zoology (London) 182:385-419.

Shigenaka, G., D.A. Coates, A.K. Fukuyama, and P.D. Roberts. 1999. Effects and trends in littleneck clams (*Protothaca staminea*) impacted by the *Exxon Valdez* oil spill. Proceedings of the 1999 International Oil Spill Conference, Seattle. American Petroleum Institute, Washington, D.C.

Sigman, D.M., and E.A. Boyle. 2000. Glacial/interglacial variations in atmospheric carbon dioxide. Nature 407:859-869.

Simenstad, C.A., J.A. Estes, and K.W. Kenyon. 1978. Aleuts, sea otters, and alternate stable state communities. Science 200(4340):403-411.

Siniff, D.B., and K. Ralls. 1991. Reproduction, survival and tag loss in California sea otters. Marine Mammal Science 7:211-229.

Siniff, D.B., T.D. Williams, A.M. Johnson, and D.L. Garshelis. 1982. Experiments on the response of sea otters, *Enhydra lutris*, to oil. Biological Conservation 23:261-272.

Small, R.J. 1998. Harbor seal investigations in Alaska. NOAA/NMFS Annual Report Award Number NA57FX0367, Juneau, Alaska.

Small, R.J., K. Hastings, and L.A. Jemison. 1999. Harbor seal investigations in Alaska. NOAA/NMFS Annual Report Award Number NA87FX0300, Juneau, Alaska.

Small, R.J., G.W. Pendleton, and K.M. Wynne. 1997. Harbor seal population trends in the Ketchikan, Sitka, and Kodiak Island areas of Alaska. In: Annual Report: Harbor seal investigations in Alaska. Alaska Department of Fish and Game, Anchorage, pp. 7-32.

Small, R.J., G.W. Pendleton, and K.M. Wynne. 2001. Harbor seal population trends in the Ketchikan, Sitka, and Kodiak areas of Alaska, 1983-1999. In: Harbor seal investigations in Alaska. Annual Report for NOAA Award NA87FX0300. Alaska Department of Fish and Game, Division of Wildlife Conservation, Anchorage, pp. 8-30.

Smith, D.R., S. Niemeyer, J.A. Estes, and A.R. Flegal. 1990. Stable lead isotope evidence of anthropogenic contamination in Alaskan sea otters. Environmental Science and Technology 24:1517-1521.

Smith, T.G., D.J. St. Aubin, and M.O. Hammill. 1992. Rubbing behaviour of belugas, *Delphinapterus leucas*, in a High Arctic estuary. Canadian Journal of Zoology 70:2405-2409.

Snarski, D. 1971. Kittiwake ecology, Tuxedni National Wildlife Refuge. Alaska Cooperative Wildlife Research Unit quarterly report, University of Alaska, Fairbanks.

Sobolevsky, Y.I., T.G. Sokolovshaya, A.A. Balanov, and I.A. Senchenko. 1996. Distribution and trophic relationships of abundant mesopelagic fishes of the Bering Sea. In: O.A. Mathisen and K.O. Coyle (eds.), Ecology of the Bering Sea: A review of Russian literature. Alaska Sea Grant College Program, University of Alaska Fairbanks, pp. 159-167.

Sogard, S.M., and B.L. Olla. 2000. Endurance of simulated winter conditions by age-0 walleye pollock (*Theragra chalcogramma*): Effects of body size, water temperature and energy stores. Journal of Fish Biology 56(1):1-21.

Sousa, W.P. 1979. Experimental investigations of disturbance and ecological succession in a rocky intertidal community. Ecological Monographs 49:227-254.

Southward, A.J., and E.C. Southward. 1978. Recolonization of rocky shores in Cornwall after the use of toxic dispersants to clean up the *Torrey Canyon* spill. Journal of the Fisheries Research Board of Canada 35:682-706.

Spraker, T.R., L.F. Lowry, and K.J. Frost. 1994. Gross necropsy and histopathological lesions found in harbor seals. In: T.R. Loughlin (ed.), Marine mammals and the *Exxon Valdez*. Academic Press, Inc., San Diego, pp. 281-312.

Springer, A.M. 1991. Seabird relationships to food webs and the environment: Examples from the North Pacific Ocean. In: W.A. Montevecchi and A.J. Gaston (eds.), Studies of high-latitude seabirds. 1. Behavioral, energetic, and oceanographic aspects of seabird feeding ecology. Canadian Wildlife Service, Ottawa, pp. 39-48.

Springer, A.M. 1998. Is it all climate change? Why marine bird and mammal populations fluctuate in the North Pacific. In: G. Holloway, P. Muller, and D. Henderson (eds.), Biotic impacts of extratropical climate variability in the Pacific: Proceedings of the Tenth 'Aha Huliko'a Hawaiian Winter Workshop, January 25-29, 1998. University of Hawaii at Manoa, School of Ocean and Earth Science and Technology, Honolulu, pp. 109-119.

Springer, A.M., and S.G. Speckman. 1997. A forage fish is what? Summary of the symposium. In: Forage fishes in marine ecosystems: Proceedings of the International Symposium on the Role of Forage Fishes in Marine Ecosystems. Alaska Sea Grant College Program, University of Alaska Fairbanks, pp. 773-805.

Springer, A.M., C.P. McRoy, and M.V. Flint. 1996. The Bering Sea Green Belt: Shelf edge processes and ecosystem production. Fisheries Oceanography 5:205-223.

Springer, A.M., J.F. Piatt, and G. Van Vliet. 1996. Sea birds as proxies of marine habitats and food webs in the western Aleutian arc. Fisheries Oceanography 5:45-55.

Springer, A.M., A.Y. Kondratyev, H. Ogi, Y.V. Shibaev, and G.B. Van Vliet. 1993. Status, ecology, and conservation of *Synthliboramphus* murrelets and auklets. In: K. Vermeer, K.T. Briggs, K.H. Morgan, and D. Siegel-Causey (eds.), The status, ecology, and conservation of marine birds of the North Pacific. Canadian Wildlife Service, Ottawa, pp. 187-201.

Springer, A.M, J.A. Estes, G.B van Vliet, T.M. Williams, D.F. Doak, E.M. Danner, K.A. Forney, and B. Pfister. 2003. Sequential megafaunal collapse in the North Pacific Ocean: An ongoing legacy of industrial whaling. Proceedings of the National Academy of Science 100:12223-12228.

St. Aubin, D.J., T.G. Smith, and J.R. Geraci. 1990. Seasonal epidermal molt in beluga whales, *Delphinapterus leucas*. Canadian Journal of Zoology 68:359-367.

Stabeno, P.J., R.K. Reed, and J.D. Schumacher. 1995. The Alaska coastal current: Continuity of transport and forcing. Journal of Geophysical Research 100:2477-2485.

Stephen R. Braund & Associates. 1995. Whittier access project subsistence technical report. In: Whittier access project revised draft environmental impact statement: Technical reports. Prepared by HDR Engineering in association with Northern Ecological Services et al. Alaska Department of Transportation and Public Facilities and Federal Highway Commission, Anchorage, pp. 1-91.

Stewart, B.S. 1997. Ontogeny of differential migration and sexual segregation in northern elephant seals. Journal of Mammalogy 78:1101-1116.

Stockmar, E.J. 1994. Diel and seasonal variability of macrozooplankton and micronekton in the near-surface of the Gulf of Alaska. Master's thesis, University of Alaska Fairbanks.

Stommel, H., and A.B. Arons. 1960a. On the abyssal circulation of the world ocean. I. Stationary planetary flow patterns on a sphere. Deep-Sea Research 6:140-154.

Stommel, H., and A.B. Arons. 1960b. On the abyssal circulation of the world ocean. II. An idealized model of the circulation pattern and amplitude in oceanic basins. Deep-Sea Research 6:217-233.

Stouder, D.J., P.A. Bisson, and R.J. Naiman (eds.). 1997. Pacific salmon and their ecosystems: Status and future options. Chapman and Hall, New York.

Sturdevant, M.V., A.C. Wertheimer, and J.L. Lum. 1996. Diets of juvenile pink and chum salmon in oiled and non-oiled nearshore habitats in Prince William Sound, 1989 and 1990. American Fisheries Society Symposium 18:578-592.

Suchanek, T.H. 1985. Mussels and their role in structuring rocky shore communities. In: P.G. Moore and R. Seed (eds.), Ecology of rocky coasts: Chapter VI. Hodder and Stoughton Educational Press, Kent, pp. 70-89.

Sugimoto, T. 1993. Subarctic gyre: Gross structure and decadal scale variations in basin scale climate and oceanic conditions. PICES Scientific Report 1:35-37.

Sugimoto, T., and K. Tadokoro. 1997. Interannual-interdecadal variations in zooplankton biomass, chlorophyll concentration, and physical environment of the subarctic Pacific and Bering Sea. Fisheries Oceanography 6:74-92.

Sundberg, K., L. Deysher, and L. McDonald. 1996. Intertidal and supratidal site selection using a geographical information system. American Fisheries Society Symposium 18:167-176.

Suryan, R.M., D.B. Irons, and J. Benson. 2000. Prey switching and variable foraging strategies of black-legged kittiwake and the effect on reproductive success. Condor 102:374-384.

Suryan, R.M., D.B. Irons, M. Kaufman, J. Benson, P.G.R. Jodice, D.D. Roby, and E.D. Brown. 2002. Short-term fluctuations in forage fish availability and the effect on prey selection and brood-rearing in the black-legged kittiwake *Rissa tridactyla*. Marine Ecology Progress Series 236:273-287.

Szepanski, M.M., M. Ben-David, and V. Van Ballenberghe. 1999. Assessment of anadromous salmon resources in the diet of the Alexander Archipelago wolf using stable isotope analysis. Oecologia 120:327-335.

Tabata, S. 1982. The anticyclonic, baroclinic eddy of Sitka, Alaska, in the Northeast Pacific Ocean. Journal of Physical Oceanography 12:1260-1282.

Taylor, C., L.K. Duffy, R.T. Bowyer, and G.M. Blundell. 2000. Profiles of fecal porphyrins in river otters following the *Exxon Valdez* oil spill. Marine Pollution Bulletin 40:1132-1138.

Thompson, R.O.R.Y., and T.J. Golding. 1981. Tidally induced upwelling by the Great Barrier Reef. Journal of Geophysical Research 86:6517-6521.

Thomson, R.E. 1972. On the Alaskan Stream. Journal of Physical Oceanography 2:363-371.

Thomson, R.E., and E. Wolanski. 1984. Tidal period upwelling with Raine Island Entrance Great Barrier Reef. Journal of Marine Research 42:787-808.

Thomson, R.E., B.M. Hickey, and P.H. LeBlond. 1989. The Vancouver Island Coastal Current: Fisheries barrier and conduit. In: R.J. Beamish and G.A. McFarlane (eds.), Effects of ocean variability on recruitment and an evaluation of parameters used in stock assessment models. Canadian Special Publication of Fisheries and Aquatic Sciences 108:265-296.

Thomson, R.E., P.H. LeBlond, and W.J. Emery. 1990. Analysis of deep-drogued satellite-tracked drifter measurements in the Northeast Pacific Ocean. Atmosphere-Ocean 28:409-443.

Thorsteinson, F.V., and C.J. Lensink. 1962. Biological observations of Steller sea lions taken during an experimental harvest. Journal of Wildlife Management 26:353-359.

Trenberth, K.E., and J.W. Hurrell. 1994. Decadal atmospheric-ocean variations in the Pacific. Climate Dynamics 9:303-319.

Trenberth, K.E., and D.A. Paolino. 1980. The Northern Hemisphere sea-level pressure data set: Trends, errors, and discontinuities. Monthly Weather Review 108:855-872.

Trillmich, F., and K. Ono. 1991. Pinnipeds and El Niño: Responses to environmental stress. Springer Verlag, Berlin.

Trites, A.W. 1990. Thermal budgets and climate spaces: The impact of weather on the survival of Galapagos (*Arctocephalus galapagoensis* Heller) and northern fur seal pups (*Callorhinus ursinus* L.). Functional Ecology 4:753-768.

Trites, A.W., P. Livingston, S. Mackinson, M.C. Vasconcellos, A.M. Springer, and D. Pauly. 1999. Ecosystem change and the decline of marine mammals in the eastern Bering Sea: Testing the ecosystem shift and commercial whaling hypotheses. University of British Columbia, Fisheries Centre Research Reports 1999, Vol. 7.

Trowbridge, C. 1995. Prince William Sound management area 1994 shellfish annual management report. Alaska Department of Fish and Game, Anchorage.

Tully, J.P., and F.G. Barber. 1960. An estuarine analogy in the sub-arctic Pacific Ocean. Journal of the Fisheries Research Board of Canada 17:91-112.

Tyler, A.V., and G.H. Kruse. 1996. Conceptual modeling of brood strength of red king crabs in the Bristol Bay region of the Bering Sea. In: High latitude crabs: Biology, management, and economics. Alaska Sea Grant College Program, University of Alaska Fairbanks, pp. 511-543.

Tyler, A.V., and G.H. Kruse. 1997. Modeling workshop on year-class strength of Tanner crab, *Chionoecetes bairdi*. Alaska Department of Fish and Game Regional Information Report No. 5J97-02, Juneau.

Underwood, A.J., and E.J. Denley. 1984. Paradigms, explanations and generalizations in models for the structure of intertidal communities on rocky shores. In: D. Simberloff et al. (eds.), Ecological communities: Conceptual issues and the evidence. Princeton University Press, Princeton, pp. 151-180.

U.S. Bureau of Economic Analysis. 2002. CA1-3: Personal income summary estimates, Alaska, 1969-1999. U.S. Department of Commerce, U.S. Bureau of Economic Analysis.

U.S. Bureau of the Census. 2001. Profiles of general demographic characteristics, 2000 census of population and housing: Alaska. U.S. Bureau of the Census.

U.S. GLOBEC (No date). U.S. GLOBEC Northeast Pacific Program Synthesis. Modeling. http://globec.oce.orst.edu/groups/nep/reports/rep16/rep16.bs.model.html, accessed July 2004.

U.S. GOOS. 2000. A position paper of the U.S. GOOS Steering Committee. Toward a national, cost-effective approach to predicting the future of our coastal environment. (U.S. Global Ocean Observing System) http://www-ocean.tamu.edu/GOOS/publications/position.html, accessed July 2004.

USDA Forest Service. 2000a. Forest health management report, forest insect and disease conditions in Alaska 1999. U.S. Department of Agriculture, Forest Service, Alaska Region and Alaska Department of Natural Resources, Division of Forestry. R10-TP-82, February 2000.

USDA Forest Service. 2000b. Chugach National Forest, proposed revised land management plan and environmental impact statement. U.S. Department of Agriculture, Forest Service, Chugach National Forest.

USEPA. 1998. Climate change and Alaska. EPA 236-F-98-007b. Washington, D.C. 4 pp.

USGS. 2000. National Water Quality Assessment Program. http://water.usgs.gov/nawqa/docs/xrel, accessed July 2004.

Valiela, I. 1995. Marine ecological processes, 2nd edn. Springer-Verlag, New York.

VanBlaricom, G.R. 1987. Regulation of mussel population structure in Prince William Sound, Alaska. National Geographic Research 3:501-510.

VanBlaricom., G.R. 1988. Effects of foraging by sea otters on mussel-dominated intertidal communities. In: G.R. VanBlaricom and J.A. Estes (eds.), The community ecology of sea otters. Springer Verlag, Berlin, pp. 48-91.

Van Pelt, T.I., J.F. Piatt, B.K. Lance, and D.D. Roby. 1997. Proximate composition and energy density of some North Pacific forage fishes. Comparative Biochemistry and Physiology A118:1393-1398.

Van Scoy, K.A., D.B. Olson, and R.A. Fine. 1991. Ventilation of North Pacific intermediate water: The role of the Alaskan gyre. Journal of Geophysical Research 96:16801-16810.

van Tamelen, P.G., M.S. Stekoll, and L. Deysher. 1997. Recovery processes of the brown alga, *Fucus gardneri* (Silva), following the *Exxon Valdez* oil spill: Settlement and recruitment. Marine Ecology Progress Series 160:265-277.

Vastano, A.C., L.S. Incze, and J.D. Schumacher. 1992. Environmental and larval pollock observations in Shelikof Strait, Alaska. Fisheries Oceanography 1:20-31.

Vaughan, S.L., C.N.K. Moores, and S.M. Gay III. 2001. Physical variability in Prince William Sound during the SEA study (1994-1998). Fisheries Oceanography 10(Suppl. 1):58-80.

Vermeer, K., and S.J. Westrheim. 1984. Fish changes in diets of nestling rhinoceros auklets and their implications. In: D.N. Nettleship, G.A. Sanger, and P.F. Springer (eds.), Marine birds: Their feeding ecology and commercial fisheries relationships. Canadian Wildlife Service, Ottawa, pp. 96-105.

Vermeer, K., S.G. Sealy, and G.A. Sanger. 1987. Feeding ecology of Alcidae in the eastern North Pacific Ocean. In: J.P. Croxall (ed.), Seabirds: Feeding ecology and role in marine ecosystems. Cambridge University Press, Cambridge, pp. 189-227.

von Huene, R.W., G.G. Shor Jr., and R.J. Malloy. 1972. Offshore tectonic features in the affected region. In: The great Alaska earthquake of 1964, Vol. 6: Oceanography and coastal engineering. National Research Council, National Academy of Sciences, Washington, D.C., pp. 266-289.

von Winterfeldt, D., and W. Edwards. 1986. Decision analysis and behavioral research. Cambridge University Press, Cambridge.

von Ziegesar, O., G. Ellis, C.O. Matkin, and B. Goodwin. 1986. Repeated sightings of identifiable killer whales (*Orcinus orca*) in Prince William Sound, Alaska, 1977-1983. Cetus 6:9-13.

Vose, D. 2000. Risk analysis: A quantitative guide. John Wiley and Sons, Chichester.

Wang, X. 1992. Interaction of an eddy with the continental slope. WHOI-92-40, Woods Hole Oceanographic Institution, Woods Hole, Massachusetts. 216 pp.

Ward, A.E. 1997. A temporal study of the phytoplankton spring bloom in Prince William Sound, Alaska. Master's thesis, University of Alaska Fairbanks.

Ware, D.M. 1991. Climate, predators and prey: Behavior of a linked oscillating system. In: T. Kawasaki, S. Tanaka, Y. Toba, and A. Tanaguchi (eds.), Long-term variability of pelagic fish populations and their environments. Pergamon Press, Tokyo, pp. 279-291.

Warren, B.A. 1983. Why is no deep water formed in the North Pacific? Journal of Marine Research 41:327-347.

Warren, B.A., and W.B. Owens. 1985. Some preliminary results concerning deep northern-boundary in the North Pacific. Progress in Oceanography 14:537-551.

Warwick, R.M. 1993. Environmental impact studies in marine communities: Pragmatical considerations. Australian Journal of Ecology 18:63-80.

Warwick, R.M., and K.R. Clarke. 1993. Comparing the severity of disturbance: A meta-analysis of marine macrobenthic community data. Marine Ecology Progress Series 92:221-231.

Welch, D.W., B.R. Ward, B.D. Smith, and P. Everson. 1998. Influence of the 1990 ocean climate shift on British Columbia steelhead (*Oncorhynchus mykiss*) and coho (*O. kisutch*) populations. In: G. Holloway, P. Muller, and D. Henderson (eds.), Biotic impacts of extratropical climate variability in the Pacific: Proceedings of the Tenth 'Aha Huliko'a Hawaiian Winter Workshop, January 25-29, 1998. University of Hawaii at Manoa, School of Ocean and Earth Science and Technology, Honolulu, pp. 77-88.

Welschmeyer, N.A., S. Strom, R. Goerjcke, G. DiTullio, L. Belvin, and W. Petersen. 1993. Primary production in the subarctic Pacific Ocean: Project SUPER. Progress in Oceanography 32:101-135.

Wendell, F.E., R.A. Hardy, and J.A. Ames. 1986. An assessment of the accidental take of sea otters, *Enhydra lutris*, in gill and trammel nets. California Department of Fish and Game, Marine Resources Technical Report 54, Long Beach.

Wespestad, V.G., L.W. Fritz, W.J. Ingraham, and B.A. Megrey. 2000. On relationships between cannibalism, climate variability, physical transport and recruitment success of Bering Sea walleye pollock, *Theragra chalcogramma*. In: Recruitment dynamics of exploited marine populations. Physical-biological interactions. ICES Journal of Marine Science 57:272-278

Western Native Trout Campaign. 2001. Imperiled western trout and the importance of roadless areas. A report by Western Native Trout Campaign, November 2001. http://www.westerntrout.org/trout/Reports/trout_report.pdf, accessed July 2004.

Westlake, R.L., and G. O'Corry-Crowe. 1997. Genetic investigation of Alaskan harbor seal stock structure using mtDNA. Alaska Department of Fish and Game, Annual Report: Harbor seal investigations in Alaska, Anchorage, pp. 205-234.

Wheeler, P.A., and S.A. Kokkinakis. 1990. Ammonium recycling limits nitrate use in the oceanic subarctic Pacific. Limnology and Oceanography 35:1267-1278.

Whitehead, J.C., and T.J. Hoban. 1999. Testing for temporal reliability in contingent valuation with time for changes in factors affecting demand. Land Economics 75.

Whitney, F.A., C.S. Wong, and P.W. Boyd. 1998. Interannual variability in nitrate supply to surface waters of the northeast Pacific Ocean. Marine Ecology Progress Series 170:15-23.

Whittaker, L.M., and L.H. Horn. 1982. Atlas of Northern Hemisphere extratropical cyclonic activity, 1958-1977. University of Wisconsin, Department of Meteorology, Madison.

Willette, T.M., R.T. Cooney, and K. Hyer. 1999. Predator foraging-mode shifts affecting mortality of juvenile fishes during the subarctic spring bloom. Canadian Journal of Fisheries and Aquatic Sciences 56:364-376.

Willette, M., M. Sturdevant, and S. Jewett. 1997. Prey resource partitioning among several species of forage fishes in Prince William Sound, Alaska. In: Forage fishes in marine ecosystems: Proceedings of the International Symposium on the Role of Forage Fishes in Marine Ecosystems. Alaska Sea Grant College Program, University of Alaska Fairbanks, pp. 11-29.

Willette, T.M., R.T. Cooney, V. Patrick, D.M. Mason, G.L. Thomas, and D. Scheel. 2001. Ecological processes influencing mortalities of juvenile pink salmon (*Oncorhynchus gorbuscha*) in Prince William Sound, Alaska. Fisheries Oceanography 10(Suppl. 1):14-42.

Willis, J.M., W.G. Pearcy, and N.V. Parin. 1988. Zoogeography of midwater fishes in the subarctic Pacific. In: T. Nemoto and W.G. Pearcy (eds.), The biology of the subarctic Pacific, Proceedings of the Japan-United States of America Seminar on the Biology of Micronekton in the Subarctic Pacific. University of Tokyo, Bulletin of the Ocean Research Institute 26:79-142.

Willmott, A.J., and L.A. Mysak. 1980. Atmospherically forced eddies in the northeast Pacific. Journal of Physical Oceanography 10.1769-1791.

Wilson, D.E., M.A. Bogan, R.L., Brownell Jr., A.M. Burdin, and M.K. Maminov. 1991. Geographic variation in sea otters, *Enhydra lutris*. Journal of Mammalogy 72:22-36.

Wilson, J.G., and J.E. Overland. 1986. Meteorology. In: D.W. Hood and S.T. Zimmerman (eds.), The Gulf of Alaska physical environment and biological resources. NOAA Ocean Assessments Division, Alaska Office, Washington, D.C., pp. 31-54

Winston, J. 1955. Physical aspects of rapid cyclogenesis in the Gulf of Alaska. Tellus 7:481-500.

Wipfli, M.S., J. Hudson, and J. Caouette. 1998. Influence of salmon carcasses on stream productivity: Response of biofilm and benthic macroinvertebrates in southeastern Alaska, U.S.A. Canadian Journal of Fisheries and Aquatic Sciences 55:1503-1511.

Wipfli, M.S., J.P. Hudson, D.T. Chaloner, and J.P. Caouette. 1999. Influence of salmon spawner densities on stream productivity in Southeast Alaska. Canadian Journal of Fisheries and Aquatic Sciences 56:1600-1611.

Witherell, D. 1999. Status and trends of principal groundfish and shellfish stocks in the Alaska exclusive economic zone, 1999. North Pacific Fishery Management Council, Anchorage.

Witherell, D., and N. Kimball. 2000. Status and trends of principal groundfish and shellfish stocks in the Alaska EEZ, 2000. North Pacific Fishery Management Council, Anchorage.

Wolfe, R.J., and L.B. Hutchinson-Scarbrough. 1999. The subsistence harvest of harbor seal and sea lions by Alaska Natives in 1998. Alaska Department of Fish and Game, Subsistence Division, Technical Paper No. 250.

Wootton, J.T. 1994. The nature and consequences of indirect effects in ecological communities. Annual Review of Ecology and Systematics 25:443-466.

Xie, L., and W.W. Hsieh. 1995. The global distribution of wind-induced upwelling. Fisheries Oceanography 4:52-67.

Xiong, Q., and T.C. Royer. 1984. Coastal temperature and salinity observations in the northern Gulf of Alaska, 1970-1982. Journal of Geophysical Research 89:8061-8068.

Yankovsky, A.E., and D.C. Chapman. 1997. A simple theory for the fate of buoyant coastal discharges. Journal of Physical Oceanography 27:1386-1401.

Yeardley Jr., R.B. 2000. Use of forage fish for regional streams wildlife risk assessment: Relative bioaccumulation of contaminants. Environmental Monitoring and Assessments 65:559-585.

Ylitalo, G.M., C.O. Matkin, J. Buzitis, M.M. Krahn, L.L. Jones, T. Rowles, and J.E. Stein. 2001. Influence of life-history parameters on organochlorine concentrations in free-ranging killer whales (*Orcinus orca*) from Prince William Sound, Alaska. The Science of the Total Environment 281(1-3):183-203.

York, A.E. 1994. The population dynamics of northern sea lions, 1975-1985. Marine Mammal Science 10:38-51.

York, A.E., R.L. Merrick, and T.R. Loughlin. 1996. An analysis of the Steller sea lion metapopulation in Alaska. In: D.R. McCullough (ed.), Metapopulations and wildlife conservation. Island Press, Washington, D.C., pp. 259-292.

Zacharias, M.A., and J.C. Roff. 2000. A hierarchical ecological approach to conserving marine biodiversity. Conservation Biology 14:1327-1334.

Zador, S.G., and J.F. Piatt. 1999. Time-budgets of common murres at a declining and increasing colony in Alaska. Condor 101:149-152.

Zheng, J., and G.H. Kruse. 2000. Recruitment patterns of Alaskan crabs and relationships to decadal shifts in climate and physical oceanography. ICES Journal of Marine Science 57:438-451.

Acronyms

A

ABC: acceptable biological catch

ABSC (USGS): Alaska Biological Science Center (Biological Resources Division): http://www.absc.usgs.gov/research/seabird&foragefish/index.html

ABWC: Alaska Beluga Whale Committee

AC: Alaska Current

AC: Arctic Council: http://www.arctic-council.org

ACC: Alaska Coastal Current

ACCE: Atlantic Climate and Circulation Experiment

ACIA (Arctic Council): Arctic Climate Impact Assessment: http://www.acia.uaf.edu

ACRC: Alaska Climate Research Center: http://climate.gi.alaska.edu

ACT: Alliance for Coastal Technologies

ADCED: Alaska Department of Community and Economic Development: http://www.dced.state.ak.us

ADCP: Acoustic Doppler Current Profilers

ADEC: Alaska Department of Environmental Conservation

ADEOS-II: Advanced Earth Observing Satellite-II

ADFG: Alaska Department of Fish and Game: http://www.state.ak.us/adfg/adfghome.htm

ADHSS: Alaska Department of Health and Social Services

ADNR: Alaska Department of Natural Resources: http://www.dnr.state.ak.us

  Division of Parks and Outdoor Recreation: http://www.dnr.state.ak.us/parks

  Division of Mining, Land and Water: http://www.dnr.state.ak.us/mlw

ADOT&PF: Alaska Department of Transportation and Public Facilities: http://www.dot.state.ak.us

AEIDC: Arctic Environmental Information and Data Center

AEPS: Arctic Environmental Protection Strategy

AEWC: Alaska Eskimo Whaling Commission

AFSC (NOAA/NMFS): Alaska Fisheries Science Center: http://www.afsc.noaa.gov/generalinfo.htm

AIS: Archival Information System

ALAMAP-C: Alabama's Monitoring and Assessment Program–Coastal

ALP (aka AL, ALPS): Aleutian low pressure system

ALPI: Aleutian low pressure index

AMAP (Arctic Council): Arctic Monitoring and Assessment Programme: http://www.amap.no

AMHS: Alaska Marine Highway System

AMMC: Aleut Marine Mammal Commission

AMMTAP: Alaska Marine Mammal Tissue Archival Project

AMNWR: Alaska Maritime National Wildlife Refuge

AMOS: Advanced Modeling and Observing System

AMSR: advance microwave scanning radiometer

ANHSC: Alaska Native Harbor Seal Commission

ANS: Alaska North Slope

ANS (EPA): aquatic nuisance species

AOC: Great Lakes areas of concern

AOSFRF: Alaskan Oceans, Seas, and Fisheries Research Foundation

APEX: Alaska Predator Ecosystem Experiment

AR (NMFS): Alaska Region

ARC: Atlantic Reference Center

ARCUS: Arctic Research Consortium of the United States: http://www.arcus.org

ARGO: Array for Real-time Geostrophic Oceanography

ARGO OPN: ARGO Ocean Profiling Network: http://www.argo.ucsd.edu

ARIES: Australian Resource Information and Environment Satellite

ARLIS: Alaska Resources Library and Information Service: http://www.arlis.org/index.html

ARMRB: Alaska Regional Marine Research Board

ARMRP: Alaska Regional Marine Research Plan

ARPA: Arctic Research and Policy Act (1984)

ASCC: Alaska State Climate Center: http://www.uaa.alaska.edu/enri/ascc_web/ascc_home.html

ASF: Alaska SAR (Synthetic Aperture Radar) Facility: http://www.asf.alaska.edu

ASLC: Alaska SeaLife Center: http://www.alaskasealife.org

ASOF: Arctic-subarctic Ocean Flux Array

ASP: amnesiac shellfish poisoning

ASTF: Alaska Science and Technology Foundation

ATSDR: Agency for Toxic Substances and Disease Registry: http://www.atsdr.cdc.gov

ATV: all terrain vehicle

AUV: autonomous underwater vehicle

AVHRR: advanced very high resolution radiometer

AVSP: Alaska Visitor Statistics Program

AWC: Anchorage Waterways Council: http://www.anchwaterwayscouncil.org

AWQ (ADEC): Division of Air and Water Quality

B

BAHC (IGBP): biospheric aspects of the hydrological cycle

BASS Task Team (PICES): Basin Scale Studies Task Team

BATS: Bermuda Atlantic time series

BBMMC: Bristol Bay Marine Mammal Council

BBNA: Bristol Bay Native Association: http://www.bbna.com

BCF: Bureau of Commercial Fisheries

BCIS: Biodiversity Conservation Information System: http://www.biodiversity.org/simplify/ev.php

BDY: beach dynamics

BEACH (EPA): Beaches Environmental Assessment, Closure, and Health Program

BIO (PICES): Biological Oceanography Committee

BOOS: Baltic Operational Oceanographic System: http://www.boos.org

BORMICON: boreal migration and consumption model

BRD (USGS): Biological Resources Division

C

C2000 (EPA): National Coastal Assessment

CAAB: codes for Australian aquatic biota

CACGP: Commission on Atmospheric Chemistry and Global Pollution

CAFF (Arctic Council): Program for the Conservation of Arctic Flora and Fauna

CalCOFI: California Co-operative Fisheries Investigation Program

CAOS: Coordinated Adriatic Observing System

CARIACO: Carbon Retention in a Colored Ocean Program

CARICOMP: Caribbean coastal marine productivity

CAST: Council for Agricultural Science and Technology: http://www.cast-science.org

CBMP: Chesapeake Bay Monitoring Program

CCAMLR: Commission for the Conservation of Antarctic Marine Living Resources: http://www.ccamlr.org

CCC (ICES/GLOBEC): cod and climate change

CCCC (PICES/GLOBEC): climate change and carrying capacity

CCF: one hundred cubic feet

CCMP (NEP): Comprehensive Conservation and Management Plan

CCS: California Current System: http://globec.oce.orst.edu/groups/nep/index.html

CDFO: Canada Department of Fisheries and Oceans: http://www.dfo-mpo.gc.ca/home-accueil_e.htm

CDOM: colored dissolved organic matter

CDQ: community development quota

CEMP (Cook Inlet Keeper): Citizens Environmental Monitoring Program

CEMP: CCAMLR Ecosystem Monitoring Program

CENR: Committee on Environment and Natural Resources: http://www.ostp.gov/NSTC/html/committee/cenr.html

CEOS: Committee on Earth Observation Satellites: http://www.ceos.org

CGOA: coastal Gulf of Alaska

C-GOOS: Coastal Panel of GOOS

CHL: chlorophyll

CHM: Clearing-House Mechanism of the Convention on Biological Diversity

CIFAR: Cooperative Institute for Arctic Research: http://www.cifar.uaf.edu

CIIMMS: Cook Inlet Information Management and Monitoring System: http://info.dec.state.ak.us/ciimms

CIK: Cook Inlet Keeper: http://www.inletkeeper.org

CIMI: Computer Interchange of Museum Information

CIRCAC: Cook Inlet Regional Citizens Advisory Council: http://www.circac.org

CISeaFFS: Cook Inlet Seabird and Forage Fish Study

CISNet: Coastal Intensive Site Network

CISPRI: Cook Inlet Spill Prevention and Response, Inc.

CiSWG (CAFF, IMCSAP, Arctic Council): Circumpolar Seabird Working Group

CLEMAN: Check List of European Marine Mollusca

CLIC: Climate and Cryosphere

CLIVAR: Climate Variability and Predictability Program

C-MAN: Coastal Marine Automated Network

CMED/GMNET: Consortium for Marine and Estuarine Disease/Gulf of Mexico Network

CMI (MMS): Coastal Marine Institute

CMM (WMO): Commission for Marine Meteorology

CNES: Centre National d'Etudes Spatiales (France)

COADS: Comprehensive Ocean-Atmosphere Data Set: http://www.cdc.noaa.gov/coads

CODAR: coastal radar

COLORS: COastal region LOng-term measurements for colour Remote Sensing development and validation

COMBINE: COoperative Monitoring in the Baltic Marine Environment

CoML: Census of Marine Life: http://www.coml.org

CONNS: Coastal Observing Network for the Near Shore

Convention on Biological Diversity: http://www.biodiv.org

COOP: Coastal Ocean Observation Panel: http://ioc.unesco.org/goos/COOP.htm

CoOP (NSF): Coastal Ocean Processes: http://www.skio.peachnet.edu/coop

COP: Coastal Ocean Program

CORE: Consortium for Oceanographic Research and Education: http://www.coreocean.org

Corexit 9500: brand name of a dispersant from Exxon

COSESPO: Coastal Observing System for the Eastern South Pacific Ocean

COTS: commercial off the shelf software

CPR (PICES): Advisory Panel on Continuous Plankton Recorder Survey in the North Pacific

CPTEC: Center for Weather Forecasts and Climate Studies (Brazil)

CRIS: Court Registry Investment System

CRP: Comprehensive Rationalization Program

CRRC: Chugach Regional Resources Commission

CRSA: Alaskan Coastal Resource Service Area, see also CIAP: http://www.ocrm.nos.noaa.gov/czm/ciap

CRTF: U.S. Coral Reef Task Force

CSCOR: Center for Sponsored Coastal Ocean Research: http://www.cop.noaa.gov

CSIRO: Commonwealth Scientific and Industrial Research Organization: http://www.csiro.au

CTD: conductivity temperature versus depth

CTW: coastal trapped waves

CU: cataloging unit

CVOA: Catcher Vessel Operational Area

CWAP: Clean Water Action Plan

CWPPRA: Coastal Wetlands Planning, Protection, and Restoration Act

CZCS: coastal zone color scanner

CZM: coastal zone management

D

DARP: Damage Assessment and Restoration Program

DARPA: Defense Advanced Research Projects Agency: http://www.darpa.mil

DBCP: Data Buoy Cooperation Panel

DBMS: database management system

DCE: 1,2-dichloroethane

DDD: dichloro bis(p-chlorophenyl)ethane

DDE: dichlorodiphenyldichloroethylene

DDT: dichlorodiphenyltrichloroethane

DEOS: Deep Earth Observatories on the Seafloor

DEOS (CORE): Dynamics of Earth and Ocean Systems

DFO: Department of Fisheries and Oceans, Canada

DGC: Division of Governmental Coordination, State of Alaska, Office of the Governor: http://www.gov.state.ak.us/dgc/CIAP/CIAPhome.htm

DIN: dissolved inorganic nitrogen

DMS: dimethylsulphide

DNMI: Norwegian Meteorological Institute (Det Norske Meteorologiske Institutt): http://met.no/english

DO: dissolved oxygen

DOC: U.S. Department of Commerce

DODS: Distributed Oceanographic Data System: http://www.unidata.ucar.edu/packages/dods and http://dods.gso.uri.edu

DOE: U.S. Department of Energy

DOI: U.S. Department of the Interior

DON QUIJOTE: Data Observing Network for the QuIJOTe

DRBC: Delaware River Basin Commission: http://www.state.nj.us/drbc/drbc.htm

E

EA/RIR: Environmental Assessment/Regulatory Impact Review

EASy: Environmental Analysis System

EBS: Eastern Bering Sea

EC: European Community

ECDIS: Electronic Chart and Display Information Systems

EC/IP (PICES): Executive Committee/Implementation Panel for CCCC

ECMWF: European Centre for Medium Range Weather Forecasting: http://www.ecmwf.int

ECOHAB (NSF): Ecology of Harmful Algal Blooms

EDOCC: ecological determinants of ocean carbon cycling

EDY: estuarine dynamics

EEZ: Exclusive Economic Zone

EEZ(A): European Economic Zone (Area)

EFH: essential fish habitat

EGB (NSF): Environmental Geochemistry and Biogeochemistry

EIOA: European Oceanographic Industry Association: http://www.eoia.org

ELOISE: European Land-Ocean Interaction Studies

EMAP: Environmental Monitoring and Assessment Program: http://www.epa.gov/emap

EMAP-E: Environmental Monitoring and Assessment Program-Estuaries

Enersperse: brand name of a dispersant

ENRI: Environment and Natural Resources Institute: http://www.uaa.alaska.edu/enri/enri_web/enrihome.html

ENSO: El Niño Southern Oscillation

EOS (NASA): Earth Observing System

EOSDIS: NASA'S EOS Data and Information System: http://spsosun.gsfc.nasa.gov/NewEOSDIS_Over.html

EPA: U.S. Environmental Protection Agency: http://www.epa.gov

ERL: effects range low (concentration of a contaminant potentially having adverse effects)

ERM: effects range medium (concentration of a contaminant associated with adverse effects on organisms)

ERMS: European Register of Marine Species

ERS-1: European Remote Sensing Satellite-1

ESA: Endangered Species Act

ESH (NSF): Marine Aspects of Earth System History

ESIP: The Federation of Earth Science Information Partners: http://www.esipfed.org

ESP: eastern South Pacific

ESRI: Environmental Systems Research Institute, ArcIMS system: http://www.esri.com/software/arcims/index.html

ETL tools: extraction, transformation, and loading tools

EU: European Union

EUMETSAT: European Organization for the Exploitation of Meteorological Satellites: http://www.eumetsat.de/en

EuroGOOS: European GOOS

EuroHAB: European harmful algae bloom

EVOS: *Exxon Valdez* Oil Spill http://www.oilspill.state.ak.us

EXDET: an Exxon laboratory test for dispersants

F

F&A (PICES): Finance and Administration Committee

FCCC: Framework Convention on Climate Change, Federal Geographic Data Committee metadata requirements: http://www.fgdc.gov/metadata/metadata.html

FDA: U.S. Food and Drug Administration

Federal Subsistence Fishery Monitoring Program, Federal Subsistence Management Program: http://www.r7.fws.gov/asm/home.html

FGDC: Federal Geographic Data Committee

FIS (PICES): Fishery Science Committee

Fishbase, FishGopher, FishNet: searchable fish databases managed by multiple organizations

FMP: fishery management plan

FOCI: Fisheries Oceanography Coordinated Investigations: http://www.pmel.noaa.gov/foci

F-R (PICES): Fundraising Committee

FY: fiscal year

G

GAIM (IGBP): Global Analysis, Interpretation and Modelling

GAK: Gulf of Alaska

GAK1: Gulf of Alaska station 1 located at the mouth of Resurrection Bay (60N, 149W)

GAP: Gap Analysis Program

GARP: genetic algorithm for rule-set production

GARS (NSF): Gulf of Alaska Recirculation Study

GBIF: Global Biodiversity Information Facility

GC (PICES): Governing Council

GCM: global climate model

GCN: Global Core Network

GCOS: Global Climate Observing System

GCRMN: Global Coral Reef Monitoring Network

GCTE: Global Change and Terrestrial Ecosystems (IGBP)

GECaFS (IGBP, WCRP, IDHP): Global Environmental Change and Food Systems

GEF: Global Environmental Facility

GEM: Gulf Ecosystem Monitoring

GEO: Global Eulerian Observations

GEOHAB: Global Ecology of Harmful Algal Blooms

GHL: guideline harvest level

GIPME: Global Investigation of Pollution in the Marine Environment

GIS: Geographic Information System

GIWA: Global International Water Assessment

GLI: global imager

GLIFWC: Great Lakes Indian Fish and Wildlife Commission: http://www.glifwc.org

GLNO: Great Lakes National Program Office

GLOBE: Global Learning and Observations to Benefit the Environment: http://www.globe.gov

GLOBEC: Global Ocean Ecosystem Dynamics: http://www.pml.ac.uk/globec

GLOBEC NEP: GLOBEC Northeast Pacific: http://globec.oce.orst.edu/groups/nep/index.html

GLORIA: Geological Long-Range Inclined Asdic

GLOSS (UN): Global Sea Level Observing System

GLWQA: Great Lakes Water Quality Agreement

GMBIS: Gulf of Maine Biogeographical Information System

GMP: Joint Gulf States Comprehensive Monitoring Program

GNP: gross national product

GOA: Gulf of Alaska

GODAE: Global Ocean Data Assimilation Experiment

GOES: Geostationary Operational Environmental Satellite

GOFS: U.S. Global Ocean Flux Study

GOOS: Global Ocean Observing System: http://ioc.unesco.org/goos

GOSIC: Global Observing System Information Center: http://www.gos.udel.edu

GPA/LBA: Global Programme of Action for the Protection of the Marine Environment from Land-Based Activities

GPO: GOOS Project Office

GPS: Global Positioning System

GSC: GOOS Steering Committee

GTOS: Global Terrestrial Observing System

GTS: Global Telecommunications System

GTSPP: Global Temperature-Salinity Pilot Project

GUI: graphical user interface

H

HAB: harmful algal bloom

HABSOS: Harmful Algal Bloom Observing System: http://www.habhrca.noaa.gov

HAPC: Habitat Areas of Particular Concern

HELCOM: Helsinki Commission-Baltic Marine Environment Protection Commission

HMAP: History of Marine Animal Populations

HMS: Hydrometeorological Service

HNLC: high nitrate, low chlorophyll waters

HOTO: Health of the Oceans

HOTS: Hawaii Ocean Time Series

HPLC: high performance liquid chromatography

I

IABIN: Inter-American Biodiversity Information Network

IAI: Inter-American Institute

IARC: International Arctic Research Center, University of Alaska Fairbanks: http://www.iarc.uaf.edu

IARPC: Interagency Arctic Research Policy Committee: http://www.nsf.gov/od/opp/arctic/iarpc/start.htm

IBOY: International Biodiversity Observation Year

IBQ: individual bycatch quota

ICAM: Integrated Coastal Area Management/Integrated Coastal Area Management Programme

ICES: International Council for the Exploration of the Sea: http://www.ices.dk

ICLARM: International Center for Living Aquatic Resources Management

ICM: Integrated Coastal Management

ICSU: International Council for Science

ICZN: International Code of Zoological Nomenclature

IFEP (PICES): Iron Fertilization Experiment Panel

IFO: intermediate fuel oil

IFP: The French Petroleum Institute: http://www.ifp.fr

IFQ: individual fishing quota

IGAC (IGBP/CACGP): International Global Atmospheric Chemistry Project

IGBP: International Geosphere-Biosphere Programme: http://www.igbp.kva.se

IGBP-DIS (IGBP): Data and Information System

I-GOOS: IOC-WMO-UNEP Committee for the Global Ocean Observing System

IGOS (NASA): Integrated Global Observing System: http://www.igospartners.org

IGOSS: Integrated Global Ocean Services System

IGS: International GPS Service for Geodynamics

IGU: International Geographical Union

IHDP (IGBP): International Human Dimensions Programme on Global Environmental Change

IJC: International Joint Commission

I-LTER: International LTER

IMCSAP (CAFF, Arctic Council): International Murre Conservation Strategy and Action Plan

IMS: Institute of Marine Science, University of Alaska Fairbanks: http://www.ims.uaf.edu

InfoBOOS: BOOS Information System

INPFC: International North Pacific Fisheries Commission: http://www.npafc.org/inpfc/inpfc.html

IOC (UNESCO): Intergovernmental Oceanographic Commission: http://ioc.unesco.org/iyo

IOCCG: International Ocean Colour Coordinating Group: http://www.ioccg.org

IODE: International Oceanographic Data and Information Exchange: http://ioc.unesco.org/iode

IOOS: Integrated Sustained Ocean Observing System

IPCC: Intergovernmental Panel on Climate Change: http://www.ipcc.ch

IPHAB: Intergovernmental Panel on HABs

IPHC: International Pacific Halibut Commission: http://www.iphc.washington.edu

IPRC: International Pacific Research Center: http://iprc.soest.hawaii.edu

IPSFC: International Pacific Salmon Fishing Commission

IRFA: initial regulatory flexibility analysis

IRIU: improved retention/improved utilization

ITAC: initial total allowable catch

ITIS: Integrated Taxonomic Information System

ITSU (IOC): Tsunami Warning System in the Pacific

IUCN: World Conservation Union

IWI (EPA): Index of Watershed Indicators

J

JCOMM: Joint Technical Commission for Oceanography and Marine Meteorology

JDBC: Java Database Connectivity

JDIMP: Joint Data and Information Management Panel

JGOFS (NSF): Joint Global Ocean Flux Study

K

KBNERR: Kachemak Bay National Estuarine Research Reserve

KRSA: Kenai River Sportfishing Association

L

LaMP (EPA): Lakewide Management Plan

LAMP: Local Area Management Plan

LATEX: Louisiana-Texas shelf study

LC50 or LC_{50}: lethal concentration of 50% of the test population

LEO: Long-term Ecosystem Observatory

LExEn (NSF): Life in Extreme Environments

LIDAR: light detection and ranging

LLP: License Limitation Program

LMR: living marine resources

LOICZ: land-ocean interactions in coastal zone

LTER (NSF): Long-term Ecological Research: http://lternet.edu

LTOP: Long-Term Observation Program: http://globec.oce.orst.edu/groups/nep/index.html

LUCC (IGBP/IHDP): Land Use/Cover Change

M

MABNET: Man and the Biosphere Network

MARBID: Marine Biodiversity Database

MARGINS (NSF): Continental Margins

MarLIN: Marine Laboratories Information Network: http://www.marine.csiro.au/marlin

MAROB: marine observation

MAST: marine science and technology

MBARI: Monterey Bay Aquarium Research Institute: http://www.mbari.org/about

MBMAP (PICES): Advisory Panel on Marine Birds and Mammals

MBNMS: Monterey Bay National Marine Sanctuary: http://montereybay.nos.noaa.gov

MEHRL: Marine Environmental Health Research Laboratory

MEL: Master Environmental Library

MEQ (PICES): Marine Environmental Quality Committee

MERIS: medium resolution imaging spectrometer

MetOp: meteorological operational

MFS: Mediterranean Forecasting System

MLD: mixed layer depth

MLML: Moss Landing Marine Laboratories: http://www.mlml.calstate.edu

MMHSRP: Marine Mammal Health and Stranding Response Program: http://www.nmfs.noaa.gov/prot_res/PR2/Health_and_Stranding_Response_Program/mmhsrp.html

MMPA: Marine Mammal Protection Act

MMRC: North Pacific Universities Marine Mammal Research Consortium

MMS: Minerals Management Service

MMS OCSES: Outer Continental Shelf Environmental Studies

MODEL (PICES): Conceptual/Theoretical and Modeling Studies Task Team

MODIS: moderate resolution imaging spectroradiometer

MODMON: Neuse Monitoring and Modeling Project

MONITOR (PICES): Monitor Task Team

MOODS (NMFS): Master Oceanographic Observational Data Set

MOOS: Ocean Observing System of the Monterey Bay Aquarium Research Institute: http://www.mbari.org/default.htm

MOS: modular optoelectronic scanner

MPA (DOC/DOI): Marine Protected Areas: http://www.mpa.gov

MPN: most probable number

MRB: maximum retainable bycatch

MSFCMA: Magnuson-Stevens Fishery Conservation and Management Act

MSVPA: multispecies virtual population analysis

MSY: maximum sustainable yield

MWRA: Massachusetts Water Resources Authority: http://www.mwra.state.ma.us

N

NA: Northern Adriatic

NABIN: North American Biodiversity Information Network

NABIS: National Aquatic Biodiversity Information Strategy

NAML: National Association of Marine Laboratories: http://hermes.mbl.edu/labs/NAML

NAO: North Atlantic oscillation

NAS: nonindigenous aquatic species

NASA: National Aeronautics and Space Administration: http://www.nasa.gov

NASA/AMSR: Advance Microwave Scanning Radiometer: http://wwwghcc.msfc.nasa.gov/AMSR

Earth Science Enterprise: http://www.earth.nasa.gov

NASA/GRACE: Gravity Recovery and Climate Experiment: http://essp.gsfc.nasa.gov/esspmissions.html

NASA/NASDA Tropical Rainfall Measurement Mission: http://modis.gsfc.nasa.gov

NASA/Salinity and Sea Ice Working Group: http://www.esr.org/lagerloef/ssiwg/ssiwgrep1.v2.html

NASQAN: National Stream Quality Accounting Network

NAWQA: National Water Quality Assessment Program: http://water.usgs.gov/nawqa

NCAR: National Center for Atmospheric Research

NCDC: National Climate Data Center: http://www.ncdc.noaa.gov

NCDDC: National Coastal Data Development Center: http://www.ncddc.noaa.gov

NCEP: National Centers for Environmental Prediction: http://wwwt.ncep.noaa.gov

NDBC: National Data Buoy Center: http://www.ndbc.noaa.gov

NDVI: normalized difference vegetation index

NEAR-GOOS: North East Asian Regional GOOS: http://ioc.unesco.org/goos/neargoos/neargoos.htm

NEMO: Naval Earth Map Observer

NEMURO: North Pacific Ecosystem Model for Understanding Regional Oceanography

NEODAT: Inter-Institutional Database of Fish Biodiversity in the Neotropics

NEP: National Estuary Program

NERR: National Estuarine Research Reserve

NESDIS: National Environmental Satellite, Data, and Information Service: http://www.nesdis.noaa.gov

NGO: nongovernmental organization

NGOA: Northern Gulf of Alaska

NGOS: North Gulf Oceanic Society: http://www.whales alaska.org

NIST: National Institute of Standards and Technology: http://www.nist.gov

NIWA: National Institute of Water and Atmosphere Research: http://www.niwa.cri.nz/index.html

NLFWA: National Listing of Fish and Wildlife Advisories

NMFS: National Marine Fisheries Service: http://www.nmfs.noaa.gov

NMMHSRP: National Marine Mammal Health and Stranding Response Program: http://www.nmfs.noaa.gov/prot_res/overview/mm.html

NMML: National Marine Mammal Laboratory

NMMTB: National Marine Mammal Tissue Bank

NMS: National Marine Sanctuary

NOAA: National Oceanic and Atmospheric Administration

NOAA HAZMAT: Hazardous Materials Program

NODC: National Oceanographic Data Center: http://www.nodc.noaa.gov

NOEL: no-effect level

NOLS: National Outdoor Leadership School

NOPP (NASA): National Ocean Partnership Program: http://www.NOPP.org

NOPPO: National Oceanographic Partnership Program Office

NORLC: National Ocean Research Leadership Council

NORPAC: North Pacific; an informal group of scientists who collated and published much of the oceanographic data from the North Pacific Ocean during approximately 1930-1965. Known as the NORPAC data, it was published in several volumes by the University of California Press.

NOS (NOAA): National Ocean Service: http://www.nos.noaa.gov

NO_x: nitrogen oxides

NPAFC: North Pacific Anadromous Fish Commission: http://www.npafc.org

NPDES: National Pollution Discharge Elimination System

NPFMC: North Pacific Fishery Management Council

NPI: North Pacific Index

NPMRP: North Pacific Marine Research Program: http://www.sfos.uaf.edu/npmr/index.html

NPO: North Pacific oscillation

NPOESS: National Polar-Orbiting Environmental Satellite System

NPPSD: North Pacific Pelagic Seabird Database

NPS: National Park Service: http://www.nps.gov

NPUMMRC: North Pacific Universities Marine Mammal Research Consortium

NPZ: nutrient-phytoplankton-zooplankton

NRA: NASA Research Announcement

NRC: National Research Council: http://www.nationalacademies.org/nrc

NRDA: natural resource damage assessment

NRT: near real time

NS&T: National Status and Trends Program

NSF: National Science Foundation

NSIPP (NASA): Seasonal-to-Interannual Prediction Program

NSTC: National Science and Technology Council: http://www.ostp.gov/NSTC/html/NSTC_Home.html

NURP (NOAA): National Undersea Research Program: http://www.nurp.noaa.gov

NVODS: National Virtual Ocean Data System: http://nvods.org

NVP: Nearshore Vertebrate Predator Project

NWI: National Wetlands Inventory

NWIFC: Northwest Indian Fisheries Commission: http://www.nwifc.wa.gov

NWP: numerical weather prediction

NWS: National Weather Service: http://www.nws.noaa.gov

O

OAR (NOAA): Oceanic and Atmospheric Research: http://oar.noaa.gov

OBIS: Ocean Biogeographical Information System

OCC: ocean carrying capacity

OCRM (NOS, NOAA): Office of Coastal Resource Management: http://www.ocrm.nos.noaa.gov

OCSEAP: Outer Continental Shelf Environmental Assessment Program

OCTET: Ocean Carbon Transport, Exchanges and Transformations: http://www.msrc.sunysb.edu/octet

OCTS: ocean color and temperature scanner

OE (NOAA OAR): Office of Ocean Exploration: http://oceanpanel.nos.noaa.gov

OECD: Organization for Economic Co-operation and Development

OFP: Ocean Flux Program

OHMSETT: Oil and Hazardous Materials Simulated Environmental Test Tank

OMB: Office of Management and Budget

ONR: Office of Naval Research

OOPC: Ocean Observations Panel for Climate

OOSDP: Ocean Observing System Development Panel

OPA 90: Oil Pollution Act of 1990

OPR: Office of Protected Resources: http://www.nmfs.noaa.gov/prot_res/prot_res.html

ORAP: Ocean Research Advisory Panel

ORNL: Oak Ridge National Laboratory: http://www.ornl.gov

OSCURS: Ocean Surface Current Simulations

OSNLR: Ocean Science in Relation to Non-Living Resources

OSPARCOM: Convention for the Protection of the Marine Environment of the North-east Atlantic

OSRI: Prince William Sound Oil Spill Recovery Institute: http://www.pws-osri.org

OSSE: Observation System Simulation Experiments

OST (EPA): Office of Science and Technology

OSTP: Office of Science and Technology Policy

OWOW (EPA): Office of Wetlands, Oceans, and Watersheds

OY: optimum yield

P

PAGES (IGBP): Past Global Change

P-BECS: Pacific Basinwide Extended Climate Study

PAH (EPA): polycyclic aromatic hydrocarbons

PAH: polynuclear aromatic hydrocarbons

PAR: photosynthetically available radiation

PC (PICES): Publication Committee

PCAST: President's Committee of Advisors on Science and Technology

PCB: polychlorinated biphenyls

PCC: Pollock Conservation Cooperative

PDO: Pacific decadal oscillation

PICES: North Pacific Marine Science Organization (not an acronym)

PIRATA: Pilot Research Array in the Tropical Atlantic

PISCO: Partnership for the Interdisciplinary Study of Coastal Oceans: http://www.piscoweb.org

PMEL: Pacific Marine Environmental Laboratory: http://www.pmel.noaa.gov

POC (PICES): Physical Oceanography and Climate Committee

POLDER: Polarization and Directionality of the Earth's Reflectances

POM: Princeton Ocean Model

PORTS/VTS: Physical Oceanographic Real-Time System/Vessel Traffic Services

POST: Pacific Ocean Salmon Tracking Project

POTW: Publicly Owned Treatment Works

PRODAS: Prototype Ocean Data Analysis System

PROFC: Programa Regional de Oceanografia Fisica y Clima

PSAMP: Puget Sound Ambient Monitoring Program

PSC: Pacific Salmon Commission: http://www.psc.org/Index.htm

PSMFC: Pacific States Marine Fisheries Commission: http://www.psmfc.org/

PSMSL (UN): Permanent Service for Mean Sea Level

PSP: paralytic shellfish poisoning

PST: Pacific Salmon Treaty

PWS: Prince William Sound

PWSAC: PWS Aquaculture Corporation: http://www.ctcak.net/~pwsac

PWSRCAC: PWS Regional Citizens Advisory Council

PWSSC: Prince William Sound Science Center

Q

QA/QC: quality assurance and quality control

QUIJOTE: Quickly Integrated Joint Observing Team

QuikSCAT: quick scatterometer (SeaWinds instrument)

R

R&D: research and development

RACE: Resource Assessment and Community Ecology

RAMS: Regional Atmospheric Modeling System

RAP: Remedial Action Plan

RCAC: Regional Citizens Advisory Council

RCRA: Resource Conservation and Recovery Act

RDP: Ribosomal Database Project

REX (PICES): Regional Experiments Task Team

RFP: request for proposals

RIDGE (NSF): Ridge Interdisciplinary Global Experiments

RLDC: Responsible Local Data Center

RMI: remote method invocation

RMP: Regional Monitoring Program

RNODC: Responsible National Oceanographic Data Center

RSN: RedSur Network

S

SAFE: Stock Assessment and Fishery Evaluation Document

SALMON (Sea-Air-Land Monitoring and Observation Network): http://www.ims.uaf.edu:8000/salmon

SALSA: Semi-arid Land Surface Atmosphere Program

SAR: synthetic aperture radar

SAV: submerged aquatic vegetation

SB (PICES): Science Board

SBIA (NSF): Shelf-basin Interactions in the Arctic

SCAMIT: Southern California Association of Marine Invertebrate Taxonomists

SCBPP: Southern California Bight Pilot Project

SCCWRP: Southern California Coastal Water Research Project

SCDHEC: South Carolina Department of Health and Environmental Control

SCDNR: South Carolina Department of Natural Resources

SCECAP: South Carolina Department Estuarine and Coastal Assessment Program

SC(-IGBP): Scientific Committee for the IGBP

SCICEX (NSF): Science Ice Exercise

SCOPE: Scientific Committee on Problems of the Environment

SCOR: Scientific Committee on Oceanic Research: http://www.jhu.edu/~scor

SCS: South China Sea

SEA: Sound Ecosystem Assessment

SEARCH: Study of Environmental Arctic Change:
http://psc.apl.washington.edu/search/index.html

SEAS: Shipboard Environmental Data Acquisition
System

SeaWiFS: Sea-viewing Wide Field-of-view Sensor:
http://seawifs.gsfc.nasa.gov

SEI: special events imager

SEPOA: Southeast Pacific Ocean Array

SERC: Smithsonian Environmental Research Center:
http://www.serc.si.edu

SERVS: Ship Escort Response Vessel System

SFEP: San Francisco Estuary Project

SFOS: School of Fisheries and Ocean Sciences,
University of Alaska Fairbanks

SG: Sea Grant: http://www.nsgo.seagrant.org

SGI: State of the Gulf Index

SHEBA (NSF): Surface Heat Budget of the Arctic
Ocean

SIMBIOS: Sensor Intercomparison and Merger for
Biological and Interdisciplinary Oceanic Studies

SIMoN: Sanctuary Integrated Monitoring Network

SJBEP: San Juan Bay Estuary Program

SLFMR: scanning low frequency microwave radiometers

SO-GLOBEC (GLOBEC): Southern Ocean Programme

SOIREE: Southern Ocean Iron Release Experiment

SOLAS: International Convention for Safety of Life at Sea

SOLAS (NRC): Surface Ocean Lower Atmosphere Study

SOLEC: State of the Lakes Ecosystem Conference

SPACC (GLOBEC): Small Pelagic Fish and Climate
Change, Specimen Banking Project

SQuID: Structured Query and Information Delivery

SSC (NPFMC): Scientific and Statistical Committee

SSE (NOAA): Sustainable Seas Expedition

SSF: Storm Surge Forecast System

SSH: sea surface height

SSLRI (NMFS, AR): Steller Sea Lion Research Initiative: http://www.fakr.noaa.gov/omi/grants/sslri

SSM/I: special sensor microwave/imager

SSS: sea surface salinity

SST: sea surface temperature

STAC: Scientific and Technical Advisory Committee

STAMP: Seabird Tissue Archival Monitoring Project

START (IGBP): Global Change System for Analysis,
Research and Training: http://www.start.org

STD: salinity temperature depth recorder

STORET System (EPA): http://www.epa.gov/storet

SVOC: semivolatile organic compounds

SWAO: South Western Atlantic Ocean

SWMP: NERRS System-Wide Monitoring Program

T

t: metric tons

TAC: total allowable catch

TAO: tropical atmosphere ocean (buoy array)

TASC (EU): Transatlantic Study of *Calanus finmarchicus*

TCE: tetrachloroethane

TCODE (PICES): Technical Committee on Data Exchange

TCP: Tropical Cyclone Programme

TEK: traditional ecological knowledge

TEMA (IOC): Training, Education and Mutual
Assistance

TMDL: total maximum daily load

TOGA: tropical ocean and global atmosphere

T/P: TOPEX/Poseidon: http://topex-www.jpl.nasa.gov

U

UAA: University of Alaska Anchorage

UAF: University of Alaska Fairbanks

UN: United Nations

UNCED: United Nations Conference on Environment
and Development

UNCLOS: United National Convention on the Law of
the Sea (Montego Bay, 1982)

UNEP: United Nations Environmental Programme

UNESCO: United Nations Educational, Scientific and
Cultural Organization: http://ioc.unesco.org/iocweb

UNFCCC: United Nations Framework Convention on
Climate Change

USARC: U.S. Arctic Research Commission

USCG: U.S. Coast Guard

USDA: U.S. Department of Agriculture

USDHHS: U.S. Department of Health and Human Services: http://www.os.dhhs.gov

USFS: U.S. Forest Service

USFWS: U.S. Fish and Wildlife Service

USGCRP (NASA): U.S. Global Climate Research Program

US GLOBEC (NSF): U.S. Global Ocean Ecosystem
Dynamics

USGS: U.S. Geological Survey: http://www.usgs.gov

USNO: U.S. Naval Observatory:
http://www.usno.navy.mil

UWA: Unified Watershed Assessments

V

VBA: vessel bycatch accounting

VENTS (NOAA): Vents Program

VIP: Vessel Incentive Program

VOC: volatile organic compounds

VOS: volunteer observing ships

W

WAF: water-accommodated fraction

WAM: wave model

WCRP (ICSU/IOC/WMO): World Climate Research Program

WDFW: Washington Department of Fish and Wildlife

WDOE: Washington Department of Ecology

WES: Waterways Experimental Station

WESTPAC: IOC Sub-Commission for the Western Pacific

WG (PICES): Working Group

WHOI: Woods Hole Oceanographic Institution

WMO: World Meteorological Organization

WMS: Open GIS Consortium's Web Mapping Server:
http://www.opengis.org/techno/specs/01-047r2.pdf

WOCE (WCRP): World Ocean Circulation Experiment:
http://www.soc.soton.ac.uk/OTHERS/woceipo/ipo.html

WODC: World Oceanographic Data Center

WOOD: World-wide Oceans Optics Database

WSRI: Wild Stock Restoration Initiative

WWW: World Weather Watch

X

XBT: expendable bathythermograph

XCDT: expendable conductivity, depth, and salinity devices

Index

(*t* = table, *f* = figure)

Kuroshio Current, 48
Kvichak River, 88

L

Labidochirus splendescens, 83*t*
Lake and Peninsula Borough, 119*t*
Laminaria, 64, 65
Lamna ditropis, 82*t*
Lampanyctus jordani, 82*t*
Lampanyctus ritteri, 82*t*
lampfish
    brokenline. See *Lampanyctus jordani*
    northern. See *Stenobrachius leucopsarus*
land use
    coastal development, 2, 16. *See also* urbanization
    logging, 16, 120, 122, 134–135
    mining, 123, 134, 138
    post-EVOS conservation and easements, 133
La Niña, 20, 23, 34
lanternfish. See *Diaphus theta; Stenobrachius leucopsarus*
    broadfin. See *Lampanyctus ritteri*
Laqueus californianus, 85*t*
Larus argentatus, 70*t*
Larus canus, 70*t*
Larus glaucescens, 70*t,* 71, 72–73
larvaceans
    crab, 93
    and fish stocks, 89, 90, 91
    food resources for, 95
    models, 140*t,* 148
    in seasonal zooplankton succession, 53
lead, 114
Lebbeus groenlandicus, 83*t*
Lepidopsetta bilineata, 82*t*
Leptasterias hexactis, 61
Leptasterias hylodes, 84*t*
Leptasterias polaris, 84*t*
Leptychaster pacificus, 84*t*
Leslie matrix, 110
Lethasterias nanimensis, 84*t*
Leuroglossus schmidti, 82*t,* 94, 97
life history
    and food-web transfers, 54
    forage species, 95*t*
    and habitat dependencies, 21
    harbor seal, 107
    herring, 88–89, 95*t*
    pollock, 90, 95*t*
    salmon, 88, 95*t*
    sea lion, 106
    sea otter, 112
    whale, 102, 104
    zooplankton, 21
light. *See* photic zone; photosynthesis; solar radiation
light-detection and ranging (LIDAR), 18, 96*t*
lightfish, 93
Limanda aspera, 54, 82*t*
Limicina pacifica, 53
limops, Akutan. See *Limopsis akutanica*
Limopsis akutanica, 84*t*
limpet. See *Lottia pelta; Tectura persona*
Line P, 50, 51
lingcod. See *Ophiodon elongatus*
lipid content of organism, 4, 18, 21, 97

Liponemis brevicornis, 83*t*
liquefied natural gas (LNG), 129, 130
Lithodes aequispinus, 83*t*
Littorina scutulata, 61
Littorina sitkana, 61
LNG. *See* liquefied natural gas
logging and timber products, 16, 120, 122, 134–135, 138
Loligo sp., 113
loon. See *Gavia immer*
Lophaster furcilliger, 84*t*
Lopholithodes foraminatus, 83*t*
Lottia pelta, 61
Luidia foliata, 84*t*
Luidiaster dawsoni, 84*t*
Lumpenus longirostris, 83*t*
Lumpenus maculatus, 83*t*
Lumpenus sagitta, 83*t*
lumpsucker
    Pacific spiny. See *Eumicrotremus orbis*
    round. See *Eumicrotremus birulai*
    smooth. See *Aptocyclus ventricosus*
lunar forcing, 1, 3*f,* 28, 30–31, 91
lunar nodal cycle, 20, 30, 91
Lunda cirrhata, 70*t,* 71, 73, 74, 78
Lycodapus sp., 83*t*
Lycodes brevipes, 83*t*
Lycodes diapterus, 83*t*
Lycodes pacificus, 83*t*
Lycodes palearis, 83*t*
Lyopsetta exilis, 82*t*

M

mackerel, Atka. See *Pleurogrammus monopterygius*
Macoma balthica, 62
macrofauna, 62
Mactromeris polynyma, 84*t*
Malacocottus zonurus, 82*t*
Mallotus villosus
    food quality of, 4, 18
    as a food resource, 70, 71, 73, 74, 93, 106, 109
    in the food web, 17, 18
    habitat for juveniles, 16
    life history, 95*t*
    predator-prey relationships, 96
    trawl surveys, 82*t*
mammals
    marine. *See* marine mammals
    terrestrial, 16, 19, 88, 99, 99, 130
management
    decision making and decision analysis, 142, 144, 145, 147
    ecosystem-based, 16, 22
    fisheries, 89, 91, 124–125, 126
    marine mammals, 101
    single-species to ecosystem-based, 16
Marine Mammal Protection Act of 1972 (MMPA), 100*t,* 101, 103, 105, 109, 133
marine mammals
    conservation, 88, 101
    effect of lower food quality, 4
    food resources for, 16, 17, 62, 97
    in the food web, 1, 3*f,* 111
    foraging behavior, 17
    general characteristics, 99–101, 100*t*
    population decline, 2, 101
    rookeries, 17, 21